The Economics of Financial Inclusion

This book offers a thorough examination of the economics of financial inclusion and management from a contemporary standpoint. It covers a vast array of financial inclusion-related topics, surveying economies around the globe and analyzing the factors that contribute to both financial inclusion and exclusion.

The Economics of Financial Inclusion discusses the role of technology, examining how technological advances have revolutionized financial services and increased access to populations previously underserved. It studies the intersection of financial inclusion and sustainability, highlighting the significance of green finance and its role in fostering inclusive and sustainable economic growth. Financial literacy and theories underlying financial inclusion efforts are examined, as is the impact of financial criminality. Further, the authors consider regional development and the extant gaps in financial inclusion as well as the urban-rural divide, investigating disparities between urban and rural areas and proposing strategies to bridge the gap. They also assess the effect of inflation and recession and discuss how monetary and fiscal policies can impact inclusion initiatives. The book concludes with a management perspective on financial inclusion, with chapters devoted to various aspects of administering inclusive financial systems. It combines theoretical insights with empirical evidence and case studies, from both developing and developed nations to illustrate the various approaches and challenges and to provide a comprehensive understanding of worldwide advancements and developments. The comparative approach provides readers with insights into diverse strategies and best practices for overcoming challenges and obstacles and for promoting financial inclusion in various economic contexts.

Overall, readers will benefit from the book's comprehensive analysis and exhaustive coverage. It is an invaluable resource for advanced students, scholars, researchers, and policymakers.

Firdous Ahmad Malik is Assistant Professor of Economics at the University of the People, Pasadena, California, USA.

Tarika Singh Sikarwar is Professor and Deputy Director at Prestige Institute of Management and Research Gwalior, India.

Routledge Studies in Development Economics

189. Cuba and the Economic Policies of Peripheral Socialism
Recent Reforms in a Historical Perspective
Vitor Eduardo Schincariol and Joana Salém Vasconcelos

190. Corruption and Economic Growth in Africa
The Impact on Development
David N. Abdulai

191. Special Economic Zones in South Asia
Structural Change, Competitiveness and Growth
Aradhna Aggarwal

192. Infrastructure Policy and Inequality
Michael A. Cohen

193. Responsible Business and Sustainable Development
The Use of Data and Metrics in the Global South
Edited by David Mhlanga and Mufaro Dzingirai

194. Unlocking Economic Development
The Unlearning Process of Nations
Ahmed Tahiri Jouti

195. Economic Shocks and Globalisation
Between Deglobalisation and Slowbalisation
Edited by Elsabé Loots

196. The Economics of Financial Inclusion
Edited by Firdous Ahmad Malik and Tarika Singh Sikarwar

For more information about this series, please visit: www.routledge.com/Routledge-Studies-in-Development-Economics/book-series/SE0266

The Economics of Financial Inclusion

Edited by Firdous Ahmad Malik and Tarika Singh Sikarwar

Routledge
Taylor & Francis Group
LONDON AND NEW YORK

First published 2025
by Routledge
4 Park Square, Milton Park, Abingdon, Oxon OX14 4RN

and by Routledge
605 Third Avenue, New York, NY 10158

Routledge is an imprint of the Taylor & Francis Group, an informa business

British Library Cataloguing-in-Publication Data
A catalogue record for this book is available from the British Library

Library of Congress Cataloging-in-Publication Data
Names: Malik, Firdous Ahmad, 1988- editor. | Singh Sikarwar, Tarika, editor.
Title: The economics of financial inclusion / edited by Firdous Ahmad Malik and Tarika Singh Sikarwar.
Description: Abingdon, Oxon ; New York, NY : Routledge, 2025. | Series: Routledge studies in development economics | Includes bibliographical references and index.
Identifiers: LCCN 2024030967 (print) | LCCN 2024030968 (ebook) | ISBN 9781032655130 (hardback) | ISBN 9781032655161 (paperback) | ISBN 9781032655185 (ebook)
Subjects: LCSH: Financial exclusion--Case studies. | Fintech--Social aspects--Case studies. | Financial services industry--Technological innovations--Case studies.
Classification: LCC HG176.55 .E36 2025 (print) | LCC HG176.55 (ebook) | DDC 332--dc23/eng/20240808
LC record available at https://lccn.loc.gov/2024030967
LC ebook record available at https://lccn.loc.gov/2024030968

ISBN: 978-1-032-65513-0 (hbk)
ISBN: 978-1-032-65516-1 (pbk)
ISBN: 978-1-032-65518-5 (ebk)

DOI: 10.4324/9781032655185

Typeset in Times New Roman
by KnowledgeWorks Global Ltd.

Contents

List of Figures

List of Tables

Contributors

Faisal Abbas is Associate Professor in the Department of Economics and Director, Center of Excellence on Population and Wellbeing Studies (CePwS), School of Social Sciences and Humanities (S3H), National University of Sciences and Technology (NUST), Islamabad, Pakistan. He is also a Sustainable Development Goals (SDG) Fellow, Center for Development Research (ZEF), University of Bonn, Germany.

Aizza Anwar has seven years of academic experience as a lecturer and researcher. She has a PhD in organization behavior and development from Universiti Sains Malaysia and served as a lecturer at the University of Management and Technology, Lahore, Pakistan. She holds a master's from Comsats Institute of Information Technology Pakistan. She has been invited as a speaker at several academic and industrial conferences in Pakistan and Malaysia. She has been part of HR Walay, Pakistan's advisory board, since 2015. She has published papers and is a reviewer of several recognized journals. Her areas of interest are human resource management, organizational behavior, leadership, digitalization, student e-learning, workplace cyberbullying, and psychological distress. For the past three years, she has served in a leadership role at the International Youth Conference in Malaysia. She is a member of the research team working on various funded projects with the Malaysian government, including the Penang Youth Development Corporation and the Penang State Government through the Majlis Mesyuarat Kerajaan (MMK) for Social Development. She has been awarded an Erasmus+ research project in Europe. She is now working on a gender equity project for the Penang State Government's MMK for Social Development.

Joe Eyong Assoua is a lecturer in the Department of Agricultural Economics and Agribusiness, part of the Faculty of Agriculture and Veterinary Medicine, University of Buea, Cameroon. He holds a PhD in agricultural economics from the University of Buea, Cameroon and has an MSc in international economics from Lund University, Sweden. He has over ten years of experience in agricultural trade, agribusiness, food systems, agri-food investment policy, and agri-food capacity development. His research and policy analysis also cuts across the analysis of food system-related policies, financial inclusion, and global value chain. He has worked on a wide range of agriculture, trade policy, and development issues with organizations such as the African Economic Research Consortium (AERC). He is an adjunct faculty at the Trade Policy Training Centre in Africa (ESAMI-TRAPCA), Arusha-Tanzania, and a consultant with the Committee Linking Entrepreneurship Agriculture Development (COLEAD). Dr Assoua has published many articles, book chapters, working papers, and more.

Akash Bag has completed his BA from the prestigious Ravenshaw University, followed by an LLB from Utkal University and LLM from KIIT University, Bhubaneswar. He was affiliated with Kalinga University, where he taught for three years before leaving in 2021 to pursue a PhD. He is currently associated with Amity University, where he is pursuing his PhD in digital forensics and cyber security. He is well-versed in subjects such as the Indian panel code jurisprudence and constitutional law. He currently works as a freelancer helping fellow scholars with research and writing. He has published papers in prestigious journals and conferences such as IEEE, Springer, IGI Global, and AIP and is currently working on projects on an international collaborative basis. Currently, he is an Assistant Professor of Law at Adamas University, Kolkata.

Ngwengeh Brendaline Beloke holds a PhD in management sciences from the University of Buea, Cameroon in the Department of Management Sciences. She is currently a part-time lecturer in the Department of Banking and Finance in the same university and HIBMAT University Institute of Buea (HUIB) where she serves as Head of the Department for Banking and Finance and coordinator of BSc courses. Dr Beloke has contributed articles in scholarly journals in the areas of stock market development and digital financial services. Her research interests are in the areas of finance, innovations, and banking. However, she is also interested in multidisciplinary and contemporary areas of research.

Mary-Juliet Bime-Egwu is part of the Department of Agribusiness Technology, College of Technology, University of Bamenda, Bamenda, Bambili, Cameroon.

Rahul Chaudhary earned his BCom Hons, MCom (IB), MPhil, BE, and PhD from Dayalbagh Educational Institute Deemed To Be University, Agra. His doctoral dissertation explored the comparative impact of central government socio-economic schemes on scheduled castes in Uttar Pradesh. Throughout his PhD, he has authored seven research papers listed in UGC Care and Scopus databases. His teaching experience encompasses courses like research methodology, fundamentals of banking, international business, and financial accounting.

Anamika Choudhary is Associate Professor at the Dr Shakuntala Misra National Rehabilitation University, Uttar Pradesh, India.

Ufual E. Daniel works in the Department of Business Management at the College of Management and Social Sciences, Covenant University, Ota, Nigeria.

Slimane Ed-Dafali is Associate Professor of Management (HDR) at the National School of Commerce and Management (ENCG), Chouaib Doukkali University, Morocco, where he conducts teaching and research activities. His current research is focused on sustainable entrepreneurship, entrepreneurial finance, business ethics, corporate responsibility, sustainable finance, and corporate governance. He has contributed to different research projects with various scholars and universities. Dr Ed-Dafali also serves as a reviewer for several reputed scientific journals.

Priti Gupta is Assistant Professor and head of the Department of Economics at Ramesh Jha Mahila College, Saharsa. She earned her PhD in economics from Banaras Hindu University. She has been involved in teaching for more than four years. Dr Priti was awarded by the ICSSR Institutional Doctoral Fellowship's Institute of Economic Growth, New Delhi. Her areas of interests are health economics, development economics, monetary economics, and public finance. Dr Gupta has published a number of research papers indexed in Scopus and UGC Care. She has participated and presented papers in various academic national and international seminars and conferences.

Wajiha Haq is Professor in the Department of Economics, School of Social Sciences and Humanities (S3H), National University of Sciences and Technology (NUST), Islamabad, Pakistan. Apart from frequently publishing on financial well-being and household resource allocation in well-reputed impact factor national and international journals, she recently published on various aspects of economic well-being linked to gender equality and health, climate change and well-being, aligned with sustainable development goals.

Daisy Mui Hung Kee is Associate Professor at the School of Management, Universiti Sains Malaysia (USM), Penang, Malaysia. She received her PhD in business and management from the University of South Australia and MBA from USM. She has published 94 ISI and Scopus-indexed journal papers. She is the Country Director of the Association of International Business and Professional Management (AIBPM) (Indonesia) and STAR Scholars Network (the United States). She is also an active keynote speaker and panelist for international conferences. In addition, Dr Kee is the coordinator for Penang Youth Development Corporation (PYDC). She was the recipient of USM's Sanggar Sanjung (2022) Award and Publication Excellence (2019–2022) by the School of Management, the Service Excellence Award (2022, 2016) by USM, and the Merdeka Award (2006) from the Australia Malaysia Business Council of South Australia (AMBCSA) by former South Australia Governor Sir Eric Neal (2006), which recognizes the Most Outstanding Malaysian University students in South Australia. She was awarded Dean's List as one of the top MBA students (2003). Dr Kee's research interests include organizational psychology, human resource management, organizational behavior, work values, leadership, and entrepreneurship. She was a visiting professor at Pusan National University in South Korea (2018). She is also the chief editor of the *Journal of Community Development in Asia*, assistant specialty chief editor of *Organizational Psychology for Frontiers in Psychology*, and senior editor for *Global Business Organizational Excellence*.

Irfan Hussain Khan is a dedicated economist and academic, with a PhD in economics and a passion for teaching and research. With over 14 years of professional experience, he has held various positions, including Visiting Lecturer of Economics at Bahauddin Zakariya University, Bahadur Layyah Campus (since 2014), NCBA Multan Campus (2019-2023), and GC University Faisalabad (2015-2018). He has also taught at Govt Degree College Choubara (2008-2009) and Prime College of Commerce (2009-2010). His expertise lies in economics, and he has taught a range of courses, including MPhil economics classes. He is committed to inspiring and educating future generations of economists and leaders.

Nidhi Jain is an Assistant Professor in Finance at the Prestige Institute of Management and Research, Gwalior, Madhya Pradesh. Currently, she is pursuing a PhD in management from Jiwaji University, Gwalior. She has completed her BCom and MBA with a dual specialization in finance and marketing, with a third position at Jiwaji University. She has a qualified UGC-NET in management. She also actively participates in research, presenting, and publishing various research papers and earning two Best Paper Presenter Awards by the International Conference of Central University, Rajasthan, and JCGS. She has also been Session Chair in various national and international conferences. Her areas of interest lie in the fields of finance, accountancy, and economics.

Sneha Kadyan is a lecturer, sociology assistant dean, JGBS-CLIP Mentorship Program Team, and member, Office of Communications & Outreach Jindal Global Business School, O.P. Jindal Global University, Sonipat, Haryana.

Sidra Khalid is an international development professional and gender and inclusion advocate with over seven years of field-based experience in research, project management, and implementation with INGOs/NGOs in programming related to women's economic empowerment, climate change, disaster management, reproductive health, and water, sanitation, and hygiene (WASH), with a focus on gender equity and social inclusion. She holds a Master of Development Practice (concentration in gender) from Emory University, USA and BA in sociology from the University of California, Berkeley, USA. In recognition of her accomplishments, she was selected as one of the recipients for Emory University's 40 Under Forty achievement award in 2023.

Ayesha Khan is CEO of Akhter Hameed Khan Foundation, a grass root non-profit organization working on women's economic and health empowerment through household and community-level interventions on gender equality, women's enterprise, and social-financial-digital inclusion in urban slums of Pakistan. By training, she is an infectious disease physician (graduate Aga Khan Medical College, Karachi Pakistan) with residency and combined fellowship in infectious diseases-MPH, USA. Dr Khan has experience working in the public sector in Pakistan (Ministry of Health in the Health Policy Unit and HIV Treatment and Care Center), and with donors and UN agencies. Her research work in the AHK-Foundation Urban Impact Lab explores the interplay of urban poverty, women's economic empowerment, population health (including family planning-SRHR agency) choices, and decision-making. Dr Khan's work has been published in international/national journals (20+ publications) and feeds into evidence-informed advocacy to government (national/provincial partners) and the private sector for changing policies and programs that enable gender equity and women's inclusion.

Anushree D. Kini is Assistant Professor, Indian Institute of Information and Technology Dharwad.

Miloudi Kobiyh has earned her PhD in economic science from the University of Caen - Basse Normandie. He is a professor eligible to supervise research in management sciences and member of LERSEM Laboratory, National School of Business and Management (ENCG) El Jadida, University of Chouaib Doukkali, El Jadida, Morocco. He is a professor of economics, statistics, and game theory. His works have been published in a number of reputed journals and international conference proceedings.

R.R. Kulkarni is a professor, Kousali Institute of Management Studies, Karnatak University, Dharwad, Karnataka, India.

Nupur Kumari is a research scholar specializing in international human rights laws. She is pursuing a PhD in international refugee law at Chanakya National Law University Patna. She has completed her LLM in the specialization of international human rights laws from the prestigious Law School of India University, Bangalore. She has also passed the UGC NET examination for teaching law subjects. She is currently working as Assistant Professor of Law at Bennett University (The Times Group), Greater Noida, India.

Hong Liang is currently a PhD candidate in strategy and organizational management at the school of management, Universiti Sains Malaysia (USM) in Malaysia. She obtained her MBA in management from INTI International University in Malaysia and participated in several high-profile conferences. In addition to her academic career, she held research assistant positions in the School of Social Science, USM.

Firdous Ahmad Malik was born in India and is currently employed by the University of People as Assistant Professor of Economics (instructor), Department of Management. Before that, he was a research fellow at the National Institute of Public Finance and Policy (NIPFP) in Delhi, India. Prior to this, he was a senior research associate at the O.P. Jindal Global University in Sonipat, Haryana's Jindal Center for the Global South. From Babasaheb Bhimrao Ambedkar University in Lucknow, India, he received his PhD. He has a master's in economics from the University of Kashmir and an MPhil in economics from Babasaheb Bhimrao Ambedkar University Lucknow. Microfinance, financial inclusion, and financial literacy are his main areas of study interest. He has articles in journals that are Scopus-indexed from Springer, Elsevier, Taylor & Francis, and others. Some of his many books include: *Financial Inclusion*

Schemes in India, Financial Behaviour of Urban Destitutes in India, Health System in Jammu and Kashmir Challenges and Opportunities, and *Asymmetry of Information and Lending Risk Livelihood Pattern of Street Vendors in India.* His forthcoming book is *Economics of Financial Inclusion*, by Routledge and *Fostering Industry-Academia Partnerships for Innovation-Driven Trade* by IGI Publishing. Microfinance, development economics, monetary economics, and public finance are his areas of expertise. To promote research among the upcoming young generation, Dr Malik is associated with specific international organizations, viz. the Young Scholars Initiative (YSI). He further contributes and promotes research by presenting and serving as session chair and review panelist in national and international conferences. For his tireless contribution to promoting young researchers, he was awarded by the Jindal Center for Global South two best paper presentations and the AIBPM Malaysian conference organizers a best reviewer award in 2023.

Mazharunnisa, MBA, MCom, MHRM, MPhil, PhD, APSET, is presently an Associate Professor, KL Business School, Koneru Lakshmaiya Educational Foundation, KL University, NTR District, Vijayawada, Andhra Pradesh. Her areas of interest are management, HRM, organizational behaviour, and economics. Dr Mazharunnisa has published a number of research papers indexed in Scopus and UGC Care. She received a UGC-sponsored Minor Research Project, 'Emotional Intelligence – A Study in Banks'. She has participated and presented papers in various academic national and international seminars and conferences.

Samiya Mubeen, BCom, MBA, PhD, is presently Associate Professor, Department of Finance, IIBS College, Bangalore. She is an academician, researcher, and co-author with a career spanning more than 15 years in management teaching with a specialization in finance. She pursued a PhD from Bangalore University in finance. She is a co-author for textbooks, and is a member of research journal editorial boards. She has published many journals and articles in finance.

Itai H. Muktar is in the Department of Business Management at the College of Management and Social Sciences, Covenant University, Ota, Nigeria.

Ch Sudipta Kishore Nanda, PhD, MCom, MBA, LLB, obtained his PhD in commerce from Utkal University, Odisha, India in 2014. Currently, he is Assistant Professor in the Department of Commerce, School of Tribal Resource Management, KISS Deemed to Be University, Bhubaneswar, Odisha. His areas of specialization are accounting and finance. He has more than 20 years of teaching experience both at the undergraduate and postgraduate levels. He has contributed 41 research papers published in UGC Care listed as national and international journals of repute. He is a life member of the All Orissa Commerce Association. Dr Nanda authored 2 textbooks and 3 edited books. He has presented 53 papers in various national and international seminars. He was an editor of *The Management Page*, a bi-annual journal. His areas of research are corporate reporting, corporate governance, and strategic financial management.

Tanya Nautiyal is a doctoral fellow in the Department of Economics, Jamia Millia Islamia, New Delhi. She is currently working as a research fellow (economics) in the Tax Policy Research Unit, Department of Revenue, Ministry of Finance. She is also a PhD scholar in Jamia Millia Islamia. Her specializations are in the areas of macroeconomics, rural development, gender inequality, tax policies, and financial inclusion. She has 2.5 years of work experience in research in tax policies, development economics, financial inclusion, and international economics.

Saima Nazir is a research scholar in the Department of Commerce, University of Kashmir, J&K, India, with a specialization in finance and management.

Norbert Ngoongeh Ngwang is part of the Department of Agribusiness Technology, College of Technology, University of Bamenda, Bambili, Cameroon.

Suvarna Nimbagal is Assistant Professor, School of Management Studies, KLE Technological University, Hubli, Karnataka, India.

Evans S. Osabuohien is Professor of Economics at Covenant University (CU), Nigeria where he has served as Head of Department (HOD) for two terms. He was first appointed in 2006, making him the youngest HOD, and later received a full professorship in 2018, becoming the youngest professor at CU. In 2020, he was recognized as 'One of the 6 Youngest Professors in Nigeria'. He is the Founding Chair of DePECOS Institutions and Development Research Centre (DIaDeRC), Nigeria where he coordinates the African Scholars Mentorship Network (ASMN) with over 600 members in Africa and globally. He founded the Centre for Economic Policy and Development Research (CEPDeR) and Regional Centre of Expertise, Ogun State (RCE Ogun) at CU in 2018. He has published five books and over 200 scholarly articles. He is a fellow of the Alexander von Humboldt Foundation (AvH) and Swedish Institute (Si). He has won numerous grants in his two decades' career and he is a visiting professor at universities in Africa and globally. He is a Global Author for Global Environmental Outlook 7th Edition (GEO-7), the flagship report of UNEP (United Nations Environmental Program). He serves as a member of the board of directors of companies in Nigeria and globally. He is a Council Member for Nigerian Economic Society (NES) where he serves as an associate editor, an associate editor for Elsevier (Heliyon-Economics), and managing editor for Springer Nature Group (Sustainable Development).

Ansumalini Panda is Assistant Professor, School of Management Studies, KLE Technological University, Hubli, Karnataka, India.

Lalit Mohan Pant has worked in the field of management and psychology since 2009. Currently, he is associated with Uttarakhand Open University Haldwani as an assistant professor in the Department of Psychology. He has 4 published books in his account and 20 research papers published in various reputed journals including UGC, Scopus, ABDC, and others.

Rachit Ranjan is Assistant Professor at the School of Management, Babu Banarasi Das University, Lucknow.

Messomo Elle Serge has been an associate professor in corporate finance since 2017. He is a teacher and a researcher in the Department of Banking and Finance at the University of Buea, Cameroon. He teaches many courses including bank regulation and governance, insurance management and practice, entrepreneurial finance, financial management, financial institutions and markets. His areas of research are microfinance, entrepreneurial finance, local public governance, and financial institution governance. He has published in many renowned journals like *Strategic Change* and *Managerial and Decision Economics*.

Muhammad Ramzan Sheikh is Professor of Economics, School of Economics, Bahauddin Zakariya University Multan, Pakistan.

Jyoti Shukla is Assistant Professor at the School of Management, Babu Banarasi Das University, Lucknow.

Tarika Singh Sikarwar has more than 17 years of experience as a training, coaching, learning, and development professional involved in management, leadership development, motivation, team building, out-of-the-box thinking, communication skills, specialist learning, and development for industry-leading multinationals across a range of industries. Her expertise includes extensive consultancy, writing, and delivery of training, along with setup and delivery of various management, leadership, communication, and strategic management qualifications. Presently, she is a professor and deputy director at Prestige Institute Management and Research, Gwalior. She is a member of management bodies like AIMA, the Indian Accounting Association, the Indian Commerce Association, and the Gwalior Management Association. She has been active in research, publishing more than 6 books with international publishers and writing more than 70 research papers in journals of international and national repute (Scopus, ABDC, WoS, UGC Care). She is a PhD guide for management and commerce at Jiwaji University.

Sana Sultan is a visiting lecturer in economics, School of Economics, Bahauddin Zakariya University Multan, Pakistan.

Aamir Ahmad Teeli is a research scholar in the Department of Economics, Central University of Tamil Nadu, India, with a specialization in macroeconomics and economic development.

Alok Tewari is a research scholar in the Faculty of Management at the Dr A.P.J. Abdul Kalam Technical University, Lucknow.

Nitesh Thakur is Assistant Professor at the Institute of Business Management, GLA University, Mathura.

Okorie E. Uchechukwu is in the Department of Economics and Development Studies, College of Management and Social Sciences, Covenant University, Ota, Ogun State.

Vimal Chandra Verma is Assistant Professor, BBA Department, Siddhartha University, Siddhartha Nagaris.

Namita Verma has been a working professional in the field of management and economics since 2000. Currently, she is associated with Uttarakhand Open University Haldwani as Assistant Professor in the Department of Economics. She has 2 published books and 15 research papers published in various reputed journals.

Nidhi Verma holds a PhD in applied business economics, focusing on the role of micro small medium enterprises in employment generation, particularly within the Agra footwear cluster. During her doctoral studies, she published several papers. Following her PhD, she transitioned into the corporate sector as a market researcher, gaining experience across various sectors like healthcare, FMCG, automotive, and cybersecurity. Presently, she serves as a market intelligence analyst, responsible for identifying and prioritizing external data sources, gathering and analyzing markets, customer and competitive data, and translating insights into actionable recommendations. Dr Verma has become the primary resource for external information related to India, actively contributing to shaping the go-to-market strategy in collaboration with India's managing director and the Market Intelligence team.

Siti Rohaida Mohamad Zainal is Associate Professor at the School of Management, the Universiti Sains Malaysia (USM). She graduated with a BBA from the University of Missouri Kansas City, USA and an MBA from USM. She joined USM in 2007 after completing her PhD at the Universiti Teknologi Mara, Shah Alam. She is involved in strategy and organisational management at USM and teaches strategic human resource management, HR analytics, leadership dynamics, and strategic leadership. Currently, she is Deputy Dean of the Academic, Career and International division. In addition to assisting in administrative work, she is active with research and publication activities, publishing in various indexed and non-indexed journals. She also leads research grants and recently was awarded a research grant from the Ministry of Higher Education. She is actively invited as a speaker for both leadership and research methodology-related topics at various institutions. She was appointed by the Malaysia Prison Department as a researcher studying the parole system. She was also appointed as a research follow for the Ministry of Human Resource Malaysia. In addition, she is very active in sharing her work experience with primary and secondary school students. Her areas of research are leadership, career management strategies, and people management strategies.

Review Board

S. no.	*Name of the Review Board*	
1.	Name Affiliation Email Research Specialization	Prof Nisha Noor Exeed College, Westford Education Group, Sharjah, UAE Noorbaloch60@gmail.com Organizational Behavior, Human Resource Management
2.	Name Affiliation Email Research Specialization	Prof. (Dr) Divya J Thakur COED, Chandigarh University, Punjab divya.minhas1331@gmail.com Business Management and Leadership Technology
3.	Name Affiliation Email Research Specialization	Dr Radhika Malhotra Institute of Management Studies, Ghaziabad radhika.narula@gmail.com Marketing
4.	Name Affiliation Email Research Specialization	Sneha Kadyan Jindal Global Business School skadyan@jgu.edu.in Economic Sociology and Gender
5.	Name Affiliation Email Research Specialization	Dr Mohd Merajuddin Inamdar National Institute of Securities Markets meraj.inamdar1@gmail.com Finance, ESG, Sustainability
6.	Name Affiliation Email Research Specialization	Tanya Nautiyal Jamia milia Islamia tanyanautiyal92@gmail.com Financial Inclusion, Development Economics
7.	Name Affiliation Email Research Specialization	Dr Sinem Koçak Independent Researcher sinemakcay@hotmail.com.tr Applied Macro Econometric

(Continued)

S. no.	*Name of the Review Board*	
8.	Name Affiliation Email Research Specialization	Lotica Surana ITM University, Gwalior lotica111surana@gmail.com Finance
9.	Name Affiliation Email Research Specialization	Laeeq Razzak Janjua WSB University, Dąbrowa Górnicza, Poland janjua.ue@gmail.com Finance, International Economics, Econometrics
10.	Name Affiliation Email Research Specialization	Saima Khuhro Dawood University of Engineering and Technology, Pakistan shinelikestar786@gmail.com Business and Innovation
11.	Name Affiliation Email Research Specialization	Faisal Abbas National University of Sciences and Technology (NUST), Islamabad, Pakistan dr.faisal@s3h.nust.edu.pk Development Economics
12.	Name Affiliation Email Research Specialization	Adedoyin Isola LAWAL Bowen University Iwo Osun State Nigeria adedoyin.lawal@bowen.edu.ng Economics
13.	Name Affiliation Email Research Specialization	Sakhi Roy Amity University roy.sakhi88@gmail.com Development Economics
14.	Name Affiliation Email Research Specialization	Syed Asif Mehdi Babasaheb Bhimrao Ambedkar University asifmehdi16@gmail.com Entrepreneurship
15.	Name Affiliation Email Research Specialization	Dr Supriya Lamba Sahdev ISBR Business School Lamba.Supriya9@gmail.com; Supriya.lamba@isbr.in Management
16.	Name Affiliation Email Research Specialization	Dr Uzma Bashir National University of Modern Languages uzma.bashir@numl.edu.pk Macroeconomics, Finance, Monetary Policy, Climate Change
17.	Name Affiliation Email Research Specialization	Padmalini Singh RV Institute of Management singhpadmalini@gmail.com Marketing and Finance

(Continued)

S. no.	*Name of the Review Board*	
18.	Name Affiliation Email Research Specialization	Mirela Panait Petroleum-Gas University of Ploiesti mirela.matei@upg-ploiesti.ro Sustainable Development, Energy Transition, CSR, Financial Inclusion, International Finance
19.	Name Affiliation Email Research Specialization	Dr Bosede Comfort Olopade Department Economics, Adeleke University Ede, Osun State, Nigeria olopadebc@gmail.com Development Economics
20.	Name Affiliation Email Research Specialization	OGEDE Jimoh Sina Olabisi Onabanjo University sinaogede@oouagoiwoye.edu.ng Financial Economics, Energy and Development Economics
21.	Name Affiliation Email Research Specialization	Dr Mandeep Kaur School of Law, Mahindra University mandeep.kaur@mahindrauniversity.edu.in Law

Part I

Conceptual and Theoretical Background

1 From Exclusion to Empowerment

Unveiling Financial Inclusion Challenges across Developing, Emerging, and Developed Nations

Anamika Choudhary

The story of development is one of persistent and incremental change that empowers people living in poverty to overcome obstacles and inequalities and flourish. Research on poverty reduction often concentrates on financial development and governance. According to economic theory, persistent inequalities too have a negative impact on the long-term development prospects of an economy. With financial exclusion, no economy can afford to develop with sustainability. When a large group of vulnerable section of population is not able to avail the formal financial services, economy whether developing, emerging, or developed loses its scope to sustain its economic growth. People from underserved communities, such as those who are disabled, migrant workers, women, or those who live in poverty and rural areas, are frequently excluded from financial services, which perpetuates inequality and limits their ability to participate in the economy. It becomes significant to understand the concept of financial exclusion and the economic theories related to it to comprehend it much better.

1.1 Economics of Financial Exclusion

It is increasingly understood that financial exclusion is a multifaceted notion that includes a wide array of obstacles to utilizing and accessing mainstream financial services. The term financial exclusion can be defined both in specific and a broad theoretical sense. Of the two meanings, one is based on banking experts' ideas of defining financial exclusion, which is primarily connected with their commitment to meeting the Reserve Bank of India's (RBI's) aim of achieving 100% financial inclusion, while the other is based on how financial economists define it so as to relate the issue of financial exclusion with other broad fundamental issues, such as social exclusion as well as economic marginalization. Obviously, the former category of definitions delivers a specific and a practical definition of financial exclusion, while the latter defines it from a theoretical framework including all aspects of financial exclusion and it is intertwined with other key areas, such as social and economic marginalization.

To track the origin of the term, the phrase "financial exclusion" was first used in the financial literature to describe a situation in which there was limited access to people to banking services due to bank closures in 1993 (Kumar, 2011). It implies

DOI: 10.4324/9781032655185-2

that initially financial exclusion was limited to the geographical accessibility of the people to banks and not the lack of banking services or insurance services. However, the term "financial exclusion" to imply the lack of accessibility to mainstream banking and insurance services started to be used since 1999.

It is no doubt that social and economic isolation are linked to financial exclusion. Some definitions of financial exclusion meaningfully include this connection.

The definition of inclusion (or, alternately, financial exclusion) has been established within the wider social inclusion (or exclusion) problem. Financial exclusion, according to one of the earliest definitions by Leyshon and Thrift (1995), is the practice of preventing members of specific socio-economic groups and individuals from accessing the financial system. Rakesh Mohan, the RBI's deputy governor, stated in a 2006 speech that "financial exclusion signifies the lack of access by certain segments of the society to appropriate, low cost, fair and safe financial products and services from mainstream providers". Similar opinions were expressed by Usha Thorat, the deputy governor of the RBI, in a speech in 2007 when she stated that "by financial exclusion we mean the provision of affordable financial services, (viz., access to payments and remittance facilities, savings loans, and insurance services) by the formal financial system to those who tend to be excluded". The emphasis has now shifted to other dimensions of exclusion, such as access, especially conditional access, technological access, etc. The geographical dimension of the problem of financial exclusion almost ceases to exist except in some uninhibited or marginally inhibited places. Since 1991, strong financial sector liberalization measures have increased competition among banks, forcing some, notably nationalized banks, to change their focus from "social and development banking" to "profit-oriented banking", again leading to a sort of exclusion of the deprived section.

People from underserved communities, such as those who are disabled, migrant workers, women, or live in poverty and rural areas, are frequently excluded from financial services, which perpetuates inequality and limits their ability to participate in the economy. In developing economies, where more than 90% of world's population is unbanked, the urgency of financial inclusion is recognized but it poses a big challenge. In developed economies, according to the Federal Deposit Insurance Corporation, FDIC (2014), 7.7% of US households, for example, did not have a bank account in 2013, and another 20% were underbanked, which means they had a bank account but also accessed alternative financial services (AFS) instead of the banking industry. There are numerous complex and multidimensional factors that are held responsible for this kind of financial exclusion. Different economies have stated different socio-economic, political, geographical, and cultural conditions for which they require a wide-ranging variety of technologies, products, and providers aptly suited for their economies (Shafi & Medabesh, 2012).

1.2 Review of Related Literature

Various studies have been conducted with respect to various aspects of financial exclusion as well as financial inclusion, the need for financial inclusion, the financial empowerment that this financial inclusion brings with itself to the deprived section of the population, the urgency of the inclusion of the excluded population in availing financial services so as to meet the sustainable development goals (SDGs) and related studies. Some of such studies are stated here.

In the paper by TijjaniMuhammad et al. (2022) they aimed to evaluate the factors that contribute to financial exclusion in northern Nigeria, including the factors that influence people's ability to receive banking services at reasonable and competitive pricing. The study utilized vulnerable group theory (religiosity and poverty) and financial literacy theory (awareness) under structural equation modelling. The survey approach was utilized in this study along with the stratified sample methodology because it offers rich and accurate data from respondents from different strata. The uniqueness of this study demonstrates that it does not use the vulnerable group theory or the financial literacy theory as justification.

M. Azimi (2022) in his analysis starts with the creation of a thorough composite financial inclusion index made up of financial service penetration, availability, and usage, as well as the estimation of heterogeneous panel data models enhanced with well-known variables. A long-term association between economic growth, financial inclusion, and the control variables in the complete panel, including income level and regional economies, is supported by the panel cointegration test results.

Biplob Kumar Nandi et al. (2022) stated that a 1% rise in the financial inclusion index results in a 0.0153%-point gain in per capita GDP for countries with low and medium levels of financial inclusion and a 0.0794%-point increase for nations with high levels of financial inclusion. According to this study, developing economies with higher levels of financial inclusion would see rapid economic growth. According to this study, nations with low and medium levels of financial inclusion may suffer from weaker levels of governance, a higher concentration of a small number of agents on the financial market, and slower economic growth. This study has greater appeal because it investigates the problem by simply using a sample of emerging economies.

T. Lal (2021): Through the use of socio-economic empowerment, his research seeks to examine the effects of financial inclusion on the economic growth of marginalized populations. The study contributes to the story of financial inclusion as it relates to the socio-economic empowerment and economic growth of underprivileged communities. It examines how marginalized populations' socio-economic circumstances may contribute to their exclusion from the nation's financial system. The study also offers important insights for policymakers, academics, and researchers at the national and international levels to develop and implement programmes that will expand the right to use financial products and services, reducing poverty incidence, income parity, social and economic empowerment, and gender- and caste-based discrimination.

Noha Emara and Mahmoud Moheildin (2020):This study's objective is to examine how financial inclusion has affected extreme poverty in a sample of 34 countries between 1990 and 2017. This study starts by estimating the impact of financial inclusion, using measures of access and usage, on the eradication of extreme poverty by 2030, the first SDG. The study's findings show that for the entire sample and the

Middle East/North Africa area, financial access initiatives have a favourable, statistically significant influence on reducing extreme poverty. The goal of this study is to evaluate how crucial financial inclusion is to ending extreme poverty by 2030, the deadline that UN member states have set for attaining the SDGs.

Peterson K. Ozili (2021): This study offers a thorough analysis of the most recent data on financial inclusion from every continent in the world. Financial inclusion is influenced and impacted by the extent of financial innovation, poverty, financial sector stability, the status of the economy, financial literacy, and regulatory frameworks that vary across nations. The main conclusions of this analysis show that financial inclusion is influenced and affected by factors such as financial innovation, poverty levels, financial sector stability, economic health, financial literacy, and regulatory frameworks that vary among nations. Finally, the issues raised in this work offer up a number of new research directions.

Shivangi Bhatia and Seema Singh (2019): The present article investigates the social, political, and economic dimensions of women's empowerment. It also conducts a test to determine whether the dimensions change as a result of financial inclusion. The results indicated that the Pradhan Mantri Jan Dhan Yojana initiative has had a positive impact on the social, political, and economic dimensions of women's empowerment, particularly for women living in slums. The study contributes to the existing body of knowledge by advancing the debate on women in urban neighbourhoods and identifying the significant need for the development of a formal financial system to expand the scope of financial inclusion.

Dinabandhu Sethi and D. Acharya (2018): This study aims to evaluate the dynamic effects of financial inclusion on economic growth across a broad spectrum of industrialized and developing nations. According to the empirical results, there is a long-term, positive correlation between financial inclusion and economic growth in 31 different nations. In addition, the panel causality test demonstrates that financial inclusion and economic growth are causally related in both directions. Thus, the study affirms that one of the primary forces behind economic growth is financial inclusion.

C. V. Reddy (2017): The objective of the current study is to assess the contribution of 12 enabling environmental variables to global financial inclusion across 55 countries. Factorial regression analysis was used to analyse the effects of each extracted factor on overall financial inclusion, and the linear multiple regression model was applied to emphasize the effects of each individual variable on overall financial inclusion. The empirical findings demonstrate that the bulk of the predictor variables under investigation significantly improve financial inclusion as a whole.

Asli Demirgüç-Kuntand Dorothe Singer (2017): Financial services can contribute to inclusive growth and economic development. This report also explores some of the obstacles to broader financial inclusion as well as potential research directions. The usage of financial goods, such as payment services, savings accounts, loans, and insurance, can support inclusive growth and economic development, according to current empirical research.

Dipasha Sharma (2016): There is a strong association between banking penetration and growth in the Indian economy. The goal of this study is to evaluate the relationship between the many facets of financial inclusion and the expansion of the developing Indian economy. Vector auto-regression (VAR) models and the Granger causality test were used in this study's design, methodology, and strategy to examine the main research question in the context of India. According to empirical findings and analysis, there is a positive correlation between economic growth and many aspects of financial inclusion, particularly banking penetration, the availability of banking services, and the use of such services for deposits. Geographic reach and economic development have a bi-directional causal relationship, according to Granger causality research, but the quantity of deposits and loans has a one-way causal relationship.

Balachandran Vivek (2016) in the paper focused on financial inclusion and on strategies to make available a range of financial products and services that meet the specific needs of the poor. His paper seeks to determine the level of financial inclusion awareness among rural women in the Tirunelveli District.

Muneeb Hussain Gattoo and S. Akhtar (2015): Gattoo and Akhtar concluded in their study that financial inclusion discussion in the emerging and developing world arises from the awareness that a robust and dynamic financial sector does not always mean increased financial access for all, regardless of socio-economic divide.

A. Miles (2015): Miles asserted in the paper that the number of people around the globe who have access to financial products and services has increased by about 20% in the past three years. Cyn-Young Park and Rogelio V. Mercado (2015) in their study stated that financial inclusion significantly reduces poverty in developing Asian economies. They developed a financial inclusion indicator in order to evaluate the impact of various macroeconomic and country-specific factors on the degree of financial inclusion in 37 developing Asian nations and examined the impact of financial inclusion on poverty and income inequality, along with other control variables. Their findings indicated that income per capita, the rule of law, and demographic factors have a significant impact on financial inclusion in developing Asia.

M. Shafi and A. Medabesh (2012): The problem of financial exclusion is severe in the country. This paper attempts to evaluate the severity of the problem of financial exclusion in the state of Jammu and Kashmir. What has been the impact of the RBI's initiatives towards greater financial inclusion, and what remains to be done to attain complete and meaningful financial inclusion, was studied in the research.

R. Cnaan et al. (2012): Social and personal deprivation contributes to financial exclusion and should be viewed as key barriers to financial inclusion. The focus was on determining whether financial inclusion has been effectively implemented in four rural South Indian locations where banks have asserted that financial inclusion is complete. They concluded that financial inclusion is not a unidimensional phenomenon and should be studied in a multidimensional manner, extending from having a bank account to utilizing modern financial instruments to their fullest extent.

1.3 Theories of Financial Exclusion

In order to provide a theoretical framework for financial exclusion, it is necessary to consider both fundamental and institutional factors. The following factors can be linked to the genesis of financial exclusion (Figure 1.1).

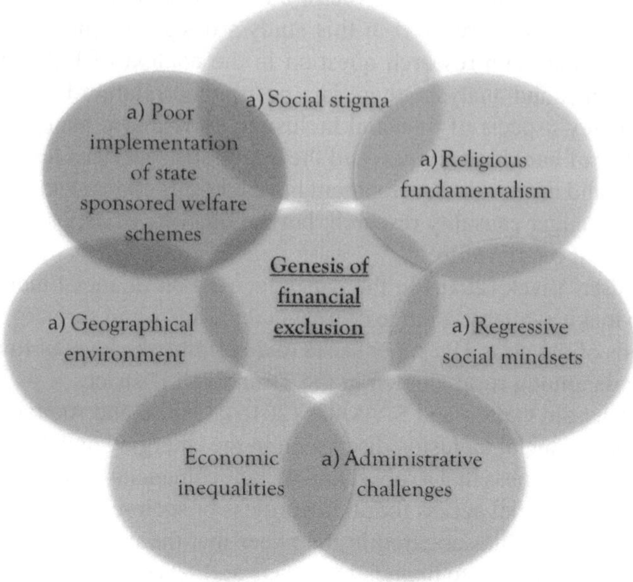

Figure 1.1 Genesis of financial exclusion

The shortage of bank branches in rural areas and the bank being majorly owned by the private owners became one of the main causes from excluding a vast section of population from accessing the mainstream financial services. Though with the nationalization of banks in 1969, the banks and its branches were opened, only some marginalized areas were excluded.

Here, we seek to identify the theoretical framework that may clarify the type of financial exclusion that results from only economic variables. The basic causes, such as a lack of income, assets, etc., must be emphasized, even though today's financial exclusion is mostly linked to factors related to technology, the financial crisis, and market-driven motivations (Kumar, 2011). Significantly there stand two theories which can better explain the process of financial exclusion (Figure 1.2).

a Free-market model
b The theory of asymmetric information

1.3.1 *Free-Market Model*

Beginning with Adam Smith, a significant number of economic theories have greatly influenced the development of the idea that the "market" is the only treatment for every economic problem. In essence, these theories contend that an unregulated economy has a natural tendency to approach the "Pareto Optimum," which is the point at which all resources are theoretically evenly distributed and used to

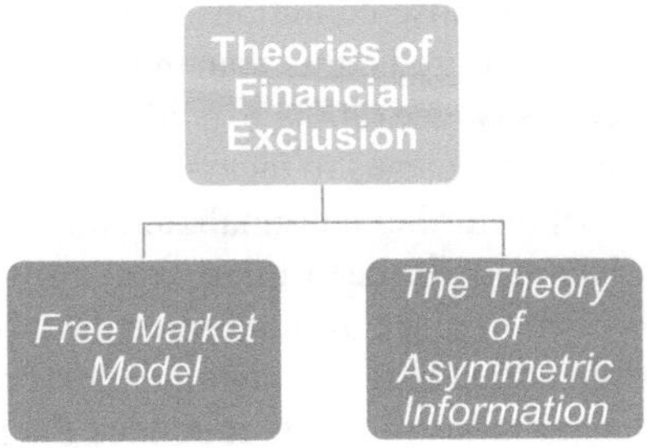

Figure 1.2 Theories of financial exclusion

ensure the greatest amount of wealth production. From the time of classical writers like Adam Smith and David Ricardo, it has been asserted that competition is possible through the "laissez faire" or the non-interventionist policy and will help to reap the benefits of eradicating any evil that an economy is likely to face. Government intervention through policy will divert economies from achieving growth and the elimination of all types of imbalances. This intellectual underpinning has served as the cornerstone for the free-market paradigm that we describe here.

Earlier the financial institutions used to deal with only financial transactions of deposit savings and lending but in the present times, financial institutions including banking institutions also participate in stock market activities to raise money for their core businesses and have started issuing their shares on the stock market with lots of publicity. The disinvestment policy of the government has propelled the commercial banks to join the upcoming private banks in flocking to the capital market to raise money. Selling out 49% of the government stake in the State Bank of India by the Finance Ministry serves as evidence of this. This seems a radical transformation placing these institutions on excellent ratings from well-known worldwide rating agencies like Standard and Poor's. *Therefore, these institutions have been compelled to refrain from issuing riskier loans as a result of the pressure to increase their stock market investing value.*

The contradiction that exists at this point is that while deregulation, in the opinion of proponents of market-driven policies, was looked upon to improve financial inclusion, *financial exclusion appears to have emerged as a serious issue.* The proponents claimed with the market-driven methods, acceptable financial products and services would emerge as a response to the market demand and would thus boost financial inclusion. But on the contrary, it led to more of financial exclusion. The reason being that as more financial products are introduced to the market, lending risk also rises, forcing banks to concentrate more on specific customer groups than on all customers. The less valued or the non-valuable customers are financially excluded and valuable customers strategically included. The vulnerable section again is deprived while the valuable ones significantly increase. The majority of private banks and new-generation banks appear to have adopted this strategy. When the banks fix a minimum amount required in opening an account, it deprives those section who could have been included in the mainstream financial system but are held back when they are unable to fulfil those conditions. This requirement actually proves that "valuable customers" are desired rather than those who want to open an account with a zero or low balance. As Boyce (2000, p. 649) rightly opines: "Customer valuation is shown to have become a means to increase shareholder income and wealth, almost inevitable at the cost of further marginalizing the poor and disadvantaged".

Financial exclusion has actually been made worse by the deregulation of the financial sector that has been in place in India since the advent of neo-liberal policies. Financial crisis when added with this deregulation process accelerates financial exclusion. The financial industry wants to reduce the risk whenever it faces a financial crisis and so it moves towards quality and affluent customer base. This economic process is described as becoming "increasingly exclusionary in response to a financial crisis founded in higher levels of competition and extreme levels of indebtedness" as stated by Leyshon and Thrift (1995, p. 312). It can thus be concluded that deregulation, liberalization and increasing high level of competition have all lead to more of financial exclusion.

In actuality, this strategic move has caused a division between customers with lower incomes or socially disadvantaged customers and customers with higher incomes, particularly in the case of the financial products to which they have accessibility. Numerous other variables, such as the recent technology breakthroughs obtained by banks and the rest of the world but not readily available to many lower-class consumers, have contributed to the intensification of this divide.

Banks may now easily target standardized clients for cross-selling their new products because of the development of a variety of financial products. Customers with low-income profiles might not be able to afford all of the things that the banks are prepared to sell. For example, in the US market, banks have been driven to look for lucrative "standardized" customers because they seem to be lower risk and are able to invest in multiple products at once. This all has led to the wide emergence of financial exclusion.

Conclusively it can be said that the "Free Market Model" may worsen the issue of financial exclusion and result in a financial space catastrophe in an economy if unchecked, as it holds that unrestrained deregulation of financial activities is driven by the desire for profit. The necessity of the hour is therefore for some sort of "intervention" to financial exclusion in the form of the requirements that the government would place on banks such as self-regulation. "Self-regulation" here refers to banking sectors whose main goals are to support the weaker segments of their clientele and grow their local economies. Institutions that have adopted this strategy have strived to increased revenue and improved financial operations efficiency.

1.3.2 The Theory of Asymmetric Information

We need to comprehend how information asymmetry stimulates and aggravates the problem of financial exclusion. There are two kinds of market-goods market and credit market. While transaction appears simpler in the goods market and less onerous, as the seller does not have to worry about who the buyer is or what happens to the commodity after the sale as long as he gets paid (Llanto, 1989), transactions in the credit market are relatively difficult and time consuming. Transactions in this market are in the nature of future contracts and endures for a longer duration. It can be explained with the help of an example. Whether it is the case of mortgage or a loan, the transaction of these products requires an amount of information whether the borrower is having a good record as a customer and his personal profile is also considered. Given this context, it makes sense that banks would devote a significant amount of their attention to finding "good" borrowers and "good" projects. The bank is concerned about the borrower's use of the loan and his compliance with the contract's terms and conditions, unlike a commodity seller who is not concerned about the financial product's consumer (Clemenz, 1986).

The asymmetric information can be seen in the context of the banks who provide loans but do not have the complete information about the buyer and thus are not sure whether these loans turn into non-performing assets. The customers here are relatively more informed of their personal capabilities, and they highlight their strengths and play with the banks by concealing their project weaknesses. The banks use screening methods as safety measure to avoid the risk of default. In doing this, it prevents the vulnerable section from using the financial services. Those borrowers who do not have a balanced information to avail the financial transaction and services are excluded from entering the financial mainstream.

1.4 Determinants of Financial Inclusion

The term "financial inclusion" is an initiative that makes sure that the regulated financial system is accessible, readily available, and used by all people. The primary definition of financial inclusion is the exclusion of a particular segment of the population.

Financial inclusion is regarded as a crucial indicator of global society's development and prosperity and an important indicator of overall growth in any economy. Previous research has identified financial inclusion as an economic tool for inclusive growth. It is consequently critical to understand the factors that influence financial inclusion. G-20 nations have emphasized financial inclusion as a means to achieve gender equality and other sustainable development objectives. Access to financial services is clearly emphasized in SDG 1, which calls for eradicating all forms of poverty. The provision of financial services to social strata that would otherwise be excluded increases their ability to ascend the economic ladder of opportunity and prosperity. Developing nations are adopting an inclusive financial model to accomplish fundamental and formative goals of empowerment and global development.

Many existing studies use financial indices derived purely on supply related data (such as the number of bank branches), which fail to incorporate demand side changes (Dev, 2006). Another study by (Beck et al., 2007) estimated that one may have multiple bank accounts and it is also possible those having accounts may not be in usage. There is still a considerable debate about how socio-economic development impacts financial inclusion. Over a four-year period, an econometric analysis using a panel data structure of 28 Indian states discovered that income, infrastructure, and employment prospects are among the most important predictors of financial inclusion (Raichoudhury, 2020). Differences in financial liberalization policies, GDP, rural population percentage, and mobile money service expansion are some macro-level differences that explain this discrepancy. Differences in literacy rates and payment methods, such as government handouts, gender, age, employment status, and ownership of a mobile phone all have a significant and favourable impact on financial inclusion. Lack of documents, trust, and money, on the other hand, are important impediments to financial inclusion.

Financial inclusion is influenced by and affected by factors such as financial innovation, poverty levels, financial sector stability, economic health, financial literacy, and regulatory frameworks that vary among nations. Developing economies with higher levels of financial inclusion would see rapid economic growth.

CRISIL (2013) developed an index called Inclusix to track the growth of Financial Inclusion in a developing economy India. Indicators included by the agency were of the supply side which included bank penetration, deposit penetration, and credit penetration. M. Sarma and J. Pais (2011) developed a multidimensional index for financial inclusion which included both the demand and supply side factors, like the number of bank branches indicates the supply side while the usage of credit and deposit accounts indicates the demand factors.

1.5 Challenges Faced by the Developing, Emerging, and Developed Economies in the Way to Financial Inclusion

Financial inclusion has taken on a central role in the public policy discourse of developing nations. The process of financial inclusion in India was launched in 1969 with the nationalization of banks. Afterwards, India employed numerous tactics, including the lead bank programme, obligatory lending to key industries, kisan credit cards, collaborating with banks to offer banking services to customers' doorsteps, and among others, to encourage financial inclusion due to the importance of financial inclusion in the provision of public services like direct benefit transfers. Thus, it is true that financial inclusion is crucial for economic growth. A portion of the population is brought into the formal channels of development and helps to save them from predatory lenders. The provision of financial services to social strata that would otherwise be excluded increases their ability to ascend the economic ladder of opportunity and prosperity.

There are many barriers to financial inclusion. They stand as challenges and must be coped up with to move away from financial exclusion towards financial inclusion and to bring the empowerment of the deprived section. Social and personal deprivation contribute to financial exclusion and should be regarded as key barriers to financial inclusion. Access to financial services influences the quality of life of the disadvantaged and enable them to increase and diversify their incomes, thereby improving their social and economic conditions. Because of a lack of financial services, a large number of poor households have to depend on their modest resources or on moneylenders, limiting their ability to actively participate in and gain the advantages of growth. Nations with low and medium levels of financial inclusion may suffer from weaker levels of governance, a higher concentration of a small number of agents on the financial market, and slower economic growth.

Informational asymmetries, difficulties in contract design and enforcement, and higher transaction costs are the primary theoretical arguments that economic theory postulates regarding the failure of financial markets in developing poor and rural areas. Low demand for such services may result from illiteracy, fewer investment opportunities in rural areas, and complicated loan contracts (Basu, 2006). When households' access to financial services is restricted, it becomes one of the primary causes of persistent inequality (World Bank, 2007). According to economic theory, persistent inequalities have a negative impact on the long-term development prospects of an economy. While establishing causality between financial development and economic growth has been arduous, with no simple answers (Gattoo & Akhtar, (2015), the evidence of a strong link between financial development and economic growth has continued to build. The interest in the financial inclusion discourse in the developing world originates from the realization that a strong and vibrant financial system does not necessarily imply expanding financial access to all across the societal divide (Honohan, 2004).

Financial inclusion has enormous potential, but it faces several challenges in moving forward. According to the most recent Global Findex report, the challenges of financial inclusion are well known: approximately two billion people, primarily in developing countries and emerging economies, lack access to the fundamental financial products and services that many of us take for granted. For people living in poverty, the inability to save, borrow, or transfer money reliably, readily, and affordably is a significant obstacle to enhancing their lives (Miles, 2015).

In recent years, both in India and around the world, financial inclusion has drawn considerable attention.

The developing economies may face the challenge of restricted access to formal financial institutions, lack of financial literacy opportunities, discriminatory lending practices, and restricted educational options contributing to exclusion of the marginalized section of the population.

The challenge in the emerging economies may include the fact that as financial services frequently have significant prices, such as minimum deposit requirements or account maintenance fees, it can restrict people with minimal financial resources. Additionally, a lot of migrants and refugees lack the paperwork needed to create bank accounts or making use of financial services. As a result, they are prevented from taking part in a formal financial system and have fewer options for saving, obtaining credit, and other financial activities.

A study by Raksmey et al. (2022) shows that macroprudential regulation has a detrimental impact on financial inclusion in developing and developed nations. While macroprudential regulation has a negative impact on the utilization of banking services in emerging or developing nations, it discourages consumers from using banking services in developed nations too, but it also makes those services more accessible.

1.6 Measures to Empower the Excluded Section in the Financial Mainstream to Achieve SDGs

1.6.1 Different Approaches to Address the Issue of Financial Exclusion

An approach belies that financial development precedes economic development. Therefore, providing the excluded section an easy access to all the financial products and services would be a strategic measure to resolve the issue of financial exclusion and bring in financial inclusion. The financial demand of the population is required to be fulfilled which would only bring an expansion of the populace in the financial mainstream thereby bringing in financial progress. Major Indian commercial banks' extensive branch development since 1969, when they were nationalized, is evidence to it. Opening No-Frill Accounts is an effort to introduce previously unbanked people to financial products in an effort to draw them into the world of finance. This is an active financial development wherein financial development leads to economic development.

Another approach is of passive financial development wherein economic development and empowerment lead to financial development. It is stated that the demand for different types of financial products suited to their needs increases when people are actively engaged in economic activities that generate employment and money. The demand for financial products from this generation will encourage the creation of financial institutions. The increasing number of informal financial institutions in the rural pockets of the nations is a result of the demand of seeking credit by the individuals at whatever costs and from whatever sources accessible to them.

Another approach states that either of the above two possibilities can take place. Any development can precede the other. No one can say which is the beginning and which is the end. Again, there is an integrationist approach which is considered as the greatest method to address the issue of financial exclusion by integrating with the labour market. This is due to the fact that once people begin working at paid employment, the revenue they generate from those positions will compel them to seek out different financial products, therefore resulting in their financial inclusion. An appropriate illustration of how integration into the job market may be a tool for financial inclusion is the Mahatma Gandhi National Rural Employment Guarantee Programme (MGNREGA), which has been effectively implemented in India. Every worker under this programme will be required to open an account with any nationalized bank in order to receive his regular pay. The pay is sent out via accounts. In this situation, a person must be in contact with the banks at all times while working under the aforementioned scheme, which will instill a habit of banking in that individual.

1.6.2 Financial Inclusion – A Holistic Line of Action

Financial inclusion is thus a holistic approach wherein a comprehensive range of financial products and services, including microloans, credit facilities, investment opportunities are included to give the form of a true financial inclusion. It is not just limited to accessibility but extends to provide the individuals with the necessary tools, resources, and knowledge to actively engage in a former financial system.

Financial inclusion is one of the perquisites to achieve the SDGs of the United Nations. It emerges as a critical enabler of sustainable development by opening up the availability of financial services, enabling the underserved, and encouraging partnership. Women are disproportionately excluded from financial services due to barriers such as difficulty in obtaining credit, unfair interest rates, and cultural biases that limit their ability to make financial decisions. It so happens that the social fabric of the developing economies is such that it limits the accessibility of women to be a part of the formal financial system. They are made to subjugate and subdue and not made to participate in the financial system in an active mode. This is one of the reasons which has deprived them from becoming financially empowered.

With financial inclusion initiatives, when the women are made to be a part of the formal financial mainstream, the process from exclusion to empowerment will hold its meaning in a real form. They need to become financial literate and realize the significance of financial empowerment. There may be certain hurdles that make them hesitate to cut the shackles of financial exclusion. Their level of literacy, their social custom to remain in the four walls of house, their indecisiveness, their hesitation to proceed on their own, their ignorance to the changing times, non-frequent banking visits, non-accessibility to the digital technology, and many such related reasons act as a challenge to transform a financial excluded economy to a financially included one.

Formal identity is difficult for women to get in many countries, which limits their ability to access important financial services like bank accounts, property ownership, credit records, and financial activities including saving, obtaining loans, and growing enterprises even in developed economies. The problem is made worse by the limited availability of essential resources like mobile phones for financial transactions. The profitability of women as a consumer segment is also frequently overlooked by financial service providers, who frequently fail to spend adequately. Financial inclusion is crucial for empowering women to break out from traditional roles, pursue their entrepreneurial dreams, and achieve financial independence in all types of economies. It helps to close the gender pay gap. Their economic involvement benefits communities in numerous capacities since they typically devote a large share of their money and resources to their families' health, education, and welfare, which improves social outcomes.in goods, services, and distribution methods that are tailored specifically to their requirements.

Additionally, financial institutions frequently overlook the need for inclusive digital platforms, affordable banking options, and assistive technologies to ensure that individuals with disabilities can properly use and access financial services. The divyang section of the population need to be facilitated to avail the banking services as an initiative to financial inclusion. Barrier free accessibility to the banks is necessary for them and more banking facilities must be provided to them so that they get empowered by being financially included. From being non-identified to getting included in the financial mainstream would require endeavours but then with proper initiatives and some policy formulations, the divyangjan population would not be financially excluded. *Through financial empowerment, people with disabilities* can obtain freedom and autonomy.

Considering the migrant workers who can also build financial security and protect the futures of their families. A lot of migrants and refugees generally lack the paperwork needed to create bank accounts and use financial services. As a result, they are prevented from taking part in a formal financial system and have fewer options for saving, obtaining credit, and other financial activities. Financial inclusion provides access to economic prospects in rural and poverty-stricken areas, helping populations to escape poverty. By enabling people to manage risks, achieve their goals, amass wealth, and protect their financial future, this catalyses empowerment.

A comprehensive range of financial products and services, including micro-loans, credit facilities, investment opportunities, and more, are included in a holistic approach that represents true financial inclusion. It goes beyond access alone, providing individuals with the necessary tools, resources, and knowledge to actively engage in a former financial system. This empowerment enables people to use inexpensive, ethical financial services that meet their unique needs and make informed judgements.

Women are disproportionately excluded from financial services due to barriers such as difficulty obtaining credit, unfair interest rates, and cultural biases that limit their ability to make financial decisions. Additionally, financial institutions frequently overlook the need for inclusive digital platforms, affordable banking options, and assistive technologies to ensure that individuals with disabilities can properly use and access financial services. The global imperative to close the gender gap in access to and use of financial services has given the search for financial inclusion enormous momentum. Through 26 active innovative financial solution initiatives, Women's World Banking facilitated access and utilization for 8.6 million women across seven countries in 2022. These remedies are absolutely necessary since financial inclusion entails more than just having access to bank accounts

1.7 Conclusion

We have the ability to address long-standing gaps while promoting gender parity, equitable society, and economic expansion by giving marginalized people access to financial services. Through financial empowerment, people with disabilities can obtain freedom and autonomy, and migrant workers can build financial security and protect the futures of their families. Financial inclusion is crucial for empowering women to break out from traditional roles, pursue their entrepreneurial dreams, and achieve financial independence. It helps close the gender pay gap. Women's economic involvement benefits communities in numerous capacities since they typically devote a large share of their money and resources to their families' health, education, and welfare, which improves social outcomes. In order to achieve the SDGs of the United Nations, financial inclusion is essential. It actively assists in realizing this. Financial services frequently have significant prices, such as minimum deposit requirements or account maintenance fees, which can be prohibitive for people with minimal financial resources. Financial inclusion emerges as a critical enabler of sustainable development by opening up the availability of banking services, enabling the underserved, and encouraging partnership.

References

Akudugu, M. A. (2013). The determinants of financial inclusion in Western Africa: Insights from Ghana. *Research Journal of Finance and Accounting*, *4*(8), 1–9. https://www.semanticscholar.org/paper/6e01239bda502d3949b006c30de50f9ed75634b7

Arshad, A. (2023). Nexus between financial inclusion and women empowerment: Evidence from developing countries. *Gender in Management: An International Journal*, *38*(4), 561–580. https://doi.org/10.1108/gm-04-2022-0125

Azimi, M. N. (2022). New insights into the impact of financial inclusion on economic growth: A global perspective. *Plos One*, *17*(11), e0277730. https://doi.org/10.1371/journal.pone.0277730

Basu, P. (2006). *Improving access to finance for India's rural poor*. World Bank Publications.

Beck, T., Demirgüç-Kunt, A., & Levine, R. (2007). Finance, inequality and the poor. *Journal of economic growth*, *12*, 27–49.

Bhatia, S., & Singh, S. (2019). Empowering women through financial inclusion: A study of urban slum. *Vikalpa*, *44*(4), 182–197. https://doi.org/10.1177/0256090919897809

Boyce, G. (2000). Valuing customers and loyalty: the rhetoric of customer focus versus the realty of alienation and exclusion of (de valued) customers. *Critical Perspectives on Accounting*, *11*, 649–689.

Clemenz,G. (1986). *Credit markets with asymmetric information*. Berlin: Springer.

Cnaan, R. A., Moodithaya, M. S., & Handy, F. (2012). Financial inclusion: Lessons from rural South India. *Journal of Social Policy*, *41*(1), 183–205.

Demirgüç-Kunt, A., & Singer, D. (2017). Financial inclusion and inclusive growth: A review of recent empirical evidence. World Bank Policy Research Working Paper (8040). https://doi.org/10.1596/1813-9450-8040

Dev, S. M. (2006). Financial inclusion: Issues and challenges. *Economic and Political Weekly*. *41*, 4310–4313.

Developed with the support of Ministry of Finance, Government of India and Reserve Bank of India (2013). Crisil Inclusix. https://www.crisil.com/content/dam/crisil/crisil-foundation/generic-pdf/CRISIL-Inclusix-Volume-I.pdf

Emara, N., & Mohieldin, M. (2020). Financial inclusion and extreme poverty in the MENA region: A gap analysis approach. *Review of Economics and Political Science*, *5*(3), 207–230.

Gattoo, M. H., & Akhtar, S. J. (2015). The development of India's financial inclusion agenda–Some lessons for Pakistan. *The Pakistan Development Review*, *54*(4), 569–583.

Honohan, P. (2004). *Financial sector policy and the poor: Selected findings and issues* (No. 43). World Bank Publications.

Kumar, D. B. P. (2011). Financial exclusion: A theoretical approach, MPRA Paper No. 89864, posted 26 August 2019.

Lal, T. (2021). Impact of financial inclusion on economic development of marginalized communities through the mediation of social and economic empowerment. *International Journal of Social Economics*, *48*(12), 1768–1793. https://doi.org/10.1108/ijse-12-2020-0830

Leyshon, A., & Thrift, N. (1995). Geographies of financial exclusion: Financial abandonment in Britain and the "US". *Transactions of the Institute of British Geographers, New Series*, *20*, 312–341.

Llanto, G. M. (1989).Asymmetric information in rural financial markets and interlinking of transactions through the self-help groups. *Journal of Philippine Development*, *28*, Vol. XVI, No. 1-e

Miles, A. (2015). Reaching the excluded responsibly: The MasterCard Foundation's strategy for financial inclusion. *Innovations: Technology, Governance, Globalization*, *10*(1-2), 3–7.

Muhammad, T., Ngah, B. B., & Obad, A. S. F. M. (2022). malhotradrneena@gmail.com. *AFEBI Islamic Finance and Economic Review*, *7*(01), 45–62. https://doi.org/10.47312/aifer.v7i01.565

Nandi, B. K., Hasan, G. Q., & Kabir, M. H. (2022). A tale of the financial inclusion-growth nexus and the degree of financial inclusion: A dynamic panel approach on selected developing countries. *Journal of Financial Economic Policy*, *14*(3), 381–402. https://doi.org/10.1108/jfep-03-2021-0071

Ozili, P. K. (2021, October). Financial inclusion research around the world: A review. In *Forum for social economics* (Vol. 50, No. 4, pp. 457–479). Routledge.

Park, C. Y., & Mercado, R. (2015). Financial inclusion, poverty, and income inequality in developing Asia (January 1, 2015). *Asian Development Bank Economics Working Paper Series No. 426*. Available at SSRN: https://ssrn.com/abstract=2558936 or http://dx.doi.org/10.2139/ssrn.2558936

Raichoudhury, A. (2020). Major determinants of financial inclusion: State-level evidences from India. *Vision*, *24*(2), 151–159.

Raksmey, U., Lin, C. Y., & Kakinaka, M. (2022). Macroprudential regulation and financial inclusion: Any difference between developed and developing countries? *Research in International Business and Finance*, *63*, 101759.

Reddy, C. V. (2017). Overall financial inclusion across 55 countries: 12 financial inclusion enabling variables. *SCMS Journal of Indian Management*, *14*(1), 14–29. https://doi.org/10.2139/ssrn.3427198

Sarma, M., & Pais, J. (2011). Financial inclusion and development. *Journal of International Development*, *23*(5), 613–628. https://doi.org/10.1002/JID.1698

Sethi, D., & Acharya, D. (2018). Financial inclusion and economic growth linkage: Some cross country evidence. *Journal of Financial Economic Policy*, *10*(3), 369–385. https://doi.org/10.1108/JFEP-11-2016-0073

Shafi, M., & Medabesh, A. H. (2012). Financial inclusion in developing countries: Evidences from an Indian state. *International Business Research*, *5*(8), 116.

Sharma, D. (2016). Nexus between financial inclusion and economic growth: Evidence from the emerging Indian economy. *Journal of Financial Economic Policy*, *8*(1), 13–36. https://doi.org/10.1108/JFEP-01-2015-0004

Shihadeh, F. H. (2018). How individual's characteristics influence financial inclusion: Evidence from MENAP. *International Journal of Islamic and Middle Eastern Finance and Management*, *11*(4), 553–574. https://doi.org/10.1108/IMEFM-06-2017-0153

Vivek, B. R. (2016). Empowering women: Uncovering financial inclusion barriers. *Advances in Social Sciences Research Journal*, *3*(3). https://doi.org/10.14738/assrj.33.1611

World Bank Research Observer. (2009). *24*(1).

2 Financial Inclusion, Concepts, and Theories

Ngwengeh Brendaline Beloke, Evans S. Osabuohien, Messomo Elle Serge, and Joe Eyong Assoua

2.1 Introduction

Financial inclusion is a growing concept that needs to be understood by practitioners and policymakers of every nation It fosters inclusive growth and helps alleviate poverty Poor people for example in India face insecurity; livelihood vulnerability and worse of it are not part of the legal protection of the state. This has caused many problems in both rural and urban sides of the country such as unemployment, lack of basic amenities and urban poverty (Malik et al., 2020). The understanding of this concept helps reduce income inequality and the gap that exists between the rich and the poor. It enables the government to work for the benefit and interest of the excluded. By making use of formal banking services, the excluded will be encouraged to save for future investments.

2.2 Divergent Views and Standard Definition of the Concept of Financial Inclusion

In an effort to determine a standard definition of the concept of financial inclusion from the perspective of a commercial bank, a critical review of the works of other authors was necessary. Even though reviewed literature reveals that there is no universally accepted definition of financial inclusion (Ishita et al., 1999), the definitional emphasis of financial inclusion varies across countries and geographies, depending on the level of social, economic and financial development of the place and priorities of social concerns.

Sinha (2009) defines financial inclusion to mean the process of ensuring accessibility to financial services, timely and adequate credit for vulnerable individuals like weaker sections and low-income groups at a cost that is affordable. To expatiate, access to finance by the poor and vulnerable groups is a prerequisite for the reduction of poverty and social cohesion. In fact, ensuring access to finance signifies a form of empowerment of the vulnerable groups. Such financial services include credit, savings, insurance and payments and remittance facilities. The primary objective of financial inclusion is to ensure that the scope of activities of the organized financial system is extended within its ambit to include people with low incomes. Through graduated credit, the effort must be to lift the

DOI: 10.4324/9781032655185-3

poor and the vulnerable from one level to another, so that they can come out of poverty.

Sama (2008) emphasized a process that facilitates the ease with which financial services could be accessed, are made available, affordable and use of the formal banking system by all the members of an economy. This definition stresses on the several dimensions of financial inclusion which includes accessibility, availability and usage of financial services. The author mentioned that banks are the gate way to the provision of basic forms of formal financial services, thus banks are often used as the analogue to financial inclusion or exclusion. The Indian Government Committee on financial inclusion began its report by defining financial inclusion to mean a process to ensure access to financial services, timely and adequate credit as needed by the poor and vulnerable groups which include the weaker sector and small income groups of an economy at an affordable price (Rangarajan Committee, 2008). The Consultative Group to Assist the Poor (CGAP) defined it as digital access to and the use of formal financial services by the excluded and underserved population. This enables individuals and businesses to access useful and affordable financial products and services that suit their needs. It includes transactions, payments, savings, credit and insurance rendered in a responsible and sustainable manner (CGAP, 2015). Kithinji (2017) defined financial inclusion as a means to foster financial access to all, at an affordable price, to various financial services and products that are delivered by banks that have the ability to sustain them. Nkuna et al. (2018) put as a process in which the vulnerable group access timely and adequate financial services at an affordable cost.

The above definitions of financial inclusion/exclusion seem attractive, but it may be surprising to know that they are limited. This is because they placed greater emphasis on access, usage, cost and less on quality provision of financial services in their definitions. Contrary to the above reviews, the World Bank Report (2015), on how to measure financial inclusion, proposes four main indicators of financial inclusion. They include accessibility indicators which measures the depth of outreach of financial services, for example; the penetration of bank branches or point of sale (POS) devices in rural areas. The second is the demand-side barriers and entails the cost borne by customers to access financial institutions or information. The third is usage indicator which reflects how clients use financial services which involves the regularity and duration of the financial product/service over time (e.g., average balance on savings, number of transactions per account, number of payments made electronically). The fourth is quality measures. It describes whether financial products and services meet clients' needs and includes the range of options made available to customers, their awareness and understanding of financial products and services. As cited in Samuel Wamba et al. (2021) the World Bank Group (2008) explained financial inclusion as a means through which individuals and businesses can access useful and affordable financial products and services that meet their financial needs through transactions such as payments, savings, credit and insurance delivery in a responsible and sustainable manner.

Based on the above explanation, this study adopts and defines financial inclusion from the supply side approach (commercial bank's perspective) and from the lens of the World Bank Report (2015), to mean the formal provision of financial services by commercial banks to facilitate the accessibility, usage, quality and cost affordable provision of financial services that meet the needs of the general population in a sustainable manner. This definition has been adopted because of the use of quality provision of financial services in a sustainable manner which is absent in most definitions. The definition corroborates with Ozili (2020), who defined it as individuals and businesses having access to financial products and services that are useful and affordable to meet their needs responsibly and in a sustainable way. Malik and Yadav (2022) also noted that this concept is not limited to having just a bank account. It entails all segments of the society participating in banking such as penetration, banking services and banking usage (Malik et al., 2021). However, access to an account is the first step to being financially included (World Bank, 2014) as cited in Kouam and Mokam (2022) followed by the use and quality of financial services (Beck et al., 2015; Sarma, 2008; Tadjudje, 2016; World Bank, 2014 as cited in Ahodode et al., nd). To support this definition in other words, Demirguc-Kunt and Levine (2008) defined financial inclusion to mean the removal of barriers in the form of price and non-price constraints from financial services and includes dimensions such as accessibility, availability, cost and range of quality of services that banks offer sustainably. This is summarized in Figure 2.1.

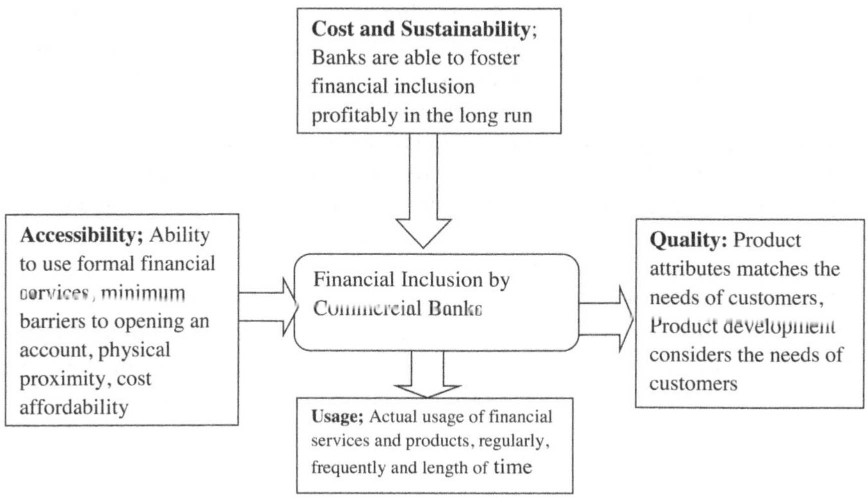

Figure 2.1 Conceptual framework for financial inclusion

Source: Researchers' adapted from World Bank Report on Financial Inclusion (2014)

2.3 Key Players in Financial Inclusion

Given their role as pillars of economic development, commercial banks find themselves at the central of fostering financial inclusion. Commercial banks play a key role in fostering financial inclusion since they operate the formal banking sector. Understanding the concept is very important. A commercial bank is a financial institution that obtains a license to accept and insure deposits from its customers and pays interest to depositors. In addition, the license permits banks to make home and commercial mortgage loans in order to render check cashing and check clearing services and also to underwrite securities such government bonds (Getter, 2016). Idiab et al. (2011) defined it as an institution involve in processing credit and lending operations, accept deposits and giving out loans. They allow the issuance of money and ease the process of payments such as automatic payments. It facilitates electronic banking services in all forms, i.e. internally and externally. It is an institution that is in charge of extending commercial loans and issuing of transaction deposits. Financial inclusion is defined as the delivery of formal banking services to the masses including the poor and the less privileged. By this, commercial banks help to reduce the wealth gap that exists between the poor and the rich. Given their financial intermediation role, they help to channel funds from the surplus to the deficit unit. Their agent banking to the rural areas contribute significantly to reaching the undeserved population. Since majority of the world's population has limited access to formal banking services, commercial banks are at the forefront of increasing the financial inclusion rate through their savings, transfers and payment functions at more affordable costs. All these are spearheaded by commercial banks and so they have a central role in encouraging financial inclusion by reducing financial exclusion (World Bank, 2022).

Developing economies have been making immense efforts to expand the frontiers of financial inclusions (Yakubu et al., 2023). Governments of the world also do have financial inclusion strategies. In Mali for example, the government in 2010 instituted the Financial Sector Development Strategy which was geared towards bringing greater alignment of the financial sectors with other sectors that drive economic growth. The government together with the central bank of Mali made it compulsory for banks to disclose their charges and commissions to the public so that they can make informed decisions in an effort to help the bank and the unsophisticated (Nkuna et al., 2018).

In Guinea, an independent, African-led organization was created to accelerate the growth of instant and inclusive payment systems for the benefit of all Africans. They believe that instant inclusive payment can play a significant role in creating mass access to financial services for the excluded adult for Africa by 2030. The introduction of M-Pesa in Kenya is the root cause of increases in financial inclusion. This service is being used for both domestic and international transactions (AfricaNenda, nd).

Apart from commercial banks, the two main players of financial inclusion in Cameroon are Mobile Telephone Network (MTN) and Orange Cameroon. With 2.8 million registered users, Orange Cameroon offers money deposits, sending and receiving money, transfers between banks accounts and mobile money. MTN's 2.6 million users also receive similar services. Their services are also used by enterprises and households for the payment of bills such as water, electricity, telephone and television. Enterprises also accept payment from customers using mobile payment services (World Bank, 2016, as cited in Ahodode et al., 2016). However, factors such as poverty and limited access to finance and education and these still prevail have slowed sustainable development of the country (Lontchi, Yang, & Su, 2022). Through the largest financial system in the Economic Comminunity of Central African State (CEMAC) regions, data on bank ownership shows 12.2 percent compared to 28 percent on average in Sub-Saharan (FINDEX survey, 2014 as cited in IMF, 2018). Banks too are playing a major role. They have developed financial products that suit the needs of the poorest populations. These initiatives include low-cost savings accounts or microcredits. They have also embraced mobile payments through their fintech partnerships (Youbi, 2023).

South Asia region is noted for low financial inclusion. Each region works hard to advance financial inclusion focusing on the unbanked. This initiative includes all segments in the society participating in banking services, banking usage as well as penetration (Malik et al., 2021). Particularly, in India, the government introduced the most notable financial inclusion programme Pradhan Mantri Jan Dhan Yojana (PMJDY) which witnessed the opening of 18 million accounts in one week in 2014 (Ozili, 2021).

The World Bank is working hard to enhance financial inclusion. They have helped countries to meet the needs of under banked and underserved. Statistics in 2012 showed that the World Bank reached 24.5 million Micro, Small and Medium Enterprises (MSME) clients with an active loan portfolio of more than $3 billion and also gave lending and technical assistance for projects to more than 70 countries worth the sum of $1.4 billion. They also support financial inclusion through capacity building and financing. Their main focus on financial inclusion is access, usage and quality. Financial infrastructure and financial consumer protection help contribute to financial sector stability and poverty alleviation (World Bank, 2013).

2.4 Financial Inclusion Theory: An Imperative

Ozili (2020) saw the need to break the silence amongst researchers who have observed recently the trend of financial inclusion amongst countries but were disturbed that this trend had an underlying theory or some principles that can guide the understanding of this concept as a pro-development initiative in the discipline of economics and finance. These theories were therefore needful to prevent financial inclusion literature from becoming porous and disconnected if there were no coherent sets of theories to develop some general principles that will guide the understanding of financial inclusion. It is the first of its kind theory on financial inclusion in the history of academic literature despite contentions from other researchers that there was no need for any financial inclusion theory considering it as a waste of time and resources. The existence of theories in financial inclusion is powerful because they can pave a way on how to achieve financial inclusion and why different ideas do exist on how to enhance financial inclusion.

In his paper, Ozili (2020) presented several theories on how financial inclusion can be fostered by focusing on those who benefit from the initiative. By beneficiaries, the author focused on those to be targeted for any financial inclusion programmes. These theories include the *Systems theory, Vulnerable group theory, Dissatisfaction theory and Public good theory. These theories are examined below;*

2.5 Financial Inclusion Theories

2.5.1 The Systems Theory of Financial Inclusion Beneficiaries

The systems theory of financial inclusion holds that the outcomes of financial inclusion are achieved through the existing subsystems such as the economic, social and financial subsystems which financial inclusion depends on and as such greater financial inclusion will have positive benefits for the systems it relies on. When there is a significant change in a subsystem (economic, financial and social), it can have a significant effect on the expected outcomes of financial inclusion. As an example, when economic agents and suppliers of financial services who are part of the economic system and financial systems are imposed regulations by regulators, this can make them put their interest in the place of users of basic financial services which may prevent them (suppliers of financial services) from offering quality and affordable financial services to users that will align with defined rules protecting these users from being exploited and from price discrimination. However, if there is a significant change at national or full system level for example, changing the existing national financial inclusion plan with a totally new plan does not make the existing subsystems to change since a change of the subsystem has to be done at the subsystem level.

The theory assumes that the success of financial inclusion agenda will depend on the efficiency and effectiveness of the subsystem. The economic, financial and social subsystems are the main beneficiaries of financial inclusion from the systems theory perspective.

The systems theory of financial inclusion is not without flaws. The theory does not recognize that factors outside the system could affect financial inclusion outcomes making it problematic. Rather, it focuses more on the effects of the system and its subsystems on financial inclusion outcomes. Thirdly, the assumption that a direct relationship exists between financial inclusion outcomes and the subsystems it relies on may not always be true.

2.5.2 Vulnerable Group Theory of Financial Inclusion Beneficiary

This theory posits that any programme geared towards financial inclusion should target the vulnerable members if the society. They should be the forefront beneficiaries of any financial inclusion initiatives. These people are seen as those who suffer the most from economic hardship and crisis situations and includes young people, women, elderly people and poor people. This can be achieved through government sponsored programmes such as government-to-person (G2P) social cash transfers into the formal bank account of vulnerable people. This will encourage other vulnerable people who do not have formal bank accounts to join the formal sector by owning one in order to benefit from the initiative of the government. This will go a long way to foster financial inclusion for vulnerable groups. If this is being carried out, vulnerable people will have the thought that they too are benefiting from equal distribution of income, which is an effort by the government to reduce income inequality. As a result, they will feel they belong and will be able to carry out transactions that will affect other segments of the society.

This theory is advantageous in reducing financial exclusion by including the vulnerable into the formal sector. The theory also points out easily financial excluded members of the society. These people can be easily identified via their income levels, age, geographical location and other demographic attributes at less cost since they can easily be figured out.

This theory is however not immune to some demerits. It does not consider financial inclusion for all. It fails to consider non-vulnerable people in the society to be considered as part of financial inclusion programmes. People who are non-vulnerable also need to be included in the formal banking sector. Not considering men as part of the vulnerable groups of people except women makes the theory to be one sided and gender bias given that both genders compete for equal opportunities. The idea behind this theory can further lead to the vulnerable having better access to formal financial services, income inequality than others over a long time period. At the end, the problem that had to be handled by the theory will be aggravated. Meaning achieving equal distribution of income may instead lead to more disparity for a given time period.

As a result of the above limitations, the Dissatisfaction theory of financial inclusion beneficiary is reviewed next.

2.5.2.1 Dissatisfaction Theory of Financial Inclusion Beneficiary

The main idea behind this theory is that it will be easier to enhance financial inclusion if focus is geared towards bringing back those who left because they were dissatisfied in the past due to factors such as online fraud, hacking of bank accounts, financial fraud, debit or credit card fraud, financial theft, long waiting hours before getting a service rendered, high cost of transaction, excessive bank charges. Meaning it is easier to persuade those who first owned formal bank accounts than those who had not had before. Financial inclusion programmes should first target those who had first owned formal bank accounts before extending to other members of the population.

This theory has its merits. It targets the problem of "voluntary financial exclusion" by using persuasive means to bring back those who left the formal financial sector as a result of dissatisfaction thus reducing the level of "voluntary financial exclusion". Again, those adults who were previously banked can easily be identified since their personal data are kept with financial institutions. Financial inclusion programmes can focus towards persuading them first to return to the financial sector. This is easier than reaching out to those who never had formal bank accounts before. More so, with this theory, there is little or no need of using public funding to enhance financial inclusion. Persuasive interpersonal skills are what is important.

The theory is however not without flaws. It prioritizes financial inclusion only for those who had ones been members of the formal financial sector and does not consider those who have never been part of the formal financial sector. Furthermore, the assumption that financial exclusion is solely caused by dissatisfaction with the rules of engagement may not always be true. There are situations where individuals can voluntarily exit the formal sector due to other reasons such as religious or personal reasons. Lastly, some individuals even though they may be dissatisfied with the formal financial sector may still have no choice but remain in the formal system due to societal and cultural expectations to live a comfortable life by owning a bank account.

2.5.2.2 Delivery Theories of Financial Inclusion

This section captures various schools of thoughts as to who should provide formal banking services to the unbanked population. Some propose the government should be at the centre (Aggarwal & Klapper, 2013; Staschen & Nelson, 2013); others think the private sector is at the best position to do it (Gabor & Brooks, 2017; Ozili, 2018) while other schools of thoughts suggest formal financial services should be a combination of the two, i.e. private and public agencies (Arun & Kamath, 2015; Pearce, 2011).

Some of these schools of thoughts are examined below.

2.5.2.3 Community Echelon Theory of Financial Inclusion

It states that the delivery of formal financial services should be done exclusively to the population through their community leaders. This is because community leaders are known to be influential and because of this can use their influence to encourage and persuade members of the community to join the formal financial sector. Members in the community trust their leaders and so will accept most proposals from them since they know any proposals from community leaders will be beneficial to them and that these proposals will uphold their values and cultures due to the strong cultural tie between community leaders and the members. By this, community leaders can easily encourage and influence members in the community to join the formal banking sector.

However, it has some flaws. Community leaders can be under due pressure to accept and make decisions that are not in the best interest of community members from promoters of financial inclusion using financial and non-financial means. Since most members of the community believe in them, decisions that do not tally with their interest can be reached.

The limitations of the above theory gave birth to the Public Service theory of financial inclusion.

2.5.2.4 Public Theory of Financial Inclusion

Authored by Ozili (2021), this theory states that financial inclusion is the public responsibility the government owes its citizens and so citizens expect the government to deliver formal financial services to them. It explains that formal financial services should be delivered by the government of all citizens through public institutions. With this theory, only the government is instrumental in ensuring formal financial services. This theory has some merits in that it assumes that financial inclusion will be achieved when the government takes responsibility for it.

This theory has some demerits. It does not think the private sector should be involved in ensuring financial inclusion. It also assumes that the programme will be funded exclusively by tax payers' money. Tax revenue may not be sufficient to fund the delivery of formal financial services since the population is large.

2.5.2.5 Special Agent Theory of Financial Inclusion

From the name, this theory states that formal financial services should be delivered to the excluded population by special agents. It argues that due to the difficulties of accessing remote communities, its people or geography, there is a need to get special agents who are specialized in rendering such services to deliver formal financial services to the unbanked. The special agent is supposed to possess the following characteristics; highly skilled and specialized, understand the peculiarities of the excluded population, identify areas of innovative improvements, understand the areas in which the excluded members live and the existing informal financial system, look for a way of integrating the informal financial systems in the community into the formal financial system. This theory depicts the principal agent relationship where the principals are the national and foreign governments, while the special agent comprises local and non-banking institution, financial institutions and technological companies or a special institution created specifically for the purpose of achieving specific financial inclusion objectives.

The theory is advantageous in that it uses the services of specialist in the promotion of financial inclusion for the excluded population. This permits the government to be focused on other pressing national issues. There is high degree of confidence by the government in the specialized agents' abilities to deliver formal financial services to the excluded population. The special agents would tend to work hand in gloves with other institutions to harness inputs so as to achieve the common goal of greater financial inclusion.

However, the theory has limitations. If the principal is the government, then the government may be tempted to choose her own agency as the specialized agent, which renders the government as both agent and principal and it will tend to defeat the purpose of special agency in delivery formal financial services because government agencies are usually inefficient.

2.5.2.6 Theories of Financial Inclusion Funding

The main idea behind these theories is who should fund financial inclusion expenditure for the excluded population? Some authors like Marshall (2004) think it should be funded using tax payers money while others propose the capitalist in the private sector should be responsible in funding since they significantly contribute in widening the income inequality gap between the poor and the rich (Mohiuddin, 2015). Others have proposed a joint funding by private and public sectors (Cobb et al., 2016; Dashi et al., 2013).

Some financial inclusion funding theories include private money theory and public theory.

2.5.2.7 Private Money Theory of Financial Inclusion

According to this theory, financial inclusion programmes should be funded using private resources from shareholders' equity capital. This is because, with private funders, there will be greater accountability from users of their funds, they will ensure that private funds are efficiently utilized and follow up to make sure that formal financial services are delivered to the excluded members of the population.

This theory has some merits. The time taken to approve private funding for financial inclusion programmes is shorter compared to long approval time required to get public funding. This is because due to the fewer approval stages for private funds application, decisions can easily be reached for approval. Again, private financiers can offer better project management skills, innovative facilities and effective risk management in attaining financial inclusion objectives. Those who do the funding can put pressure on private contractors to ensure they complete their programme in good time while ensuring high quality.

This theory is not without demerits. It is very costly to raise private funds to fund financial inclusion projects. Using private funds to fund financial inclusion programmes can increase the private interest at the expense of poor people and excluded population. Government control over financial inclusion infrastructure may be lost due to partial or full ownership by private investors.

2.5.2.8 Public Theory of Financial Inclusion

From the name, it implies that an inclusion programmes should be funded by the state using public money (tax payers' fund). This means financial inclusion programmes should be financed from government budgets. According to Dashie et al. (2013), there is a growing evidence that public funding for financial inclusion is growing faster than private funding.

These are the merits of the public funding theory of financial inclusion; the government will tend to tax the rich in order to generate resources for the financial inclusion programmes for the benefit of all. With this method, there will be equal distribution of wealth reducing the gap between the poor and the rich for the benefit of the poorer segment of the population and the excluded. Secondly, it is less costly to raise funds through this method. By using public money, self-interest individuals will be prevented from hijacking the agenda for their sole benefits.

The theory however has some demerits. If there is lack of proper planning by the government, it will lead to over spending on the financial inclusion programme and this will ultimately lead to inefficiency. The use of public resources to fund financial inclusion programmes can lead to unnecessary delays in reaching the excluded population arising from disbursing funds, delays caused by lobbying for funds due to the political environment. If the tasks for financial inclusion programmes are assigned to incompetent agent or institution, it will lead to inefficiency. This usually arises when the government appoints an already existing agency who has its own statutory duty. It may be overburdened with the additional duties of promoting financial inclusion agenda.

2.6 Conclusion

Financial inclusion has become an important development priority for countries all over the world (Wamba et al., 2021). To promote economic growth and empowerment of citizens, it has taken the centre stage in the development agenda of most economies (Izquierdo & Tuesta, 2015; Park & Mercado, 2018). The main objective of this paper was to review theories and concepts in financial inclusion. Financial inclusion is an important aspect of inclusive growth and sustainability in every nation. Its significance is seen as it tends to reduce the disparity of income distribution between the rich and the poor through its funding programmes.

Financial inclusion concept has been the priority of most governments around the world. Particularly, the Indian Government has made efforts geared towards nationalization of banks, building up of robust branch networks of scheduled commercial banks, co-operatives and regional rural banks; introduction of mandated priority sector lending targets and lead bank schemes; formation of self-help groups just to ensure poverty in the nation is reduced (Malik & Yadav, 2022). It also assists in poverty alleviation by enabling the financially excluded have access to formal banking services (Ozili, 2020). This paper has reviewed theories related to financial inclusion; it has examined theories related to who is more competent in delivering this programme and the best sources of funds for the programme. It has also noted that the marginal benefit from owning a formal bank account is very important in enhancing financial inclusion. If the benefits of using formal accounts become negative and unbearable, the affected bank adults may either discontinue or exit the formal banking sector which may push a financially included adult becoming unbanked again (Ozili, 2021).

This paper therefore recommends a collective effort by practitioners and policymakers in promoting financial inclusion agenda that will ensure efficiency, cost affordability, sustainability and fairness in the provision of formal financial services. It calls on the government of nations to be at the centre of this agenda. They are to work for the general interest of all those excluded from formal financial services.

References

Aggarwal, S., & Klapper, L. (2013). Designing government policies to expand financial inclusion: Evidence from around the world. *The Journal of Finance*, *56*(3), 1029–1051.

Ahodode, C., Okala, E., & Bayiha, Y. (2016). Financial inclusion, financial innovation and enterprise performance. African Economic Research Consortium (AERC) Final Report.

Arun, T., & Kamath, R. (2015). Financial inclusion: Policies and practices. *IIMB Management Review*, *27*(4), 267–287.

Cobb, J. A., Wry, T., & Zhao, E. Y. (2016). Funding financial inclusion: Institutional logics and the contextual contingency of funding for microfinance organizations. *Academy of Management Journal*, *59*(6), 2103–2131.

Dashi, E., Lahaye, E., & Rizvanolli, R. (2013). Trends in International Funding for Financial Inclusion. CGAPbrief Washington, D.C.: World Bank Group. http://documents.worldbank.org/curated/en/578651468338439171/Trenda-in-international-funding-for-financial-inclusion

Demirguc-Kunt, A., & Levine, R. (2008). Finance, Financial Sector Policies and Long-Run Growth. World Bank Policy Research Working Paper No. 11. https://doi.org/10.1596/1813-9450-4469

Gabor, D., & Brooks, S. (2017). The digital revolution in financial inclusion: International development in the fintech era. *New Political Economy*, *22*(4), 423–436.

IMF (2018). Financial Inclusion in Cameroon. IMF e-Library. https://www.elibrary.imf.org

Izquierdo, N. C., & Tuesta, D. (2015). Factors that matter for financial inclusion: Evidence from Peru. Aestimatio, *The IEB International Journal of Finance*, *10*, 10–31. DOI:10.5605/IEB.10.1

Malik, A. F., & Yadav, D. K. (2022). Financial inclusion schemes and changing socio economic status of poorest of the poor. In *Financial inclusion schemes in India* (pp. 109–130). Singapore: Springer Nature Singapore.

Malik, F. A., Yadav, D. K., Adam, H., & Omrane, A. (2020). The urban poor and their financial behavior: A case study of slum dwellers in Lucknow (India). In *Sustainable entrepreneurship, renewable energy-based projects, and digitalization* (pp. 305–315). Boca Raton: CRC Press.

Malik, F. A., Yadav, D. K., Lone, N. A., & Adam, H. (2021). An investigation into the dynamics of financial inclusion in south Asian countries. *Pakistan Economic and Social Review*, *59*(2), 231.

Marshall, J. N. (2004). Financial institutions in disadvantaged areas: A comparative analysis of policies encouraging financial inclusion in Britain and the United States. *Environment and Planning A*, *36*(2), 241–261.

Mohiuddin, S. (2015). Private Sector Leadership in Financial Inclusion. Corporate Citizenship Center, U.S. Chamber of Commerce Foundation. Available at https://www.uschamberfoundation.org/.

Kouam & Mokam (2022). The Impact of Financial Inclusion on Cameroon's Economic Growth. https://nkafu.org/

Nkuna, O., Lapukeni, A., Kaude, P., & Kabango, G. (2018) The role of commercial banks on financial inclusion in Malawi. *Open Journal of Business and Management*, *6*, 812–832. https://doi.org/10.4236/ojbm.2018.64061.

Ozili, K. P. (2021). Financial inclusion-exclusion paradox: How banked adults become unbanked again. *Financial Internet Quarterly*, *17*(2), 44–50.

Ozili, P. K. (2018). Impact of digital finance on financial inclusion and stability. *Borsa Istanbul Review*, *18*(4), 329–340.

Ozili, P. K. (2020). Theories of Financial Inclusion. http://dx.doi.org/10.2139/ssrn.3526548.

Park, C.-Y., & Mercado, R. (2018). *Financial inclusion: New measurement and cross-country impact assessment*. ADB Economics Working Paper Series (No.539). Metro Manila: Asian Development Bank.

Pearce, D. (2011). Financial inclusion in the Middle East and North Africa: Analysis and roadmap recommendations. Washington: The World Bank.

Staschen, S., & Nelson, C. (2013). The role of government and industry in financial inclusion. https://doi.org/10.1596/978-0-8213-8927-0_ch3

Wamba, S., Queiroz, M., Blome, C., & Sivarajah, U. (2021). Fostering financial inclusion in a developing country: Predicting user acceptance of Mobile Wallets in Cameroon. *Journal of Global Information Management (JGIM)*, 29(4). https://doi.org/10.4018/JGIM.20210701.oa9.

World Bank (2013). Financial Inclusion: Helping Countries Meet the Needs of the Under-Banked and Under-Served. https://www.worldbank.org/

World Bank (2022). Financial Inclusion: Financial inclusion is a key enabler to reducing poverty and boosting prosperity. https://www.worldbank.org/en/topic/financialinclusion

Yakubu, I., Abdulazi, M., Bunyaminu, A., & Bashiru, S. (2023). Drivers of Financial Inclusion: Insights from Sub-Saharan Africa. https://doi.org/10.3390/economies11050146.

Youbi, K. (2023). Financial Exclusion in Cameroon: A Challenge for Financial Inclusion. https://www.linkedin.com/pulse/financial-exclusion-cameroon-challenge-inclusion-jacques-k-youbi/

Part II

Role of Technology in Financial Inclusion

3 Digital Financial Inclusion of Women in Pakistan

Evidence from Global Findex Database

Wajiha Haq and Faisal Abbas

3.1 Introduction

In this age of artificial intelligence, the world's problems are yet fundamental and the contemporary world faces the problem of access to financial services and also financial inclusion.[1] The severity of the issue of financial services access and inclusion (especially in rural and remote areas) is daunting. One can gauge this problem by looking at startling statistics, i.e., around one-quarter (24%) of the population is financially excluded globally, as only 76% of the population have accounts with banks or other financial institutions including mobile service providers. Majority of those without bank accounts and/or access to financial services are either females, farmers or rural residents. The unbanked population is not evenly distributed geographically and/or demographically, suggesting that the problem is region-specific and not gender-neutral. The problem of access to financial services via bank is severe in remote rural locations as well as far-flung areas. As it is rather difficult for bank to open up their branches, Digital finance can be one solution in this particular context. Digital finance[2] provides services to unbanked population, provides access to financial services and promotes inclusion of otherwise excluded population specifically females. Pakistan is one of those seven countries, globally, that are facing the challenges of digital financial access and inclusion (Demirgüç-Kunt et al., 2022).[3]

Financial inclusion simply means that individuals have easy and equitable access, usage and availability of the formal financial system to avail financial services (Dev, 2006; Sarma & Pais, 2011). Empirical literature emphasizes that financial inclusion is a tool that helps in economic development (Kim et al., 2018; Sulong & Bakar, 2018), poverty reduction (Churchill & Marisetty, 2020; Inoue, 2019), social progress (Banerjee & Francis, 2014) and gender equality (Abdu et al., 2015). Financial inclusion facilitates investment, capital accumulation and wealth creation and eventually positively stimulates economic growth (Kim et al., 2018; Van et al., 2021) and hence development. Financial inclusion provides economic freedom and helps to reduce poverty. By having access to finance and financial services, low-income individuals can borrow, save and invest money, and the aggregate impact is depicted by a reduction in poverty (Churchill & Marisetty, 2020; Inoue, 2019). Technology use in financial services may help create ease in access, usage and

DOI: 10.4324/9781032655185-5

availability of these services. The digital financial inclusion (DFI) thus refers to using digital services and technology to include financially excluded individuals in a cost-effective manner and tailoring services according to their needs (Ray et al., 2022). Digital financial services are a tool to increase participation of marginalized groups by catering their needs (Tay et al., 2022).

Globally around 1.4 billion individuals are unbanked out of which 115 million are in Pakistan. The majority of the unbanked across globe are poor, less educated, women and out of labor force. In Pakistan half of the unbanked population are women (Demirgüç-Kunt et al., 2022). It is of no surprise as in Pakistan, the gender gap in labor force participation rate (the labor force as a % of the working ag population) according to ILOSTAT (2021) is around 57.4%. As those women who are working, their main stay is in the informal sector which is more or less why females have less access to financial services. Hence, women's access to financial services is limited, and therefore the problem of financial inclusion is aggravated for women in Pakistan.

Of note, women matter for improving financial inclusion (Malik et al., 2021). Financial inclusion is also improved by better socioeconomic status (Ahmad Malik & Yadav, 2022). Generally, women face hurdles in having equal education, access to digital resources and financial literacy which becomes the cause of deteriorated economic freedom. A more educated woman can accumulate and manage finances more easily than their counterparts. They spend more time on education and work and, hence, have fewer number of children which not only decreases their dependency ratio but also use finance efficiently (Klasen & Lamanna, 2009). Women have less confidence and skill to manage finances which becomes a hurdle to their financial freedom (Ghosh & Vinod, 2017). By understanding the severity of the problem and investigating the hurdles leading to it, government can address the issue through data-driven informed policy interventions (Ali & Abdullah, 2020; Manzoor et al., 2021).

The problem of financial inclusion has been studied for Pakistan in order to find the solution. For example, Ibtasam et al. (2018)) studied women financial inclusion in Pakistan by focusing on their knowledge, access and decision-making. Using mix methods approach and collecting data from 51 participants using semi-structured interviews, Ibtasam et al. (2018) studied barrier to access DFI with gender lens. Their study discussed the sociocultural and gender-based (both men and women views) barrier to access digital financial services in Pakistan. Another study (Zulfiqar et al., 2016)) empirically examines the role of financial inclusion and significance for economic growth of Pakistan using probit regression model and Global Findex data 2014. Their empirical investigation found the determinants of borrowing in order to understand the financial inclusion phenomenon. The study of Zulfiqar et al. (2016) also investigated barrier to financial inclusion and determinants of various sources of borrowing. Their study concluded that lack of money and formalities in financial services access are significant barrier to financial services access The DFI has also been studied qualitatively (Kemal, 2019; Khan & Jaffar, 2021) to understand the indigenous hurdles to financial inclusion but yet we need enough evidence spatially (across space and time and together) to understand the DFI through surveys where the understanding may be generalizable.

The objective of this chapter is to investigate the severity of the problem by calculating the DFI and to dissect the DFI genderwise. Furthermore, it tends to investigate the DFI of women and factors that are driving it. This will help in designing an effective policy with targeted interventions for increasing the financial inclusion of women through digital platforms by providing them ease of access and usage. The focus on women will not only help them in increasing their economic freedom by having access to digital financial freedom but also in sustainable development. The focus on underserved marginalized groups will help in achieving the sustainable development goals (SDGs) 1, 2, 3, 8, 12 and 17.[4]

3.1.1 Digital Financial Inclusion and Gender Parity in Pakistan

Pakistan is a lower middle-income country with a Gross Domestic Product (GDP) at current market price of US dollar 341 billion (PKR 84658 billion), with a per capita income of US dollar 1568 and according to recent census with a population of 241.49 million (fifth most populous country in the world) people (GoP, 2023). With macroeconomic, financial and political instability that Pakistan economy is facing, in the year 2022, country faced devastating floods that impacted 33 million people and their livelihoods across the country (GoP, 2023).

Nevertheless, the economy of Pakistan tried to expand social and economic services to the people across breadth and width. One such facility is to access financial services in urban and rural areas as well as for men and women alike. Despite many efforts over the years in digitizing the financial services as well as providing mobile banking Pakistan still faces immense issues related to gender parity and rural penetration when it comes to banking and other financial services. According to one estimate, only 4% women had bank account in Pakistan in the year 2008 which rose to 18% in 2020 (an increase of more than four times) in two decades (WFID Partnership, 2022). Therefore, there is huge potential for extending financial services to 82% of the remaining women clientele. It is estimated to generate potentially banking revenue of about US dollar 650 million (WFID Partnership, 2022). Although financial inclusion as well as DFI in Pakistan is increasing slowly, nevertheless, gender gaps still persist and these gaps are wider for rural and uneducated women in Pakistan (PCSW, 2020). Of note, access to finance is critical for economic growth, poverty reduction, achieving financial stability and above all equitable distribution of opportunities. With very low level of population having access to banking and financial services and financial literacy for the use of digital financial services Government of Pakistan in 2015 announced National Financial Inclusion Strategy (NFIS-2015). The aim of the NFIS was to improve financial services access in rural and urban areas but also for women.[5] Financial deepening improves economic resilience of an economy. Furthermore, banks dominate the financial sector of Pakistan for about three-fourth (74%) of the total assets possessed by financial sector and the balance (26%) is by non-banking sector.[6] Additionally, in 2014 Pakistan had per

1000 adults 333 bank accounts compared to 979 in south Asian region (IMF, 2017). ATM machine coverage increased by about nine times and active mobile money account increased by about 17 times over six years (from 2011 to 2016) in Pakistan. Nevertheless, this coverage is low in rural areas and specifically for women in rural areas (IMF, 2017).

According to State Bank of Pakistan (SBP) Access to Finance Survey 2015 adult population with bank account increased from 11% in 2008 to about 16% in the year 2015. No doubt that this average is well below the regional average of south Asian countries (46%). The financial inclusion index (FII) in 2014 places Pakistan on 135th number out of 142 countries globally.[7] This FII for men, in Pakistan, is twice as high (66%) as for women pointing toward strong gender disparity while FII is 30% for south Asian countries (Aslan et al., 2017).

Making financial services available widely across length and breadth of country two things are important; first, education, so people know about the financial services as well as able to use these digital platforms; second, availability of mobile network and internet services. If we look at the education statistics of Pakistan, according to Pakistan Social Living Standard Measurement Survey (PSLM-2019–20) about two-third (67%) of the population ever attended primary schools and completed their education up till grade five, a little less than half (47%) attended and completed lower secondary education and 23% attended upper secondary education. Sixty percent of the total population that has ever attended school, 70% are males and 50% are females. In the year 2020–21 literacy rate of Pakistan was 62.8% (54% rural versus 77.3% urban Pakistan), whereas it was 73.4% for males (67.2% rural and 83.5% urban male) and 51.9% (40.8% for rural and 70.8% for urban) for females (GoP, 2023). Rural disparity is prevalent in terms of education in Pakistan. According to Global Gender Gap Report (2023)[8] Pakistan ranks at 142 out of 146 countries of the world. All other south Asian neighbors are performing better than Pakistan except Iran (143rd) and Afghanistan (rank 146th). Pakistan's gender parity score is 0.575 where as it is 0.634 for South Asia region. As women face inequality in terms of access to education and hence the financial services it is important improve gender parity in education by providing more education to women and girls as well as increasing their level of awareness through digital platforms and internet access specifically in rural Pakistan. In the year 2014, there were meager two million subscribers for broadband services in Pakistan which increased to 128 million in the year 2022 (with a broadband penetration of 54.1%) (GoP, 2023). Furthermore, mobile services contribute 97.6% of the broadband penetration in Pakistan. Gender gap with respect to access to mobile phone and its usage in Pakistan as 38% of the women are less likely to own mobile phone and almost 49% less likely to use mobile Internet.[9] This is why Government of Pakistan has initiated with the help of PTA, UNESCO, Global Mobile Communication Systems (GSMA) and Alliance for Affordable internet (A4AI) to overcome barrier for women to access mobile phone and broadband services. Additionally, as there is a huge gender gap in access to financial services, government also announced branchless banking, provoking all the mobile phone service providers in Pakistan to promote this Assan Mobile Account (AMA) for their customers and resultantly seven million people across the country open up AMA account using mobile phone services (GoP, 2023).

This section is followed by Section 3.2: Data and methodology, explaining the research design, Section 3.3: Results, obtained after analysis and Section 4,4: Conclusion.

3.2 Data and Methodology

3.2.1 Data

In this chapter, we employ the Global Financial Inclusion (Findex) database (2021) by World Bank and Pakistan[10] as a case in point to study the determinants of the severity of DFI and understand the factors affecting it. This survey is the most demand comprehensive data available which contains the data on how people manage, save and borrow money and manage their risk. This national representative survey is collected through face-to-face interviews. The data is collected through 2-stage stratified sampling. In order to collect the data, initially the primary sampling units (PSUs) are selected based on geography and population size. On second stage, the sample is collected either based on probability proportion to sample size or random sampling. For this round, 1002 individuals were interviewed across Pakistan.[11] This data is collected from adults of the age 15 years or above from urban and rural areas of the country.

3.2.2 Constructing Digital Financial Index Variable

In order to achieve the objective of this study, DFI was calculated using two indicators of access and usage with six dimensions in total following Khera et al. (2022). In this study, only DFIDFI is calculated based on the indicators used by the mentioned study covering the aspects of access and usage. In our study, we do not combine DFI to the traditional financial inclusion in contrast to Khera et al. (2022).[12] DFI is different from traditional financial inclusion as the former focuses on digital platforms of financial access while the later focuses on traditional modes of payment. DFI is measured through indicator of access which has two dimensions including mobile subscription measured through mobile phone ownership and access to internet. The dimensions for the second indicator namely "usage" include four dimensions which are having mobile money account, using internet to make payment, using mobile phone to receive salary/wages and using mobile phone to make utility payments. The construction of variable is depicted in Figure 3.1.

The survey in use for this study has data on the dimensions described in Figure 3.1. The respondent responds with closed ended option including Yes and No.

We have used Alkire Foster Methodology (Alkire et al., 2011)[13] to calculate DFI by giving equal weights to each indicator and equal weights to dimension within each indicator.[14] The weights are indicated in brackets in Figure 3.1.

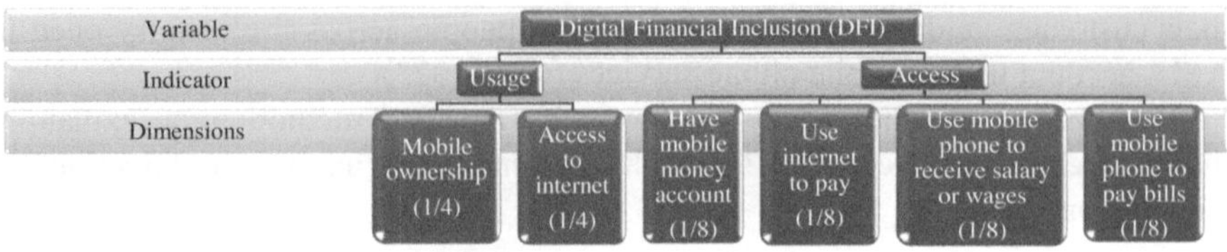

Figure 3.1 Construction of variable of digital financial inclusion

Source: Authors

The other variables used are gender (male/female), region (urban/rural), income category (income quintiles), account in financial institution (yes/no), education (completed primary or less/completed secondary/completed tertiary or more) and financially worry. The survey contains questions about, "for which one of the financial issues, individual is most financially worried". We have used weights to calculate the descriptive statistics.

3.2.3 *Empirical Technique*

We have used mixed-effects generalized linear model (GLM)[15] in order to test the random variation existing at regional level.

$$y_{ij} = \beta_0 + \beta_1 x_{ij1} + \beta_2 x_{ij2} \ldots + \beta_n x_{ijn} + u_i + \varepsilon i_{ij}$$

In this equation, *yij* represents the dependent variable (digital FII) for the *i*th group (region) at the *j*th observation. The data may have a hierarchical structure[16] due to sampling technique with multiple observations (*j*) nested within each group (*i*). x_{ij1}, x_{ij2}, ..., x_{ijp} are the predictors. *βetas* are the fixed-effect coefficients, representing the impact of the corresponding independent variables on the dependent variable. These coefficients are constant across all groups. *ui* represents the random effects or group-specific intercepts. *εij* is the error term, representing the residual variation or noise in the model not explained by the fixed and random effects. The predictors used to model the variation in DFI are gender, region, education, income, financial account holding and financial worry. The results are displayed in Table 3.4 where we tested the predictors for the whole sample containing male and female in Model 1, added interaction of gender and region in Model 2 and lastly analyzed the effect of these predictors for females in the sample in Model 3. We have checked the robustness of model through Akaike Information Criteria (AIC) and Bayesian Information Criteria (BIC).

3.3 Results

The sample used to analyze has 1002 observations. The sample has 499 females and 503 males. Mean age of the population is around 34 ranging between 15 and 93. The detailed descriptive statistics are shown in Table 3.1.

Table 3.1 Descriptive statistics

Variable	*Frequency*	*Percentage*
Respondent education level		
Completed primary school or less	718	72
Completed secondary school	229	23
Completed tertiary education or more	56	6
Within-economy household income quintile		
Poorest 20%	199	20
Second 20%	201	20
Middle 20%	201	20
Fourth 20%	201	20
Richest 20%	201	20
Respondent working status		
In the workforce	447	45
Out of the workforce	555	55
Region of residence		
Rural	395	39
Urban	607	61
Has an account at a financial institution		
No	839	84
Yes	163	16
Total	1002	100

Source: Authors' own calculation based on World Bank Global Findex data 2021.

Table 3.2 depicts that 63% of the population have mobiles but 70% do not have internet access which indicates the infrastructural flaws and underserved situation. The usage is very less. Only 9% of the population have mobile money account. Around 6% of population use internet to pay and get salary and wages using mobile phone, respectively. Around 5% of the population use mobile to make payments of utility bills. The situation of usage is much worse than access which may be due to attitude, awareness and literacy. Overall pattern is relatively worse in rural areas than urban areas.

If we see the distribution of DFI across females as depicted in Figure 3.2, the dismal situation of females is much evident.

Figures 3.3 and 3.4 show dismal situation of women education-wise and region-wise in order to supplement Figure 3.2. Figure 3.3 shows that at every level of education the mean DFI of women is lesser than men. Furthermore, Figure 3.4 depicts that in rural areas the mean DFI of females is lesser than their counterparts.

When we see genderwise distribution of dimensions in Figure 3.5, it becomes evident that women lag behind men in both usage and access. The histogram shows the presence of usage and access.

There are only 257 individuals who have DFI score greater than one-third (0.33). It is of great importance to study different factors which may affect DFI and can help in targeted policy interventions. Data shows that women remain more

Table 3.2 Descriptive statistics of dimensions of digital financial inclusion

Dimensions	*Overall sample*	
	Frequency	*Percentage*
Access		
Mobile ownership		
No	371	37
Yes	631	63
Internet access		
No	700	70
Yes	302	30
Usage		
Has mobile money account		
No	916	91
Yes	86	9
Use internet to pay		
No	944	94
Yes	58	6
Use mobile to pay utility		
No	505	94
Yes	31	6
Use mobile to receive wage		
No	212	95
Yes	11	5
Total	1002	100

Source: Authors' own calculation.

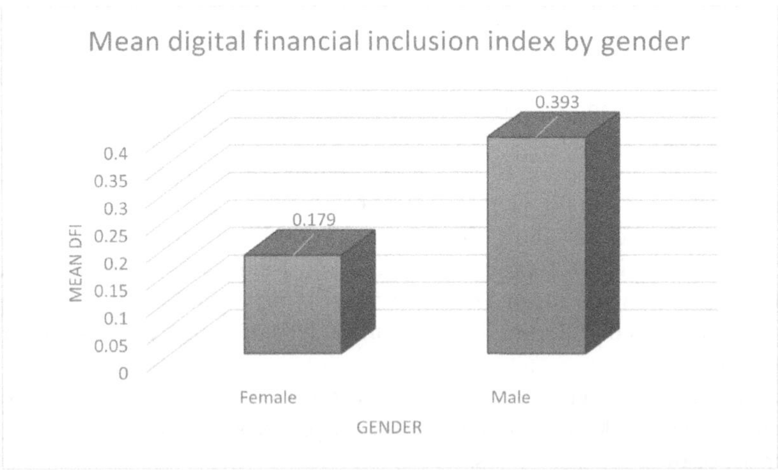

Figure 3.2 Mean DFI by gender

Source: Authors

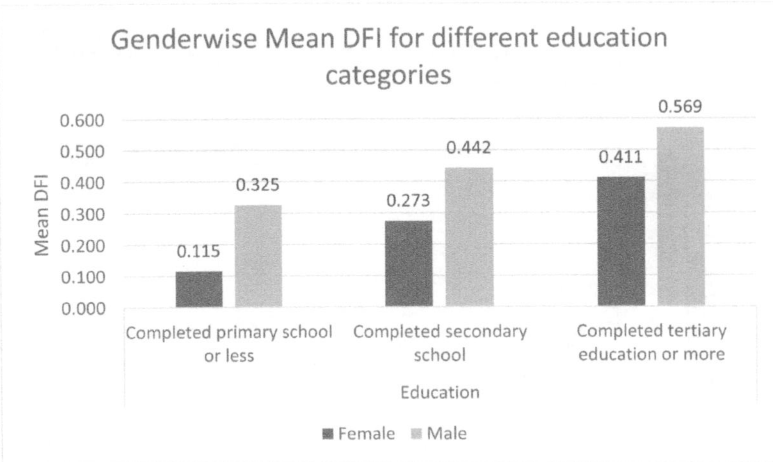

Figure 3.3 Mean DFI of male and female by their level of education

Source: Authors

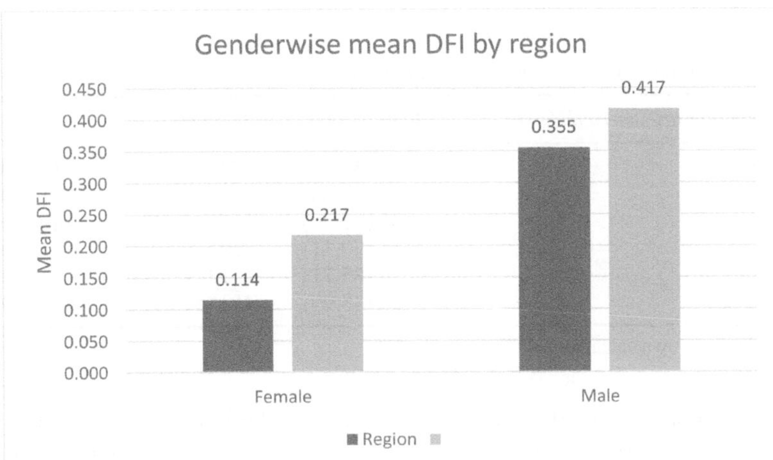

Figure 3.4 Mean DFI of male and female by region of residence

Source: Authors

financially worried due to old age, education fees and payment of utility bills than men, which is evidence of the need for financial inclusion in Pakistan. The frequency distribution is shown in Table 3.3.

The association of different factors with DFI is checked through mixed-effects GLM, and the results of the multivariate regression model are presented in the Table 3.4.

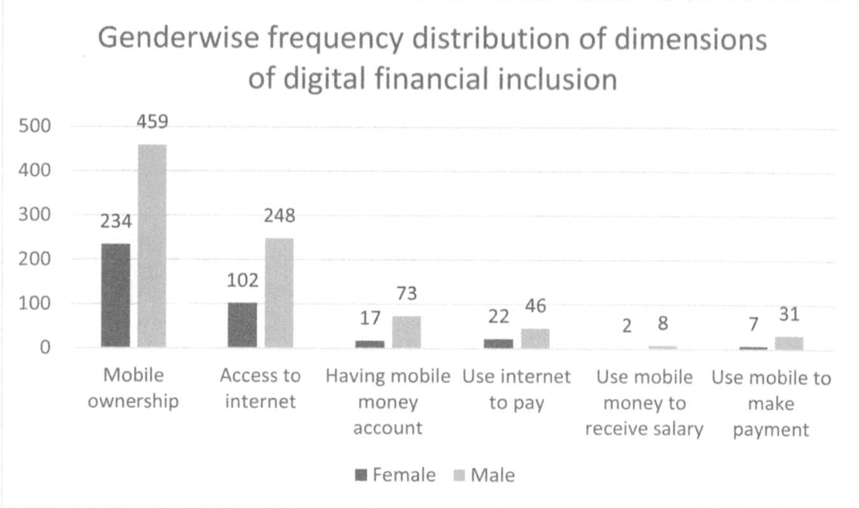

Figure 3.5 Genderwise distribution of dimensions of DFI

Source: Authors

Table 3.3 Genderwise distribution of financial worry

Mostly financially worried due to	*Female (%)*	*Male (%)*	*Total (%)*
Old age	83 (53.21)	73 (46.79)	156 (100)
Medical cost	121 (37.69)	200 (62.31)	321 (100)
Bills	180 (52.94)	160 (47.06)	340 (100)
Education	45 (70.31)	19 (29.69)	64 (100)
(DK)	6 (85.71)	1 (14.29)	7 (100)
Total	435 (48.99)	453 (51.01)	888 (100)

Source: Authors' own calculation.

Table 3.4 shows the effect of various factors on DFI. We have estimated three different models for our regression analyses. In *Model 1* which is our model for estimation of total sample in which we did not distinguish anything else but just included all the variables as it is. In *Model 2* we included an interaction term of gender of the head of the household with that of region of residence. The aim is to depict if there is any rural-urban divide in access to digital financial services for male and/or female. In our *Model 3*, we estimated only for female headed households. This is done to empirically examine the gender inclusion aspect of the digital financial services. Also, a number of studies examined this gender dimension of financial services nevertheless a few studied the impact of DFI and women. In our estimated *Model 1*, it is estimated that that male and individuals living in urban areas have significantly higher DFI than their counterparts. Gender and region independently affect the DFI. The interaction of gender and region was tested in Model 2 which

Table 3.4 The effect of various factors on DFI using mixed-effects GLM

Variables	*Model 1*	*Model 2*	*Model 3*
Gender *(male)*	0.17***	0.19***	–
Base category: Female	(0.015)	(0.022)	
Region (Urban)	0.0444***	0.061***	0.054***
Base category: Rural	(0.012)	(0.017)	(0.017)
Gender*Region	–	–0.0334	
Base category: Male living in urban area vs others		(0.0243)	
Age	–0.0015***	–0.00147***	–0.00018
	(0.0005)	(0.00051)	(0.00072)
Education – Base category: Primary or less completed			
Secondary school completed	0.121***	0.120***	0.161***
	(0.013)	(0.0134)	(0.019)
Tertiary or more completed	0.200***	0.198***	0.274***
	(0.0247)	(0.0247)	(0.0396)
Income – Base category: First quintile			
Second quintile	–0.0273	–0.0278	0.0330
	(0.0203)	(0.0203)	(0.0281)
Third quintile	–0.0285	–0.0290	0.0149
	(0.0189)	(0.0189)	(0.0266)
Fourth quintile	–0.0248	–0.0243	0.0143
	(0.0191)	(0.0191)	(0.0270)
Fifth quintile	0.00681	0.00661	0.0303
	(0.0190)	(0.0190)	(0.0272)
Employment status (working)	–0.0194	–0.0192	–0.0313
Base category: Out of work	(0.0148)	(0.0148)	(0.0238)
Financial institution account holding (Yes)	0.129***	0.130***	0.144***
Base category: No	(0.0160)	(0.0160)	(0.0276)
Financial worried – Base category: Old age			
Medical cost	–0.0109	–0.00856	–0.0262
	(0.0175)	(0.0175)	(0.0248)
Bills	–0.0231	–0.0216	–0.0292
	(0.0171)	(0.0171)	(0.0229)
Education	–0.00217	–0.00258	–0.0239
	(0.0266)	(0.0265)	(0.0325)
Constant	0.185***	0.173***	0.107**
	(0.0304)	(0.0316)	(0.0432)
Random intercept variations			
Region level	–27.74*	–28.03	–27.71
	(15.87)	(3.391)	(17.19)
Individual level	–1.757***	–1.758***	–1.786***
	(0.0237)	(0.0237)	(0.0339)
Log-likelihood	299.469	300.839	159.229
Observations	887	887	434
Number of groups	2	2	2

Standard errors are in parentheses. Statistical level of significance: *** $p < 0.01$, ** $p < 0.05$, * $p < 0.1$.

shows that a male in urban area is not significantly different from its counterparts. With increasing age, the DFI significantly reduces. Educated people and individuals having account at traditional financial institutions have significantly higher DFI than their counter parts. The direction of relationship of these faction and association is the same for females as well as depicted in *Model 3*. For females, age is not a predictor of DFI. Region level variances are significant which means that there are some factors specific to rural urban divide that affects the DFI of individuals; however, this variation is insignificant for women model and when we account for moderation of gender at regional level. The multilevel model suggests that there are some region level factors that contribute to DFI in addition to factors that are common to both urban and rural areas as evident by random regional variation of *Model 1* of Table 3.4. We did not find significant variation in regional characteristics when we estimated for only females in *Model 3*.

3.4 Conclusion

In this digital age, the world is facing problem of access to financial services as well as digital financial services specifically women and residents of rural areas. This divide is visible in developing countries in general and countries of South Asia in particular. Pakistan is a south Asian country with huge gender digital divide as well as low access to digital financial services and which is evident from the fact that large population is unbanked and among them highest proportion is of women. Therefore, it is imperative to analyze the factors that are responsible for DFI specifically of women. Digital platforms can play a vital role by providing cheaper solutions for paying bill, saving, borrowing and managing finances. It is an important platform for women as they can provide them ease to manage things from home or during their work. In Pakistan, where women are less empowered to take their own decision, the provision of digital platforms will help them to take financial decision easily. In this study we have used Global Findex 2021 survey data and found that males have significantly higher inclusion than females. Women are lagging in every dimension of DFI. Income does not determine the DFI for the population. People who have accounts in financial institutions have higher DFI than others whereas policy needs to target more underserved. Women are mostly worried about payments and digital platform can easily facilitate and empower them and financially include them.

3.4.1 Policy Implications

Providing easy access and usage of financial system to women, we can foster the growth of the economy by empowering them and providing them with opportunities which will make them eventually a productive participant of the society. Proactively gender sensitive policy response is required. DFI is also vital to achieve SDGs of zero poverty, reducing gender inequality and improving the quality of education.

Acknowledgments

We would like to thank National University of Sciences and Technology for supporting us to do this research.

Declaration of Conflicting Interests

The author(s) declared no potential conflicts of interest.

Funding

The author(s) received no financial support for this research and/or publication of this article.

Notes

1 Financial inclusion (FI) provides individuals as well as businesses alike greater and smooth access to affordable and meaningful financial services and products to meet their requirement like payments, transactions, credit and insurance, savings. Also the financial system makes sure that the services delivered in a sustainable as well as responsible manner. FI enables seven out of seventeen SDG goals (https://www.worldbank.org/en/topic/financialinclusion/overview).

2 Digital finance (DF) means financial application and services are available on internet or any other IP network or through mobile network services. DF includes peer-to-peer lending and crowd funding and it usually represents fairness and inclusivity. Furthermore, DF offers more freedom compare to traditional financial system by breaking the boundaries and enabling users to be efficient and mobile (Hu & Zheng, 2016).

3 These seven countries are India, China, Pakistan, Indonesia, Egypt, Bangladesh and Nigeria. Cumulatively more than half of world's unbanked population live in these seven countries. Four of these countries have more than 100 million population estimated as unbanked with highest number in India (230 million) followed by China (130 Million) and Pakistan with 115 million and Indonesia with 100 million populations with no bank account (Demirgüç-Kunt et al., 2022).

4 SDG1: End poverty in all its forms everywhere for all people. SDG2: End hunger, achieve food security and improved nutrition and promote sustainable agriculture. SDG3: Ensure healthy lives and promote well-being for all at all stages. SDG8: Promote sustained, inclusive and sustainable economic growth, full and productive employment and decent work for all. SDG12: Ensure sustainable consumption and production patterns. SDG17: Strengthen the means of implementation and revitalize the global partnership for sustainable development. Government of Pakistan in one of its parliamentary resolution declare SDGs as national development goals (NDGs) and set priority list for these SDGs as priority area I, II and III. Priority area I includes SDG goals 2, 3 and 8. Priority area II includes SDG 1 and 17. Priority area III includes SDG 12 (for details, see https://www.sdgpakistan.pk/web/sdgs).

5 For details see State Bank of Pakistan, 2018. "National Financial Inclusion Strategy – Government's 100-days Agenda" (www.finance.gov.pk/NFIS.pdf).

6 Banking sector of Pakistan consists of Islamic banks public sector commercial banks, private commercial banks, foreign banks branches, specialized banks and Microfinance Banks. Whereas non-banking sector comprised Insurance Companies, Asset Management Companies, Mutual and Pension funds, Portfolio Management, REIT, Leasing

Companies, Modarabas, Investment Banking and MFIs, National Saving Schemes (NSS), and Development Finance Institutions.

7 This FII is developed by Aslan et al. (2017) using indicators of access and use of financial services (see for details Aslan et al., 2017).

8 Global Gender Gap Index combines four dimensions, i.e., economic participation and opportunity, Educational attainment, Health and survival and Political empowerment. For details of global gender parity index and its components.

9 https://www.unesco.org/en/articles/unesco-collaborate-pakistan-telecommunication-authority-digital-inclusion-and-gender-mainstreaming#:~:text=According%20to%20the%20Global%20Mobile,likely%20to%20use%20mobile%20internet (accessed 15 August 2023).

10 In the Global Findex data 2021, Azad Jammu and Kashmir (AJK) and Gilgit Baltistan (represents approximately 5% of total population of Pakistan) is excluded. Furthermore, gender-matched sampling was used during the final stage of selection with margin of error 4.1 and design effect 1.72 (see for details page 188 of the report and URL https://www.worldbank.org/en/publication/globalfindex).

11 For details of what questions were asked by the global Findex data 2021 please see the link https://thedocs.worldbank.org/en/doc/62b680b8e92d0f3631cfe82728b00a39-0050062022/original/Findex-2021-Questionnaire.pdf.

12 Khera et al. (2022) in their study use data of 52 developing countries for the period of 2014–2017. They calculate DFI and then combine it with traditional financial inclusion based on literature to calculate overall FII.

13 Akire Foster Methodology is a comprehensive approach that allows inclusivity and provides holistic tool for measuring the intensity and composition of the phenomenon with temporal comparability. This approach is originally used to measure Multidimensional Poverty Index. It involves choosing dimensions (e.g., health, education and living standards), deciding indicators within those dimensions (e.g., malnutrition, child mortality), setting cutoffs for deprivation, collecting data, identifying deprived individuals, and aggregating their deprivations into a single score

14 Assigning equal weights provide ease and transparency by avoiding judgments in aggregation. Sen's Human Development Index has used this technique (Anand & Sen, 2003). Atkinson et al. (2002) mention "the interpretation of the set of indicators is greatly eased where the individual components have degrees of importance that, while not necessarily exactly equal, are not grossly different" (see also Alkire & Foster, 2011; Atkinson, 2003).

15 Mixed-effects GLM is a generalization of the linear model. Unlike linear model which require normalization of response variable, it allows for more variety of distribution of data and provides robust results. In addition, the hierarchical nature of the data requires the use of the mixed-effect model.

16 The hierarchal data does not have independent observation, but they are clustered within different groups. If such data is analyzed with level models, they may give biased results. For that matter, we use multilevel models for analysis.

References

Abdu, M., Buba, A., Adamu, I., & Muhammad, T. (2015). Drivers of financial inclusion and gender gap in Nigeria. *The Empirical Econometrics and Quantitative Economics Letters (EEQEL)*, *4*(4), 186–199.

Ahmad Malik, F., & Yadav, D. K. (2022). Financial inclusion schemes and changing socio economic status of poorest of the poor. In *Financial inclusion schemes in India* (pp. 109–130). Singapore: Springer Nature Singapore.

Ali, H., & Abdullah, R. (2020). Fintech and financial inclusion in Pakistan: An exploratory study. In Enhancing financial inclusion through Islamic finance (Vol. I, pp. 159–192).

Alkire, S., & Foster, J. (2011). Counting and multidimensional poverty measurement. *Journal of Public Economics*, *95*(7), 476–487. https://doi.org/10.1016/j.jpubeco.2010.11.006.

Alkire, S., Roche, J., Santos, M., & Seth, S. (2011). Multidimensional Poverty Index 2011: brief methodological note. Oxford Poverty & Human Development Initiative (OPHI).

Anand, S., & Sen, A. (2003). *Concepts of human development and poverty: A multidimensional perspective*. Oxford: Oxford University Press.

Aslan, G., Deléchat, C., Newiak, M., & Yang, F. 2017. "Inequality in Financial Inclusion and Income Inequality." IMF Working Paper 17/236, International Monetary Fund, Washington, DC. Available at https://www.elibrary.imf.org/view/journals/001/2017/236/article-A001-en.xml.

Atkinson, A. B. (2003). Multidimensional deprivation: Contrasting social welfare and counting approaches. *The Journal of Economic Inequality*, *1*, 51–65.

Atkinson, T., Cantillon, B., Marlier, E., & Nolan, B. (2002). Social Indicators: The EU and Social Inclusion. https://doi.org/10.1093/0199253498.001.0001.

Banerjee, S., & Francis, G. (2014). Financial inclusion and social development. *International Journal of Scientific Research and Management*, *2321*(3418), 13–18.

Churchill, S. A., & Marisetty, V. B. (2020). Financial inclusion and poverty: A tale of forty-five thousand households. *Applied Economics*, *52*(16), 1777–1788.

Demirgüç-Kunt, A., Klapper, L., Singer, D., & Ansar, S. (2022). *The global findex database 2021: Financial inclusion, digital payments, and resilience in the age of COVID-19*. Washington, DC: World Bank Publications, World Bank.

Dev, S. M. (2006). Financial inclusion: Issues and challenges. *Economic and Political Weekly*, *41*(41) 4310–4313.

Ghosh, S., & Vinod, D. (2017). What constrains financial inclusion for women? Evidence from Indian micro data. *World Development*, *92*, 60–81. https://doi.org/10.1016/j.worlddev.2016.11.011.

GoP (2023). Economic Survey of Pakistan, Economic Advisor's Wing, Ministry of Finance, Government of Pakistan, Islamabad.

Hu, B., & Zheng, L. (2016). Digital finance: Definition, models, risk, and regulation. In B. Hu, Z. Yin, & L. Zheng (Eds.) *Development of China's financial supervision and regulation*. New York: Palgrave Macmillan. https://doi.org/10.1057/978-1-137-52225-2_2.

Ibtasam, S., Razaq, L., Anwar, H. W., Mehmood, H., Shah, K., Webster, J., …, Anderson, R. (2018). *Knowledge, access, and decision-making: Women's financial inclusion in Pakistan*. Paper presented at the Proceedings of the 1st ACM SIGCAS Conference on Computing and Sustainable Societies.

ILOSTAT, ILO modelled estimates, November 2021. Available at https://www.ilo.org/infostories/en-GB/Stories/Employment/barriers-women#global-gap/gap-labour-force

IMF (2017). Pakistan: Selected Issues. International Monetary Fund Country Report No. 17/213 Washington, DC. Available at https://www.imf.org/en/Publications/CR/Issues/2017/07/13/Pakistan-Selected-Issues-45079

Inoue, T. (2019). Financial inclusion and poverty reduction in India. *Journal of Financial Economic Policy*, *11*(1), 21–33.

Kemal, A. A. (2019). Mobile banking in the government-to-person payment sector for financial inclusion in Pakistan. *Information Technology for Development*, *25*(3), 475–502.

Khan, I., & Jaffar, K. H. (2021). Searching for the Binding Constraint to Digital Financial Inclusion in Pakistan: A Decision Tree Approach. Washington, DC: Center for Global Development.

Khera, P., Ng, S., Ogawa, S., & Sahay, R. (2022). Measuring digital financial inclusion in emerging market and developing economies: A new index. *Asian Economic Policy Review*, *17*, 213–230. https://doi.org/10.1111/aepr.12377.

Kim, D.-W., Yu, J.-S., & Hassan, M. K. (2018). Financial inclusion and economic growth in OIC countries. *Research in International Business and Finance*, *43*, 1–14.

Klasen, S., & Lamanna, F. (2009). The impact of gender inequality in education and employment on economic growth: New evidence for a panel of countries. *Feminist Economics*, *15*(3), 91–132.

Malik, F. A., Yadav, D. K., Lone, N. A., & Adam, H. (2021). An investigation into the dynamics of financial inclusion in south Asian countries. *Pakistan Economic and Social Review*, *59*(2), 231.

Manzoor, R., Javed, A., Ahmed, V., & Rauf, A. (2021). Digital financial services in Pakistan: Opportunities, challenges and suggestions. *Journal of Finance & Economics Research*, *6*(2), 1–16. Retrieved from https://www.ncbi.nlm.nih.gov/pmc/articles/PMC9538238/pdf/JOFI-77-2949.pdf.

PCSW (2020). Generating data to advance women's social and economic wellbeing in Pakistan. Policy Brief prepared by PCSW with support from DFID and UNFPA. Available at https://pcsw.punjab.gov.pk/system/files/financial.pdf.

Ray, S. M., Peter, J., & Thakur, V. (2022). Digital Financial Inclusion and Literacy from a G20 Perspective. https://doi.org/10.56506/UXOQ1249.

Sarma, M., & Pais, J. (2011). Financial inclusion and development. *Journal of International Development*, *23*(5), 613–628.

Sulong, Z., & Bakar, H. (2018). The role of financial inclusion on economic growth: Theoretical and empirical literature review analysis. *Journal of Business & Financial Affairs*, *7*(4), 2167–0234.

Tay, L.-Y., Tai, H.-T., & Tan, G.-S. (2022). Digital financial inclusion: A gateway to sustainable development. *Heliyon*. 8(6).

Van, L. T.-H., Vo, A. T., Nguyen, N. T., & Vo, D. H. (2021). Financial inclusion and economic growth: An international evidence. *Emerging Markets Finance and Trade*, *57*(1), 239–263.

WFID Partnership (2022). Towards Women's Financial Inclusion: a Gender Data Diagnostic of Pakistan. Report prepared by Financial Alliance for Women, Data 2X, Women Financial Inclusion Database. Available at https://financialallianceforwomen.org/download/towards-womens-financial-inclusion-a-gender-data-diagnostic-of-pakistan/.

World Economic Forum (2023). Global Gender Gap Report 2023: Insight report. Available at https://www3.weforum.org/docs/WEF_GGGR_2023.pdf

Zulfiqar, K., Chaudhary, M. A., & Aslam, A. (2016). Financial inclusion and its implications for inclusive growth in Pakistan. *Pakistan Economic and Social Review*, *54*(2), 297–325.

4 The Adoption of FinTech Services in Morocco

Confronting the Challenges and Opportunities

Miloudi Kobiyh, Slimane Ed-Dafali, Firdous Ahmad Malik, and Sneha Kadyan

4.1 Introduction

The banking and financial sector is a strategic sector for economic development, providing necessary capital for the economy. Financial globalization has fostered innovation in the sector, with the emergence of services like GAFA and FinTech players. These players utilize new technologies and novel business models to provide innovative financial services, reviving the sector's offerings in the past two decades. Digitization in banking has revolutionized services, leveraging globalization and internet disruption (Aglietta, 2017). Traditional institutions are now integrating these innovations, transforming banks into mobile entities. This modern organizational model facilitates change through mobile technologies, transforming banks into mobile entities (Abou Shakra, 2019).

The FinTech sector combines digital technology with financial services to create new models, processes, and products (De Vauplane, 2015). This disruptive approach disrupts traditional consumption habits and offers more accessible and cost-effective services (Awais et al., 2023). It involves startups and companies transforming the financial sector through innovative use of information technologies, aiming to break away from old consumption habits and create new, more accessible services (Barz et al., 2023). FinTech has become a significant part of the banking and financial sector, offering services through information technology. Initially, the concept began in the 1990s with remote banking services, but faced challenges due to low internet penetration and a lack of familiarity with computer technologies. The 2008 financial crisis accelerated the growth of FinTech, leading to the proliferation of digital tools and the reinvention of banking and financial services. Web giants like Google and Facebook use collected data to access strategic sectors (Lee & Shin, 2018). Leveraging this immense amount of individual customer data allows for a more efficient understanding of customer needs, enabling the offering of more tailored products that meet their requirements (Mieszala, 2015).

The digital revolution has transformed the banking sector, making services more accessible online and enabling customers to perform operations more efficiently and cost-effectively. This has led to online banking, which differs from traditional banking by offering entirely digital services. However, security and trust

DOI: 10.4324/9781032655185-6

are crucial elements in online operations. Traditional banks have developed collaboration strategies with FinTech actors to address customer needs and optimize processes while maintaining human interaction. This cooperative logic allows both sectors to share costs and risks related to digital technology research. Digitalization in Morocco contributes to strengthening the country's industrial, economic, and social emergence. FinTech services are diverse, focusing on borrowing money, investment, and commercial transactions. They leverage innovation and cutting-edge technology to enhance financial services and support businesses, stakeholders, and clients (Siddik et al., 2023).Traditional financial institutions are adapting to digital transformation, enabling them to tailor their strategies and optimize relationships with clients. This has led to a reimagining of the relationship between institutions and clients. The chapter explores consumer adoption of digital financial services and the ecosystem that has allowed traditional institutions to integrate this new dimension for innovation, sustainability, and longevity (Barz et al., 2023).

Specifically, the focus is on examining consumers' reactions to various digital financial services, as well as their role in improving customer relationships. The aim is to discuss the results obtained to confirm or refute the overall enthusiasm surrounding the new players in the FinTech sector and the competition they pose to the traditional banking sector. By addressing these questions, the intention is to gain a comprehensive understanding of the FinTech landscape in Morocco and Africa, exploring how consumers perceive digital transformation, their level of trust, and the larger implications for the financial sector and sustainability challenges. From this perspective, the objective of this chapter is to elucidate, in the first section, the role of the digitalization process in the emergence of the FinTech phenomenon and the general enthusiasm for this sector. Subsequently, in the fifth section, we address the overall trend of the phenomenon in the African continent, and in the sixth section, we examine the relationship between this phenomenon and sustainability challenges.

4.2 Digital Transformation in Banking: Challenges and Issues

In the past, the measurement of wealth relied primarily on material factors such as physical capital and raw materials. Currently, technological innovations play a crucial role in economic efficiency and the behavior of the economy. They are now demanded as a key factor for the success of a company or, more broadly, an economy. This is why economic sectors have a strong interest in taking these innovations into account in their operations, especially their role in establishing new practices capable of addressing several challenges that today's economic system faces (Laperche & Uzunidis, 2011). Innovation stimulates economic growth through the development of innovative enterprises. The digital revolution has brought about major changes that impact various sectors, particularly the financial sector (Simon, 2015). Indeed, the financial sector is influenced by multiple demands related to the proliferation of new technologies (Cichowlas, 2015). These innovations affect financial services and attract a growing number of customers, thereby increasing their profitability (Abou Shakra, 2019). As a result, thanks to innovations, financial institutions can continually improve the efficiency of their investments (Hikmi & Parnaudeau, 2008). This is why technological innovation is a priority and a strategic area for the entire financial sector. Furthermore, the emergence of the internet and the widespread use of the web have led to new consumption habits and generated new needs. This digitalization has empowered customers to be well informed and increasingly demanding. This technology is disruptive in the sense that it breaks away from previous models of service provision. These are disruptive innovations that have compelled the traditional financial sector to reinvent itself with the emergence of new digitally driven services that revolutionize the conventional mode of organizing activities (De Vauplane, 2015). Information technology has significantly aided the sector in streamlining routine operations and expanding its services, which can enhance access to various financial services (Abou Shakra, 2019). Consequently, these technological innovations indeed compel all players active in the finance ecosystem to innovate to adapt to this new environment. The objective is to offer customers a more personalized mode of consumption. This behavior change is driven by the FinTech scholars and marks this disruptive evolution (De Vauplane, 2015). Simultaneously, the expansion of information technologies has triggered technological disruptions and changes that forced the sector to reorganize and adapt to the new context (Cichowlas, 2015). As a result, banks found themselves compelled to integrate these technological innovations to address the evolution of their environment, marked by the new competition from these new players. They thus mobilized significant human and financial resources to promote the adoption of new digital tools that have become central intermediaries in the customer relationship. One thing is certain, the emergence of these new intermediaries presents an opportunity to provide financial services that can reduce the costs of financial intermediation (Havrylchyk & Verdier, 2017). In this regard, daily, FinTech sector players announce innovations that address a need for proximity, accessibility, and simplicity (Mieszala, 2015). This will likely create a dynamic of repositioning for these players (Lavayssière, 2015). This is why traditional players find themselves compelled to align with their customers' choices regarding digital technology and adopt information technologies, allowing them to remain competitive (Cichowlas, 2015). These disruptive innovations emerged in the 1990s and gained momentum in the 2000s. They are innovative companies with projects that differ from one another but converge in their disruptive approach to financial services. The majority are Anglo-Saxon, with a few being French (Mieszala, 2015). They operate under a business model related to the use of information technologies and later spread to the rest of the world after the major financial crisis of 2008. Indeed, this financial crisis led to significant issues of trust, especially in traditional banks and their services (Debernardi, 2018). This situation has brought about a change in consumer behavior, with an increasing shift toward online usage. Customers are turning to these solutions that are cheaper and better suited to their needs. Moreover, this crisis context created feelings of mistrust toward the entire financial sector, which persisted even after the crisis (De Vauplane, 2015). The rise of these startups is based on the development of innovative technologies and significant investments initiated by these startups in the field.

This fusion of technology and finance has allowed these actors to offer services that are cheaper than those provided by the traditional sector and exhibit a certain level of economic efficiency. Indeed, in the 1980s and 1990s, banks professionalized their marketing through the use of new information and communication technologies (ICT). Banking became more widespread, allowing them to sell more effectively to each customer (Simon, 2015). The use of the internet and smartphones, along with their various applications that marked the last decade, accelerated, especially after the 2008 crisis, highlighting the expansion of mobile finance. As a result, the traditional organizational structure of the financial system has undergone significant changes (De Vauplane, 2015). In this regard, crowdfunding, which experienced significant growth starting from the context of the economic and financial crisis of 2008, is a very significant example of using the internet in the financial domain. It is a form of collaborative funding that allows project creators to find alternative sources of financing. Since its inception, crowdfunding has expanded remarkably worldwide (Hemdane, 2016). These platforms offer a genuine source of funding and are more broadly situated within the FinTech sector (Havrylchyk & Verdier, 2017). This example of crowdfunding platforms is one of the most developed forms of FinTech. However, not all platforms are limited to crowdfunding. They can also engage in other activities such as issuing financial securities, financing loans, and providing financial advice (Havrylchyk & Verdier, 2017). As a result, the development of platforms and social media has given rise to new forms of investment opportunities for savers. A second, more illustrative example of this new sector is a FinTech player that represents a significant competitor to the banking system. One such example is PayPal, which offers secure and free online money transfers, a primary activity of the banking system. This is precisely why FinTech are driving a new form of competition that poses substantial challenges for the traditional financial sector. The business model of the financial industry is changing and will continue to evolve further with the development of these disruptive technological tools. Consequently, FinTech herald a new paradigm in which digital technology is the driving force of innovation in the field of finance (Wonglimpiyarat, 2018). This is why these actors present themselves as a revolutionary innovation capable of triggering transformative changes in the traditional financial market. They can significantly contribute to democratizing financial services. Therefore, in the long run, the ongoing revolution could lead to the disruption of the intermediation role played by traditional financial institutions. Simultaneously, digital transformation is a challenge that strongly impacts modern economies. In developing countries, with the widespread penetration of the internet and mobile telecommunications, new entrants offer undeniable opportunities to enhance financial inclusion and promote economic and social development.

This is especially true if these new players seek to be customer-centric, responsible, and supportive. Therefore, accessing financial services through new technology is an asset that encourages mobilizing investments to have a positive impact on clients and society (Wonglimpiyarat, 2018). These are also changes that disrupt the way the entire sector's business is approached, moving toward more optimization of internal exchange flows and those between financial institutions and their partners. This digitization will benefit banks by allowing them to adjust their models and gain in terms of efficiency, relevance, and proximity to their customers (Mieszala, 2015). The changes are notably cultural and social, as the paradigm shift requires transitions that are both economic and social. Information technology also provides the means for individual transactions between peers, which also reflects changes in mindsets (Debernardi, 2018). However, it appears that the digitalization of financial institutions also brings concerns and resistance, often stemming from the fear of change. Indeed, this demands change management skills that require deploying more agile methods. Fear is also tied to security and perceived complexity. Therefore, implementing technological innovations needs to be carried out according to regulatory laws to control the process. Nevertheless, all trends suggest that this technological agility will pave the way for regulatory frameworks to create a more favorable environment, leveraging its numerous benefits for the economy and society.

4.3 Coopetition in the Banking and Financial Sector: Collaborating in a Competitive Context

The democratization of internet usage and the widespread adoption of smartphones have facilitated the creation of opportunities for the emergence of a sector that has successfully transformed innovations into an economic model. The technological disruption caused by FinTech operators is based on the convergence of various types of innovations in the field of financial technology. The spread of their offerings is both alternative, simple, and cost-effective. This process requires the support of central banks, governments, and investors to evolve the sector collectively and sustainably. Traditional players have no choice but to integrate this process and incorporate these tools into their value chain. This is why established institutions have embarked on patterns of collaboration and partnerships with FinTech actors to become more agile and compete with other players in the sector (Abou Shakra, 2019). The categories of FinTech actors include small and medium FinTech startups (technological startups offering financial solutions or services), BigTech companies (such as GAFAM in the United States) and large telecommunications companies, banks offering digital financial services, FinTech-bank partnerships, and digital banks (100% digital banks). New technologies such as machine learning, artificial intelligence, predictive behavioral analysis, and data-driven marketing are the cornerstone of the FinTech revolution. The FinTech ecosystem encompasses a multitude of sectors, including Insurtech dedicated to insurance, Regtech which offers technological solutions to address regulatory constraints, and neo-banks. As a result, the financial system has been profoundly disrupted by both digital transformation and evolving customer behaviors, along with the multitude of cooperations and collaborations with these startups.

In other words, even though the structure of the financial industry is fundamentally shaken, traditional financial actors have implemented strategies of collaboration with the FinTech startup sector to cope with competitiveness and reconnect with customers seeking these more streamlined and agile remote services (Lee & Shin, 2018).

Indeed, previous studies have confirmed that cooperation with online operators leads to the development of new financial services and facilitates the digital transition. At the same time, FinTech operators must create services that are different from those offered by traditional financial institutions (Wonglimpiyarat, 2018).

In this regard, the cooperation between the two sectors offers a multitude of advantages: cost reduction, access to partner networks, shortened time-to-market, and strengthening credibility and trust among all actors. Thus, worldwide, traditional institutions are increasing their partnerships and investments in FinTech startups to quickly access their IT expertise and technological innovation capabilities.

Moreover, relying on partnerships with digital solution providers is less costly than trying to develop more expensive technological solutions in-house. Several partnership opportunities have emerged for traditional actors (banks, insurers, and investment funds), with a greater focus on mobilizing savings and investing in research and development (Hemdane, 2016). Simultaneously, their market share is still substantial, and they can offer their advantages stemming from advancements in customer experience (Mieszala, 2015).

These actors have become a necessity for the financial sector to ensure its ability to survive, compete, and keep up with digital progress (Abou Shakra, 2019). These actors operating in the FinTech domain constitute the main drivers of the digital revolution. This is why these collaborations are crucial to prevent any dysfunction in the financial sector, as the rational behavior of private actors at the microeconomic level can deteriorate the situation for all actors at the macroeconomic level (Aglietta, 2017). In summary, on one hand, established players will need FinTech startups to benefit from their technological advancements and expertise in obtaining structured customer data (Mieszala, 2015). Moreover, the sector has simultaneously witnessed a strengthening of prudential constraints, meaning that FinTech actors need the involvement of other sector entities to enter the market.

Thus, with the reinforcement of prudential constraints, there are synergies to be developed among actors to define and bring to life a viable and sustainable development project through collective action. From the perspective of traditional actors, it can unfold by mutually developing technology with startups, accelerating the maturity of startups through corporate incubators, directly acquiring certain startups, or developing financial technology internally (Lee & Shin, 2018). Simultaneously, one of the main challenges of this paradigm shift is the transformation of human resources through the development and realignment of skills, as well as the emergence of new skill requirements. Similarly, effective management of a collaborative project paves the way for complementary skills and mobilizes the necessary expertise and resources for innovation (Maillefert & Robert, 2020). Therefore, this new path of cooperation serves as a crucial lever to develop or attract new skills well suited to the novel roles demanded by technological innovation.

4.4 Financial Integration and FinTech: Global Trend in Morocco

In Morocco, FinTech operators are developing tentatively. Financial technology is gradually entering the country, attracting various actors from both the public and private sectors. Recent years have witnessed the growth of digital solutions offered by Moroccan banks to their customers, leading to an increasing number of remote operations. This digitalization is impacting customer relationship management strategies. Hence, other entities have a strong interest in integrating ICT into their interactions with customers. The rise of smartphones and the increasing use of various applications have amplified the use of the web among the Moroccan population, particularly for checking their accounts and gathering information about different offers. The success of this digital usage is largely attributed to the pursuit of simpler access to services provided by the sector, driven by a desire for autonomy. In this context, the Moroccan financial sector is striving to meet the expectations of its clientele, which has become increasingly demanding and is constantly in search of the best solutions. In this regard, crowdfunding has gained popularity as an alternative means of financing businesses worldwide (Wonglimpiyarat, 2018). This funding strategy could provide developing countries with $93 billion annually by 2025, with the Middle East and North Africa region having a potential annual potential of $5.6 billion (Hemdane, 2016). Consequently, the digital transformation in the financial domain offers opportunities for the country to become a pioneer in the new industry on the African continent. Even though the startup sector in Morocco is still struggling to flourish due to regulations that have yet to fully accommodate innovation, Bank Al-Maghrib has repeatedly expressed its intention to support these players by implementing regulatory measures to facilitate their operations. The introduction of regulatory measures can help regulate the financial sector, which has been revolutionized by technological innovations and digital transition. Particularly, Morocco stands as one of the few countries on the continent making tangible efforts to enact a law aimed at facilitating the activity of crowdfunding. In the face of these challenges, the digital sector is poised to provide real solutions. The movement can only accelerate with the establishment of incubators that welcome ideas and innovations capable of enhancing financial integration (Simon, 2015). Indeed, Morocco possesses several advantages that enable the development of its FinTech sector. Notably, the country boasts a high-quality telecom infrastructure with internet speeds that position Morocco as a leader in the digital realm within its region. Furthermore, the mobile penetration rate is quite high, providing an opportunity across various sectors. As of 2018, 4G coverage in Morocco exceeds 95%, and internet access surpasses 45% (CUA/OCDE, 2021). Morocco has also embarked on the path of digital transformation since the early 21st century, quickly realizing the significance of digital transition that could play a decisive role in the country's economic development. Consequently, on September 14, 2017, Framework Law No. 61-16 was enacted, leading to the establishment of the Digital Development Agency (ADD).[1] Its mission is to establish a regulatory framework for digital products and services that promote digitalization and encourage innovation for sustainable and inclusive digital inclusion.

In this regard, Bank Al-Maghrib has adopted Law 103-12, which represents a significant breakthrough that could put an end to the banking monopoly and allow non-banking service providers to offer their solutions to promote financial inclusion. Specifically, Bank Al-Maghrib aims to promote alternative models capable of reaching the most excluded populations at lower costs and with services that are better suited to their specific needs. Similarly, the development of financial innovations has been at the center of actions taken by the Central Bank of Morocco. In order to promote innovation and playing a key role in the FinTech ecosystem, Bank Al-Maghrib has launched many programs as part of its strategic programs. The "One Stop Shop FinTech" platform is one of these initiatives; it was created to operate as a single regulatory point of contact and provide legal and regulatory advice to FinTech businesses looking to enter the market. This one-stop shop has helped more than 60 FinTech startups through regulatory requirements since it was established in 2019 (Bank Al-Maghrib, 2022). In 2021, 19 FinTechs sought guidance, with 42% Moroccan and 58% foreign. Among them, 23% aimed for a payment institution license (Bank Al-Maghrib, 2022). By being a single point of contact within the Bank, this one-stop shop has the main role of supporting, advising, and guiding innovative companies in the legal and regulatory aspects. This unique platform aims to be accessible, fostering an open dialogue with the regulator and the entire FinTech sector looking to offer innovative services in the Moroccan financial landscape (Bank Al-Maghrib, 2021).

However, the banking sector in Morocco has long adopted client proximity strategies to reach even the most remote citizens, aiming to address the low banking penetration rate and the lag in financial inclusion. Nevertheless, despite their effectiveness, these strategies have resulted in significant costs over the past decade, which weigh heavily on the profitability of these operations. Hence, approaches have emerged that involve developing FinTech operators as part of a national financial inclusion strategy. Thus, the sector is witnessing the emergence of a multitude of services that are taking shape. In 2016, the BCP Group embarked on an ambitious project for a large-scale digital transformation, aiming to accelerate the trend of innovations to discover high-potential technologies. These are digital and computer-based innovations that enable customers to explore new ways of investing, saving, and obtaining credit (Havrylchyk & Verdier, 2017). Thanks to FinTech, the flow of cash, credit, deposits, investments, salaries, government-to-person (G2P) transfers, and peer-to-peer (P2P) transactions, among others, at the national and regional levels, was maintained without endangering people's lives during the COVID-19 crisis (UNDP, 2021). In this context, the role of collaborations in the development of the FinTech sector in Morocco could play a pivotal role. The shifting power dynamics in the banking and financial sector have compelled traditional players to view FinTech startups as part of a beneficial digital transformation strategy for all stakeholders. This is why traditional financial actors may initiate alliance strategies with these emerging players to capitalize on their technological advancements and address any lag they might have in integrating innovations. These strategies lead to the introduction of new financial services, similar to countries that are advanced in this field (Lee & Shin, 2018). However, Morocco lags in the area of mobile payments. This is why the establishment of a national mobile payment platform is also promising. In addition to this, the demands of interoperability technology between the banking sector and payment institutions contribute to this effort. This will position Morocco as a regional digital hub by enhancing digital export offerings, reducing the digital divide, and transforming key sectors of the national economy (CUA/OCDE, 2021). In this context, the sector is anticipating significant growth in FinTech due to the impetus provided by Law 103.12, particularly related to the digitalization of banking institutions and mobile banking. Similarly, the digitalization process promotes a better organization of work. In Morocco, Technopark Morocco (located in Casablanca, Rabat, Tanger, and Agadir) hosts 280 Moroccan startups and small- and medium-sized enterprises (SMEs), employing nearly 2,000 individuals with an average age below 30 years, contributing to over 10% of the national ICT (excluding telecom) turnover, and witnessing a turnover of more than 60 new startups each year. The development and expansion of this technological park can be achieved through "clusterization" policies that support the digital economy and successful digital transformation (CUA/OCDE, 2021). Consequently, the sector offers opportunities to incubate innovation and support these new players with innovative ideas. However, to overcome the slowness that characterizes sector development, there is a need to accelerate the implementation of regulatory support to foster the ecosystem of startups specialized in the digital sector and expedite initiatives in this field. As a result, these startups can take advantage of this environment and expand, helping to develop their local brand. This safeguards the national digital market, making it more competitive against foreign products.

However, a significant number of activities carried out by FinTech can pose risks that could impact the stability of the financial system. In this regard, the accumulation of vulnerabilities could threaten financial stability, raising new questions regarding the regulation of competition policy (Verdier, 2016). Given the importance of this system, the establishment of appropriate regulatory measures to protect consumers conducting transactions through the FinTech sector becomes a necessity. Bank Al-Maghrib is thus required to continue its efforts in the direction of a more adaptable and appropriate regulation for the startup ecosystem inside the Moroccan financial landscape. Moreover, realizing that FinTech goes beyond the scope of the Central Bank alone, Bank Al-Maghrib has strengthened its role as a market catalyst by joining an expanded ecosystem, encompassing other regulators in the financial sector, relevant public institutions, and a variety of private actors who are also interested in FinTech development. Many of these stakeholders are highly active organizations in the field and, in collaboration with Bank Al-Maghrib, aim to promote financial innovation and foster this ecosystem in the digital era (Bank Al-Maghrib, 2021). To respond to these new demands and issues of the digital age, Morocco's current banking and financial model, as well as its structure and operation, must be fundamentally rethought (De Vauplane, 2015). This adaptation can take the form of collaborations or partnerships, but it can also manifest through policies to reposition skills within the sector. It's also a promotional tool that allows these projects to have an impact beyond Morocco's borders. The future of this new sector is closely linked to the utilization of "big data" and algorithms; however, this demands accompanying plans to mitigate the risks that can arise from various irregularities (Havrylchyk & Verdier, 2017).

4.5 Moroccan Consumer Response toward FinTech Services: The Role of Trust

Although digital tools have the advantage of being used to reduce costs and improve services, in Morocco, customers remain physically attached to their financial institutions. For example, they prefer to go to the bank branch where they expect personalized service, appreciation, and high-quality solutions provided by the staff. This reveals that despite digital offering more autonomy and independence, the dominant relationship in the financial sector remains one of proximity that provides welcoming and high-value advice (Lavayssière, 2015). However, digital evolution allows for a paradigm that combines the best of human interaction and digital tools (Mert & Ed-Dafali, 2022; Mohiuddin et al., 2022). Integrating new digital practices with quality advice and the friendliness offered by staff can contribute to increasing transactions and strengthening financial services. The aim is to anchor and enhance financial inclusion, allowing broad populations to access FinTech services (Abou Shakra, 2019). The goal is to facilitate various transactions (bank-to-bank transfers, real-time balance checks, check ordering, contact with financial advisors, financing simulations, and bill and tax payments), to create new services and thereby address emerging needs. FinTech lenders can reduce information asymmetry and providing loans to low-income households and small businesses that traditional banks may not assist due to information scarcity.

FinTech platforms have also developed savings instruments that allow households to pool their savings and channel them to households and businesses in need. Loans granted to households globally amounted to \$76 trillion in 2015, \$170 trillion in 2016, and \$275 trillion in 2017. Meanwhile, loans to businesses for the same years were \$49 trillion, \$99 trillion, and \$125 trillion. This demonstrates the potential of this instrument in improving financing and financial inclusion, which can extend to other areas such as insurance, wealth management, and cross-border payments (including remittances) (IMF, 2020). Moreover, the development of the financial sector is crucial to ensure economic efficiency due to its contribution to domestic savings mobilization. It also facilitates the better flow of capital, enhances liquidity, and reduces the costs of banking and financial transactions (Lane, 2010). In this regard, Bank Al-Maghrib is expected to implement a monitoring policy aimed at accelerating the dedicated support framework for this sector. These measures have become a necessity to promote, on one hand, the provision of financial services, and on the other hand, to accelerate the financial inclusion of Moroccan households. Bank Al-Maghrib is working toward co-creating a FinTech ecosystem, channeling efforts, and creating synergy between the various initiatives proposed by different financial actors, particularly with the public/private sector and various financial regulators. Bank Al-Maghrib is actively involved in the cooperative creation of a FinTech ecosystem with the goal of coordinating and syncing the activities of various financial actors. Regarding the partnership with CDG Invest through its "212 Founders" fund, the objective is to provide comprehensive support for the development of FinTech in Morocco and to consolidate Moroccan initiatives to create a cohesive ecosystem for investors and entrepreneurs operating in the FinTech sector. Bank Al-Maghrib will be responsible for assisting CDG Invest and the FinTech supported by this program in the regulatory aspects of their projects. On the other hand, CDG Invest's primary mission will be to support FinTech project founders in structuring and implementing their projects, providing them access to international-level expertise (Bank Al-Maghrib, 2022). However, the weight of cultural heritage contributes to the slow pace of digital transformation in Morocco. It makes traditional actors less receptive to these innovative initiatives despite their numerous advantages. Among the solutions to address this challenge, it is important to enhance financial education in the habits and behaviors of consumers. The goal is to achieve a high level of financial inclusion, covering most Moroccan households. Similarly, such education will facilitate access to other financial services.

The development of FinTech can only be ensured through trust in the integrity and security of digital finance (CUA/OCDE, 2021). This provides decision-makers with the opportunity to understand how to address challenges and overcome obstacles, both in terms of regulatory and operational aspects that underlie digitization in this field. These elements also enable the formulation of recommendations to strengthen the position of these actors in the Moroccan economy and reinforce their role in the country's development. Among the recommendations for a new development model in Morocco is the creation of centers of excellence dedicated to future technologies (e.g., AI, big data, blockchain, agritech, biotech, 5G, and FinTech). The regulation should be adapted to promote the emergence of innovative companies capable of growing in the domestic market and expanding internationally, such as FinTech, mobile payment, crowdfunding, etc. (CESE, 2019). The perception of these tools depends on several variables that play a crucial role in their acceptance and expansion in the country. In this regard, motivations are diverse, specifically related to cultural, social, and economic factors that drive the adoption of these FinTech services. The primary goal is to facilitate the use of these new services within the Moroccan social context and to assess the potential that the Moroccan economy and its ecosystems hold, allowing these new players to fully play their role in stimulating the economy and enhancing financial and social inclusion. It's also about exploring elements related to these tools, such as service transparency, trust, ease of use, refinement, pricing, and quality. These elements facilitate the expansion of these services and enhance their potential in the country's development. To summarize, the financial sector's commercial and financial performance are significantly influenced by digital transformation. It is hoped that the digitalization of services will result in significant time savings, increased placement in the marketplace, and rewarding customer relationships. This may make it possible to allocate resources most effectively while raising the standard of living for everyone (Cichowlas, 2015).

4.6 FinTech in Africa: Current State and Prospects

In the African context, there are several potential opportunities for FinTech to improve financial inclusion: it is fast, convenient, and cost-effective. The business models are innovative, offering tailor-made customer services with enhanced security. As for the development of FinTech on this continent, a report from PwC Morocco in partnership with Casablanca Finance City reveals that African FinTech represent only 2% of all finance-related startups worldwide. Despite this, FinTech startups on the African continent raised over $335 million in the first half of 2021, which is twice as much as the entire previous year. FinTech accelerators are expected to have in-depth expertise in digital technologies, entrepreneurship, and digital business models, a network of qualified/certified mentors, angel investors, institutional investors, venture capital firms, and government startup support programs (UNDP, 2021). African FinTech tend to combine multiple services by offering a diverse range of offerings such as money transfers, digital payments, remote banking, and loans. Simultaneously, within the innovative business ecosystem, the FinTech sector attracts the most investors in Africa. Implementing any initiatives in this direction has the potential to accelerate the sector's development to make it a prominent player on the continent. In this regard, foreign experiences have shown that it's often traditional financial institutions that initiate the first steps to facilitate collaboration between the traditional and digital sectors. This collaboration has fostered an ecosystem where platforms are developed to enable financial operators to digitize and reach a broader customer base. The verticals of the financial services industry and their constituent elements within FinTech include the following segments: Digital Banking or BankTech (banking services via mobile phone, online banking, data-driven finance, SME financing, alternative credit assessment, personal finance, and risk management); Financial Sales and Trading, Investment and Wealth Management or WealthTech (robotic/automated advisory, securities sales and trading, portfolio management, risk management); Transactional Financial Services (PayTech, payment gateway, e-wallet, money transfers, digital currency, currency exchange) (UNDP, 2021). For African and other developing and emerging countries, these FinTech services offer opportunities to stimulate economic and social development and enhance financial inclusion. In developing and emerging countries, 1.2 billion people have gained access to financial services through technology. The potential of FinTech in emerging economies by 2025 is estimated at 6% of Gross Domestic Product (GDP) and 95 million new jobs. Since 2008, global investments in the sector have accelerated, reaching $135.7 billion in 2019 compared to $25 billion in 2016. Globally, the growth of FinTech lender assets in 2021 was $195 billion for the banking FinTech sector and $275 billion for the non-banking FinTech sector. Regarding the African continent, in the eight countries of the West African Economic and Monetary Union (WAEMU) – Benin, Burkina Faso, Côte d'Ivoire, Guinea-Bissau, Mali, Niger, Senegal, and Togo – the number of FinTech is 128. While FinTech is vibrant in East Africa and parts of Southern Africa, it is just beginning to gain momentum in the WAEMU region. FinTech startups are often undercapitalized and primarily focus on the initial level of services related to payments, money transfers, and digital/mobile wallets and accounts (UNDP, 2021). Despite evolving regulations, FinTech can effectively implement compliance controls to operate and innovate within the framework of existing regulations (Barz et al., 2023). Digital credit, savings, and insurance services are not yet widely available in the WAEMU region. Among the 128 identified FinTech startups in the region, only 12 marginally offer alternative financing services (crowdfunding/investment), which remain very limited and concentrated mainly in Côte d'Ivoire and Senegal (UNDP, 2021). FinTech, which is rapidly gaining ground in Central Africa, could facilitate access to financing for young entrepreneurs. With a 30.1% level of banking penetration in 2017, Central Africa has the lowest rate on the entire continent. However, mobile payment has experienced remarkable growth in recent years, despite its recent introduction. In 2019, the volume of mobile payment transactions reached USD 1.8 billion, compared to only $200 million in 2010 in this region of Africa. The pooling of resources from the public and private sectors could lead to significant cost savings. The region is expected to invest USD 2.9 billion to achieve complete 4G coverage by 2025. Over the period from 2015 to 2019, the telecommunications sector in Central Africa invested an average of USD 750 million per year in infrastructure projects of this type (CUA/OCDE, 2021). In North Africa, digital transformation presents numerous opportunities but also generates new risks for economies, requiring the implementation of appropriate policies. To strengthen the emergence of the FinTech sector, it's important to develop digital skills and support entrepreneurship and innovation. This includes relaxing regulatory constraints, bridging the infrastructure gap with advanced countries, modernizing education, and training systems, and supporting public-private partnerships (PPPs) (CUA/OCDE, 2021). In this region of Africa, Egypt, Morocco, and Tunisia are the three countries where FinTech-specialized startups are most prominent. Their development should align with policies to enhance digital infrastructure and connectivity. While North Africa is the most connected region on the continent, there is still a need to improve the regulatory environment to expedite digital finance development. For instance, the 4G coverage rate reached 83% in 2020. However, in 2018, it was only 68%, and only 35.7% of the rural population had internet access compared to 53.9% in urban areas (CUA/OCDE, 2021). One of the catalytic events supporting FinTech and digital startups is the example of the South African Innovation Summit. The SA Innovation Summit serves as a negotiation platform for the technology startup community, connecting them with funders, large and small companies, and relevant support services/platforms such as student activation, inventor activation, hackathons, collaboration platforms for programming, acceleration programs, Match & Invest for investor-entrepreneur connections, Pitching Den for presenting business plans to investors, and events to prepare for participation in the World Start-up Cup in Silicon Valley (PNUD, 2021). In summary, FinTech catalyzes digital transformation in Africa, although resistance to change remains a significant constraint to this transformation and the development of its FinTech sector. However, promoting financial inclusion and encouraging the development of the digital finance ecosystem through policies and events, such as organizing days focused on financial education and financial inclusion, is important (Bank Al-Maghrib, 2022). Furthermore, the ecosystem supporting FinTech remains underdeveloped, particularly in terms of venture capital, government support policies, and supportive institutions such as accelerators and business incubators. The emergence of FinTech startups has catalyzed new financing models for SMEs that are better suited to their needs and profiles. FinTech bring three levels of benefits to the economy and SMEs: efficiency and competitiveness gains for SMEs, improved access to financing and transactional financial services for SMEs, and facilitation of other socio-economic sectors (PNUD, 2021). It is evident that

FinTech is reshaping the financial landscape and holds tremendous potential to enhance financial inclusion. Today's FinTech companies have experienced phenomenal growth in terms of volume, investments, and market penetration. However, on a global level, 90% of these FinTech fail (Barz et al., 2023). Therefore, FinTech, investors, and various partners need to understand the factors that lead to success. While culture is crucial at the maturity stage, factors such as communication, compliance ease, and customer orientation are essential for the sector's development and positioning within the financial industry (Barz et al., 2023). Finally, this sector alone is not sufficient to address the various gaps in access to financial services. This improvement can be complemented by targeted policy initiatives such as strengthening regulations and financial infrastructure, promoting financial and digital education, and standardizing FinTech products, among others, which are necessary to address these challenges. Additionally, the importance of global collaboration and coordination cannot be understated, as they are necessary for sharing knowledge, reaching international agreements, and promoting best practices.

4.7 FinTech and Sustainability: Challenges for Sustainable Innovation

In the financial domain, issues of economic sustainability are of considerable interest. In this realm, FinTech companies can be considered key agents of sustainability and responsible investment. They have the potential to influence the socio-environmental performance of countries. This calls for both theoretical and empirical collaboration to better understand the relationship between FinTech and sustainability (Mertzanis, 2023). However, digital finance often disrupts existing financial practices, necessitating a reallocation of capital toward environmentally friendly investments, leading to an evolution toward sustainable approaches. This convergence between financial technology and sustainability is referred to as "Green FinTech" (Merello et al., 2022). According to Pizzi et al. (2021), the current literature has not adequately explored the link between FinTech and the adoption of sustainable models, especially in the context of SMEs. They seek to understand whether the benefits of implementing FinTech solutions for SMEs can accelerate the transition to more equitable and sustainable economic models. Additionally, Merello et al. (2022) have highlighted the agency problem for FinTech actors as sustainable enterprises. As the financial appetite of shareholders increases, efforts toward sustainability within these companies may decrease, potentially undermining sustainable strategies and long-term value creation. Their study also explores the facilitative role of FinTech in SMEs transitioning toward circular economic models. Recently, Lisha et al. (2023) demonstrated how financial development contributes to maintaining a sustainable environment. By quantifying the impact of digital finance growth on sustainable energy usage, the findings of their study encourage investment in green technologies, ultimately leading to sustainable development. Moreover, the FinTech sector can be utilized by businesses to incentivize customers to participate in green financing projects by offering rewards for sustainable behaviors (Awais et al., 2023). However, challenges to achieving sustainable economic activity include transparency, security, and traceability of information, all of which are aspects that the FinTech sector can contribute to. As FinTech solutions continue to evolve while aligning with sustainability goals, their influence on environmental performance may increase. This demonstrates that there are links between FinTech tools and sustainability. FinTech contributes to sustainable development by supporting the responsible use of resources, and its development can have a positive relationship with the use of renewable energy. Indeed, the use of renewable energy sources in the extraction of materials used in various types of technology, coupled with the use of financial technology, helps reduce dependence on fossil fuels (Lisha et al., 2023). Moreover, FinTech also encompasses cloud computing, which offers opportunities for sustainable business operations with higher efficiency. Thus, FinTech supports green finance activities to help protect the environment from the impacts of productive activities and significantly reduce harmful emissions (Awais et al., 2023). Moreover, higher levels of funding, secure infrastructures, and the availability of new technologies are, on average, associated with greater social and environmental performance (Mertzanis, 2023). As a result, collaboration and supportive policies can further enhance the FinTech's contribution to environmental sustainability. Peer-to-peer (P2P) financing, which enables SMEs and investors to fund social or sustainable projects, is an example of how this industry, particularly through lending, offers alternative pathways for obtaining financial resources. The FinTech sector plays a role as an instrument of social financing and green financing by serving informal businesses and providing insurance that protects small farmers from climate risks, as is the case in Africa. Additionally, it can offer solutions for financing renewable energy, lease-to-own options for production equipment for small farmers, "buy now, pay later" contract financing, and more (PNUD, 2021). The FinTech sector, as an industry that has evolved under the impact of Industry 4.0, also has the potential to play a significant role in helping SMEs transition to a more sustainable business model (Siddik et al., 2023). Their business model represents fertile ground for this approach, and the sustainable SME model could be activated by leveraging scientific knowledge and practitioner-driven contributions from the FinTech industry. These elements demonstrate that FinTech serves as a tool for ecological modernization that can enhance business performance in terms of sustainability. Therefore, investigating innovative technology adoption in the Moroccan context, Ed-Dafali et al. (2023) argued that Industry 4.0 innovations play a crucial role in achieving sustainable competitive advantage. Continuous innovation and digital connectivity are vital for sustainable business performance and efficiency (Pizzi et al., 2021). However, it takes time for FinTech solutions to support environmental sustainability to become widely used since they must first raise awareness, develop trust with investors and consumers, and win their support. Thus, these actors need sufficient time to develop and enhance their offerings, attract a substantial user base, and establish partnerships (Mertzanis, 2023). The emphasis on sustainability and eco-friendly investments within FinTech organizations is anticipated to continue increase as a result of increased consumer and investor concerns regarding the environmental impact of their investments. Finding the financial benefits associated with this change is necessary for creating a more sustainable society. Moreover, exploring the potential of FinTech and digital technologies in advancing the shift toward more sustainable economic models appears to be a promising direction for future research (Pizzi et al., 2021). In light of the assumed environmental impact of the digital financial services industry, it's critical to evaluate how FinTech companies support sustainability and raise the value of the sector.

4.8 Conclusion

The financial industry has been significantly impacted by the digital revolution, allowing it to better understand its clients and offer tailored financial services. This has led to increased profitability and financial inclusion, making the FinTech sector a growth engine for economic advancement. The rapid growth of social media and internet usage has provided opportunities for the development of the FinTech sector, which can reduce costs and provide tailored products. The Covid-19 pandemic has demonstrated the viability of providing services remotely via digitalization, highlighting the transition from digital to cognitive eras. Traditional institutions have adopted hybrid models by investing in new digital technology, and the Moroccan financial sector is exploring the possibilities offered by new technologies to improve processes through innovative approaches. Bank Al-Maghrib faces challenges in implementing digitalization and ensuring robust regulations to prevent uncontrolled drift or abusive use of customer trust.

Fostering collaboration between legislators, financial institutions, and FinTech specialists is essential for improving underserved individuals access to financial services in developing countries. Digitalization has the potential to prompt a rethinking of new management approaches for financial institutions, fostering a spirit of complementarity and cooperation between traditional and digital sectors. The FinTech industry is a rapidly developing topic with the potential to advance research in other areas. Future research should involve various experts in formulating metrics to gauge the effect of FinTech on banking and finance performance, as well as examine the importance of financial education and its influence on the industry's growth.

Note

1 https://www.add.gov.ma/.

References

Abou Shakra, N. (2019). « *L'impact de la FinTech dans la restructuration du secteur bancaire au Liban », thèse de doctorat en Sciences Économiques*. Amiens, France: Université de Picardie Jules Verne. theses.hal.science/tel-03691888/file/TheseAbouShakra.pdf.

Aglietta, M. (2017). Finance globale, cycle financier et stabilité macroéconomique. *Revue d'économie financière*, *127*(3), 223–236. https://doi.org/10.3917/ecofi.127.0223.

Awais, M., Afzal, A., Firdousi, S., & Hasnaoui, A. (2023). Is FinTech the new path to sustainable resource utilisation and economic development? *Resources Policy*, *81*, 103309. https://doi.org/10.1016/j.resourpol.2023.103309.

Bank Al-Maghrib (2021). Rapport annuel sur les infrastructures des marchés financiers et les moyens de paiement, leur surveillance et l'Inclusion Financière-Exercice 2020. www.bkam.ma/Publications-et-recherche/Publications-institutionnelles/Rapport-annuel-sur-les-infrastructures-des-marches-financiers-et-les-moyens-de-paiement-leur-surveillance-et-l-inclusion-financiere.

Bank Al-Maghrib (2022). Rapport annuel sur les infrastructures des marchés financiers et les moyens de paiement, leur surveillance et l'Inclusion Financière-Exercice 2021. www.bkam.ma/Publications-et-recherche/Publications-institutionnelles/Rapport-annuel-sur-les-infrastructures-des-marches-financiers-et-les-moyens-de-paiement-leur-surveillance-et-l-inclusion-financiere

Barz, L., Lindeque, S., & Hedman, J. (2023). Critical success factors in the FinTech world: A stage model. *Electronic Commerce Research and Applications*, *60*, 101280. https://doi.org/10.1016/j.elerap.2023.101280.

CESE (2019). Le Nouveau Modèle de Développement du Maroc- Contribution du Conseil Economique, Social et Environnemental. www.cese.ma/media/2020/10/CESE-Nouv_Modele_de_Devt-f-3.pdf.

Cichowlas, A. (2015). Technologie et transformation des services bancaires: l'exemple de technovision de Capgemini. *Revue d'économie financière*, *120*(4), 35–56. https://doi.org/10.3917/ecofi.120.0035.

CUA/OCDE (2021). Dynamiques du développement en Afrique 2021: Transformation digitale et qualité de l'emploi, CUA, Addis Abeba/Éditions OCDE, Paris. https://doi.org/10.1787/cd08eac8-fr.

De Vauplane, H. (2015). Les nouveaux acteurs de la finance. *Revue d'économie financière*, *2*(118), 27–35. https://doi.org/10.3917/ecofi.118.0027.

Debernardi, C. (2018). Les nouvelles technologies du monde financier. *Paysans & société*, *3*(369), 34–38. https://doi.org/10.3917/pes.369.0034.

Ed-Dafali, S., Al-Azad, M. S., Mohiuddin, M., & Reza, M. N. H. (2023). Strategic orientations, organizational ambidexterity, and sustainable competitive advantage: Mediating role of industry 4.0 readiness in emerging markets. *Journal of Cleaner Production*, *401*, 136765.

Fond Monétaire International (FMI) (2022). Global Financial Stability Report—Shockwaves from the War in Ukraine Test the Financial System's Resilience. Washington, DC, April. www.imf.org/en/Publications/GFSR/Issues/2022/04/19/global-financial-stability-report-april-2022.

Havrylchyk, O., & Verdier, M. (2017). L'intermédiation financière à l'époque des FinTech: le rôle des plateformes de crowdlending. *Revue d'économie financière*, *3*(127), 207–222. https://doi.org/10.3917/ecofi.127.0207.

Hemdane, T. (2016). Le crowdfunding, une innovation pour financer le développement du Maroc. *Techniques financières & développement*, *3*(124), 27–34. https://doi.org/10.3917/tfd.124.0027.

Hikmi, A., & Parnaudeau, M. (2008). Le rôle du financement bancaire dans le processus d'innovation: le cas de quatre pays européens. *Vie & Sciences de l'entreprise*, *1*(178), 91–112. https://doi.org/10.3917/vse.178.0091.

Lane, P. R. (2010). Innovation et mondialisation financière. *Revue d'économie du développement*, *18*(4), 121–152. https://doi.org/10.3917/edd.244.0121.

Laperche, B., & Uzunidis, D. (2011). Responsabilité sociale et profit – repenser les objectifs de l'entreprise. *La revue des sciences de gestion*, *46*(247–248), 111–120. https://doi.org/10.3917/rsg.247.0111

Lavayssière, B. (2015). Les modèles économiques bouleversés par le digital. *Revue d'économie financière*, *4*(120), 57–66. https://doi.org/10.3917/ecofi.120.0057.

Lee, I., & Shin, Y. J. (2018). FinTech: Ecosystem, business models, investment decisions, and challenges. *Business Horizons*, *61*(1), 35–46. https://doi.org/10.1016/j.bushor.2017.09.003.

Lisha, L., Mousa, S., Arnone, G., Muda, I., Huerta-Soto, R., & Shiming, Z. (2023). Natural resources, green innovation, FinTech, and sustainability: A fresh insight from BRICS, *Resources Policy*, *80*, 103119. https://doi.org/10.1016/j.resourpol.2022.103119.

Maillefert, M., & Robert, I. (2020). Nouveaux modèles économiques et construction de la durabilité territoriale. Illustrations à partir d'une analyse de l'action collective. *Natures Sciences Sociétés*, *28*(2), 131–144. https://doi.org/10.1051/nss/2020031.
Merello, P., Barberá, A., & De la Poza, E. (2022). Is the sustainability profile of FinTech companies a key driver of their value? *Technological Forecasting and Social Change*, *174*, 121290, https://doi.org/10.1016/j.techfore.2021.121290.
Mert, G., & Ed-Dafali, S., (2022). Digital human resources management. In F. Özsungur (Ed.), *Managing the digital workplace in the post-pandemic: A companion for study and practice*. Taylor & Francis. https://doi.org/10.4324/9781003283386-8.
Mertzanis, C. (2023). FinTech finance and social-environmental performance around the world. *Finance Research Letters*, *56*, 104107. https://doi.org/10.1016/j.frl.2023.104107
Mieszala, J. C. (2015). La révolution technologique des systèmes financiers: l'exemple de la banque de financement et d'investissement. *Revue d'économie financière*, *2*(118), 53–66. https://doi.org/10.3917/ecofi.118.0053
Mohiuddin, M., Azad, M. S. A., Ahmed, S., Ed-Dafali, S., & Reza, M. N. H. (2022). Evolution of industry 4.0 and its implications for international business. In J. W. M. Mohiuddin, M. S. A. Azad, & S. Ahmed (Eds.), *Global trade in the emerging business environment*. London: IntechOpen.
Pizzi, S., Corbo, L., & Caputo, A. (2021). FinTech and SMEs sustainable business models: Reflections and considerations for a circular economy. *Journal of Cleaner Production*, *281*, 125217. https://doi.org/10.1016/j.jclepro.2020.125217.
PNUD (2021). Cartographie des stratégies et modèles de financement réussis pour les MPME et les entreprises du secteur informel, y compris le soutien à leur redressement et à leur résilience dans le contexte de la pandémie de COVID-19. www.undp.org/sites/g/files/zskgke326/files/migration/africa/066ff14b640063747e6413bb31024fda14aa82b23139db72d18bd93123199fa7.pdf.
Siddik, A. B., Rahman, M. N., & Yong, L. (2023). Do FinTech adoption and financial literacy improve corporate sustainability performance? The mediating role of access to finance. *Journal of Cleaner Production*. https://doi.org/10.1016/j.jclepro.2023.137658.
Simon, P. (2015). Nouvelles technologies et services financiers. *Revue d'économie financière*, *4*(120), 199–210. https://doi.org/10.3917/ecofi.120.0199.
Verdier, M. (2016). Les développements récents de la littérature sur les plates-formes. *Revue économique*, *67*(HS1), 25–38. https://doi.org/10.3917/reco.hs01.0025.
Wonglimpiyarat, J. (2018). Challenges and dynamics of FinTech crowd funding: An innovation system approach. *The Journal of High Technology Management Research*, *29*(1), 98–108. https://doi.org/10.1016/j.hitech.2018.04.009.

5 An Empirical Study on the Adoption of Fintech Services in Fostering Economic Growth

Mediating the Role of Digital Technology

Smita Nadiger, Anushree D. Kini, R.R. Kulkarni, Suvarna Nimbagal, and Ansumalini Panda

5.1 Introduction

India's financial industry has experienced remarkable growth, and the country is advancing technologically. The national government wants to encourage the financial industry's shift to digital technology. These include lowering expenses and obstacles, boosting competitiveness and efficiency, reducing information asymmetry, and expanding access to financial services (Feyen et al., 2021). Financial technology (fintech) gives customers clear and quick services in the age of digitization. The opportunity to deliver more efficient and inclusive financial services while simultaneously promoting economic growth is presented by the digitalization of financial services. The way that businesses execute their transactions has altered as a result of fintech services. Today's consumers participate digitally in payments and business transactions. With dependable and secure financial services, fintech helps to decrease fraud and boost security. Building better consumer banking and financial goods and services is made possible by digital finance. Fintech provides the benefits of getting better services and lower prices to customers. For fintech players, it gives the benefits of simplifying the transaction chain, reducing operational and capital costs, and freezing the information flow. For a country, it provides the benefits of encouraging the transmission of economic policies (Safitri, 2019). India's financial inclusion is progressing at an average rate; more initiatives are needed to invest in banking infrastructure, particularly for the nation's rural areas; the nation is performing worse than expected when the findings of the financial inclusion index are taken into account (Malik & Yadav, 2019) due to the fact that over 70% of Indians reside in rural regions, most consumer adoption of fintech services (AFS) occurs in metro and tier 1 and II metropolitan centers. Furthermore, a sizable portion of the Indian populace lacks sufficient banking, and it is challenging to encourage a mentality change from in-person to online transactions. Financial services offered online are frequently linked to fraud and online scams.

Fintech provides consultancy services, insurance services, and online bank account opening. They provide a significantly better experience due to their speed

DOI: 10.4324/9781032655185-7

and low cost. Fintech adoption makes financial transactions easy and secure. The new entrants of fintech can increase efficiency and lower the costs of financial services. Fintech companies have the natural benefit of employing cutting-edge new technology to offer these underserved groups customized products, digital payments database financing, and insurance. The expansion of fintech in India can be attributed to two factors: ongoing government measures that foster growth and increased internet connectivity in rural areas in the upcoming years. Together with business associations, legislators and regulators worked diligently to create regulations. The fintech system in India is seeing remarkable growth and momentum. Financial inclusion has always benefited from the industry; fintech companies will have a clear chance to lead innovations, alliances, and changes for long-term, equitable economic growth. The entire finance segment has seen a significant transformation as a result of technological advancement, which has altered how financial institutions previously conducted business. One of the cutting-edge technologies utilized to enhance conventional financial practices and provide efficient financial service solutions that keep up with the most recent technological trends is fintech. A result of the variety of financial advances and important investment in new technology, new firms are entering the financial market in recent years. Using fintech services using digital technology involves complex technology collaboration and human interaction. Fintech developments have only been the subject of a small number of studies incorporating the technology acceptance model (TAM) and resource-based view (RBV) theory. Thus, our study focuses on understanding the influence of fintech services with the interaction of digital technology fostering economic growth. Firstly, this paper empirically investigates the use of fintech services. Next, the fintech on fostering economic growth is observed. Lastly, our research is focused on the mediating role of digital technology. For this reason, TAM and RBV model are applied.

The objectives of the study are as follows

1 To empirically investigate the available financial services
2 To examine the connection between the promotion of fintech, adoption of technology, and economic expansion
3 To investigate the mediating role of digital technology

5.2 Literature Review

The Technology Acceptance paradigm, which describes and forecasts system utilization, is undoubtedly a very popular paradigm. According to Davis (1986), there are several factors that can be used to explain why users are motivated to use a system, including perceived usefulness (PU), perceived ease of use (PEOU), and attitude toward using the system (Chuttur, 2009). TAM was used to explain how customers would react to innovation used in a variety of settings (Zaineldeen et al., 2020). Potential users who believed the new technology would benefit them in the long run and improve job performance were said to have a high perception of usefulness (Khatri et al., 2020). In both required and optional circumstances,

PU improves a person's goal (Verkasalo et al., 2010). It also affects how someone feels about utilizing technology (Austermann et al., 2014; Nath et al., 2014). When fintech services are more valuable for their effort or are easier to utilize, their attitude toward using fintech services improves (Khatri et al., 2020). How this technology might enhance performance, boost productivity, boost effectiveness, facilitate transactions, and benefit businesses can all be used to gauge PU (Purnamasari et al., 2020).

Financial services offered online are frequently linked to fraud and online scams. The growth of information and communication technology (ICT), which is pervasive in most corporate sectors and helps users cut costs, is an engine of growth (Hu et al., 2019) because of their user-friendliness, friendliness of operations, and simplicity of application program download, fintech services will have an impact on how customers feel about utilizing them (Khatri et al., 2020). PEOU is a measure of how much a person thinks utilizing a technology would be effortless (Nunkoo, Juwaheer, & Rambhunjun, 2013; Purnamasari et al., 2020). The most significant factor influencing whether customers would utilize fintech services is the level of positive and negative appraisal of those services by customers. Customers will be more enthusiastic about using the fintech service if they can complete transactions in real time and without any constraints on time or place, or efficiently, simply, and rapidly get pertinent information about businesses (Chuang et al., n.d.). Users' positive perception of fintech services is influenced by their perception of their advantages as being practical and simple to use (Khatri et al., 2020). Risk, privacy, utility, perceived usability, user innovation, and government backing are all factors that are becoming more and more significant (Hu et al., 2019). Customers must have confidence in a system's services before they can be sure that their transactions are secure and safe from online threats. The model also has the following four important moderators: age, experience, gender, and willingness to use (Ahmad & Tajul Urus, 2021).

Technologies can have a positive impact (Awais et al., 2023), and investments in corporate social responsibility can be encouraged by financial technologies (Liu et al., 2021) improving the societal sustainability performance of businesses (Irtyshcheva, 2021). As a Greenfield industry for fostering start-ups and novel ideas, fintech promotes job creation and so helps to lower the unemployment rate (Ben Romdhane et al., 2023; Kammoun et al., 2020). When traditional banks work with fintech firms and incorporate their own fintech into their business models, their profitability is increased (Basdekis et al., 2022).

The term "resources" refers to all of a firm's assets, capabilities, organizational processes, firm qualities, information, and knowledge. According to RBV, a company can be thought of as a combination of organizational, human, and physical resources (Hadjira, 2021). According to the RBV, possession and control of strategic assets determine whether organizations produce greater profits and have a competitive advantage over others (Madhani, 2010). The organization's routines, procedures, and culture all incorporate organizational competencies (Collis & Montgomery, 1995; David-West et al., 2018). Traditional banks and the fintech sector have gradually moved from being competitors to working together more.

Early on in the development of the fintech industry, platform and technology companies engaged in the payment industry in an environment with lax regulations, which stimulated the growth of financial services. Along with the development of the fintech industry, relevant applications are developed by fintech companies and also banks (Zhao et al., 2022). Start-up businesses that also provide some of the alternative sources of financial services are finding it easier to launch thanks to the growth of fintech capabilities (FC) and related technologies (Martinčević, 2020). In the process of developing capabilities, resources in the form of information technology (hardware, software) and business resources (people, money, information, and relationships) would be necessary (Dukeov et al., 2018). Financial progress aids in boosting the use of renewable energy sources (Li et al., 2023).

When resources help companies capitalize on market opportunities or reduce market risks, they are valuable (Hadjira, 2021). Valuable resources are termed strategic assets (Madhani, 2010). Fintech companies revolutionize the financial sector through IT-enabled resources. Resources and the manner they are combined differentiate businesses from one another, which in order enables a business to obtain a competitive edge (Madhani, 2010). Resource sharing has the potential to produce a lot of fruit. According to Max Bomer and Schwienbacher (2018), fintech companies are likely to need a wide variety of resources to develop and thrive, ranging from funding to human capital and access to financial and technological networks. The speed generated by both the innovations inside the business ecosystem and the enabling capabilities, which are feasible to see as dynamic capabilities and the banks, seems to be the source of the competitive advantage created through the open innovation process. There was a lot of talk about merging the client base and trust of the banks with the speed of the fintechs, which would suggest that there are benefits to pooling resources. However, utilizing Lavie's 2006 theory and expanding the resource-based paradigm to additionally consider network resources However, a corporation can gain a competitive advantage based on the RBV by using the theory put forward by Lavie (2006) and his extension of the RBV to also incorporate network resources (Jonsson Holm & Andersson 2018).

Numerous studies have demonstrated that using digital financial services has an impact on equitable growth strategies and poverty reduction, which in turn has consequences for long-term economic growth (David-West et al., 2018; Karlan, Kendall, Mann, Pande, Suri, & Zinman, 2016; Park & Mylenco, 2015; Zulfiqar, Chaudhary, & Aslam, 2016). RBV, fintech, and digitalization when combined effectively can have a substantial favorable effects on economic expansion and prosperity. The extent and application of ICTs have had a significant impact on modern life as a result of digitalization (Li et al., 2023). Fintech showcases important chances to enhance the financial industry (Arner et al., 2020). This is significant since both the financial sector and the health of the whole economy and the environment are connected (Afzal et al.). Fintech has been viewed as an expansion of the conventional or traditional financial sector. The sector is playing a wider and more inclusive role in reforming all businesses toward value creation (Awais et al., 2023). Even while the function of regional digital economies in economic development is evident, it is indisputable that there are still disparities in the size of these economies and their effects on high-quality economic development (Ding et al., 2021).

5.3 Theoretical Framework

5.3.1 The Technology Acceptance Model (TAM)

TAM is a theoretical framework widely used in information systems and technology adoption studies. TAM attempts to explain people's acceptance and adoption of new technologies by taking into account their PU and simplicity of use.

"Perceived Usefulness (PU)": This is the degree to which a user believes that implementing a specific technology would improve their performance and productivity. Users assess the potential benefits and advantages offered by the technology in achieving their goals and objectives.

"Perceived Ease of Use (PEOU)": This factor relates to the user's perception of the ease with which they can learn and use the technology. It encompasses factors such as the simplicity of the user interface, the intuitiveness of the system, and the effort required to interact with the technology.

Users' intents to adopt a technology are shaped by their impressions of its usefulness and simplicity of use, according to TAM. Furthermore, extrinsic factors such as social influence, facilitating conditions, and individual traits influence users' opinions regarding the utility and simplicity of usage.

TAM posits that users' intentions to adopt a technology directly impact their actual usage behavior. In other words, the stronger the intention to adopt, the more likely the individual is to use the technology. Furthermore, the model suggests that the relationship between intentions and actual usage is mediated by the users' attitude toward using the technology.

Extensions of the TAM have incorporated additional variables to enhance the model's explanatory power, such as perceived enjoyment, subjective norms, and trust. These extensions aim to capture the broader social and contextual factors that influence technology adoption and usage. It provides a valuable framework for researchers and practitioners to analyze and design technology interventions that align with users' needs and preferences.

Overall, the TAM offers a systematic and comprehensive approach to understanding the reasons that influence users' acceptance and adoption of technology, making it a valuable model for studying the AFS and their impact on economic growth

5.3.2 Resourced-Based Utilization

The resource-based model is a theoretical framework that can be applied to examine the implementation of fintech services and its impact on fostering economic growth. This model emphasizes the role of resources and capabilities within an organization as key determinants of competitive advantage and performance. In the context of fintech adoption, the resource-based model can help identify the resources and capabilities that enable organizations to effectively leverage fintech services for economic growth.

Identifying Key Resources: The resource-based model suggests that organizations possess unique resources that can provide a competitive advantage. In the context of fintech adoption, these resources can include financial capital, technological infrastructure, data assets, human expertise, and customer relationships. Understanding the resources available to organizations is crucial for assessing their readiness and potential for adopting fintech services.

Evaluating Resource Utilization: The model emphasizes the effective utilization of resources to create value. Organizations need to identify how their existing resources can be combined and leveraged to adopt and integrate fintech services successfully. This involves evaluating the compatibility between resources and FC, assessing the need for additional resources, and developing strategies for resource allocation and management.

Building Fintech Capabilities: The resource-based model highlights the importance of developing capabilities that allow organizations to effectively adopt and utilize fintech services. FC may include technological skills, data analytics expertise, regulatory compliance knowledge, and customer engagement strategies. Building these capabilities may require investments in training, hiring specialized talent, or partnering with external entities possessing the required expertise.

Enhancing Competitive Advantage: The resource-based model suggests that organizations can achieve a competitive advantage through the strategic deployment of unique resources and capabilities. Fintech adoption, when combined with well-aligned resources and capabilities, can differentiate organizations from competitors, improve operational efficiency, enhance customer experience, and foster economic growth. This can result in increased market share, profitability, and overall organizational performance.

Continual Resource Renewal: The resource-based approach emphasizes the importance of organizations constantly renewing and upgrading their resources and skills in order to respond to changing market conditions and technological breakthroughs. Fintech services evolve rapidly, and organizations must proactively invest in updating their resources, acquiring new technologies, and developing innovative capabilities to maintain a competitive edge.

By applying the resource-based model to the AFS, researchers and practitioners can gain insights into how organizations can leverage their unique resources and capabilities to foster economic growth. This analysis can help guide decision-making processes, resource allocation strategies, and the development of effective adoption and implementation plans for fintech services.

5.3.3 Fintech Services

The AFS, like any other technological innovation, is influenced by a variety of factors that can be organized into a model to better understand the process. Here's a basic conceptual model of the AFS:

External environment factors consist of economic, regulatory, and market competition. The overall economic conditions, including income levels, economic stability, and access to financial resources, can impact the AFS. Government regulations and policies related to fintech can either promote or hinder its adoption. The presence of other fintech providers and traditional financial institutions in the market influences consumers' choices.

Technological factor consists of innovation, usability and security and privacy parameters. Innovation is the degree of novelty and perceived technological advancement of the fintech service influences its adoption. Usability is the ease of use and user-friendliness of the fintech application affects adoption rates. Security and privacy of fintech services is the perceived security risks and concerns about the privacy of personal financial information impacts adoption.

Individual characteristics that influence the fintech services are perceived benefits, perceived risks and attitude and beliefs. The perceived advantages of using the fintech service, such as convenience, cost savings, and efficiency, drive adoption. The potential drawbacks, such as data breaches or financial losses, hinder adoption. Personal attitudes and beliefs toward technology, finance, and change can influence the willingness to adopt fintech services.

The AFS is influenced by social factors such as peer recommendations, social norms and media and marketing. Positive reviews and recommendations from friends, family, or colleagues encourage adoption. Societal expectations and norms regarding technology usage and financial practices play a role. The portrayal of fintech services in the media and through marketing efforts also shapes the perceptions and decisions.

Facilitating conditions that support AFS are digital literacy, access to technology and education. Digital literacy is the level of understanding and comfort with digital technologies enabling or impeding adoption. The availability of devices and internet connectivity is essential for using fintech services. Access to information about the benefits and usage of fintech services facilitates adoption.

Barriers to AFS are financial exclusion, lack of trust, and cultural factors. The financial exclusion is due to access to traditional financial services that can either encourage or inhibit fintech adoption. Distrust in technology or financial institutions could act as a barrier. The cultural norms and practices related to finance and technology affect the fintech adoption rates. Based on the balance between perceived benefits, risks, and individual characteristics, an individual makes a decision to adopt or reject the fintech service. After adoption, the individual's satisfaction with the fintech service and their continued usage will depend on the actual experience and fulfillment of expectations as put forth in the theoretical model in Figure 5.1.

H1: "Perceived Usefulness has a positive impact on the adoption of fintech services".

H2: "Perceived ease of use has a positive impact on the adoption of fintech services".

H3: "Fintech capabilities has a positive impact on the adoption of fintech services".

H4: "Resources renewal has a positive impact on the adoption of fintech services".

H5: "Resource utilization has a positive impact on the adoption of fintech services".

H6: "Digital technology mediates the relationship between the adoption of fintech services and economic growth".

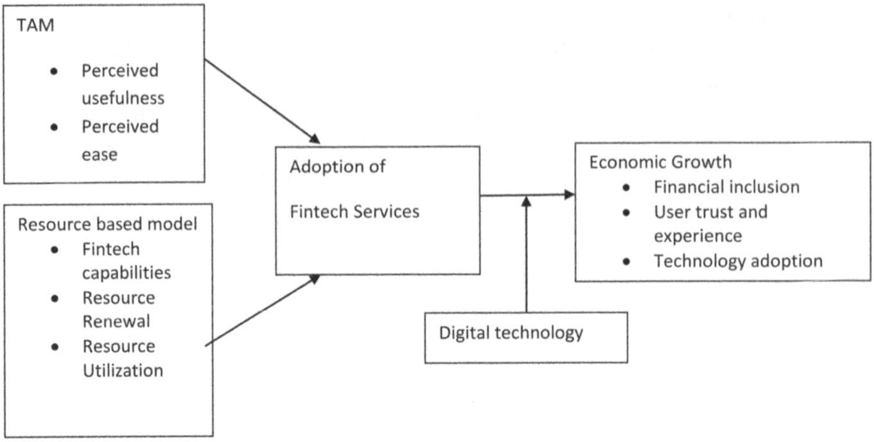

Figure 5.1 Conceptual model of adoption of fintech services

Source: Authors' own

Based on the above theoretical model the following measurement items were developed as shown in Table 5.1.

5.4 Research Methodology

Used Smart PLS 3.3.3 to assess the structural model and test the proposed hypotheses in this investigation (Irtyshcheva, 2021). The descriptive statistical findings of 410 surveys examined respondents' demographic variables and use of fintech (Hiremath et al., 2023). The hypotheses were tested using inferential statistics in

Table 5.1 Measurement instrument

Latent variables	*Measurement items*	*Sources*
"Perceived usefulness" (PU)	• "Using Fintech can meet my service needs. • Fintech services can save time • Fintech services can improve efficiency • Overall, fintech services are useful to me • It is easy to use fintech services"	Lockett et al. and Huh et al.
"Perceived ease of use" (PEOU)	• I find the fintech service easy to use • The interface of the fintech service is clear and straightforward • I can quickly become skillful in using the fintech service • Interacting with the fintech service is uncomplicated • I feel confident using the fintech service even if I have limited technological knowledge	Lockett et al. (2009) and Huh et al. (2010)

(*Continued*)

Table 5.1 (Continued)

Latent variables	*Measurement items*	*Sources*
Resource-based model	Fintech capabilities (FC) • The fintech firm possesses specialized technological knowledge and expertise • The fintech firm has developed unique fintech solutions that differentiate us from competitors • The fintech firm is capable to provide customized solutions to diverse customer needs Resource renewal (RR) • The fintech firm actively seeks new technological advancements to refresh the offerings • The fintech firm regularly updates and upgrades the fintech solutions to remain competitive • The fintech firm demonstrates agility in adapting to changes in the fintech landscape Resource utilization (RU) • The fintech firm efficiently allocates resources to different areas • The fintech firm optimizes the allocation of human resources based on the requirements of fintech projects	Authors' own compilation
Adoption of fintech services (AFS)	• I am likely to adopt fintech services if I see positive reviews from trusted sources • I worry about the potential negative consequences of using fintech services • I believe that fintech services maintain a high level of data security • Using fintech services would help me save time and effort	
Digital technology (mediation) (DT)	• Digital technology usage enhances my perception of how easy it is to use fintech services • The more I use digital technology, the more I perceive fintech services as user-friendly • Digital technology improves my access to valuable financial information	
Economic growth (EG)	• I actively seek out opportunities to integrate fintech solutions into my daily financial routines • The adoption of fintech is an integral part of staying current with technological trends • I consider technology adoption to be a key factor in optimizing my financial interactions and decisions	

the quantitative method (Asif et al., 2023). Statistical tests are used to verify the relationship's existence and strength. The Structure Equation Model (SEM) is the primary statistical technique used to examine the impact of fintech on financial inclusion and test the hypotheses (Goswami et al., 2022)

Table 5.2 displays the demographic and fintech usage characteristics of the respondents. People between the ages of 26 and 35 make up the majority of the population. The biggest amount (50.0%) accounted for employed people using the fintech services the most. In terms of usage frequency, frequent users (64%) accounted for a comparatively significant share, indicating the rate of popularization of fintech service. Fintech acceptance is currently pretty high, and research into the factors influencing their adoption is important.

5.4.1 Research Design

The research methodology used for studying the AFS is survey method where customers of fintech companies are respondents who respond to the standardized questionnaires. These questionnaires used the abovementioned measurement items about the factors such as digital adoption that influences the economic growth. Surveys through questionnaires provide quantitative data that would be analyzed using Smart PLS. A structured questionnaire was used that covered all the aspects of fintech adoption, usage patterns, user perceptions, and satisfaction using Likert scales, multiple-choice questions, to capture quantitative data. The survey was distributed online, targeting individuals who use or have experienced with fintech services.

5.4.2 Data Collection

The online survey method was used to collect the primary data for the study that incorporated the population of all the people who have used or using fintech services, 410 respondents have given their inputs through the questionnaire from the users of fintech services. The authors used simple random sampling technique for their research.

5.4.3 Descriptive Statistics

Table 5.2 Demographic characteristics

Demographic variable		*Frequency*	*Percentage*
Gender	Male	243	59.3%
	Female	167	40.7%
Age	18–25	56	13.7%
	26–35	201	49.0%
	36–45	68	16.6%
	46–55	59	14.4%
	>=56	26	6.3%

(*Continued*)

Table 5.2 (Continued)

Demographic variable		*Frequency*	*Percentage*
Employment status	Student	25	6.1%
	Employee	206	50.2%
	Business	179	43.7%
Education	Less than degree	120	29.3%
	Degree	241	58.8%
	PG or more	49	12.0%
Annual income	Less than 800,000	59	14.4%
	800,000–1,500,000	298	72.7%
	Greater than 150,000	53	12.9%
Fintech service usage	Never	24	5.9%
	Occasionally	125	30.5%
	Frequently	261	63.7%

Source: Authors' calculations.

5.4.4 *Scale Reliability and Validity Findings*

The model was tested using confirmatory factor analysis, which encompassed tests for discriminant validity, convergent validity, and internal consistency reliability. The degree of consistency or stability of the measurement outcomes, which illustrates the dependability of the questionnaire items, is known as reliability (Henseler et al., 2009). Cronbach's alpha and composite reliability (CR) were used in this article to confirm the data's internal consistency. Fornell and Larcker specify that the sample's Cronbach's alpha (CR) should be greater than 0.8 and that its CR should be more than 0.7 (Garson, 2016). Table 5.3 demonstrates that all latent variables' CR, average variance extracted (AVE), and Cronbach's alpha were greater than the critical thresholds, indicating that the model had satisfactory reliability and validity.

Validity comprises both discriminant and convergent validity and describes how well the model fits the survey data. The CR, the loading of associated measurable variables, and the AVE of the latent variable represent the degree of correlation of multiple indicators for a given variable. Both the sample's AVE values and the loadings of the quantifiable variables need to be greater than 0.7.The evidence for each construct's convergent validity is shown in Table 5.3. Discriminant validity signifies the absence of a correlation between each variable; that is, each variable's measurements may be distinguished from others. If the AVE is higher than the square of the interscale correlation, the model supports it. As can be shown in Table 5.4, the AVE was therefore consistently higher than the squared interscale correlation, indicating strong discriminant validity for each variable.

5.4.5 *Hypothesis Testing*

Structural Equation Modelling (SEM) is a statistical method that uses the variables' covariance matrix to look at correlations between the variables. It is a crucial tool for multivariate data analysis as well. This section examined the fintech service adoption model empirically using sample data analysis and tested the hypothesis

Table 5.3 Validity and reliability of the scale

Constructs	*Item*	*Factor loading*	*AVE*	*CR*	*Cronbach's alpha*
"Perceived Usefulness" (PU)	PU1	0.725	0.811	0.984	0.873
	PU2	0.764			
	PU3	0.812			
	PU4	0.811			
"Perceived Ease of Use" (PEOU)	PEU1	0.751	0.798	0.976	0.911
	PEU2	0.851			
	PEU3	0.794			
	PEU4	0.756			
	PEU5	0.814			
Resource-based model –FC	FC1	0.864	0.698	0.879	0.819
	FC2	0.875			
	FC3	0.805			
Resource-based model –RR	RR1	0.794	0.843	0.977	0.856
	RR2	0.874			
	RR3	0.745			
Resource-based model –RU	RU1	0.731	0.915	0.885	0.895
	RU2	0.741			
Adoption of fintech services (AFS)	AFS1	0.753	0.863	0.888	0.913
	AFS2	0.711			
	AFS3	0.841			
	AFS4	0.864			
Digital technology (mediation) (DT)	DT1	0.766	0.932	0.845	0.902
	DT2	0.781			
	DT3	0.832			
Economic growth (EG)	EG1	0.841	0.874	0.917	0.814
	EG2	0.791			
	EG3	0.726			

Source: Authors' calculations.

Table 5.4 Discriminant validity

Construct	*PU*	*PEU*	*FC*	*RR*	*RU*	*AFS*	*DT*	*EG*
PU	0.846							
PEU	0.751	0.864						
FC	0.354	0.941	0.916					
RR	0.655	0.364	0.641	0.965				
RU	0.754	0.91	0.124	0.911	0.941			
AFS	0.741	0.641	0.872	0.345	0.714	0.841		
DT	0.412	0.841	0.645	0.385	0.845	−0.314	0.873	
EG	0.645	0.345	0.723	0.445	0.641	−0.125	0.756	0.845

Source: Authors' calculations.

using the structural equation model and sample data, which came after the validity and reliability analysis. The standardized path coefficient () and the t value were produced using Smart Partial Least Squares (PLS) 4.0 and used to evaluate the study's assumptions. At the p 0.05 confidence level, the coefficient test is significant if $t > 1.96$. The test results for the hypothesis are displayed in Figure 5.2.

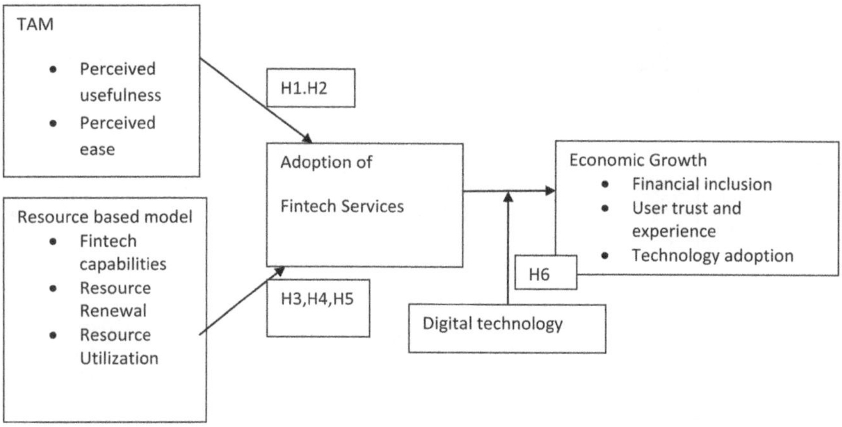

Figure 5.2 Structural results of the proposed model

Source: Authors' own

5.5 Result and Findings

The analysis revealed with empirical evidence that Perceived Usefulness (PU) ($\beta = 0.178$, t = 3.339), Financial Capabilities (BI) ($\beta = 0.132$, t = 2.852), Resource Renewal (TRU) ($\beta = 0.101$, t = 2.122), Resource Utilization (GS) ($\beta = 0.315$, t = 5.584), and UI ($\beta = 0.270$, t = 6.322) all had a substantial beneficial influence on Attitude (ATT). Their t values were used as the t value threshold for hypothesis testing (David-West et al., 2018), where t values are more than 1.96, implying that hypotheses H1, H6, H5, H10, and H12 are supported. BI ($\beta = 0.256$, t = 4.925), significant impacts were exerted by PR ($\beta = -0.025$, t = 6.251), GS ($\beta = 0.295$, t = 5.625), and UI ($\beta = 0.200$, t = 4.669) (Hair et al.,2013). From the empirical analysis, it has been identified Trust TRU, and their t values were all more than 1.96, implying that H7, H9, H11, and H13 were supported. Perceived Ease of Use (PEU) had a t value more than 1.96, while the former ($\beta = 0.741$, t = 18.397) had a substantial impact on conceptual model (Figure 5.3).

As a result of the latter's influence, hypothesis H3 was supported. TRU was an important intermediate in the interaction of BI, GS, and UI since ATT ($\beta = 0.793$, t – 25.410) had a statistically significant influence on dependent variables. Because ATT ($\beta = 0.793$, t = 25.410) had a substantial influence on INT, the t value of ATT for INT was larger than 1.96, suggesting that H4 was significant. However, PEU ($\beta = 0.086$, t = 1.306) and PR ($\beta = 0.006$, t = 0.204) showed no significant effects on ATT, and their t values for ATT were less than 1.96, indicating that hypotheses H2 and H6 were not supported.

From the above analysis it could be derived that hypothesis1 (PU and AFS) is supported, hypothesis 2 (perceived ease and AFS) is not supported empirical analysis. Fintech services are independent of the degree of complexity that users perceive them to be (Irimia-Diéguez et al., 2023). Moreover, other three hypotheses as mentioned H3, H4, and H5 (FC, RR, RU connecting with adoption of Fintech

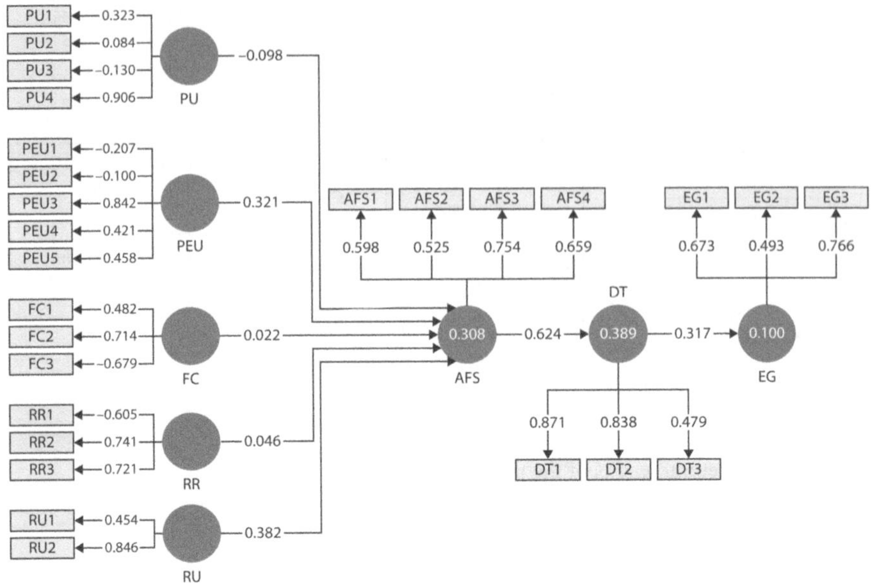

Figure 5.3 Structural equation path analysis

Source: Authors' own

services) were supported by analysis. At last, hypothesis 6 such as interconnection of Digital technology on economic growth is also supported by the empirical evidence. It implies that the adoption of fintech and circular economy strategies by businesses are favorably correlated. The present discovery aligns with other research that indicated a robust impact of Industry 4.0 technology, such as fintech, on companies' adoption of circular economy strategies. We note that increased access to financing significantly stimulates circular economy activity (Irtyshcheva, 2021).

5.6 Discussion

The findings of the study have several inferences that illuminate the use of fintech services and provide valuable insights for both researchers and practitioners. All the factors have a positive impact on the AFS. These places of interest in promoting fintech services that offer clear benefits are easy to use and demonstrate technological expertise. Fintech companies can focus on developing user-friendly interfaces, personalized solutions, and regular updates to improve adoption rates. Perceived risks, such as concerns about data security and potential negative consequences, were found to impact adoption negatively. This implies that fintech providers should prioritize addressing security concerns and implementing robust privacy measures. Educating users about the security protocols and measures in place can help mitigate these concerns and build trust. The mediating role of digital technology between fintech adoption and economic growth suggests that the more users embrace digital technology, the more likely they are to adopt fintech services. This highlights the interconnectedness of technology adoption and its effect on the financial ecosystem. The implications of the study provide valuable guidance for various stakeholders in the fintech ecosystem, helping them make informed decisions to foster adoption, address challenges, and contribute to the growth of the fintech industry.

This research study offers several theoretical contributions that contribute to the broader understanding of related concepts. These contributions have the potential to advance academic knowledge and provide valuable insights into the field. Here are some potential theoretical contributions based on the study. This study presents a comprehensive conceptual model that identifies and organizes the factors influencing fintech adoption. This model is providing researchers with a clear structure to build upon. By integrating external environment factors, technological factors, individual characteristics, social factors, facilitating conditions, and barriers to adoption, your model offers a holistic perspective on the complex dynamics that shape fintech adoption decisions. This integrated method helps us comprehend the complex aspects of technology adoption on a deeper level. One noteworthy theoretical contribution is the incorporation of digital technology as a mediator between the adoption of fintech and economic growth. This emphasizes how crucial technology integration and digital literacy are to the uptake of fintech and overall economic growth.

This study applies a resource-based model to the context of fintech adoption, providing an updated look at how FC, RR, and RU influence adoption decisions. This application helps to apply and extend recognized theoretical frameworks in the financial industry. The assessment of reliability and validity of measurement constructs adds to the understanding of research methodology in the fintech adoption domain. The application of these concepts contributes to the rigor of research practices in this field. By collecting and analyzing data from real-world fintech users, this study provides empirical evidence of the relationships proposed in the conceptual model. These insights contribute to the empirical body of knowledge on fintech adoption and can guide future research efforts.

Based on the findings of the study, there are several practical recommendations that can be derived for fintech companies, policymakers, and other stakeholders involved in the fintech ecosystem. These recommendations are aimed at leveraging the insights gained from the research to enhance adoption rates, address challenges, and promote the growth of the fintech industry. Governments and organizations can encourage digital literacy programs to facilitate fintech adoption, potentially boosting economic growth. Government policymakers can use these findings to better understand the factors influencing fintech adoption and tailor regulatory frameworks that encourage innovation while ensuring consumer protection and data security. Fintech companies can use the insights from this study to refine their business strategies, improve their service offerings, and design effective marketing campaigns.

The sample of 410 respondents is small, and the demographics may not be fully representative of all potential fintech consumers. To improve the ability to generalize findings, future studies might strive for larger and more diverse populations. The cross-sectional design of this study provides an outline of the relationships at a single point in time. Longitudinal research could provide insights into the dynamics of fintech adoption over time, as well as how determinants alter as the fintech market grows. Individuals who are less digitally oriented or do not have internet access may be excluded if only online surveys are used. Future study could use a combination of methodologies to capture a broader diversity of opinions.

5.7 Policy Implications

The creation of facilities and technology infrastructure that help eliminate information asymmetry and opacity in the loan supply should be a top priority for policymakers. Over time, financial development and institutional quality have a major role in economic growth and development (Malik et al., 2021). Policymakers should consider the ethical implications of fintech, particularly regarding the use of artificial intelligence and big data. Regulations may be needed to ensure ethical behavior and the responsible use of data. To foster economic growth, policymakers should support initiatives that enhance financial inclusion through fintech. This might include measures to ensure that underserved populations have access to digital financial services.

5.8 Conclusion

This research paper used a quantitative research approach and statistical methods including regression and "Structural Equation Modeling" to examine the relationship between fintech promotion, digital technology adoption, and economic growth. The present research is focused on the mediating role of digital technology. For this reason, TAM and RBV model are applied. Through the empirical research, the influence of fintech services with the interaction of digital technology fostering the economic growth is found. Digital technology as a mediator between fintech adoption and economic growth indicates in embracing digital technology by more users by adapting more fintech services. Everyone agrees that financial inclusion is essential to reducing poverty, fostering balanced economic growth, and preserving economic stability (Asif et al., 2023) The various stakeholders in fintech ecosystem can make informed decisions to foster adoption, address challenges, and contribute to the growth of fintech industry.

Conflicts of Interest

The authors declare that there is no conflict of interest.

Acknowledgment

The researchers would like to express their gratitude to the re-viewers for their efforts to improve the quality of this paper.

Funding

This research has not received external funding.

References

Africa N. (2023). The State of Instant and Inclusive Payment in Africa SIIPS 2022, Case Study https://www.africanenda.org/en/publications/siips-2022-case-study-pesalink-kenya?__geom=%E2%9C%AA

Ahmad, S., Tajul Urus, S., & Syed Mustapha Nazri, S. N. F. (2021). Technology acceptance of financial technology (fintech) for payment services among employed fresh graduates. Asia-Pacific Management Accounting Journal (APMAJ), *16*(2), 27–58. https://doi.org/10.24191/APMAJ.V16i2-02.

Arner, D., Buckley, R., Zetzsche, D., & Veidt, R. (2020). Sustainability, FinTech and financial inclusion. *European Business Organization Law Review*, *21*, 7–35. https://doi.org/10.1007/s40804-020-00183-y.

Asif, M., Khan, M. N., Tiwari, S., Wani, S. K., & Alam, F. (2023). The impact of fintech and digital financial services on financial inclusion in India. *Journal of Risk and Financial Management*, *16*(2), 122. https://doi.org/10.3390/jrfm16020122.

Awais, M., Afzal, A., Firdousi, S., & Hasnaoui, A. (2023). Is fintech the new path to sustainable resource utilisation and economic development? *Resources Policy*, *81*, 103309. https://doi.org/10.1016/j.resourpol.2023.103309.

Afzal, A., Rasoulinezhad, E., & Malik, Z. (2022). Green finance and sustainable development in Europe. *Economic research-Ekonomska istraživanja*, *35*(1), 5150–5163.

Bomer, M., & Schwienbacher, A. (2018). Resource-based perspective of VC investments in fintech. *SSRN Electronic Journal*. https://doi.org/10.2139/ssrn.3312793.

Basdekis, C., Christopoulos, A., Katsampoxakis, I., & Vlachou, A. (2022). FinTech's rapid growth and its effect on the banking sector. *Journal of Banking and Financial Technology*, *6*(2), 159–176. https://doi.org/10.1007/s42786-022-00045-w.

Beck, T., Senbet, L., and Simbanegavi, W.(2015). Financial Inclusion and Innovation in Africa: An Overview. *Journal of African Economies*, *24*(suppl_1), i3–i11. https://doi.org/10.1093/jae/eju031

Ben Romdhane, Y., Kammoun, S., & Loukil, S. (2023). The impact of fintech on inflation and unemployment: The case of Asia. *Arab Gulf Journal of Scientific Research*. https://doi.org/10.1108/AGJSR-08-2022-0146

Consultative Group to Assist the Poor (CGAP). (2015). Making financial services meet the needs of the world's most vulnerable. https://www.cgap.org/

Collis D. J., & Montgomery C. A. (1995). Competing on resources: Strategy in the 1990s. *Harvard Business Review*, 73(4), 118–128.

Chuang, L.-M., Liu, C.-C., & Kao, H.-K. (2016). The Adoption of Fintech Service: TAM perspective. International Journal of Management and Administrative Sciences, *3*(7), 1–15.

Chuttur, M. (2009). "Overview of the Technology Acceptance Model: Origins, Developments and Future Directions," Indiana University, USA. Sprouts: Working Papers on Information Systems, 9(37). http://sprouts.aisnet.org/9-37

Dashi, E., Lahaye, E., and Rizvanolli, R. (2013). Trends in International Funding for Financial Inclusion. https://www.cgap.org/sites/default/files/Brief-Trends-in-International-Funding-for-Financial-Inclusion-Dec-2013.pdf

David-West, O., Iheanachor, N., & Kelikume, I. (2018). A resource-based view of digital financial services (DFS): An exploratory study of Nigerian providers. *Journal of Business Research*, *88*, 513–526. https://doi.org/10.1016/j.jbusres.2018.01.034

Davis, F.D. (1986). A Technology Acceptance Model for Empirically Testing New End-user information Systems: Theory and Results. Doctoral Dissertation, MIT Sloan School of Management, Cambridge, MA.

Ding, C., Liu, C., Zheng, C., & Li, F. (2021). Digital economy, technological innovation and high-quality economic development: Based on spatial effect and mediation effect. *Sustainability*, *14*(1), 216. https://doi.org/10.3390/su14010216

Dukeov, I., Bergman, J.-P., Heilmann, P., Platonov, V., & Jaschenko, V. (2018). How do a firm's age and size affect its organizational innovation? Journal of Innovation Management, 6(3), 98. https://doi.org/10.24840/2183-0606_006.003_0005

Feyen, E., Frost, J., Gambacorta, L., Natarajan, H., & Saal, M. (2021). Fintech and the digital transformation of financial services: Implications for market structure and public policy. BIS papers.

Getter, D. (2016). Overview of Commercial (Depository) Banking and Industry Conditions. Congressional Research Service. In forming the legislative debate since 1914. https://sgp.fas.org/crs/misc/R44488.pdf

Goswami, S., Sharma, R. B., & Chouhan, V. (2022). Impact of financial technology (Fintech) on financial inclusion (FI) in rural India. *Universal Journal of Accounting and Finance*, *10*(2), 483–497. https://doi.org/10.13189/ujaf.2022.100213.

Hadjira, C. (2021). Resource Based View and competitiveness: An empirical study of the. Post-Print hal-03453864, HAL. https://ideas.repec.org/p/hal/journl/hal-03453864.html.

Hiremath, S., Prashantha, C., Panda, A., & Hiremath, G. (2023). Digitisation and artificial intelligence in retailing sector – Key drivers. In P. Tyagi, S. Grima, K. Sood, B. Balamurugan, E. Özen, & T. Eleftherios (Eds.), *Contemporary studies in economic and financial analysis* (pp. 215–232). Emerald Publishing Limited. https://doi.org/10.1108/S1569-37592023000110B014

Hu, Z., Ding, S., Li, S., Chen, L., & Yang, S. (2019). Adoption intention of fintech services for bank users: An empirical examination with an extended technology acceptance model. *Symmetry*, *11*(3), 340. https://doi.org/10.3390/sym11030340

Huh, H. J., Kim, T. (Terry), & Law, R. (2009). A comparison of competing theoretical models for understanding acceptance behavior of information systems in upscale hotels. *International Journal of Hospitality Management*, *28*(1), 121–134. https://doi.org/10.1016/j.ijhm.2008.06.004

Idiab, A., Idiab, M Haron, S., and. Ahmad, S. (2011). Commercial Banks & Historical Development. *Journal of Applied Sciences Research*, *7*(7): 1024-1029, 2011. ISSN ISSN 1819-544X https://www.aensiweb.com/old/jasr/jasr/2011/1024-1029.pdf

Irimia-Diéguez, A., Velicia-Martín, F., & Aguayo-Camacho, M. (2023). Predicting fintech innovation adoption: The mediator role of social norms and attitudes. *Financial Innovation*, *9*(1), 36. https://doi.org/10.1186/s40854-022-00434-6

Irtyshcheva, I. (2021). The effect of digital technology development on economic growth. *International Journal of Data and Network Science*, 25–36. https://doi.org/10.5267/j.ijdns.2020.11.006.

Ishita, G. (2018). Challenging the dominant narratives of a Digital Financial Inclusion. https://escholarship.org/content/qt6wv2s3fx/qt6wv2s3fx_noSplash_534a946e9a48795b6583728662a60fed.pdf

Jonsson Holm, E., & Andersson, F. (2018). Building Competitive Advantage Through Open Innovation: A case study in the financial technology sector.

Kammoun, S., Loukil, S., & Loukil, Y. B. R. (2020). The Impact of FinTech on Economic Performance and Financial Stability in MENA Zone: In N. Naifar (Ed.), *Advances in Finance, Accounting, and Economics* (pp. 253–277). IGI Global. https://doi.org/10.4018/978-1-7998-0039-2.ch013

Karlan, Dean S., Karlan, Dean S., Kendall, Jake, Mann, Rebecca, Pande, Rohini, Suri, Tavneet, & Zinman, Jonathan, Research and Impacts of Digital Financial Services (September 27, 2016). HKS Working Paper No. RWP16-037, Available at SSRN: https://ssrn.com/abstract=2844388 or http://dx.doi.org/10.2139/ssrn.2844388.

Khatri, A., Gupta, N., & Parashar, A. (2020). Application of technology acceptance model (TAM) in fintech services. *International Journal of Management*, 11(12). https://doi.org/10.34218/IJM.11.12.2020.328

Kithinji, E. (2017). Effects of Digital Banking Strategy on Financial Inclusion Among Commercial Banks in Kenya. http://hdl.handle.net/11295/102435

Li, C., Razzaq, A., Ozturk, I., & Sharif, A. (2023). Natural resources, financial technologies, and digitalization: The role of institutional quality and human capital in selected OECD economies. *Resources Policy*, *81*, 103362. https://doi.org/ 10.1016/j.resourpol.2023.103362.

Liu, B., Ju, T., & Gao, S. S. (2021). The combined effects of innovation and corporate social responsibility on firm financial risk. *Journal of International Financial Management & Accounting*, *32*(3), 283–310.

Lockett, A., Thompson, S., & Morgenstern, U. (2009). The development of the resource-based view of the firm: A critical appraisal. *International journal of management reviews*, *11*(1), 9–28.

Lontchi, C., Yang, B., and Su, Y. (2022). The Mediating Effect of Financial Literacy and the Moderating Role of Social Capital in the Relationship between Financial Inclusion and Sustainable Development in Cameroon. https://doi.org/10.3390/su142215093

Madhani, Pankaj M., Resource Based View (RBV) of Competitive Advantage: An Overview (March 26, 2010). RESOURCE BASED VIEW: CONCEPTS AND PRACTICES, Pankaj Madhani, ed., pp. 3–22, ICFAI University Press, Hyderabad, India, 2009, Available at SSRN: https://ssrn.com/abstract=1578704

Malik, F., & Yadav, D. K. (2019). How inclusive is financial inclusion in India? *SSRN Electronic Journal*. https://doi.org/10.2139/ssrn.3308572.

Malik, F. A., Yadav, D. K., Lone, N. A., & Adam, H. (2021). An investigation into the dynamics of financial inclusion in south Asian countries. *Pakistan Economic and Social Review*, *59*, 231–251.

Martinčević, I., Črnjević, S., & Klopotan, I. (2020). Fintech Revolution in the Financial Industry. In *Proceedings of the ENTRENOVA-ENTerprise research In NOVAtion Conference* (Vol. 6, No. 1, pp. 563–571).

Purnamasari, P., Pramono, I. P., Haryatiningsih, R., Ismail, S. A., & Shafie, R. (2020). Technology acceptance model of financial technology in micro, small, and medium enterprises (MSME) in Indonesia. *The Journal of Asian Finance, Economics and Business*, *7*(10), 981–988. https://doi.org/10.13106/JAFEB.2020.VOL7.NO10.981.

Rangarajan Committee. (2008). Report of the Committee on Financial Inclusion. https://www.findevgateway.org/sites/default/files/publications/files/mfg-en-paper-report-of-the-committee-on-financial-inclusion-jan-2008.pdf

Safitri (2019). *Advances in Social Science, Education and Humanities Research, volume 436*, 1st Borobudur International Symposium on Humanities, Economics and Social Sciences (BIS-HESS 2019).

Sarma, M. (2008). Index of Financial Inclusion. Working Paper No. 215. *Indian Council for Research on International Economic Relations* https://www.icrier.org/pdf/Working_Paper_215.pdf

Sinha, D. R. P. (2009). Commercial bank performance in financial inclusion: A bilateral comparison model. https://www.researchgate.net/profile/Ram-Sinha/publication/228200250_Commercial_Bank_Performance_in_Financial_Inclusion_A_Bilateral_Comparison_Model/links/004635323dde21f64d000000/Commercial-Bank-Performance-in-Financial-Inclusion-A-Bilateral-Comparison-Model.pdf

Tadjudje, W. (2016). Mutual bonding and financial inclusion in Africa. Organization for the Harmonisation of Business Law in Africa. https://www.ohada.org/en/mutual-bonding-and-financial-inclusion-in-africa/

World Bank. (2014). Global Financial Development Report. https://books.google.cm/books?hl=en&lr=&id=GEcXAgAAQBAJ&oi=fnd&pg=PP2&dq=World+Bank+Report+(2014).+Digital+Financial+Inclusion.&ots=4X4etzREVk&sig=CazOFJlJ6WvvARLWocSIz8OQhbQ&redir_esc=y#v=onepage&q=World%20Bank%20Report%20(2014).%20Digital%20Financial%20Inclusion.&f=false

Verkasalo, H., López-Nicolás, C., Molina-Castillo, F. J., & Bouwman, H. (2010). Analysis of users and non-users of smartphone applications. *Telematics and Informatics*, *27*(3), 242–255. https://doi.org/10.1016/j.tele.2009.11.001

Zaineldeen, S., Hongbo, L., Koffi, A. L., & Hassan, B. M. A. (2020). Technology acceptance model' concepts, contribution, limitation, and adoption in education. *Universal Journal of Educational Research*, *8*(11), 5061–5071. https://doi.org/10.13189/ujer.2020.081106.

Zhao, J., Li, X., Yu, C.-H., Chen, S., & Lee, C.-C. (2022). Riding the FinTech innovation wave: FinTech, patents and bank performance. *Journal of International Money and Finance*, *122*, 102552. https://doi.org/10.1016/j.jimonfin.2021.102552.

Zulfiqar, K., Chaudhary, M. A., & Aslam, A. (2016). Financial inclusion and its implications for inclusive growth in Pakistan. Pakistan Economic and Social Review, 54(2), 297–325.

Part III

Global Perspectives of Financial Inclusion

6 Redefining Economic Landscape

Financial Inclusion Perspectives from Global Contexts

Nishath Anjum, Md. Saidur Rahaman, M.M. Tahmid Ahsan, Md. Masud Rana, and Md. Mizanur Rahman

6.1 Introduction

FI (*FI*), a widespread concept, denotes that everyone in the society should have access to reasonable financial services, which are customized to their own circumstances (Ayyagari & Beck, 2015). These services include banking, credit, savings, loans, insurance, etc. FI services guide individuals in managing their money efficiently, generating capital, investing in profitable schemes, increase earnings, overcoming poverty, and avoiding risk with full control (Khan et al., 2022). The driving forces of FI in any nation are determined by the social or macroeconomic factors, characteristics of banks, financial service providers, and infrastructural facilities. Moreover, the cost of delivering financial services to the mass community and favorable policies offer a vital part in fostering a positive climate for FI (Naceur et al., 2015). While developed countries prioritizing effective FI through multifaceted strategies, under-developed nations face multitude of challenges in achieving FI (Choudhary & Kamboj, 2017).

Successful initiatives have accelerated FI improvement worldwide. The efforts to achieve FI may vary across nations and regions, but the ultimate goal is same, i.e. to enable every citizen to join the institutional financial system (Le et al., 2019). The core objective of this chapter is to explore the global perspectives of FI focusing on Asia, G20, and the BRICS countries. The research provides a comprehensive understanding of the efforts made to promote FI across diverse economies, ranging from advanced financial systems to nations with limited access to such services. In addition, the chapter addresses the FI challenges and the opportunities across developed and under-developed regions. The author tries to provide some suggestions based on current challenges to improve the state of global FI. The study is, therefore, seeking the attention of collaborative efforts involving governments, financial institutions, international agencies, and fintech companies regarding effective regulatory frameworks, policy changes, and innovative solutions to ensure effective FI across nations.

This chapter unfolds in eight sections, each dissecting distinct facets of global FI. Sections 6.1 and 6.2 delineate introductory insights and offer a sweeping view of institutional financial services worldwide. Section 6.3 delves into Asian FI, spotlighting Bangladesh, Pakistan, Nepal, Sri Lanka, Afghanistan, Thailand, and

DOI: 10.4324/9781032655185-9

the Philippines. Sections 6.4, 6.5, and 6.6 intricately examine FIs in G20 nations, BRICS countries, and across developed and under-developed regions. Section 6.7 dissects challenges and opportunities of FI, while Section 6.8 culminates by proposing suggestions to enhance global FI, backed by policy implications and conclusive insights from the study.

6.2 Institutional Financial Inclusion Service across Nations

Banks are performing the prominent role in providing financial services and the accessibility of fundamental banking services is the pre-condition for FI in any nation. FI of an economy can be estimated by the percentage of the population who have account in a bank (Demirgüç-Kunt & Singer, 2017). Again, having simply a bank account may not indicate FI if there exists additional hurdles that limiting individuals from fully utilizing those accounts (Diniz et al., 2013). People with an unutilized bank account regarded as ‘unbanked’ or ‘marginally banked’ who are being equitable to financially excluded people (Sharma, 2016). Subsequent to the bank, ***Microfinance Institutions (MFIs)*** are popular means of expanding FI services, especially in the developing and under-developed nations. MFIs provide small loans and other monetary services tailored to the needs of poor income group people (Ahmed, 2009). They operate with a focus on social impact, reaching out to underserved communities and offering accessible financial products. MFIs often employ group lending methodologies, where borrowers collectively guarantee each other’s loans, fostering social cohesion and community development (Ahlin et al., 2011). Following the MFIs, ***Community-Based Organizations (CBOs)***, same as the cooperatives, particularly contribute to FI in under-developed nations. These organizations are creating a silent revolution by mobilizing savings and provide credit facilities and other finance-related services to fulfill the specific demands of their community members. It promotes financial literacy, encourages savings behavior, and provides a platform for community members to pool resources and collectively address their financial needs (Arcand & Fafchamps, 2012). Finally, ***International Development Agencies*** including NGOs and multilateral organizations play an active role in expanding financial access across nations. They provide financial support, technical assistance, and capacity-building programs to local institutions and governments. These agencies facilitate the development of inclusive financial systems by promoting policy reforms, supporting financial infrastructure development, and implementing programs that target FI. They also foster partnerships between public and private sector entities to leverage resources and expertise (Gabor & Brooks, 2020).

6.3 Financial Inclusion in Asia

Asia, the largest continent of the world, consists of countries like India, Sri Lanka, Bangladesh, Pakistan, Nepal, China, Indonesia, Thailand, Saudi Arabia, Malaysia, etc. (Ratnawati, 2020). The continent is diverse in terms of varying level of economic status of the countries including the richest countries with inclusive financial systems like Japan or South Korea, as well as countries with poor economic status having substantial discrepancies in financial service coverage like Afghanistan or Maldives (Cicchiello et al., 2021; Morsy, 2020; Nagpal et al., 2020). Such disparity continues to pose major obstacles for FI service providers.

Bangladesh has made improvements in FI through the promotion of the MFIs (Uddin et al., 2017), which provides smaller amount grants to the lower-income-level individuals particularly women (Raihan et al., 2017). MFIs also ensure to help the borrowers in achieving financial literacy and entrepreneurial knowledge aiming to elevate the position of the marginalized people in Bangladesh (Mia et al., 2019). Bangladesh government implemented initiatives like the Digital Financial Services (DFS) program to leverage mobile or internet banking networks to extend financial services in agrarian areas. ***Pakistan*** has achieved a noteworthy development in FI through various policy measures and technological innovations. The government established Pakistan Microfinance Investment Company (PMIC) to support the growth of institutions related with microfinancing (Kemal, 2019) to bring all excluded people under FI. The introduction of branchless banking through mobile money services has facilitated to solve the problem of mobility as well as turned to be very effective for the people in rural areas (Zulfiqar et al., 2016). The biometric verification system has also enhanced the security system and the effectiveness of financial transaction. ***Nepal*** still has a greater number of people excluded from financial services facing several disparities (Dhungana & Kumar, 2015). Nepal Rastra Bank's (NRB) formulated some long-term strategies like the Directed lending model, the Cooperative model, the FINGOs model, the Project-Based micro-credit model, and the wholesale microfinance approaches. Nepal emphasized on expanding financial aid with through wholesale lending institutions such as the rural microfinance development center and the small farmer development bank ltd that provide collateral-free microcredit to the needy (Pant, 2016). ***Sri Lanka*** has made a notable progress in expanding financial services coming out of the barriers posed by bureaucracy and infrastructure. It has implemented a well-established formal financial structure through the development of national FI strategy (Arandara & Gunasekera, 2020; Jeewananda et al., 2021). The Central Bank of Sri Lanka has come up with initiatives like the 'Rata Purama LANKA QR' code, which promotes digital payments in a safe and customer friendly way. Community development intuitions also introduced welfare programs such as Janasaviya, Divineguma, and Samurdhi. ***Afghanistan*** emerged from decades of conflict with a shattered financial system. The country faced immense challenges including inad equate infrastructure, limited income people, and unavailability of cost-effective financial assistance (Azimi, 2020). The government and international organizations are collaborating to establish an effective financial system in Afghanistan (Zahidi & Khan, 2019). Banks and microfinance institutions are also trying hard to increase access for financial services in both formal and informal ways. ***Thailand's*** way to the pursuit of inclusive finance is predominantly led by the government. Along with banks, there are many state financial institutions (SFIs), non-banking financial institutions (NBFIs), saving cooperatives, and credit unions, which provides loan with low interest to the poor (Tambunlertchai, 2015). The BACC and the GSB are among the biggest microfinance providers in the world dominating the Thailand's SFIs. The national e-payment was approved in the country to help people in distant area and the OTC (Over the Counter Service) introduced to pay the bills in a convenient way (Lewis & Lewis, 2017). ***Philippines*** made an effective FI with a mix of a favorable regulatory framework and robust market backing (Operana, 2016). Its microfinance strategies are more diverse regarding micro deposits and micro insurance (Llanto, 2015). Philippines exemplifies how technology advancements, when combined with efficient business strategies and supportive regulations from the government, provide affordable financial services to all. Efforts are being made to build a comprehensive credit information system to include client data from a variety of economic entities that will be accessible to the public.

6.4 Financial Inclusion in G20

G20 is a very familiar name in the global arena including countries as, the US, Australia, Germany, China, the UK, Canada, India, Indonesia, France, Italy, etc. The G20 nations focused on regulatory reforms in order to facilitate FI (Khan et al., 2022). They have implemented measures to promote responsible finance, consumer protection, and fair competition. They made notable international cooperation such as the G20 Global Partnership for Financial Inclusion – GPFI (Tian & Li, 2022). Furthermore, G20 countries engage in capacity-building programs to assist developing nations through technical assistance, knowledge sharing, and financial support (Shaw, 2023). Collectively, G20 have the potential to drive systemic change and create an enabling environment for FI worldwide.

The ***United States*** with a strong financial system have established a planned banking network throughout the country (Yogo et al., 2022). The government has encouraged the establishment of Community Development Financial Institutions, which particularly provides services to lower-income group people (Marshall, 2004). They have initiatives like the Community Re-investment Act, which mandated banks to provide loans to poor income populations. Technological advancements like internet banking have even more expanded financial access throughout the nation. The ***United Kingdom*** promoting competition and innovation in financial services with the widespread adoption of digital banking, contactless payments, and allowing clients to safely share financial transaction data with allowed third parties (Lewis & Lindley, 2015). The Financial Conduct Authority (FCA) has taken steps to promote responsible lending and consumer protection, guaranteeing the availability and reasonable cost of financial services (Esoimeme, 2020). The government has launched the Financial Inclusion Policy Forum, which brings together stakeholders to address financial exclusion issues. ***Canada*** with well-planned financial policies aims to ensure all individuals have access to basic banking services and affordable credit (Normand Bourgault, 2014). However, other alternatives sources of finance such as cheque cashers, title loan stores, rent-to-own shops, and payday loan providers occupy a greater role in Canada's monetary industry as they meet the people's demand for small dollar or temporary loans. The government implemented Financial Consumer Agency of Canada (FCAC) to protect consumers and promote financial literacy. The Community Economic Development Investment Fund and the Social Finance Fund support community-driven initiatives (Rohan, 2016). ***Germany*** has promoted the establishment of huge number of microfinance organizations throughout the nation to offer financial support to the people who cannot always afford to get to the banks. German government implemented a number of programs to increase financial awareness, particularly among vulnerable groups and emphasized the importance of financial education in schools (Neuberger, 2015). German program GPFI-Global Partnership for Financial Inclusion aims at boosting resilience, enhancing sustainability and embracing accountability (GPFI, 2017). ***Indonesia***'s attempts to develop FI have been remarkable along with the planned infrastructural development and effective government strategies (Jahan et al., 2019). The accomplishments of its core programs, TabunganKu (My Savings) and People's Business Credit, demonstrate Indonesia's improvement in FI services (Kurniasari et al., 2021). The initiatives taken by the privately owned bank Rakyat Indonesia to connect with people having no bank account highlight the crucial role of private sector in promoting FI.

6.5 Financial Inclusion in BRICS

The BRICS nations (Brazil, Russia, India, China, and South Africa) have made notable progress in advancing FI (Dou & Li, 2022). This alliance has started making revolutionary move as launching new currency and expanding activities across other nations (Khandare, 2019). The well-established banking infrastructure, extensive digital networks, and financial technology enable individuals to access financial services conveniently and manage their finances remotely which has accelerated the FI services in BRICS nations (Barik & Pradhan, 2021).

Brazil has made a good stride in FI through initiatives such as Bolsa Família Program, which supplies limited income households with conditioned cash payments, and Cadastro Único, a unified registry, helps identify individuals eligible for social benefits (Diniz et al., 2013). The federal government supported the physical existence of government-owned banks all around the nation and permitted credit unions for dissolving inequalities among regions (Kalliala, 2016). The Banco para Todos (Banks for All) initiative started correspondent banking channels allowing banks partnering with enterprises like lottery merchants, pharmacies, post office, and others to provide unique FI services (Fonseca & Matray, 2022). ***Russia*** faced many obstacles in attaining FI like undercapitalization, territorial discrepancies, imbalanced income, and dependence on external markets (Gorshkov, 2017). Despite a slight rise in the Global Findex Indicators, Russians out of financial services remain high. The government implemented diligent efforts to enhance digital infrastructure, facilitate electronic payments, and enhance financial education (Imaeva et al., 2014). Russia introduced a comprehensive credit reporting system to promote responsible lending and make financing more accessible. In collaboration with the World Bank and OECD, it established the Financial Literacy Trust Fund to encourage global studies on finances. ***India*** achieved tremendous growth in advancing FI. The implementation of Pradhan

Mantri Jan Dhan Yojana (PMJDY) provides universal availability of financial services (Agarwal et al., 2017; Agarwala et al., 2022; Cnaan et al., 2012). The Aadhaar biometric identification system facilitates easier account opening and verification while the Unified Payments Interface (UPI), the very first biometrically scanned unique identity initiative, allows unbanked people to use credit and other financial services. The central bank has launched the Kisan Credit Card for providing small loans to the poor farmers (Sharma, 2016). ***China*** with well-developed banking and non-bank institutions ensured the availability of financial services like deposits, loans, mortgages, retirement savings, and remittances at competitive rates (Chen & Yuan, 2021; Khan & Rehan, 2022). The government adopted measures to support microcredit programs and encourage the expansion of rural financial institutions (Ma & Li, 2021). China's financial liberalization made it possible for new market actors including agro-related banks, village township banks, and postal savings banks to extend their offerings into remote areas. The changes also led to the development of certain new services, like SME Board, ChiNext, and innovative funding markets for SMEs (Lu et al., 2020). ***South Africa*** has focused on promoting FI with the advancements of smart devices, enhanced security levels and continual technological improvements (Matsebula & Yu, 2020). The government-implemented initiatives such as the Financial Sector Code (FSC) aim to transform the monetary sector and ensure access to greater financial services for excluded groups. The Financial Sector Transformation Council (FSTC) in compliance with the nation's FI policy has also set many business requirements (Shipalana, 2019). Moreover, Private sector's attempt is evidenced by the implementation of the Mzansi Initiative, an account with low cost designed to increase access to transactional banking.

6.6 Financial Inclusion Perspectives from Developed and Under-Developed Regions

Developed countries of the world, including the Germany, the US, Canada, the UK, and others, have always been on upper hand in terms of using the FI services in an effective way (Grohmann & Menkhoff, 2017). These nations have leveraged their robust financial system, an extensive networking, technology, and digital innovation to promote FI. They are in a favorable condition because they have a higher percentage of individuals with bank accounts and have awareness regarding financial services. The establishment of comprehensive regulatory frameworks, public-private partnerships, and the adoption of digital banking solutions are notable progress of developed nations (Ye & Kulathunga, 2019). The governments take many initiatives like working closely with financial institutions, regulators, and non-profit organizations to ensure the facilitation of cost-effective financial assistance to underserved populations. They are also promoting responsible lending practices, consumer protection, and transparency in financial transactions (Yoshino et al., 2020). By embracing diversity, enhancing accessibility, and fostering financial education, developed nations strive to create inclusive systems that empower all individuals to participate fully in the economy.

Contrary, in under-developed countries, where a large number of people do not have access to regular financial amenities, achieving FI becomes a pivotal goal. Many under-developed countries face challenges in establishing a robust financial infrastructure, including physical bank branches and digital payment networks (Cicchiello et al., 2021). The people of these countries do not have enough ability to maintain a bank account of their own. In nations with low development, a substantial percentage of the citizens lack the identification and documentation necessary to get formal FI services. They do not even have adequate financial literacy, which impedes individuals' understanding of financial services (Ye & Kulathunga, 2019). In addition, the lower income of the population creates barriers to access traditional financial services, which often require regular deposits and steady employment records. Cultural beliefs and practices can also influence people's perceptions of formal financial institutions leading them to rely on informal methods of saving and lending within communities. Therefore, FI in under-developed countries is a multifaceted endeavor that requires concerted efforts from governments, financial institutions, NGOs, and the private sector.

6.7 Key Challenges and Opportunities of Financial Inclusion in Asia, G20, and BRICS Nations

FI in Asia is a mixed landscape, with advanced economies demonstrating high levels of access, while developing and under-developed economies face significant challenges. Limited access to formal financial services, lack of financial literacy, income inequality, political instability, and lack of infrastructural facilities are the challenges here (Rillo, 2014; Siano et al., 2020). Large segment of Asian population does not even have a bank account, which makes them lag behind from being financially included. In many under-developed regions, access to the digital facilities is uneven due to several disparities. They also struggle with regulatory concerns while extending financial access (Cnaan et al., 2012). Some Asian countries are trying to put in a game-changing effort to address these challenges with efficiency. The key opportunities for Asian countries are their hardest effort to grow and their large number of excluded population who can be brought under the system.

The G20 nations have made notable progress in advancing FI through various initiatives, still, challenges persist in the area of national strategies, financial education programs, and regulatory reforms (Yogo et al., 2022). The creation of innovative financial goods and services has aided in the extension of banking services across the G20, nonetheless, offering simple and inexpensive monetary assistance to the deprived marginalized people remains the greatest challenge. The opportunities could be gained through international cooperation. By sharing best practices, knowledge, capacity, and collaborating on innovative solutions, the G20 nation can address cross-border challenges, such as remittances, digital identity, and regulatory harmonization (Barik & Sharma, 2019). Developing common approaches among the G20 nations can contribute to advance inclusive FI system globally.

Finally, the BRICS countries took unique approaches to achieve FI, but the barriers lie both in terms of accessibility and actual use (Dou & Li, 2022). The common challenges include reaching underserved populations, enhancing financial literacy, addressing geographic disparities, promoting responsible lending and ensuring equitable access to loan (Tay et al., 2022). The opportunity for BRICS nations lies in the fact that most of their citizens have bank accounts and basic banking knowledge. BRICS countries can make concrete development through effective strategic alliance; through tailored strategies and international cooperation, they can assure that the advantages of FI reach all individuals and communities, regardless of their socioeconomic status or geographical location.

6.8 Suggestions to Improve Financial Inclusion in Global Contexts

Nations throughout the globe are attempting to achieve universal FI realizing its significance for national development. Addressing the challenges and overcoming the obstacles that stop marginalized populations from getting institutional financial services is the necessity of time. Much progress has been achieved in financial inclusion but there is still plenty to do to reach the universal FI target (Barik & Pradhan, 2021).

1 Governments should establish supportive regulatory environment ensuring consumer protection and responsible lending. Regulations should be proportionate and inclusive, allowing growth of alternative financial service providers. Flexible rules, easy procedure, and low costs can encourage low-income individuals to get financial assistance.
2 Financial education initiatives should be integrated into education system and tailored to the specific needs of populations. Establishing financial mentorship program is imperative for vulnerable groups to learn digital banking and make financial choices.
3 Investing in digital infrastructure is essential for securing widespread access to digital banking services. Mobile wallet and internet banking can be a very effective tool for reaching remote people particularly for the countries with high population rate.
4 Collaboration between governments, financial institutions, and non-profit organizations is crucial for strengthening FI. Public-private partnerships can leverage resources, expertise, and networks to implement effective strategies.
5 Encouraging innovation and research on FI can lead to the development of effective solutions. Policymakers should support initiatives that explore new technologies, alternative credit scoring models, and innovative financial services.
6 Addressing the demands of financial aid for low-income people and small businesses is essential for reducing inequality. Implementing policies that empower every individual and ensure equal right to monetary services is integral for comprehensive growth.
7 Regular monitoring and evaluation of FI efforts are essential to track progress, identify gaps, and make informed decisions. Robust data collection, analysis, and reporting mechanisms should be established to measure the impact of interventions.

6.9 Policy Implications

Addressing the challenges and overcoming the obstacles that stop marginalized populations from getting institutional financial services is the necessity of time. Integrating everyone into the world of FI services is evident and significant, especially for those who are still excluded from having access to these services. Policymakers, financial institutions, and stakeholders must evaluate the study outcomes and put into practice the suggestions in order to accomplish the worldwide FI goal. Individuals should also collaborate and play a critical role in advancing FI on a global scale, creating a more all-encompassing model of economic development and significantly lowering poverty around the world.

6.10 Conclusion

FI is crucial in establishing a solid foundation of financial infrastructure, which subsequently facilitates economic progress for a nation. Though many successful initiatives being taken aiming to improve the FI scenario worldwide including the national financial assistance programs, the promotion of microfinancing organizations in growing economies, and the adoption of digital banking solutions, etc., still some issues must be resolved immediately to unlock the maximum potentiality of FI in global contexts. Each nation and region faces unique challenges in promoting FI, such as addressing rural urban differences, enhancing financial literacy, overcoming regulatory hurdles, and reaching marginalized populations. Contrary, opportunities exist in leveraging technology, fostering partnerships, and tailoring approaches to local contexts. People's access to appropriate credit is a prerequisite for sustainable FI in any country. Recognizing the significance, every government is attempting to achieve universal financial accessibility. This chapter provides insights into FI services across different nations seeking attention for joint efforts and effective strategies to accelerate the progress fostering around the globe.

Author Contributions

All the authors worked together on the plan, approach, and finalized version of this study. The theoretical literature review and crafting the content across various sections were all significantly influenced by each contributor. Moreover, each author took turns reviewing and revising the chapter to provide a unified and thorough presentation of the findings.

Funding

There was no external funding used for this study.

Data Availability Statement

A data availability declaration is not applicable since this study is based on a literature review rather than primary data gathering.

Acknowledgments

Sincere appreciation is expressed to the authors of the cited works, which strengthened the basis of this chapter. Reviewers' and editors' suggestions were important in improving the paper's rigorousness and coherence. The academic community as a whole is thanked for creating a climate conducive to the free exchange of ideas that has allowed this study to move forward.

References

Agarwal, S., Alok, S., Ghosh, P., Ghosh, S., Piskorski, T., & Seru, A. (2017). Banking the unbanked: What do 255 million new bank accounts reveal about financial access? Columbia Business School Research Paper (17–12).

Agarwala, V., Sahu, T. N., & Maity, S. (2022). Efficiency of public sector banks in achieving the goal of PMJDY and PMMY. *International Journal of Economics and Business Research*, *24*(1–2), 234–256.

Ahlin, C., Lin, J., & Maio, M. (2011). Where does microfinance flourish? Microfinance institution performance in macroeconomic context. *Journal of Development Economics*, *95*(2), 105–120.

Ahmad Malik, F., & Yadav, D. K. (2022a). Financial inclusion schemes and changing socio economic status of poorest of the poor. In *Financial inclusion schemes in India* (pp. 109–130). Singapore: Springer Nature Singapore.

Ahmed, S. (2009). Microfinance institutions in Bangladesh: Achievements and challenges. *Managerial Finance*, *35*(12), 999–1010.

Arandara, R., & Gunasekera, S. (2020). Financial Inclusion and Inclusive Growth: What Does It Mean for Sri Lanka? World Bank Policy Research Working Paper (9204).

Arcand, J. L., & Fafchamps, M. (2012). Matching in community-based organizations. *Journal of Development Economics*, *98*(2), 203–219.

Ayyagari, M., & Beck, T. (2015). Financial inclusion in Asia: An overview. *Asian Development Bank Economics Working Paper Series* (449).

Azimi, M. N. (2020). Hypothesizing resurgence of financial inclusion to reduce poverty in Afghanistan. *Journal of Business and Management Revolution. Okinawa, Japan*, *1*(1), 10–13.

Barik, R., & Pradhan, A. K. (2021). Does financial inclusion affect financial stability: Evidence from BRICS nations? *The Journal of Developing Areas*, *55*, 341–356.

Barik, R., & Sharma, P. (2019). Analyzing the progress and prospects of financial inclusion in India. *Journal of Public Affairs*, *19*(4), e1948.

Chen, W., & Yuan, X. (2021). Financial inclusion in China: An overview. *Frontiers of Business Research in China*, *15*(1), 1–21.

Choudhary, K., & Kamboj, S. (2017). A study of financial literacy and its determinants: Evidence from India. *Asian Journal of Accounting Perspectives*, *10*(1), 52–72.

Cicchiello, A. F., Kazemikhasragh, A., Monferrá, S., & Girón, A. (2021). Financial inclusion and development in the least developed countries in Asia and Africa. *Journal of Innovation and Entrepreneurship*, *10*(1), 1–13.

Cnaan, R. A., Moodithaya, M. S., & Handy, F. (2012). Financial inclusion: Lessons from rural South India. *Journal of Social Policy*, *41*(1), 183–205.

Demirgüç-Kunt, A., & Singer, D. (2017). Financial inclusion and inclusive growth: A review of recent empirical evidence. World Bank Policy Research Working Paper (8040).

Dhungana, B. R., & Kumar, P. (2015). The status of financial inclusion in Nepal. *Pacific Business Review International*, *7*(8), 51–59.

Diniz, E., Cernev, A., & Porto de Albuquerque, J. (2013). Mobile platform for financial inclusion: The case of an unsuccessful pilot project in Brazil. In Proceedings of SIG GlobDev Sixth Annual Workshop, Milan, Italy December (Vol. 14).

Dou, D., & Li, L. (2022). Does sustainable financial inclusion and energy efficiency ensure green environment? Evidence from BRICS countries. *Economic Research-Ekonomskaistraživanja, 35*(1), 5599–5614.
Esoimeme, E. E. (2020). Balancing anti-money laundering measures and financial inclusion: The example of the United Kingdom and Nigeria. *Journal of Money Laundering Control, 23*(1), 64–76.
Fonseca, J., & Matray, A. (2022). Financial inclusion, economic development, and inequality: Evidence from Brazil. *Journal of Financial Economics*, 156, 103854.
Gabor, D., & Brooks, S. (2020). The digital revolution in financial inclusion: International development in the fintech era. In *Material cultures of financialisation* (pp. 69–82). Abingdon: Routledge.
Gorshkov, V. A. (2017). Financial inclusion in Russia: Challenges for the promotion of long-term savings and investment. *The Journal of Comparative Economic Studies, 12*, 121–133.
GPFI (2017). Global Partnership for Financial Inclusion (GPFI) Germany 2017 Priorities Paper. Access from https://www.gpfi.org/publications/global-partnership-financial-inclusion-gpfi-germany-2017-priorities-paper.
Grohmann, A., & Menkhoff, L. (2017). Financial literacy promotes financial inclusion in both poor and rich countries. *DIW Economic Bulletin, 7*(41), 399–407.
Imaeva, G., Lobanova, I., & Tomilova, O. (2014). Financial inclusion in Russia: the demand-side perspective. Consultative Group to Assist the Poor, World Bank, Moscow, 37–40.
Jahan, M. S., De, J., Jamaludin, M. F., Sodsriwiboon, P., & Sullivan, C. (2019). *The financial inclusion landscape in the Asia-Pacific region: A dozen key findings*. Washington: International Monetary Fund.
Jeewananda, W. S., Jeewantha, J., & Karunasena, D. M. (2021). Customer Adoption of Quick Response (QR) Based Payment System at Badulla District in Sri Lanka. Available at SSRN 3913154.
Kalliala, O. (2016). Credit union correspondents and financial inclusion in Brazil: an exploratory study (Doctoral dissertation).
Kemal, A. A. (2019). Mobile banking in the government-to-person payment sector for financial inclusion in Pakistan. *Information Technology for Development, 25*(3), 475–502.
Khandare, V. B. (2019). Financial inclusion: Empirical study of BRICS countries. *International Journal of Social Science and Economic Research, 4*(5), 3319–3334.
Khan, M. A., & Rehan, R. (2022). Revealing the impacts of banking sector development on renewable energy consumption, green growth, and environmental quality in China: Does financial inclusion matter? *Frontiers in Energy Research, 10*, 940209.
Khan, N., Zafar, M., Okunlola, A. F., Zoltan, Z., & Robert, M. (2022). Effects of financial inclusion on economic growth, poverty, sustainability, and financial efficiency: Evidence from the G20 countries. *Sustainability, 14*(19), 12688.
Kurniasari, F., Gunardi, A., Putri, F., & Firmansyah, A. (2021). The role of financial technology to increase financial inclusion in Indonesia. *International Journal of Data and Network Science, 5*(3), 391–400.
Le, T. H., Chuc, A. T., & Taghizadeh-Hesary, F. (2019). Financial inclusion and its impact on financial efficiency and sustainability: Empirical evidence from Asia. *Borsa Istanbul Review, 19*(4), 310–322.
Lewis, S., & Lewis, D. R. (2017). Financial inclusion in Thailand: Innovations and challenges. (hokuga.hgu.jp), 19–43.
Lewis, S., & Lindley, D. (2015). Financial inclusion, financial education, and financial regulation in the United Kingdom, ADBI Working Paper, No. 544, Asian Development Bank Institute (ADBI), Tokyo.
Llanto, G. (2015). Financial inclusion, education, and regulation in the Philippines, ADBI Working Paper, No. 541, Asian Development Bank Institute (ADBI), Tokyo.
Lu, Z., Wu, J., & Liu, J. (2020). Bank concentration and SME financing availability: The impact of promotion of financial inclusion in China. *International Journal of Bank Marketing, 38*(6), 1329–1349.

Ma, J., & Li, Z. (2021). Does digital financial inclusion affect agricultural eco-efficiency? A case study on China. *Agronomy*, *11*(10), 1949.

Marshall, J. N. (2004). Financial institutions in disadvantaged areas: A comparative analysis of policies encouraging financial inclusion in Britain and the United States. *Environment and Planning A*, *36*(2), 241–261.

Matsebula, V., & Yu, D. (2020). An analysis of financial inclusion in South Africa. *African Review of Economics and Finance*, *12*(1), 171–202.

Mia, M. A., Lee, H. A., Chandran, V. G. R., Rasiah, R., & Rahman, M. (2019). History of microfinance in Bangladesh: A life cycle theory approach. *Business History*, *61*(4), 703–733.

Morsy, H. (2020). Access to finance – Mind the gender gap. *The Quarterly Review of Economics and Finance*, *78*, 12–21.

Naceur, M. S. B., Barajas, M. A., & Massara, M. A. (2015). *Can Islamic banking increase financial inclusion?* Washington: International Monetary Fund.

Nagpal, A., Jain, M., & Jain, A. (2020). Determining the role of digital technology, governance and institutions in advancing financial inclusion in BRICS nations using probit regression analysis. *Journal of Social and Economic Development*, *22*, 443–459.

Neuberger, D. (2015). Financial inclusion, regulation, and education in Germany, ADBI Working Paper, No. 530, Asian Development Bank Institute (ADBI), Tokyo.

Normand Bourgault, D. B. A. (2014). The moderating role of risk, security and trust applied to the TAM model in the offer of banking financial services in Canada. *Journal of Internet Banking and Commerce*, *19*, 1–21.

Operana, B. (2016). Financial inclusion and financial stability in the Philippines. Published Masters Dissertation. Graduate School of Public Policy (GraSPP). The University.

Pant, B. (2016). Financial inclusion in Nepal: Policy review and prescriptions. *NRB Economic Review*, *28*(2), 1–18.

Raihan, S., Osmani, S. R., & Khalily, M. B. (2017). The macro impact of microfinance in Bangladesh: A CGE analysis. *Economic Modelling*, *62*, 1–15.

Ratnawati, K. (2020). The impact of financial inclusion on economic growth, poverty, income inequality, and financial stability in Asia. *The Journal of Asian Finance, Economics and Business (JAFEB)*, *7*(10), 73–85.

Rillo, A. D. (2014). Overview of financial inclusion in Asia. *Financial Inclusion in Asia: Country Surveys*, 1–5. //efaidnbmnnnibpcajpcglclefindmkaj/https://www.adb.org/sites/default/files/publication/154220/adbi-book-financial-inclusion-asia.pdf

Rohan, S. (2016). Investor brief: Promoting financial inclusion in Canada's financial services sector. Vancouver: Shareholder Association for Research and Education.

Sharma, D. (2016). Nexus between financial inclusion and economic growth: Evidence from the emerging Indian economy. *Journal of Financial Economic Policy*, *8*(1), 13–36.

Shaw, P. (2023). Financial Inclusion and SDGs in G20: Accelerating Entrepreneurship and Creating Jobs in Post-Pandemic Economic Recovery. India & the G20: Legacy & Prospects for Multilateralism amidst a Polycrisis, 43.

Shipalana, P. (2019). Digitising financial services: A tool for financial inclusion in South Africa?

Siano, A., Raimi, L., Palazzo, M., & Panait, M. C. (2020). Mobile banking: An innovative solution for increasing financial inclusion in Sub-Saharan African countries: Evidence from Nigeria. *Sustainability*, *12*(23), 10130.

Tian Y., & Li, L. (2022). https://idp.springer.com/authorize/casa?redirect_uri=https://link.springer.com/article/10.1007/s11356-022-19618-9&casa_token=AiibwB_xPAgAAAA-A:4ymUDthJK8japNTv7DErRvgsyYwUaEPMw3bjzXXiOtGKrTJG5SCkiY7Xk-zLx1pWUtQvkTlV4VNsAtx40KI

Tambunlertchai, K. (2015). Financial inclusion, financial regulation, and financial education in Thailand.

Tay, L. Y., Tai, H. T., & Tan, G. S. (2022). Digital financial inclusion: A gateway to sustainable development. *Heliyon*, *8*, 1–10.

Uddin, A., Chowdhury, M. A. F., & Islam, M. N. (2017). Determinants of financial inclusion in Bangladesh: Dynamic GMM & quantile regression approach. *The Journal of Developing Areas*, *51*(2), 221–237.

Ye, J., & Kulathunga, K. M. M. C. B. (2019). How does financial literacy promote sustainability in SMEs? A developing country perspective. *Sustainability*, *11*(10), 2990.

Yogo, M., Whitten, A., & Cox, N. (2022). Financial inclusion across the United States. Available at SSRN 3934498.

Yoshino, N., Morgan, P. J., & Long, T. Q. (2020). Financial literacy and fintech adoption in Japan (No. 1095). ADBI Working Paper Series.

Zahidi, S., & Khan, W. (2019). Financial inclusion and its effect on alleviation of poverty: A case of Afghanistan. *Kardan Journal of Economics and Management Sciences*, *2*(3), 15–26.

Zulfiqar, K., Chaudhary, M. A., & Aslam, A. (2016). Financial inclusion and its implications for inclusive growth in Pakistan. *Pakistan Economic and Social Review*, *54*(2), 297–325.

Part IV

Financial Inclusion and Regional Development

7 Financial Inclusion Policy Implication of Financial Knowledge

Evidence from India

Rahul Chaudhary and Nidhi Verma

7.1 Introduction

The Indian banking industry has shown tremendous growth in volume and complexity over the last decade or so. Despite making significant improvements in all areas relating to financial viability, profitability and competitiveness, there are concerns that much needed banking services have not reached underprivileged sections. In this context, efforts are being made as financial inclusion can truly lift financial condition and standards of life of the poor and disadvantaged (Leeladhar, 2006; Subbarao, 2009a; Thorat, 2007).

The study performed by Sarma (2008) attempted to construct Index of Financial Inclusion, based on three aspects of financial inclusion, namely, penetration of banking system, its availability to users and its actual usage for a cross section of countries for 2004. The index was aggregative in nature that preserves same weight for all three components.

Financial inclusion as a comprehensive and holistic process of ensuring access to financial services and timely and adequate credit, particularly by vulnerable groups such as weaker sections and low-income groups at an affordable cost in a fair and transparent manner (Financial Inclusion Committee Report, 2008). Financial inclusion or inclusive financing is the delivery of financial services at affordable costs to sections of disadvantaged and low-income segments of society. Financial inclusion means that individuals and businesses have access to useful and affordable financial products and services that meet their needs – transactions, payments, savings, credit and insurance delivered in a responsible and sustainable way (World Bank, 2017) Karmakar (2007) has described microfinance needs and concepts in India in his book *Rural Credit and Self-Help Groups*.

Financial inclusion is described as “the process of assuring vulnerable groups, such as weaker parts and low-income groups, affordable access to financial services, timely and enough financing” (Reserve Bank of India, Committee on Financial Inclusion, Chairman Dr. C. Rangarajan, 2008). The Committee on the Medium-Term Path to Financial Inclusion (Chairman Shri Deepak Mohanty, RBI, 2015) has defined financial inclusion as “convenient access to a basket of basic formal financial products and services that should include savings, remittance, credit, government-sponsored insurance, and pension products to small and marginal

DOI: 10.4324/9781032655185-11

farmers and low-income households at a reasonable cost with adequate protection, gradually supplemented by social cash transfer aside from improving access to formal funding for small and marginal businesses by relying more heavily on technology to minimize costs and improve service delivery".

"The literal meaning of the two phrases, inclusive growth, refers to both the pace and structure of economic growth; it simply shows broad-based, shared, and pro-poor growth. "The phrase 'inclusive' should be regarded as a process of including the excluded as actors whose participation is essential in the very design of the development process, not simply as welfare targets of development programs," according to the Planning Commission. In a simpler and wider sense, it means that inclusive growth as a strategy of economic development should not only aim at equitable distribution of growth benefits but also at creating economic opportunities along with equal access to them for all. In this study, an effort is made to understand the inclusive growth phenomenon, its need, and financial inclusion as an instrument for improving it, with a focus on the extent with which it occurs in Indian states.

New Delhi, that the process of financial inclusion is an attempt to bring the weaker and vulnerable sections of society with in the ambit of the organized financial system. It may, therefore, be defined as the process of enabling access to timely and adequate credit and other financial services for vulnerable groups such as the weaker section and low-income groups at affordable cost. The access to finance by the poor is a prerequisite for poverty reduction and sustainable economic development of a country according to Chitraand Selvam (2013). Financial inclusion is an effective policy tool for inclusive growth. In the same view, Dr. C. Rangarajan (2008) has stated in the report on financial inclusion that financial inclusion must be taken up in a mission mode and suggested the participation of all the stakeholders and beneficiaries in bringing policy changes and undertaking promotional initiatives for achieving 100% financial inclusion in India. Even after controlling for several other factors underlying economic growth, Levine (1997) observed that countries with larger banks and more active stock markets grew faster over future decades. Access to money by all parts of society is also critical (Levine, 1997; Pande & Burgess, 2003). Finance has the potential to help people get out of poverty. A well-developed financial system that is open to everybody minimizes information and transaction costs and has an influence on saving rates, investment decisions, technological innovation, and long-term growth rates (Beck et al., 2009). According to research by Binswanger and Khandker (1995) and Pande and Burgess (2003), India's rural branch expansion initiative reduced rural poverty and increased non-agricultural employment.

Financial inclusion has been more prominent in recent years in terms of public policy. Many countries, including India (Government of India, 2008) and the United Kingdom (UK) (2006), as well as international institutions such as the United Nations (2006) and the World Bank (2008, 2009), have established task forces or committees to better understand and extend financial inclusion. These researches provide light on a variety of financial inclusion issues. However, these papers have not yet adequately covered the measurement component of financial inclusion. One of the primary goals of development economics is to figure out how to get people out of poverty. Access to finance has long been regarded as a crucial component in helping people to transform their production and employment activities and thus escape poverty (Aghion & Bolton, 1997; Banerjee, 2001; Banerjee & Newman, 1993; Pande & Burgess, 2003; Yunus, 1999).

Because India's economy and society are so diverse, it is critical to pay close attention to financial inclusion assessment. Few academics have attempted to quantify certain dimensions of financial inclusion. Honohan (2007) used data on the number of banking and microfinance institution (MFI) accounts for over 160 countries to calculate the percentage of adults who use formal financial intermediaries, which he then associated with inequality (Gini Coefficient) and poverty. Sarma (2008) created a Financial Inclusion Index for 55 countries based on aggregate banking indicators such as the number of accounts, bank branches, and total credit and deposit as a percentage of GDP.

The policymakers in India have been focusing on financial inclusion of rural and semi-rural areas, primarily for three most pressing needs:

> Creating a platform for inculcating the habit to save money – The lower income category has been living under the constant shadow of financial duress mainly because of the absence of savings. The absence of savings makes them a vulnerable lot. Presence of banking services and products aim at providing a critical tool to inculcate the habit to save. Capital formation in the country is also expected to be boosted once financial inclusion measures materialize, as people move away from traditional modes of parking their savings in land, buildings, bullion, etc.
>
> Providing formal credit avenues – So far, the unbanked population has been vulnerably dependent on informal channels of credit like family, friends and moneylenders. Availability of adequate and transparent credit from formal banking channels shall allowthe entrepreneurial spirit of the masses to increase outputs and prosperity in the countryside. A classic example of what easy and affordable availability of credit can do for the poor is the microfinance sector.
>
> Plug gaps and leaks in public subsidies and welfare programmes – A considerable sum of money that is meant for the poorest of poor do not actually reach them. While this money meanders through large system of government bureaucracy much of it is widely believed to leak and is unable to reach the intended parties. Government therefore, is pushing for direct cash transfers to beneficiaries through their bank accounts rather than subsidizing products and making cash payments. This laudable effort is expected to reduce government's subsidy bill (as it shall save that part of the subsidy that is leaked) and provide relief only to the real beneficiaries. All these efforts require an efficient and affordable banking system that can reach out to all.

Therefore, as per Rangarajan Committee (2008) report, financial inclusion is the process of ensuring access to financial services and timely and adequate credit where needed by vulnerable groups such as weaker sections and low-income groups at affordable cost. Broadly speaking, financial inclusion is delivery of banking services at affordable cost to vast sections of disadvantaged and low-income groups. Goals of financial inclusion can be met by initiative of banking sector to cut across various strata of society, regions, gender, and income and encourage public to embrace banking habit. Also, Reserve Bank of India (RBI), as chief regulator, has intervened for success of financial inclusion by various enactments, financial literacy drives, leveraging technology, etc. In addition to banking system, Indian financial network consists of Indian postal department, insurance companies; self-help groups (SHGs), civil society organizations (CSOs), non-banking financial companies (NBFCs), non-government organizations (NGOs), MFIs, which are vital financial intermediaries.

7.2 Rational of the Study

Financial inclusion is a critical component of a country's economic development and poverty alleviation efforts. It is the process of ensuring that all individuals and businesses have access to and can effectively use a wide range of financial services, including banking, credit, insurance, and savings. India, as one of the world's largest and most diverse economies, has made significant strides in advancing financial inclusion in recent years. However, achieving comprehensive financial inclusion remains a complex challenge.

This study seeks to examine the relationship between financial knowledge and financial inclusion in the Indian context and to draw important policy implications from the findings. The rationale for conducting this research can be outlined as follows:

1 Economic and Social Significance: Financial inclusion has the potential to reduce poverty, enhance economic growth, and improve the overall well-being of individuals. It is essential to understand the factors that contribute to or hinder financial inclusion, and the role of financial knowledge in this process. By analysing these factors within the Indian context, this study contributes to the broader understanding of financial inclusion's significance in emerging economies.

2 Knowledge Gap: Although there is a growing body of research on financial inclusion in India, there remains a significant knowledge gap concerning the relationship between financial knowledge and financial inclusion. This study aims to bridge this gap by investigating how financial knowledge, or the lack thereof, impacts an individual's or household's access to and use of financial services.

3 Policy Relevance: Policymakers in India are continually working to enhance financial inclusion, as evidenced by initiatives such as the Pradhan Mantri Jan Dhan Yojana (PMJDY). To formulate effective policies, it is crucial to understand the role of financial knowledge in improving financial inclusion. This research provides empirical evidence to inform policy decisions, helping policymakers design more targeted and efficient strategies.

4 Behavioural Insights: An individual's financial behaviour is influenced by their level of financial knowledge. This study aims to explore how increased financial knowledge can positively impact financial behaviours such as savings, investment, and responsible borrowing. Insights from this research can inform financial education programmes and campaigns.
5 Methodological Approach: The study employs empirical evidence to establish a causal relationship between financial knowledge and financial inclusion. It utilizes quantitative and qualitative data, surveys, and analysis to provide a comprehensive understanding of the dynamics involved.

7.3 Review of Literature

Knowledge of finances, often known as financial literacy, is an essential component of personal finance that has a significant influence on the overall financial well-being of individuals. An analysis of the research papers published in this field reveals various important results and patterns, including the following: To begin, there is a substantial knowledge gap among individuals about financial matters, with many people missing a fundamental understanding of topics such as creating a budget, saving money, and investing. This lack of understanding can lead to poor decision-making around finances, which in turn can raise a person's vulnerability to experiencing financial difficulties. In addition, the study underlines the significance of early financial education and the favourable impact that it has on the financial results of individuals throughout the course of their lifetime. According to a number of studies, individuals who receive financial education at a younger age are more likely to acquire healthy financial habits and to make educated decisions throughout their lives.

Financial expertise adopting appropriate financial behaviour, according to various academics, heavily depends on one's financial literacy (Allgood & Walstad, 2016; Mountain et al., 2020). Financially literate people are those who can utilize their knowledge to make the right judgements for the efficient management of their financial resources (Asaad, 2015; Robb & Woodyard, 2011).

Numerous studies have evaluated the degree of financial literacy among students, young people, and the broader community in this respect. Some authors (Keown, 2011; Lalonde & Schmidt) selected the popular Jump$tart questionnaire, while others (Allgood & Walstad, 2016; Kim et al., 2019, 2020; Potrich & Vieira, 2018; Shen et al., 2016) created comparable questions that relate to a body of financial knowledge or to some of its components. The outcomes are consistent across all scenarios: individuals have a generally low level of financial literacy.

While this has inspired a number of writers to become interested in financial literacy as a way to enhance financial behaviour, mixed outcomes have been attained. For instance, Xiao et al. (2011), Allgood and Walstad (2016), and Mountain et al. (2020) discovered a favourable relationship between financial knowledge and financial behaviour, whereas Borden et al. (2008) and Tang et al. (2015) discovered that financial knowledge is insufficient to alter financial behaviour. Despite these discrepancies, we contend that having a solid understanding of finances has a good impact on both financial confidence and behaviour (H_{2a} and H_{2b}).

Furthermore, the present study examines the correlation between financial literacy and retirement planning. The study conducted by Lusardi and Mitchell (2007) underscores the correlation between elevated levels of financial literacy and the propensity to make well-informed decisions on retirement planning. This finding underscores the significance of financial education in ensuring the attainment of a secure and prosperous retirement. This article posits the necessity of establishing a more precise and comprehensive delineation of financial literacy within the framework of a multifaceted and dynamic economic landscape. Remund (2010) argues that it is crucial to develop a precise and thorough comprehension of financial literacy in order to properly inform educational initiatives. The present study aims to investigate the influence of financial literacy and financial education on individuals' subsequent financial behaviours. The study reveals that enhanced financial literacy is associated with a greater propensity for responsible financial decision-making and behaviours.

The book titled *Nudge* explores the use of behavioural economics principles in several sectors, such as personal finance, with the aim of promoting improved decision-making. The paper examines the notion of "choice architecture" as a means of influencing decision-making, as discussed by Thaler and Sunstein (2008). The concept of "scarcity" explores the psychological aspects of scarcity and its influence on the process of decision-making. The study conducted by Mullainathan and Shafir (2013) provides insight into the impact of financial limitations on individuals' cognitive capacity, resulting in less than optimal decision-making in financial matters. The present study aims to integrate the Technology Acceptance Model (TAM) and the Theory of Planned Behaviour (TPB) by incorporating the constructs of perceived risk and perceived benefit. The present study investigates the determinants that impact the adoption of internet banking by including the TAM and the TPB. The study conducted by Lee and Jun (2007) examines the impact of perceived risks and advantages on the adoption of internet banking. This study aims to examine the factors influencing the adoption of mobile banking in Spain. This study provides valuable insights into the various aspects that exert influence on individuals' decision-making processes when it comes to utilizing mobile banking services. According to the study conducted by Serrano-Cinca, Gutiérrez-Nieto, and López-Palacios in 2015, the present research provides an analysis of the findings derived from the pilot study conducted by the Organization for Economic Co-operation and Development (OECD) and the International Network on Financial Education (INFE) pertaining to the assessment of financial literacy (Serrano-Cinca et al., 2015). According to Atkinson and Messy (2012), this study offers valuable perspectives on the creation of instruments and measures for evaluating financial literacy on a worldwide scale. This paper provides an analysis of findings from a comprehensive global financial literacy survey administered by Standard & Poor's Ratings Services. The provided analysis presents a complete perspective on global financial literacy levels. Klapper et al. (2015) conducted a study. The present study investigates the efficacy of financial education and counselling initiatives in enhancing individuals' financial literacy and behavioural outcomes. This implies that these programmes remain viable options for improving financial literacy. According to Collins and O'Rourke (2010), The Dilemma of Prioritising Prices or Knowledge Acquisition What are the factors that influence the demand for financial services in emerging markets? This study examines the determinants of financial services demand, with a particular emphasis on emerging markets. The study conducted by Cole et al. (2011) investigates the relative influence of pricing and knowledge on financial service utilization. This study examines the enduring impacts of compulsory financial education requirements in high schools on individuals' financial conduct and savings patterns. This statement underscores the long-lasting influence of financial education. According to Bernheim et al. (2001), this research examines the phenomenon of financially unstable households and explores the potential repercussions associated with this condition. The study conducted by Lusardi et al. (2011) presents empirical evidence about the susceptibility of specific households, highlighting the policy implications for mitigating financial fragility.

7.3.1 *Objective of the Study*

1 To examine the level of financial knowledge among different segments of the Indian population in relation to PMJDY

7.3.2 *Research Framework*

The proposed research model is as in Figure 7.1.

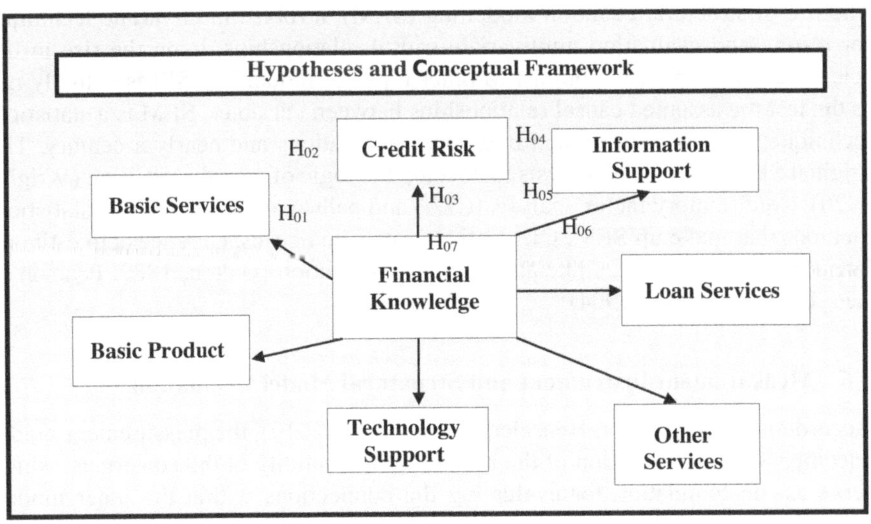

Figure 7.1 Research framework

7.4 Research Methodology

The data collection process included the following steps: the first draft of the questionnaire is prepared by reviewing the relevant studies, financial inclusion, financial knowledge, financial literacy, banking services, etc., for content validation. Before they filled out the questionnaire, participants were asked about their financial knowledge and PMJDY scheme.

Secondly, we reviewed the questionnaire to validate the measurement scales, content, and suitability of the wording of the questions. Next, the questionnaire is administered offline and online through a Google form over six months (December 2022–May 2023). The screening criteria for the respondents include having an account on SNS like Facebook, Instagram and Twitter, Gmail and other online mode. The study used convenience and snowball sampling, as this sampling method is economical, convenient and very useful for measuring the relationships among different occurrences and situations. We received a total of 209 responses, but only 100 of those were considered suitable for further analysis. And research uses the smart PLS 4.2 for analysis

$$FK = \lambda 1 * BP + BS + CR + IS + LS + OTS + T + \delta 1 + \varepsilon 1$$

FK represents the observed variable.
$\lambda 1$ represents the factor loading, which reflects the relationship between the latent variable and FK.
$\delta 1$ represents the intercept or mean of income.
$\varepsilon 1$ represents the error term for income.

7.5 Results and Discussion

The use of structural equation modelling (SEM), a robust multivariate technique for testing and evaluating multivariate causal relationships, is on the rise in the scientific community. In contrast to other types of modelling, SEMs actually put to the test the assumed causal relationships between variables. SEM is a statistical technique that has been refined over three generations and nearly a century. The original SEMs used path analysis to develop the logic of causal modelling (Wright, 1920). Confirmatory factor analysis (CFA) and path analysis are the two statistical methods that make up SEM. Originating in psychometrics, CFA seeks to estimate latent psychological traits like attitude and satisfaction (Galton, 1889; Pearson & Lee, 1903; Spearman, 1904).

7.6 Measurement Instrument and Structural Model Evaluation

According to Vinzi, Chin, Henseler, and Wang in (2010), the measurement model encompasses the evaluation of the reliability and validity of the constructs, which serve as the foundation for evaluating the connections within the inner model. Measurement model evaluation serves as a confirmatory assessment of measurement theory (Vinzi et al., 2010). The measurement theory elucidates the manner

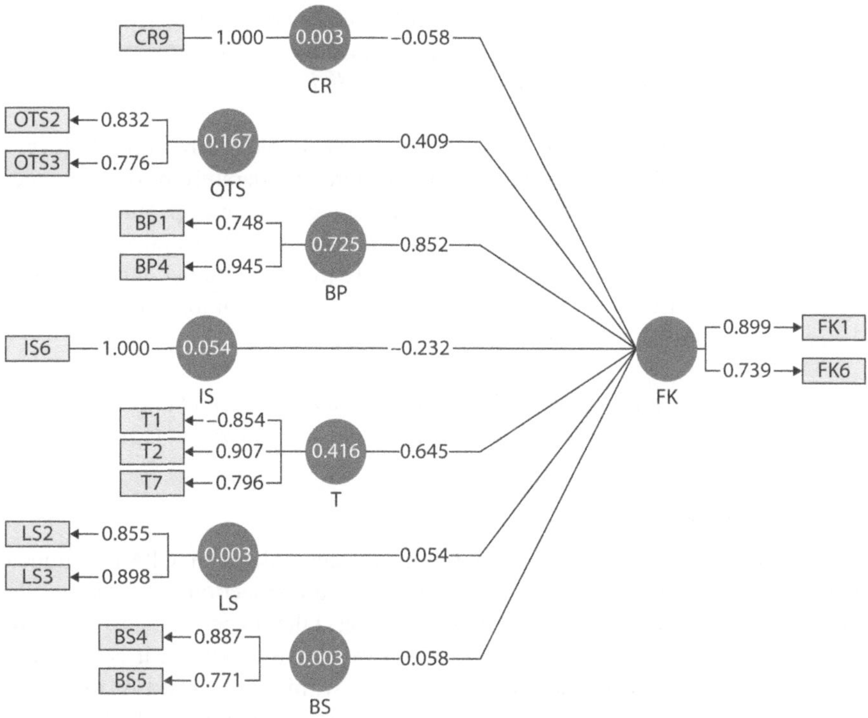

Figure 7.2 Measurement model

in which measurement variables serve as representations of the constructs defined within a given model. Once the reliability and validity of the construct have been established, the subsequent stage involves evaluating the outcomes of the structural model. This entails examining the predictive capabilities of the model and the interrelationships among the constructs. The assessment of the structural model is conducted in a systematic manner (Figure 7.2).

7.7 Hypotheses

Study provides an in-depth analysis of the links between financial knowledge, attitude and behaviour, based on the Austrian contribution to the OECD/INFE survey on financial literacy. Our analysis gives evidence of causal effects of financial knowledge on financial behaviour, using a new instrument based on respondents' newspaper reading habits. We confirm that the selection bias is likely negative, i.e. we would underestimate the causal effect of knowledge on behaviour in a classical regression setting (Fessler et al., 2020).

H_{01}: *There is no relation between financial knowledge and basic product.*
H_{02}: *There is no relation between financial knowledge and basic service.*

H_{O3}: *There is no relation between financial knowledge and credit risk.*
H_{O5}: *There is no relation between financial knowledge and loan service.*
H_{O6}: *There is no relation between financial knowledge and other services.*

The results of the research show that individuals have a reasonable level of financial literacy. Most of the individuals exhibited moderately positive financial behaviour. It is also observed that financial literacy can enhance people's skills and abilities to make more informed choices and ultimately lead to a positive financial behaviour (Thavva, 2021). The findings indicate that the internet and Televisions are the most effective source in creating financial literacy among millennials and Generation Z (Tiwari & Yadav, 2022)

H_{O4}: *There is no relation between financial knowledge and innovation support.*
H_{O7}: *There is no relation between financial knowledge and technology.*

7.8 Measurement Model

To assess the measurement component of the conceptual model, CFA is conducted initially. The CFA method is utilized to establish a connection between a collection of observed variables and the latent variable(s) that underlie them. Given that the scales utilized in this study were derived from prior research, it is imperative to ascertain the appropriateness of these factors within the context of the present study. The findings of the measurement model, as presented in Table 7.1, demonstrate that all latent constructs were sufficiently loaded, adhering to the benchmark values established in previous studies. The constructs utilized in this study exhibit a Cronbach's alpha coefficient exceeding 0.7, suggesting that the assessed constructs

Table 7.1 Measurement model

Construct	*Latent variable*	*Factor loading*	*Cronbach's alpha*	*CR*	*AVE*
Basic product	BP1	0.748	0.657	0.839	0.726
	BP4	0.945			
Basic services	BS4	0.887	0.560	0.816	0.690
	BS5	0.771			
Credit risk	CR9	1.000	0.580	0.588	0.567
Information support	IS6	1.000	0.523	0.678	0.657
Loan services	LS2	0.855	0.700	0.869	0.768
	LS3	0.898			
Other services	OTS2	0.832	0.457	0.786	0.647
	OTS3	0.776			
Technology support	T1	0.854	0.813	0.889	0.728
	T2	0.907			
	T7	0.796			
Financial knowledge	FK1	0.899	0.540	0.806	0.677
	FK6	0.739			

possess a satisfactory level of reliability (Nunnally, 1978). All items within the construct exhibited factor loadings exceeding 0.7, indicating that the constructs demonstrated favourable convergent validity and adhered to the established benchmark factor loading threshold of 0.6 (Hair et al., 2010). All composite reliability (CR) values exceeded the threshold level of 0.7, indicating high internal consistency reliability. Similarly, all average variance extracted (AVE) values surpassed the threshold level of 0.5, indicating satisfactory convergent validity.

7.9 Structural Model Findings

Structural model refers to subsequently confirming the fitness of the measurement model, the next step is to use the structural model to test the research hypotheses defined in the study. The result showed that H1(FK -> BP): The relationship between FK and BP is found to be positive and significant. The high T-Statistic suggests a strong and statistically significant positive relationship between FK and BP. H2(FK -> BS): The relationship between FK and BS is found to be positive and significant. While the path coefficient is positive, the T-Statistic indicates a weaker relationship compared to BP. H3(FK -> CR): The relationship between FK and CR is found to be negative and insignificant. The path coefficient is negative, but the T-Statistic does not reach a level of significance. H4(FK -> IS): The relationship between FK and IS is found to be negative and insignificant. The path coefficient is negative, and the T-Statistic indicates some significance, although it is weaker compared to BP. H5(FK -> LS): The relationship between FK and LS is found to be positive and significant. However, the T-Statistic suggests a relatively weak relationship compared to BP and T. H6(FK -> OTS): The relationship between FK and OTS is found to be positive and significant. The T-Statistic indicates a reasonably strong and statistically significant positive relationship. H7(FK -> T): The relationship between FK and T is found to be positive and highly significant. The exceptionally high T-Statistic indicates a very strong and statistically significant positive relationship (Table 7.2).

Furthermore, this study reveals that FK has varying relationships with different dependent variables. While FK shows positive and significant relationships with BP, BS, LS, OTS and T, it exhibits negative and insignificant relationships with CR and IS. The strength and significance of these relationships differ among the variables, with the strongest positive relationship observed between FK and T, as indicated by the highest T-Statistic. These findings provide valuable insights into the associations between FK and the dependent variables under investigation.

7.10 Policy Implication

The significance of financial knowledge in several areas, such as education, consumer protection and financial regulation, necessitates careful consideration of its policy consequences. The following are many significant policy issues arising from financial knowledge:

Table 7.2 Hypotheses testing

Variables	*Hypotheses*	*Path coefficient*	*Mean*	*STDEV*	*T-Statistics*	*Decision*
FK->BP	H1	0.852	0.861	0.020	43.148	Positive and significant
FK->BS	H2	0.058	0.091	0.102	0.570	Positive and significant
FK->CR	H3	–0.058	–0.058	0.122	0.477	Negative and insignificant
FK->IS	H4	–0.232	–0.232	0.078	2.988	Negative and insignificant
FK->LS	H5	0.054	0.054	0.118	0.457	Positive and significant
FK->OTS	H6	0.409	0.408	0.110	3.711	Positive and significant
FK->T	H7	0.645	0.643	0.072	8.903	Positive and significant

It is imperative for governments and financial institutions to allocate resources towards the implementation of comprehensive financial education initiatives that cater to individuals across all age groups. These initiatives encompass a range of activities such as curriculum design, seminars, online materials, and community engagement aimed at enhancing individuals' financial literacy and understanding.

The implementation of financial education in schools should start at an early stage. The inclusion of financial ideas in the curriculum throughout the early stages of education facilitates the cultivation of positive financial habits and the acquisition of decision-making abilities among pupils. This, in turn, diminishes the probability of encountering financial difficulties in the future.

It is imperative for policymakers to implement regulatory frameworks and consumer protection measures in order to ensure the safeguarding of persons from financial goods and services that may possess a level of complexity beyond their full comprehension. Potential solutions that can be implemented are enhanced disclosure requirements, limitations on interest rates, and regulatory actions targeting predatory lending practices.

It is imperative for financial authorities to guarantee that financial institutions offer comprehensive and comprehensible information on their goods and services. This may encompass the process of establishing uniform language, costs, and conditions inside financial contracts, hence facilitating customers' ability to effectively evaluate various goods.

Governments have the capacity to institute default savings and retirement schemes for its employees, shown by the practice of automatically enrolling individuals in retirement savings accounts. This incentivizes individuals to engage in long-term financial planning, regardless of their low understanding of financial concepts.

Policymakers possess the capacity to facilitate the provision of accessible and reasonably priced financial counselling and advisory services that are impartial in nature, therefore assisting individuals in making well-informed choices pertaining to their finances. These services have the ability to provide individuals with guidance in the areas of debt management, retirement planning, and prudent investment strategies.

Periodic evaluations of the populace's financial literacy skills might facilitate the identification of domains necessitating further educational initiatives and interventions by policymakers. The aforementioned data has the potential to provide valuable insights for the development of tailored programmes.

Policymakers possess the ability to provide individuals various incentives aimed at improving their financial literacy, including tax benefits and employer-endorsed financial education initiatives. In addition, regulatory authorities should actively engage in the oversight of financial institutions to guarantee adherence to disclosure and transparency mandates. It is imperative to implement enforcement measures against institutions that participate in misleading or unfair practices.

It is imperative for policymakers to endorse and prioritize research endeavours aimed at assessing the efficacy of diverse financial education programmes and initiatives. Systematic assessments can aid in ascertaining the efficacy of various strategies in enhancing financial knowledge and behaviour.

7.11 Conclusion

Financial knowledge is a multifaceted area of study with significant implications for individuals, households, and society as a whole. The literature reviewed here underscores its importance, the various factors influencing it, and the ongoing efforts to enhance financial literacy and education to improve financial well-being and decision-making. Researchers and policymakers continue to explore ways to bridge the gaps in financial knowledge and promote greater financial literacy among diverse populations.

Furthermore, this study will shed light on the relationship between financial knowledge and financial inclusion in India, offering valuable insights for policymakers and stakeholders. By addressing the policy implications of enhancing financial knowledge, this research aims to contribute to more effective financial inclusion strategies and ultimately improve the financial well-being of India's diverse population.

Acknowledgements

We like to extend our heartfelt appreciation to all individuals who have made valuable contributions towards the successful completion of this research work. We would like to express our gratitude to our adviser, Dr. Firdous Malik, for their important counsel, knowledge, and continuous support throughout the study process. The guidance provided by their mentor significantly improved the calibre and comprehensiveness of their endeavour.

Conflict of Interest

No conflicts between the authors.

References

Aghion, P., & Bolton, P. (1997). A theory of trickle-down growth and development. *The Review of Economic Studies*, *64*(2), 151–172. https://econpapers.repec.org/article/ouprestud/v_3a64_3ay_3a1997_3ai_3a2_3ap_3a151-172.html

Allgood, S., & Walstad, W. B. (2016). The effects of perceived and actual financial literacy on financial behaviors. *Economic Inquiry*, *54*(1), 675–613. https://doi.org/10.1111/ecin.12255.

Asaad, C. T. (2015). Financial literacy and financial behavior: Assessing knowledge and confidence. *Financial Services Review*, *24*(2), 101–118.

Atkinson, A., & Messy, F. A. (2012). Measuring financial literacy: Results of the OECD/International network on financial education (INFE) pilot study. In OECD working papers on finance, insurance and private pensions. Paris: OECD Publishing.

Banerjee, A. V. (2001). Contracting Constraints, Credit Markets and Economic Development. Retrieved from https://papers.ssrn.com/sol3/papers.cfm?abstract_id=306990

Banerjee, A. V., & Newman, A. F. (1993). Occupational choice and the process of development. *Journal of Political Economy*, 101(2), 274–298. http://dx.doi.org/10.1086/261876

Beck, T., Demirguc-Kunt, A., & Honohan, P. (2009). Access to financial services: Measurement, impact, and policies. The World Bank Research Observer, *24*(1), 119–145. https://doi.org/10.1093/wbro/lkn008

Beck, T., Demirgüç-Kunt, A., & Levine, R. (2009). Financial Institutions and Markets Across Countries and Over Time - Data and Analysis. World Bank Policy Research Working Paper No. 4943, Available at SSRN: https://ssrn.com/abstract=1414705

Bernheim, B. D., Garrett, D. M., & Maki, D. M. (2001). Education and saving: The long-term effects of high school financial curriculum mandates. *Journal of Public Economics*, *80*(3), 435–465.

Binswanger, H. P., & Khandker, S. R. (1995). The impact of formal finance on the rural economy of India. *The Journal of Development Studies*, *32*(2), 234–262. https://doi.org/10.1080/00220389508422413

Borden, L. M., Lee, S.-A., Serido, J., & Collins, D. (2008). Changing college students' financial knowledge, attitudes, and behavior through seminar participation. *Journal of Family and Economic Issues*, *29*(1), 23–40. https://doi.org/10.1007/s10834-007-9087-2.

Burgess, R., & Pande, R. (2003). Do rural banks matter. Evidence from the Indian social banking experiment. Evidence from the Indian social banking experiment (August 2003), 2. https://core.ac.uk/download/pdf/7119523.pdf

Chithra, N., & Selvam, M. (2013). Determinants of Financial Inclusion: An Empirical Study on the Inter-State Variations in India. Available at SSRN: https://ssrn.com/abstract=2296096 or http://dx.doi.org/10.2139/ssrn.2296096

Cole, S., Sampson, T., & Zia, B. (2011). Prices or knowledge? What drives demand for financial services in emerging markets? *Journal of Finance*, *66*(6), 1933–1967.

Collins, J. M., & O'Rourke, C. M. (2010). Financial education and counseling—Still holding promise. *Journal of Consumer Affairs*, *44*(3), 483–498.

Fernandes, D., Lynch, J. G., & Netemeyer, R. G. (2014). Financial literacy, financial education, and downstream financial behaviors. *Management Science*, *60*(8), 1861–1883. https://doi.org/10.1287/mnsc.2013.1849.

Fessler, P., Silgoner, M., & Weber, R. (2020). Financial knowledge, attitude and behavior: Evidence from the Austrian Survey of Financial Literacy. *Empirica*, *47*, 929–947. https://doi.org/10.1007/s10663-019-09465-2.

Galton, F. (1889). Personal identification and description. *Journal of Anthropological Institute of Great Britain and Ireland*, *18*, 177–191.

Hair, J., F., Rolph, E. A., Barry J. B., & William, C. B. (2010). Multivariate data analysis: A global perspective (Vol. 7). Upper Saddle River: Pearson.

Keown, L.-A. (2011). The financial knowledge of Canadians. *Statistics Canada*, *11*, 1–12. http://en. copian.ca/library/research/stats/financial_knowl edge/financial_knowledge.pdf

Kim, K. T., Anderson, S. G., & Seay, M. C. (2019). Financial knowledge and short-term and long-term financial behaviors of millennials in the United States. *Journal of Family and Economic Issues*, *40*(2), 194–208. https://doi.org/10.1007/s10834-018-9595-2

Klapper, L., Lusardi, A., & van Oudheusden, P. (2015). Financial Literacy Around the World: Insights from the Standard & Poor's Ratings Services Global Financial Literacy Survey. Global Financial Development Report 2015/2016: Long-Term Finance, 141–157.

Lee, J. H., & Jun, S. Y. (2007). Factors influencing the adoption of internet banking: An integration of TAM and TPB with perceived risk and perceived benefit. *Electronic Commerce Research and Applications*, *6*(3), 182–193.

Leeladhar, V. (2006). RBI. https://rbidocs.rbi.org.in/rdocs/Bulletin/PDFs/68236.pdf

Levine, R. (1997). Financial development and economic growth: Views and agenda. *Journal of Economic Literature*, *35*, 688–726. https://www.researchgate.net/publication/4722931_Financial_Development_And_Economic_Growth_Views_And_Agenda

Lusardi, A., & Mitchell, O. S. (2007). Baby boomer retirement security: The role of planning, financial literacy, and housing wealth. *Journal of Monetary Economics*, *54*(1), 205–224.

Lusardi, A., Schneider, D. J., & Tufano, P. (2011). Financially fragile households: Evidence and implications. *Brookings Papers on Economic Activity*, *43*(2), 83–150.

Mountain, T. P., Kim, N., Serido, J., & Shim, S. (2020). Does type of financial learning matter for young Adults' objective financial knowledge and financial behaviors? A longitudinal and mediation analysis. *Journal of Family and Economic Issues*, *42*(1), 1–20 https://link.springer.com/article/10.1007/s10834-020-09689-6

Mullainathan, S., & Shafir, E. (2013). *Scarcity: Why having too little means so much*. London: Macmillan.

Pearson, K., & Lee, A. (1903). On the laws of inheritance in man: I. Inheritance of physical characters. *Biometrika*, *2*(4), 357–462.

Potrich, A. C. G., & Vieira, K. M. (2018). Demystifying financial literacy: A behavioral perspective analysis. *Management Research Review*, *41*(9), 1047–1068. https://doi.org/10.1108/MRR-08-2017-0263

Rangarajan Committee (2008). Report of the Committee on Financial Inclusion. Government of India.

RBI (2015). Report on the Committee on Medium-term Path on Financial Inclusion. December. https://rbidocs.rbi.org.in/rdocs/PublicationReport/Pdfs/FFIRA27F4530706A41A0BC394D01CB4892CC.PDF (last accessed on September 22, 2017).

Remund, D. L. (2010). Financial literacy explicated: The case for a clearer definition in an increasingly complex economy. *Journal of Consumer Affairs*, *44*(2), 276–295.

Robb, C. A., & Woodyard, A. S. (2011). Financial knowledge and best practice behavior. *Journal of Financial Counseling and Planning*, *22*(1), 60–70. https://psycnet.apa.org/record/2011-18553-005

Sarma, M. (1970). *Index of financial inclusion*. EconStor. https://www.econstor.eu/handle/10419/176233

Serrano-Cinca, C., Gutiérrez-Nieto, B., & López-Palacios, L. (2015). Determinants of mobile banking adoption in the case of Spain: A nationwide empirical study. *Telematics and Informatics*, *32*(1), 1–14.

Thaler, R. H., & Sunstein, C. R. (2008). *Nudge: Improving decisions about health, wealth, and happiness*. New Haven: Yale University Press.

Thavva, S. (2021). A study on financial literacy and financial behaviour. *ResearchGate*. https://www.researchgate.net/publication/349238535_A_Study_on_Financial_Literacy_and_Financial_Behaviour.

Tiwari, A., & Yadav, A. (2022). A study of financial literacy and financial behaviour among millennials and generation Z. Zenodo (CERN European Organization for Nuclear Research). https://doi.org/10.5281/zenodo.7251292.

Vinzi, V. E., Chin, W. W., Henseler, J., & Wang, H. (2010). Handbook of partial least squares: Concepts. Dordrecht: Springer Science & Business Media.

World Bank (2017). Financial Literacy in India: A Demand-Supply Gap Analysis.
Wright, S. (1920). The relative importance of heredity and environment in determining the piebald pattern of guinea-pigs. *Proceedings of the National Academy of Sciences*, *6*(6), 320–332.
Xiao J.J., & Porto, N. (2017). Financial education and financial satisfaction. *International Journal of Bank Marketing*. *35*(5):805–817. doi: 10.1108/IJBM-01-2016-0009.
Yunus, M. (1999). Banker to the Poor: Micro-Lending and the Battle Against World Poverty. USA: PublicAffairs.

8 From Empowerment to Inclusion

Unveiling the Path for Women in South Punjab (Pakistan)

Muhammad Ramzan Sheikh, Irfan Hussain, and Sana Sultan

8.1 Introduction

To improve financial inclusion and the socioeconomic development of countries, women's empowerment plays an essential role (Duflo, 2012). Financial inclusion, which is understood to be the availability and utilization of formal financial services by both individuals and enterprises, is a recognized fundamental factor in economic growth and the eradication of poverty (Demirgüç-Kunt & Klapper, 2012). On the other hand, women empowerment encloses the improvement of women's economic, social and political capabilities that enable them to participate in social, economic, and political activities and decision-making processes (Mehra, 1997). These two ideas come together to produce enormous advantages for economies and communities (Malik & Yadav, 2022).

Empowering women in terms of financial inclusion can lead to numerous significant benefits (Malik & Yadav, 2022b). It can help in ending the cycle of poverty by empowering women to accumulate wealth by saving, investing, and other means, thereby enhancing their own and their families' financial well-being (Duflo, 2012). The financial inclusion of women can benefit the whole economy by promoting innovation and entrepreneurship as well as a more equitable distribution of resources.

Women's involvement in financial decision-making has also been associated with better household financial management, better child health and education outcomes, and greater overall family welfare (Kabeer, 2005). Women who have access to financial services are better able to manage risks and deal with unforeseen circumstances, which in turn helps them be more resilient to economic shocks. Supporting women's financial inclusion can help advance social justice and gender equality (Arshad, 2023). Societies can lessen the likelihood that women will experience financial shocks and improve their ability to allocate resources wisely by enabling them to use formal financial services. Economic empowerment of women can end the cycle of intergenerational poverty and advance sustainable development.

Women's financial inclusion can also help keep financial systems resilient and stable overall. By encouraging a more equitable distribution of financial resources and lowering the concentration of financial operations, a diversified and inclusive

DOI: 10.4324/9781032655185-12

financial landscape that actively includes women, can reduce systemic risks (Siddik, 2017). Women's empowerment not only promotes a more fair society but also improves the economy as a whole by increasing its resilience to shocks. As a result, supporting women's financial inclusion is not only a matter of social justice but also a crucial strategic move in the development of more reliable and long-lasting financial institutions (Aziz et al., 2022).

Financial inclusion and women's empowerment are related, with each strengthening the advantages of the other. Financial inclusion for women provides significant advantages for economic development, poverty reduction, and gender equality (Malik et al., 2020). Achieving both individual and community prosperity requires acknowledging the significance of women's active engagement in economic activities and granting them equitable access to financial services (Bhatia & Singh, 2019).

The study holds significant importance as it pioneers an in-depth exploration of the less developed areas of South Punjab, Pakistan, shedding light on a critical but often overlooked aspect of development – women's financial inclusion and empowerment. By adopting the financial inclusion index as the dependent variable and encompassing a comprehensive array of independent variables such as women's social, political, and economic empowerment indices, educational awareness, sociocultural factors, regulatory and policy landscape, and technological infrastructure, the study offers a holistic understanding of the challenges and opportunities faced by women in the region. As South Punjab faces multifaceted developmental disparities, this study stands as a guiding beacon, providing actionable insights for policymakers, researchers, and stakeholders alike to formulate targeted interventions that can pave the way for gender-inclusive economic growth and social progress.

8.2 Literature Review

Table 8.1 shows the summary of the studies on women's empowerment and financial inclusion.

The literature on women empowerment and financial inclusion demonstrates that a variety of theoretical approaches, various sample sizes, and estimation methods are used. All the studies show that there is a positive link between women's empowerment and financial inclusion.

8.3 Conceptual Framework

In this section, we establish the conceptual framework that underpins our study, highlighting the key indicators of women's economic empowerment and their influence on financial inclusion. Figure 8.1 illustrates women's empowerment and other key determinants along with financial inclusion.

Women's economic, social, and political empowerment influence financial inclusion as suggested by feminist economic theory, human development theory, and social capital theory. The gender differences in economic opportunity, resources,

Table 8.1 Studies on the women's empowerment and financial inclusion

Reference(s)	*Country/area*	*Time Period/ observation*	*Methodology*	*Main results*
Islam (2014)	Bangladesh	One hundred and sixty women: 2012	Multiple regression analysis	In terms of income generation, saving motivation, the development of household assets, and overall poverty reduction, microcredit fostered financial inclusion and played a vital role in the empowerment of low-profile rural women
Saddik (2017)	Bangladesh	Five hundred rural women living in the Kurigram and Gaibandha district of Bangladesh for the year 2017	Preliminary analysis and Chi-square test	There is a positive relationship between financial inclusion and women's empowerment
Eton et al. (2018)	Lango sub-region, Northern Uganda	One hundred and twenty-six women	Chi-square test	There was an association between women's empowerment and financial inclusion
George and Thomachan (2018)	India	One hundred women: 2017	Chi-square test	There was an association between participation in decision-making, access to loans, access to insurance, and women's empowerment
Bhatia and Singh (2019)	Ludhiana, India	Two hundred and eighteen slums: 2018	One-way ANOVA	Financial inclusion positively affects women's social, political, and economic empowerment

(Continued)

Table 8.1 (Continued)

Reference(s)	*Country/area*	*Time Period/ observation*	*Methodology*	*Main results*
Aziz et al. (2022)	South Asian countries	Eight South Asian countries: 2004–2017	Multivariate model	Gender and the use of financial services seem to be closely associated and women are less likely than men to have a bank account in countries where religious constraints prevent them from working for a living
Jedi (2022)	Iraq	2011–2021	Descriptive statistics	The study found a strong relationship between financial inclusion and women empowerment in Iraq
Pal et al. (2022)	India	Seven hundred and seventy-four women: 2021	Logistic regression	Women's empowerment through financial inclusion is significantly influenced by their earning position, involvement in household financial decision-making, and participation in social welfare programs; nevertheless, the safety of their funds is seen as an inconsequential aspect
Ghosh (2022)	India	Twenty-two areas: 2013–2015	Cragg-Double hurdle model	Political empowerment improves financial inclusion
Arshad (2023)	Developing countries	2004–2019	GGM estimation method	The influence of financial inclusion on women's empowerment is positive

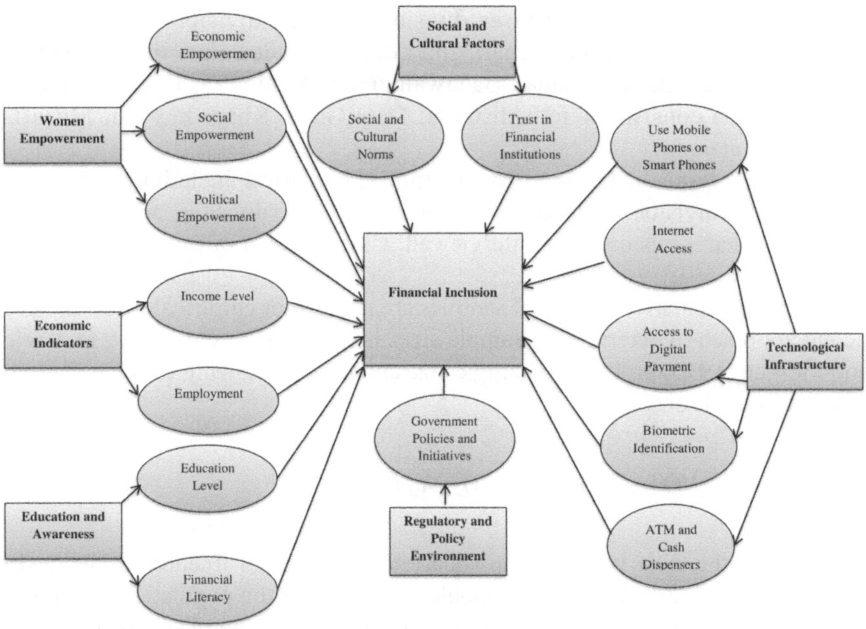

Figure 8.1 Key indicators and their direct impact on financial inclusion

and decision-making authority are highlighted by feminist economics. Women's economic empowerment, including income generating and asset ownership, is considered a way to strengthen women's autonomy in financial concerns and to challenge established gender norms. According to the human development concept, empowering people – including women – leads to societal advancement in general. People's capacities are improved by empowerment in the economic, social, and political realms, and this has a favorable effect on their access to necessities like financial resources, healthcare, and education. The ability to manage one's finances, interact with financial institutions, and contribute to economic progress is improved for empowered women. According to social capital theory, community ties, trust, and social networks are important for facilitating access to opportunities and resources. The social empowerment of women via knowledge and awareness improves their capacity to connect with others, learn about financial services, and make wise financial decisions. These networks can be a great help in negotiating the financial system's intricacies.

8.4 Data Source and Sampling Design

Primary sources are used to gather the data for the present study. Data for this study are taken from a survey of the Multan, Bahawalpur, and DG Khan Divisions of South Punjab (Pakistan). We have used the proportional sampling method in this work. The population sample is drawn from eleven randomly chosen rural areas across all three divisions. Multan division consists of four districts: Multan, Khanewal, Vehari, and Lodhran. Bahawalpur division consists of three districts: Bahawalnagar, Bahawalpur, and Rahim Yar Khan. Dera Ghazi Khan division consists of four districts: Dera Ghazi Khan, Layyah, Muzaffargarh, and Rajanpur.

In the 11 rural areas, 384 women from 11 districts including 135 women from Multan division, 121 women from Bahawalpur division, and 128 women from DG Khan division were interviewed. Closed-ended questions make up the questionnaire.

Since representative statistical samples are needed for empirical research, an efficient approach to determining sample sizes is required. To close the gap, Krejcie and Morgan (1970) produced a sample size chart. The following formula is used to calculate sample size:

$$s = X^2 NP(1-P) + d^2(N-1) + X^2 P(1-P)$$

where X^2 is the table value of Chi-square for 1 degree of freedom at the desired confidence level (3.841), N is the population size, P is the population portion (assumed to be 0.50 since this would provide the maximum sample size), and d is the degree of accuracy expressed as a proportion (0.05).

By using the Krejcie and Morgan (1970) formula, which recommends that 384 is the sample size to estimate the sample size for a finite population of 1000000 or more, we have determined the sample size (Table 8.2). To determine the proportionate sample size, the following formula is used:

$$S = \frac{Rural\ Population\ in\ division_i}{Total\ Population\ in\ all\ Divisions} \times 384$$

8.5 Model Specification and Methodology

The following model illustrates the factors influencing financial inclusion, encompassing variables including the women's social empowerment index, women's political empowerment index, and women's economic empowerment index, as well

Table 8.2 Sample size determination

Division	*Rural population*	*Sample size (based on rural population)*	*Sample taken in actual*
Multan	6,263,028	6,263,028/17,852,980 × 384 = 135	140
Bahawalpur	5,629,048	5,629,048/17,852,980 × 384 = 121	130
DG Khan	5,960,904	5,960,904/17,852,980 × 384 = 128	130
Total population in all divisions	17,852,980	384	410

as a composite of economic indicators, educational awareness, social and cultural dynamics, regulatory and policy frameworks, and technological infrastructure.

$$\text{FI} = \text{f}\begin{pmatrix} \text{WEEI, WSEI, WPEI, INC, EMP, EDU, FINL, SCN, TFI, GPI,} \\ \text{MOB, INT, DPP, BIOI, ATM} \end{pmatrix} \tag{8.1}$$

The econometric form of the model is:

$$\begin{aligned} \text{FI} = {} & \beta_0 + \beta_1\text{WEEI} + \beta_2\text{WSEI} + \beta_3\text{WPEI} + \beta_4\text{INC} + \beta_5\text{EMP} + \beta_6\text{EDU} \\ & + \beta_7\text{FINL} + \beta_8\text{SCN} + \beta_9\text{TFI} + \beta_{10}\text{GPI} + \beta_{11}\text{MOB} + \beta_{12}\text{INT} \\ & + \beta_{13}\text{DPP} + \beta_{14}\text{BIOI} + \beta_{15}\text{ATM} + \varepsilon \end{aligned} \tag{8.2}$$

The study uses ordinary least square (OLS) technique to estimate the above model. Table 8.3 shows the abbreviation, description and measurement of variables used in this study.

8.6 Results and Discussions

8.6.1 An Elementary Data Analysis

In this section, we delve into an introductory exploration of data analysis, laying the foundation for deeper insights and understanding in the following sections.

Table 8.4 reveals a distinct pattern in women's empowerment levels across the economic, social, and political dimensions in South Punjab. Women classified as having "No Empowerment" exhibit the highest counts in all three dimensions: economic (80), social (81), and political (101).

As empowerment increases, the counts decrease consistently. Remarkably, the transition from "Less Empowerment" to "Empowerment" sees a reduction in counts for each dimension, indicating a shift toward higher empowerment. The trend continues as empowerment levels rise, with the lowest counts observed in the "Highly Empowerment" category. The patterns observed in Table 8.4 are visually reinforced by the corresponding pie charts in Figures 8.2–8.4.

Table 8.5 analyzes the counts for women's empowerment distribution in Multan across economic, social, and political dimensions. The table reveals a mixed scenario of women's empowerment in the Multan region across the three dimensions. While the majority of women fall into the "Moderate Empowerment" category across all three aspects, it is noteworthy that a smaller number of women are classified as "Highly Empowered" in economic, social, and political spheres.

On the other hand, a considerable portion of women still face limited empowerment, as indicated by the counts in the "No Empowerment" and "Less Empowerment" categories. This suggests that efforts may be needed to enhance women's

Table 8.3 Variables: abbreviation, description, and measurement

Variables	*Abbreviation*	*Description of variables*	*Measurement*
Financial inclusion	FI	It represents the mean of five indicators that have been assessed on a binary scale of 0 and 1	Continuous
Women economic empowerment index	WEEI	It is the average of ten indicators that have been on a binary scale of 0 and 1	Continuous
Women social empowerment index	WSEI	It represents the average of seven indicators that have been evaluated on a binary scale of 0 and 1	Continuous
Women political empowerment index	WPEI	It denotes the mean of eight indicators that have been estimated on a binary scale of 0 and 1	Continuous
Income level	INC	It refers to a woman's earnings from various sources.	Continuous
Employment	EMP	A woman is engaged in paid work or occupation to earn a living.	0 for unemployed 1 for employed
Financial literacy	FINL	It is the capacity to understand and manage financial matters of a woman	0 for No 1 for Yes
Social and cultural norms	SCN	It signifies the mean of two indicators that have been appraised using a binary scale of 0 and 1	Continuous
Trust in financial institutions	TFI	Whether the woman has trust in the financial institution or not	0 for No 1 for Yes
Government policies and interventions	GPI	Whether the government implements initiatives to improve access to financial services for underserved populations	0 for No 1 for Yes
Use mobile phones and smart phones	MOB	Whether a woman uses mobile phones and smartphones	0 for No 1 for Yes
Internet access	INT	Whether a woman has access to internet services or not	0 for No 1 for Yes
Access to digital payment platform	DPP	Whether a woman has access to a digital payment platform or not	0 for No 1 for Yes
Biometric identification	BIOI	It represents the mean of two indicators that have been assessed on a binary scale of 0 and 1	Continuous
ATMs and cash dispensers	ATM	It represents the mean of four indicators that have been assessed on a binary scale of 0 and 1	Continuous

Table 8.4 Distribution of women empowerment in South Punjab

Status	*Economic*	*Social*	*Political*
No empowerment	80	81	101
Less empowerment	75	85	98
Empowerment	68	69	66
Moderate empowerment	109	115	56
Highly empowerment	52	34	63

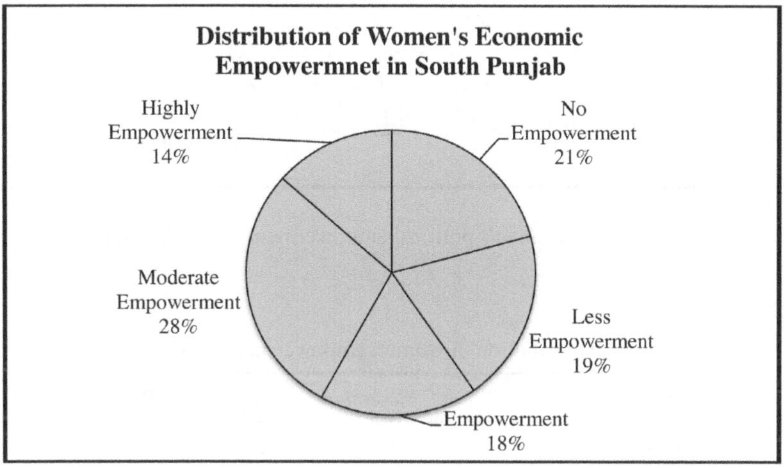

Figure 8.2 Distribution of women's economic empowerment in South Punjab

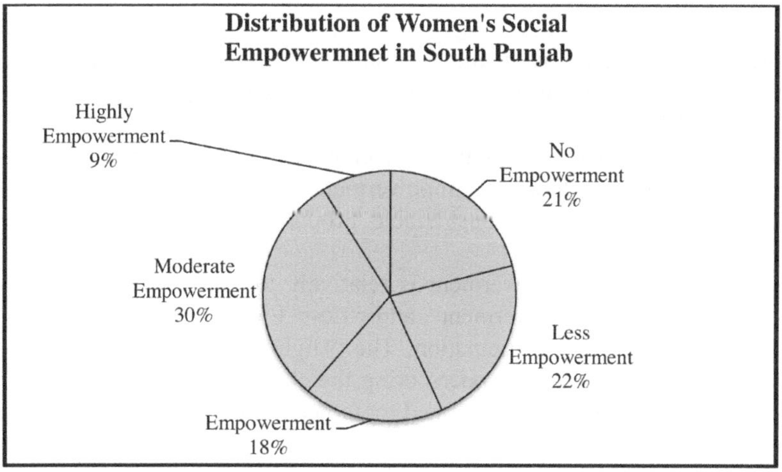

Figure 8.3 Distribution of women's social empowerment in South Punjab

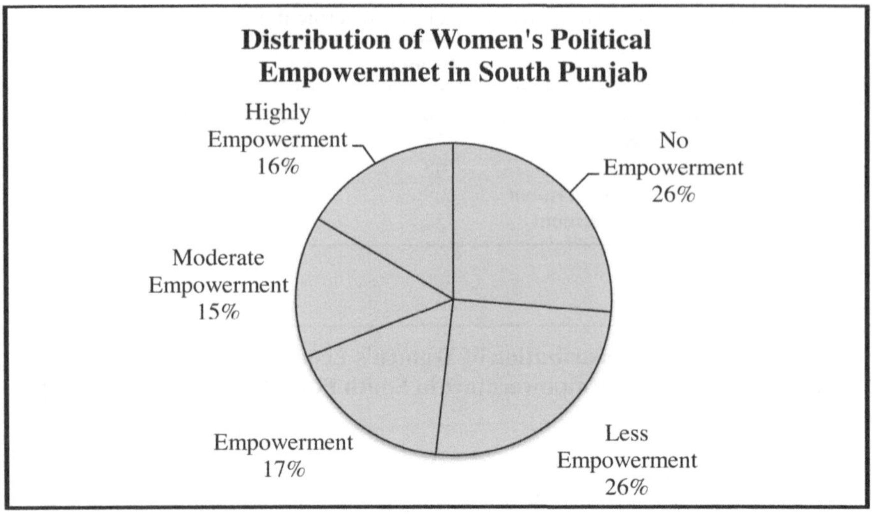

Figure 8.4 Distribution of women's political empowerment in South Punjab

Table 8.5 Distribution of women empowerment in Multan

Status	*Economic*	*Social*	*Political*
No empowerment	24	25	32
Less empowerment	22	27	32
Empowerment	21	15	22
Moderate empowerment	62	57	31
Highly empowerment	6	11	18

empowerment, particularly in the economic and political domains. The trends identified in Table 8.5 find visual validation through the pie charts presented in Figures 8.5–8.7.

Table 8.6 illustrates distinct patterns in women's empowerment distribution within Bahawalpur. "Moderate Empowerment" is prominent in economic and social aspects, indicating a considerable proportion experiencing intermediate empowerment.

However, political empowerment is relatively lower, with most women falling under the "No Empowerment" and "Less Empowerment" categories, reflecting limited political participation. The "Highly Empowerment" category is consistently less represented, underscoring the challenges in achieving extensive empowerment. This highlights the need for targeted efforts to enhance political engagement and elevate empowerment levels for women in Bahawalpur. The trends discerned from Table 8.6 find visual confirmation through the pie charts presented in Figures 8.8–8.10.

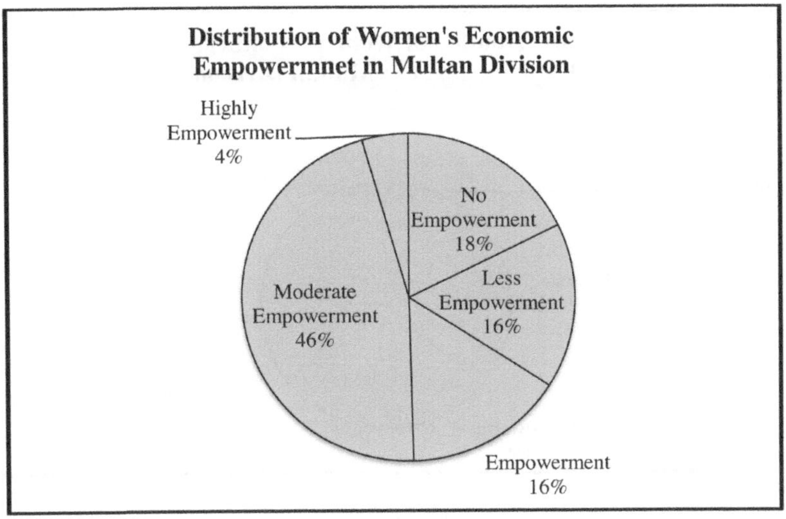

Figure 8.5 Distribution of women's economic empowerment in Multan division

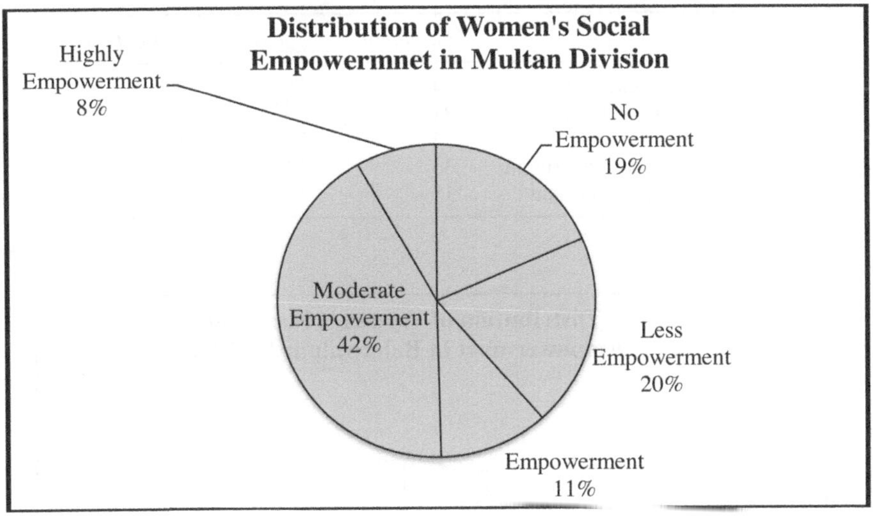

Figure 8.6 Distribution of women's social empowerment in Multan division

Table 8.7 outlines the distribution of women's empowerment in DG Khan across economic, social, and political dimensions and uncovers intriguing insights. The pattern of empowerment distribution in DG Khan appears distinct from the Bahawalpur region. In terms of economic and social empowerment, "Less Empowerment" is prevalent, suggesting that a substantial number of women possess limited influence in these domains.

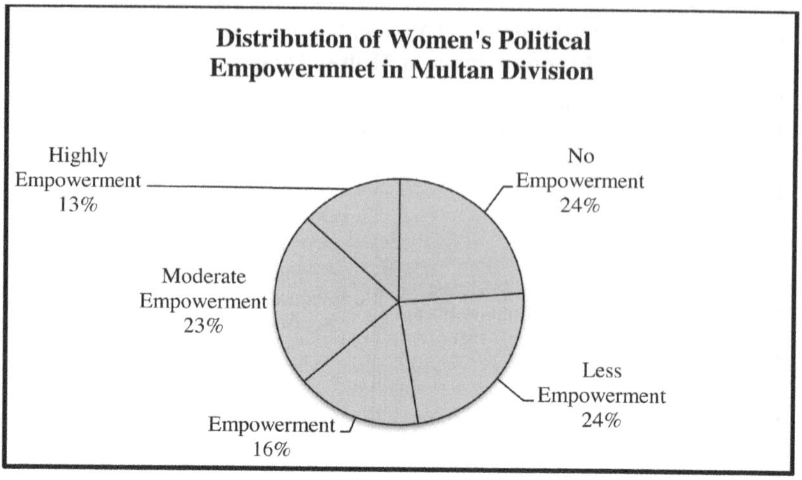

Figure 8.7 Distribution of women's political empowerment in Multan division

Table 8.6 Distribution of women empowerment in Bahawalpur

Status	*Economic*	*Social*	*Political*
No empowerment	24	25	34
Less empowerment	21	27	33
Empowerment	23	23	21
Moderate empowerment	35	34	17
Highly empowerment	18	12	16

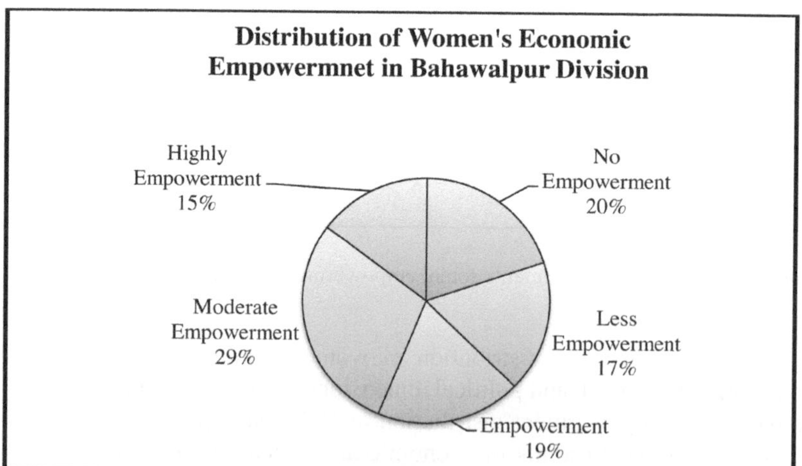

Figure 8.8 Distribution of women's economic empowerment in Bahawalpur division

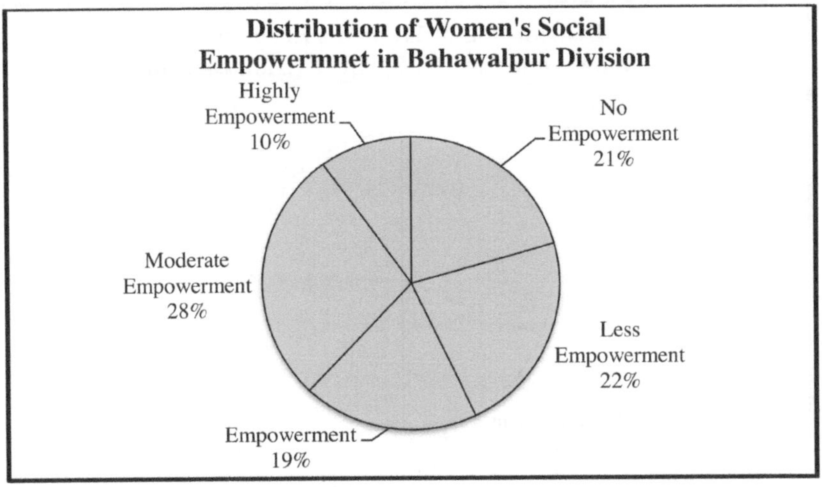

Figure 8.9 Distribution of women's social empowerment in Bahawalpur division

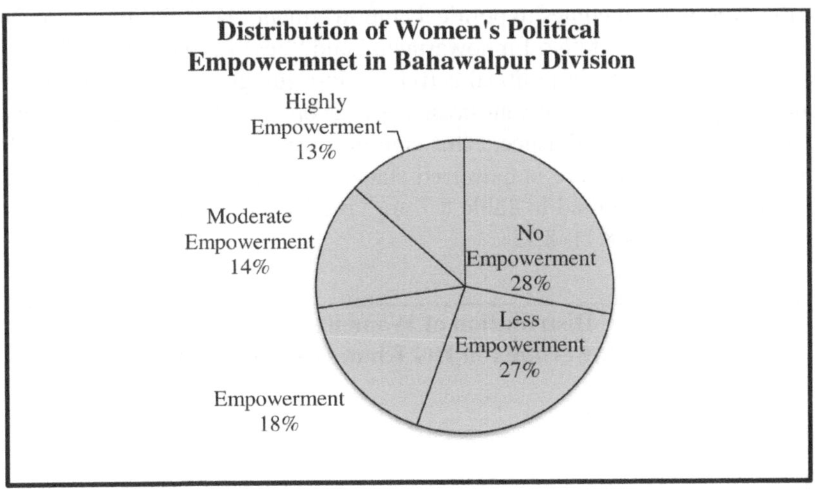

Figure 8.10 Distribution of women's political empowerment in Bahawalpur division

Table 8.7 Distribution of women empowerment in DG Khan

Status	*Economic*	*Social*	*Political*
No empowerment	32	31	35
Less empowerment	32	31	33
Empowerment	24	31	23
Moderate empowerment	12	24	8
Highly empowerment	28	11	29

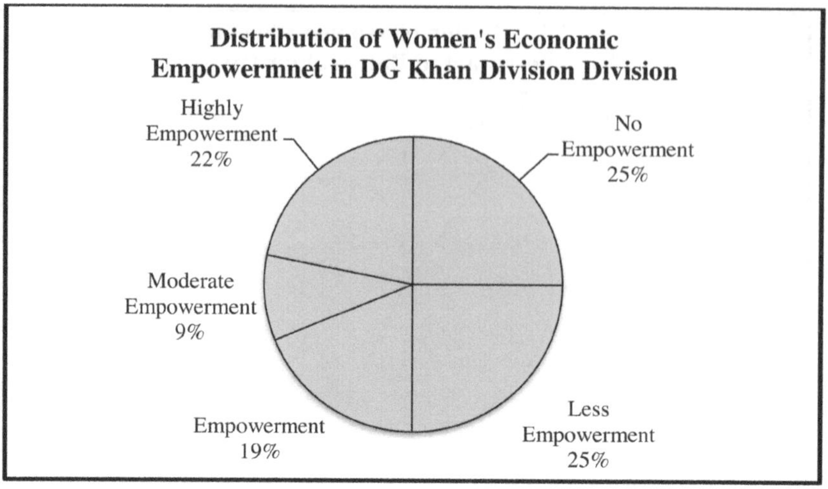

Figure 8.11 Distribution of women's economic empowerment in DG Khan division

However, when it comes to political empowerment, the majority of women fall under the categories of "No Empowerment" and "Less Empowerment," implying restricted participation in political activities. Intriguingly, the "Highly Empowerment" category has a significant presence in economic and political aspects, but not as much in the social aspect. This signifies a potential economic and political inclination toward a more empowered status for some women in the DG Khan area. The trends identified in Table 8.7 are visually underscored by the pie charts presented in Figures 8.11–8.13

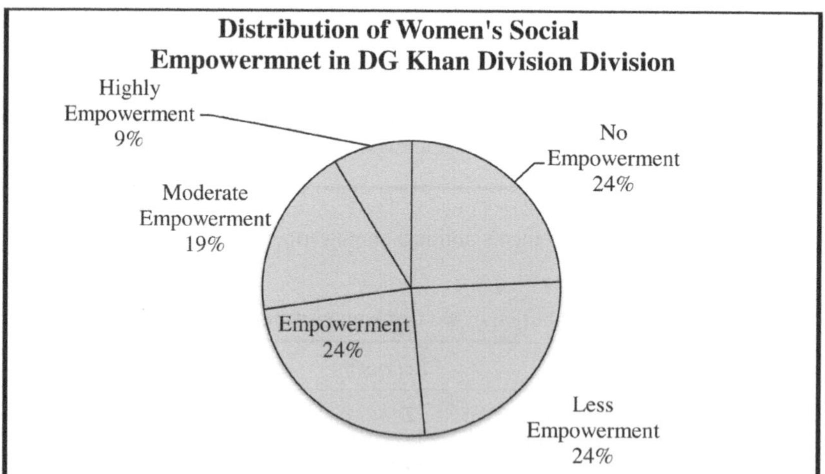

Figure 8.12 Distribution of women's social empowerment in DG Khan division

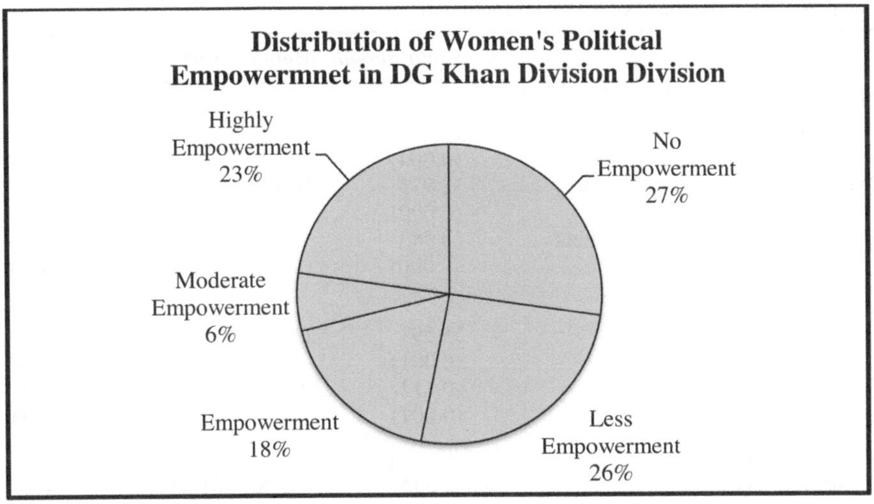

Figure 8.13 Distribution of women's political empowerment in DG Khan division

8.6.2 Econometric Analysis of the Determinants of Financial Inclusion

After performing an elementary analysis, we have conducted an econometric analysis. The OLS regression analysis is used to investigate the impact on financial inclusion. Table 8.8 presents the determinants of financial inclusion across different regions. Women's economic, social, and political empowerment is positively associated with financial inclusion across all regions, and this relationship is highly statistically significant.

A possible reason for this is that economic empowerment gives women the abilities, opportunities, and resources they need to fully engage in economic activity. Women are better able to invest in businesses that generate income, amass assets, and develop financial resilience when they get access to financial services like credit, savings, and insurance. Economic empowerment increases women's capacity to interact with formal financial institutions, boosting their financial inclusion (Duflo, 2012; Kabeer, 2005). Women can participate more actively in decision-making processes within their households and communities through transforming gender norms as part of social empowerment. Women are more likely to be acknowledged as genuine economic agents as their social status rises, making it easier for them to acquire financial services. According to studies by Malhotra et al. (2002) and Duflo (2012), social empowerment enables women to efficiently navigate and use financial resources, supporting their financial inclusion.

The participation of women in political processes and their representation in decision-making bodies are essential components of political empowerment. Marginalized women will gain from policies and activities encouraging financial inclusion that are more likely to be developed and put into practice as the political influence of women increases. Women's greater political participation promotes policies that

Table 8.8 Determinants of financial inclusion

Variables	*South Punjab*	*Multan*	*Bahawalpur*	*DG Khan*
Women's empowerment				
Women's economic empowerment	12.765	3.661	13.003	6.930
	(0.004)	(0.073)	(0.005)	(0.000)
Women's social empowerment	12.975	18.903	11.772	11.280
	(0.000)	(0.003)	(0.000)	(0.000)
Women's political empowerment	8.543	7.843	2.671	6.669
	(0.000)	(0.001)	(0.003)	(0.001)
Economic indicators				
Income level	25.591	23.126	18.450	19.352
	(0.001)	(0.000)	(0.000)	(0.000)
Employment	0.112	0.132	0.156	0.213
	(0.001)	(0.003)	(0.000)	(0.013)
Education and awareness				
Education level	2.345	1.970	1.652	1.431
	(0.001)	(0.020)	(0.030)	(0.021)
Financial literacy	4.907	4.743	3.187	1.207
	(0.000)	(0.000)	(0.000)	(0.008)
Social and cultural factors				
Social and cultural norms	5.765	3.966	3.517	3.964
	(0.004)	(0.000)	(0.000)	(0.008)
Trust in financial institutions	0.907	0.704	0.456	0.345
	(0.001)	(0.010)	(0.032)	(0.065)
Regulatory and policy environment				
Government policies and initiatives	3.225	3.125	2.698	2.449
	(0.000)	(0.001)	(0.000)	(0.000)
Technological infrastructure				
Use of mobile phones and smart phones	0.995	0.105	0.102	0.552
	(0.001)	(0.000)	(0.0001)	(0.000)
Internet access	0.812	0.673	0.601	0.769
	(0.000)	(0.009)	(0.000)	(0.000)
Access to digital payment platforms	0.927	0.355	0.402	0.858
	(0.000)	(0.000)	(0.000)	(0.000)
Biometric identification	5.699	4.407	4.515	4.635
	(0.000)	(0.000)	(0.000)	(0.000)
ATMs and cash dispensers	4.978	3.225	2.227	2.265
	(0.040)	(0.060)	(0.090)	(0.020)
Model summary				
Model	*R-Square*		*Durbin-Watson*	
	0.290		1.717	

address gender-based barriers and help to create an atmosphere that is supportive of financial inclusion (Chatterjee & Duflo, 2004; Ghosh, 2022).

Financial inclusion, a pivotal aspect of economic development, is positively influenced by women's income levels in all regions which is highly statistically significant (Malik et al., 2021). People tend to be more financially literate as their income increases, which allows them to make wise judgments about formal financial services like savings accounts, investments, and insurance (Grohmann et al., 2018). A person's ability to meet collateral criteria for loans is also made possible by an increase in income (Demirguc-Kunt & Klapper, 2012). This makes it easier for them to get credit from formal financial institutions. This encourages investment and entrepreneurship, which helps the economy expand.

Higher income levels also increase demand for a variety of financial services. Financial institutions have increased their product selection to meet the needs of customers with higher incomes since they need a wider range of financial products (Beck et al., 2007a). In this setting, initiatives designed to increase income levels can significantly support financial inclusion, enabling people to successfully utilize formal financial services and promoting economic growth.

Employment is playing a positive impact in promoting financial inclusion which is highly statistically significant in all regions, contributing to enhanced access to and usage of financial services among individuals and households. People are more able to interact with conventional financial institutions like banks and credit unions as they establish stable sources of income through work. They are better able to get credit, open and keep bank accounts, save money, invest it, and manage their money more skillfully because of their greater financial stability (Malik & Yadav, 2022a). Furthermore, work frequently promotes financial education and awareness by exposing people to the numerous financial goods and services available, giving them the knowledge and authority to decide what is best for their financial well-being. According to a study by Demirgüç et al. (2012), those who are employed are more likely to have access to formal financial services, demonstrating the link between financial inclusion and employment. Beebe (2020) emphasized the link between employment possibilities and increased engagement in the formal financial sector in a similar manner.

Education level has been shown to have a positive influence on financial inclusion in all regions which is highly statistically significant, mainly because of its complex effects on people's financial knowledge, talents, and decision-making ability. People who have completed more schooling are better able to comprehend financial ideas, traverse complex financial systems, and make wise financial decisions (Hastings et al., 2013). Education also promotes analytical thinking, which helps people evaluate different financial products and services, find good options, and stay away from predatory tactics (Cole & Shastry, 2009). Education also encourages digital literacy, which is important for gaining access to and using contemporary digital financial tools, platforms, and services that are essential to boosting financial inclusion. Moreover, educated people are more likely to be aware of their financial rights and obligations, which boosts their confidence when interacting with financial organizations and services (Lusardi & Mitchell, 2011).

Financial literacy level indeed exerts a positive influence on financial inclusion in all regions which is highly statistically significant. There are several associated causes behind this occurrence. First of all, people who have greater levels of financial literacy are better able to comprehend and circumnavigate the complexities of financial products and services, empowering them to make wise choices regarding their financial well-being (Lusardi & Mitchell, 2011). As a result, they are more likely to use different financial instruments including credit, insurance, and savings accounts, increasing their access to the established financial system. Improved financial literacy encourages better money management techniques by encouraging saving and investing habits (Hastings et al., 2013). As a result, people are more likely to engage in banking operations and look for ways to accumulate wealth. Last but not least, higher financial confidence is frequently accompanied by increased financial literacy, lowering the psychological obstacles that may prevent people from seeking out financial services (Cole & Shastry, 2009).

Social and cultural norms have a positive impact on financial inclusion by influencing people's attitudes, behaviors, and choices on how they access and use financial services. These conventions foster a climate where community members are encouraged to participate financially. Shared values, attitudes, and practices that place a premium on financial security and stability frequently catalyze the acceptance of inclusive financial practices. For instance, financial inclusion might be viewed as a way to improve the welfare of the entire society in collectivist countries, where social assistance is highly prized. Cultural values that encourage collaboration, reciprocity, and trust might increase the use of financial services since people are more willing to transact when they feel safe and comfortable. Cultural values that value saving money for the future and supporting family members may encourage people to use financial services like insurance and savings accounts, which will strengthen their financial resilience. It is important to match financial programs and regulations with local cultural contexts to promote more inclusivity, as evidenced by the beneficial association between social and cultural norms and financial inclusion.

Financial inclusion is being positively facilitated by trust in financial institutions, which increases people's willingness to interact with and use formal financial services. Trust encourages underbanked and unbanked populations to participate in the established financial system. People are more inclined to open bank accounts, apply for credit, and use other financial products and services when they believe that financial institutions are trustworthy and open. Numerous causes can be identified for this occurrence. First off, trust maintains the confidentiality of personal and financial information and reduces perceived dangers related to financial transactions. Second, people are more likely to spend money on financial education and seek advice from organizations they trust, which results in better financial literacy and decision-making. Furthermore, trust can lessen the stigma attached to asking for financial aid, encouraging marginalized and vulnerable communities to utilize financial services without worrying about being taken advantage of. Because of this, increasing financial inclusion and fostering socioeconomic growth depend on fostering trust in financial institutions (Lusardi & Mitchell, 2011).

Government programs and policies positively affect financial inclusion which is highly statistically significant, because they improve underprivileged and marginalized groups' access to financial resources and services. People and communities are more likely to interact with and participate in formal financial institutions when they have faith in their government's commitment to equitable economic development. By encouraging people to use government-provided banking services, savings programs, and credit choices, trust fosters a climate that makes it less likely that they will turn to unofficial, frequently exploitative financial arrangements. This phenomenon has its roots in the idea of social capital, according to which trust in governmental institutions fosters cooperation, lowers transaction costs, and makes it easier to disseminate information, which raises financial literacy and awareness. Specifically targeted programs including subsidized credit programs, mobile banking services, and microfinance schemes have demonstrated greater success in expanding financial inclusion in nations with higher levels of government confidence, as demonstrated by transparent and effective policies. This successful partnership serves as a reminder of the value of trust as a motivator for expanding financial inclusion, supporting inclusive economic growth, and assisting in the eradication of poverty.

The variable presence of technological infrastructure, such as bank offices and ATMs, which are crucial for providing financial services, is a major factor in this issue. According to Kunt and Klapper (2012), proximity to these facilities is essential since it lowers the obstacles to accessing financial services, particularly in remote or rural locations. Geographical location can also impact the accessibility of digital infrastructure, such as cell networks and internet connectivity, which are crucial for enabling mobile banking and other digital financial services. The importance of digital access in increasing financial inclusion, especially in areas with few brick-and-mortar banking options, is highlighted by research by Suri and Jack (2016). In addition, cultural and contextual elements linked to geography might affect financial attitudes and behaviors. For instance, local norms and traditions can affect people's desire to interact with official financial institutions, according to Zeller and Sharma (1998). Additionally, being close to economic centers and markets might make it easier for people to find work and generate income, improving their financial capacities and increasing their likelihood of participating in the formal financial system (Beck et al., 2007b).

Due to their broad use and adoption in many economies, mobile phones and smartphones have considerably improved financial inclusion. Several important variables contribute to the phenomena of mobile phones favorably promoting financial inclusion. First, mobile phones offer an affordable and effective platform for delivering financial services to underserved people, making it possible for them to have access to fundamental banking, payment systems, and other financial tools. This is especially true in underdeveloped nations with weak traditional banking infrastructure. Second, the widespread use of mobile devices eliminates geographical obstacles and lessens the need for physical presence at brick-and-mortar branches, enabling quick and convenient access to financial services. Digital wallets and mobile banking apps make it easier to complete transactions and send money, encouraging savings and building a culture of sound money management. Additionally, through educational apps and content, mobile phones support campaigns to promote financial literacy, equipping users with the knowledge they need to make wise financial decisions. Mobile technology and financial inclusion have a synergistic link that has been extensively researched and accepted (Aker & Mbiti, 2010; Jack & Suri, 2014). Conclusion: by facilitating access, convenience, and education and bridging the gap between informal and formal financial systems, mobile phone and smartphone use has significantly affected financial inclusion.

Access to the internet positively influences financial inclusion in all regions which is highly statistically significant, through improved financial literacy and easy access to financial services. People no longer need to be physically close to traditional banks to use digital banking, mobile payments, and online lending platforms because of internet access (Sanderson et al., 2018). Additionally, a variety of financial knowledge and educational materials are available online, enabling people to manage their money and make wise financial decisions (Lusardi & Mitchell, 2011).

Access to digital payment platforms has positively influenced financial inclusion in all regions which is highly statistically significant. Digital payment systems offer a practical and affordable solution for people to handle their financial services, particularly in underdeveloped or rural places. They make it possible for customers to conduct transactions, manage their finances, and obtain credit without relying on conventional brick-and-mortar banks. Research, such as a Kunt et al. (2018) study, which discovered that digital payments boost access to financial services among the unbanked population, supports this. Additionally, digital payment systems minimize transaction costs and entry barriers, promoting broader financial inclusion, according to the World Bank Group (2019).

Biometric identification positively influences financial inclusion in all places which is highly statistically significant. By offering a safe and practical way to verify people's identities, biometric technologies, like fingerprint or iris scanning, improve financial accessibility, particularly in areas with limited access to conventional identification documents or where illiteracy rates are high (Aker & Mbiti, 2010). Biometric identification makes it easier for those without official identification to access financial services by lowering fraud, streamlining the account opening procedure, and facilitating transactions (Karlan & Zinman, 2011). Providing banking services to disadvantaged people promotes financial inclusion and aids in the decrease of poverty and the expansion of the economy.

ATMs and cash dispensers positively influence financial inclusion in all places which is highly statistically significant. Particularly in remote or underdeveloped areas, these facilities offer more convenience and ease of access to financial services. They promote a sense of economic involvement by making it possible for people without traditional bank accounts to carry out essential financial operations like cash withdrawals and balance checks. The idea of physical access as a foundational element of financial inclusion and this reality is consistent. Further research supports the critical function of ATMs in fostering financial inclusion by showing a correlation between increased ATM density and better financial access and usage (Fanta & Makina, 2019).

8.7 Conclusions

In conclusion, the study delves into the intricate relationship between women empowerment and financial inclusion within the rural areas of South Punjab (Pakistan). By using a comprehensive approach that took into account social, political, and economic aspects of empowerment, we examined data gathered from 384 women across 11 chosen rural areas. The findings show a strong relationship between women's empowerment and their ability to access financial services. Women who have higher degrees of authority and control throughout the range of social, political, and economic empowerment are more likely to reap benefits from financial services. This link emphasizes the interconnectedness of women's financial well-being and their diverse empowerment.

The study also has pinpointed important factors that significantly influence women's financial inclusion in South Punjab. Economic factors such as income and employment prospects have emerged as key enablers for promoting women's engagement with formal financial systems. Education and awareness play a vital role that enabling women to navigate financial inclusion. Furthermore, it is discovered that social and cultural dynamics have a substantial impact on how capable women are of making decisions and having financial independence.

8.8 Policy Implications

However, regulatory policies and technological infrastructure have also proven to be significant determinants of financial inclusion. In addition to technological improvements like mobile banking and digital payment systems, policies encouraging gender equality and financial inclusion are essential for closing the financial gender gap. The following policy implications are suggested:

- The policymakers may implement a framework for policy that includes support for women-centric entrepreneurship, accessible banking services, and targeted financial education for women.
- To improve women's access to formal financial institutions, property rights should be strengthened and women's organizations should be involved.
- The planners may devise policies to adopt digital platforms, spread the word, and promote broader financial inclusion to give women more economic power.

Acknowledgments

The authors are grateful for comments from two anonymous referees. "We would also like to inform that as authors, we did not receive any funding for this research project."

Disclosure Statement

No potential conflict of interest was reported by the authors.

References

Ahmad Malik, F., & Yadav, D. K. (2022a). Financial inclusion schemes and changing socio economic status of poorest of the poor. In *Financial inclusion schemes in India* (pp. 109–130). Singapore: Springer Nature Singapore.

Ahmad Malik, F., & Yadav, D. K. (2022b). Impact of recent financial inclusion schemes on status of financial inclusion in India: Secondary data analysis. In *Financial inclusion schemes in India* (pp. 37–51). Singapore: Springer Nature Singapore.
Aker, J. C., & Mbiti, I. M. (2010). Mobile phones and economic development in Africa. *Journal of Economic Perspectives*, *24*(3), 207–232.
Arshad, A. (2023). Nexus between financial inclusion and women empowerment: Evidence from developing countries. *Gender in Management: An International Journal*, *38*(4), 561–580.
Aziz, F., Sheikh, S. M., & Shah, I. H. (2022). Financial inclusion for women empowerment in South Asian countries. *Journal of Financial Regulation and Compliance*, *30*(4), 489–502.
Beck, T., Demirgüç-Kunt, A., & Levine, R. (2007a). Finance, inequality and the poor. *Journal of Economic Growth*, *12*, 27–49.
Beck, T., Demirguc-Kunt, A., & Peria, M. S. M. (2007b). Reaching out: Access to and use of banking services across countries. *Journal of Financial Economics*, *85*(1), 234–266.
Beebe, N. H. (2020). A complete bibliography of publications in computer networks (Amsterdam, Netherlands: 2010–2019).
Beebe, B. (2022). "Shut Up and Take My Money!": Revenue Chokepoints, Platform Governance, and Sex Workers' Financial Exclusion. *International Journal of Gender, Sexuality and Law*, *2*(1), 140–170.
Bhatia, S., & Singh, S. (2019). Empowering women through financial inclusion: A study of urban slum. *Vikalpa*, *44*(4), 182–197.
Cole, S. A., & Shastry, G. K. (2009). *Smart money: The effect of education, cognitive ability, and financial literacy on financial market participation* (pp. 09–071). Boston: Harvard Business School.
Demirguç-Kunt, A., & Klapper, L. F. (2012). Financial inclusion in Africa: An overview. *World Bank policy research working paper* (6088).
Duflo, E. (2012). Women empowerment and economic development. *Journal of Economic Literature*, *50*(4), 1051–1079.
Eton, M., Mwosi, F., Ogwel, B. P., Edaku, C., & Obote, D. (2018). Financial inclusion and women empowerment in Uganda a case of Lango Sub Region, Northern Uganda. *Economics, Commerce and Trade Management: An International Journal (ECTIJ)*, *2*(1), 1–11.
Fanta, A. B., & Makina, D. (2019). The relationship between technology and financial inclusion: Cross-sectional evidence. In *Extending financial inclusion in Africa* (pp. 211–230). Cambridge: Academic Press.
George, B., & Thomachan, K. T. (2018). Financial inclusion and women empowerment: A gender perspective. *International Journal of Research-Granthaalayah*, *6*(5), 229–237.
Ghosh, S. (2022). Political empowerment of women and financial inclusion: Is there a link? *Social Sciences & Humanities Open*, *5*(1), 100267.
Grohmann, A., Klühs, T., & Menkhoff, L. (2018). Does financial literacy improve financial inclusion? Cross country evidence. *World Development*, *111*, 84–96.
Hastings, J. S., Madrian, B. C., & Skimmyhorn, W. L. (2013). Financial literacy, financial education, and economic outcomes. *Annual Review of Economics*, *5*(1), 347–373.
Islam, M. S. (2014). Microcredit, financial inclusion and women empowerment nexus in Bangladesh. *Asian Development Studies*, *3*(2), 6–15 ISSN 2304-375X.
Jack, W., & Suri, T. (2014). Risk sharing and transactions costs: Evidence from Kenya's mobile money revolution. *American Economic Review*, *104*(1), 183–223.
Jedi, F. F. (2022). The relationship between financial inclusion and women's empowerment: Evidence from Iraq. *Journal of Business and Management Studies*, *4*(3), 104–120.
Kabeer, N. (2005). Gender equality and women's empowerment: A critical analysis of the third millennium development goal 1. *Gender & Development*, *13*(1), 13–24.

Karlan, D., & Zinman, J. (2011). Microcredit in theory and practice: Using randomized credit scoring for impact evaluation. *Science*, *332*(6035), 1278–1284.
Krejcie, R. V., & Morgan, D. W. (1970). Determining sample size for research activities. *Educational and Psychological Measurement*, *30*(3), 607–610.
Lusardi, A., & Mitchell, O. S. (2011). *Financial literacy and planning: Implications for retirement wellbeing* (No. w17078). Cambridge: National Bureau of Economic Research.
Malhotra, A., Schuler, S. R., & Boender, C. (2002, June). Measuring women's empowerment as a variable in international development. In *Background paper prepared for the world bank workshop on poverty and gender: New perspectives* (Vol. 28, p. 58). Washington: The World Bank.
Malik, F. A., & Yadav, D. K. (2022). *Financial inclusion schemes in India*. Berlin: Springer.
Malik, F. A., Yadav, D. K., Adam, H., & Omrane, A. (2020). The urban poor and their financial behavior: A case study of slum dwellers in Lucknow (India). In *Sustainable entrepreneurship, renewable energy-based projects, and digitalization* (pp. 305–315). Boca Raton: CRC Press.
Malik, F. A., Yadav, D. K., Lone, N. A., & Adam, H. (2021). An investigation into the dynamics of financial inclusion in south Asian countries. *Pakistan Economic and Social Review*, *59*(2), 231.
Mehra, R. (1997). Women, empowerment, and economic development. *The Annals of the American Academy of Political and Social Science*, *554*(1), 136–149.
Pal, M., Gupta, H., & Joshi, Y. C. (2022). Social and economic empowerment of women through financial inclusion: Empirical evidence from India. *Equality, Diversity and Inclusion: An International Journal*, *41*(2), 294–305.
Sanderson, A., Mutandwa, L., & Le Roux, P. (2018). A review of determinants of financial inclusion. *International Journal of Economics and Financial Issues*, *8*(3), 1.
Siddik, M. N. A. (2017). Does financial inclusion promote women empowerment? Evidence from Bangladesh. *Applied Economics and Finance*, *4*(4), 169–177.
Suri, T., & Jack, W. (2016). The long-run poverty and gender impacts of mobile money. *Science*, *354*(6317), 1288–1292.
World Bank Group (2019). *Women, business and the law 2019: A decade of reform*. Washington: World Bank.
Zeller, M., & Sharma, M. (1998). *Rural finance and poverty alleviation* (No. 8). Washington: International Food Policy Research Institute (IFPRI).
Islam, M. S. (2014). Microcredit, financial inclusion and women empowerment Nexus in Bangladesh. *Stud*, *3*(2), 6–15.
Jedi, F. F. (2022). The relationship between financial inclusion and women's empowerment: evidence from Iraq. *Journal of Business and Management Studies*, *4*(3), 104–120.
Demirgüç-Kunt, A., & Klapper, L. F. (2012). Financial inclusion in Africa: an overview. *World Bank policy research working paper*, (6088).

9 Survival in the Era of COVID-19

A Qualitative Exploration of Micro and Small Enterprises (MSE) Operating within Pakistan's Informal Economy

Sidra Khalid and Ayesha Khan

9.1 Introduction

The economic consequences of COVID-19 have been devastating for countries across the globe. Fallout from the pandemic triggered economic shocks worldwide, with halted travel and trade, business contractions, and soaring unemployment (Nicola et al., 2020). Nation-wide lockdowns, border closures, and government-mandated social-distancing policies aimed at curbing the spread of the virus inevitably had a domino effect on livelihoods, thrusting millions into financial duress and further exacerbating poverty and inequities. Strict control measures contributed to market volatility and disruptions in consumer spending and supply chain, drastically changing the economic landscape for businesses and patrons alike. Developing countries have been more vulnerable to these crisis-induced negative economic impacts, and within countries, small-scale businesses have especially been hard hit.

Small-scale businesses like micro and small enterprises (MSEs) represent most of the business population in low- and low-middle-income countries. They play a critical role in developing economies by stimulating job and wealth creation, essentially forming the backbone of the economy. Despite the recognition that businesses and enterprises are key players for a nation's growth and development, majority of MSEs in developing countries operate within the informal economy. The informal economy refers to all economic activities by workers or economic units that are not legally regulated or socially protected (Chen, 2012). This lack of social and legal protections makes informal MSEs more vulnerable than their formal counterparts. Globally, 61% of all workers are informally employed (approximately 2 billion workers), among which 64% have their own business (ILO, 2018). In South Asia in particular, 88% of employment comprises informal employment (ILO, 2018).

Pakistan has a large number of MSEs constituting its informal entrepreneurial landscape. With the ninth largest workforce in the world (CIA World Factbook, 2017), the country's informal sector accounts for 72.5% of employment outside agriculture (Pakistan Bureau of Statistics, 2021). Informal businesses are spread across Pakistan in both rural and urban areas and can mostly be found in manufacturing, retail, and trade and service sectors (Shafi et al., 2020, p. 1). Weak institutional and regulatory systems (e.g., only 2.3% of the country's workforce is

DOI: 10.4324/9781032655185-13

unionized, Shaikh, 2019), low gross domestic product (GDP) growth, increased tax burdens, and a growing youth labor force have contributed to the steady rise in informal businesses and employment (Çiçek & Elgin, 2010). Further, Pakistan's informal sector is predominately concentrated among the low-skilled, low-income, and less-educated population, who are already more prone to poverty.

Even before the pandemic began in 2020 (2019), Pakistan's economy was fragile with projected growth at 2.5% (IMF, 2019), growing debt, rising inflation, low tax collection, and a per capita GDP of USD 1288 (The World Bank, 2020). It had been estimated that Pakistan would lose 18.5 million jobs as a direct result of COVID-19, with growth dipping into negatives and the poverty rate potentially increasing from 27% to 43%, driving millions below the poverty line (Moeen et al., 2020). Operating against this volatile economic backdrop, Pakistan's MSEs have been pushed into further financial fragility since the onset of COVID-19. A survey conducted by the Small and Medium Enterprises Development Authority (SMEDA) of SMEs across Pakistan found more than 90% had experienced a reduction in operations and disruptions in the supply chain, around 50% had laid off employees, and 89% reported facing financial issues (Seth et al., 2020). Businesses wished for tax relief from the government, leniency in loan repayment, relaxation in utility and rent payments, and salary support to retain employees (Seth et al., 2020). MSEs in the informal economy would face even bleaker realities. Businesses operating informally are unable to access available government support that may have otherwise provided some relief.

Pakistan's informal sector contributes one-third to its GDP (The World Bank, 2021), yet the informal economy is underserved by public and government sector services and more vulnerable to information asymmetry about opportunities, services, and resources compared to its formal counterpart. Enterprises operating within this context have narrower margins and fewer safety nets for dealing with economic crises and are the least well positioned to mitigate financial setbacks. Many of them operate in low-income areas to begin with, which tend to lack proper resources and formal structures of support, making it harder for MSEs to achieve their full economic potential regardless of high business acumen and drive.

Within this context, this study examined how inform MSEs in Pakistan responded to the economic impact of COVID-19, specifically exploring the implications of the pandemic on their entrepreneurial activity and crisis management strategies. To answer this question, the research looked at how MSEs were operating pre- and post-COVID-19, what coping strategies were used, and what formal or informal safety nets were available and availed.

9.2 Methodology

This qualitative study took place in Islamabad and Rawalpindi, Punjab, Pakistan, from August to September 2020, three months after the government lifted the lockdown imposed from mid-March to early June 2020. Participants represent various sectors, including general stores, hair salons, bakeries, eateries, and garment shops.

We draw on Webb et al. (2020) and Williams and Horodnic's (2016) definitions of informal employment, focusing on MSEs operating outside formal employment and tax regulations but considered legitimate if registered and complying with business laws.

9.2.1 Sample and Recruitment

Self-employed male enterprise owners were selected through purposeful random, a method chosen for its efficiency when facing constraints in time, resources, and information access (Suri, 2011). Seven key industrial zones in Islamabad/Rawalpindi (Dhok Hassu, Pirwadhai, Satellite Town, Westridge, and Sectors I-9, I-10, and I-11) were identified as economic hubs. Five external mappers used tablet-based data collection software (SurveyCTO) to record GPS coordinates and identify around 300 enterprises within these zones. Enterprises were categorized according to The Pakistan Standard Industrial Classification (PSIC), aligning with the UN's International Standard Classification (ISIC). Table 9.1 summarizes the breakdown of selected MSEs interviewed by industry category.

MSEs were identified based on the number of employees, focusing on this criterion over annual turnover or assets due to its ease of measurement. In the informal sector, businesses are often hesitant to disclose financial details, fearing potential reporting to authorities. While MSE definitions vary among Pakistan's economic institutions, this study classified enterprises with 0–2 employees as micro and those with 3–10 employees as small. These parameters were selected to encompass individual business owners (with at least one other employee or partner), who are excluded from institutional definitions (Jassim & Khawar, 2018). Of the 300 identified enterprises, 30 were randomly selected for interviews, distributed across industrial zones and enterprise sizes. Eligible enterprises had to be in operation for at least a year, and interviews were conducted directly with the owners.

9.2.2 Sample Rationale

MSE owners from various categories (transport, hospitality, services, retail, etc.) were interviewed to capture a comprehensive view of COVID-19's impact on

Table 9.1 Breakdown of study MSEs by industry category

Industry category	*Micro*	*Small*	*Total*
Accommodation and food service activities	7	2	9
Administrative and support service activities		1	1
Construction/utilities/contracting		2	2
Information and communication		1	1
Personal service activities	5		5
Wholesale and retail trade	4	7	11
Electricity, gas, steam, and air conditioning supply		1	1
Total	**16**	**14**	**30**

businesses. While women entrepreneurs in the informal economy have been significantly affected by the pandemic (HÉTFA, 2020; Manolova et al., 2020), Pakistan's low rates of women entrepreneurship, mainly home-based or contributing family workers, posed challenges for their inclusion in the study (ILO, 2018). Social norms limiting female entrepreneurship made it more practical to focus on interviewing male enterprise owners, ensuring a more diverse representation of industries in commercially accessible areas.

9.2.3 *Analysis*

Thematic analysis was used to systematically identify patterns and themes, examining both explicit and implied verbal cues and context. The research team transcribed and translated detailed notes from each recording, organizing them in a matrix. Analysis centered on questionnaire themes, using both deductive and inductive coding. The interview guide served as the analytical index's foundation, establishing main categories, and incorporating emergent themes. Once the final thematic framework was developed and agreed upon, the research team compared themes across all participants, providing a clearer conceptual picture.

9.2.4 *Ethical Considerations*

Before each interview verbal consent to participate in the audio-recorded interview was obtained from each participant. The researchers explained the purpose of the study and emphasized confidentiality and the participant's right to withdraw from the interview at any time.

9.3 Findings

Of the total 30 MSEs[1] interviewed, 16 were micro-enterprises and 14 were small. Four of the 30 were formally registered businesses and included in the analysis to provide comparative insight. The majority of enterprise owners were semi-educated (up to 10 years, matric level or lower), while only one had a master's degree. Table 9.2 summarizes the main findings of the pandemic's impacts and how MSEs responded.

9.3.1 *Operating in the Informal Sector – Business Operations before the Pandemic*

9.3.1.1 *Motivation for Startup and Initial Challenges – Low Savings and Margins to Begin With*

All participants acknowledged the challenges of starting a business but expressed a prevailing belief that entrepreneurship is preferable to seeking a salaried job. Their limited education was seen as a barrier to well-paying jobs, reinforcing the choice to pursue business. Even the sole well-educated owner with a master's

Table 9.2 Summary of qualitative findings

Pre-Pandemic	*Impact of COVID-19*	*Responses/coping strategies*
• Low savings and margins to begin with • Low expectations for business growth • Reliance on informal social networks for hiring • Hesitancy toward formal registration • Distrust of financial institutions • Low digital literacy • Little to no business planning	• Fewer earnings • Low sales • Loss of customers • Disruption in supply chain • Transport closures • Shorter business hours due to lockdown • Difficulty paying shop rent	• Little to no change to business model or marketing strategies • No shift to digital platforms • Followed safety protocols (mask, sanitizer, social distancing) • Delivery or home services (made difficult with police patrolling) • Salary cuts to employees • Frustration with government • Poor awareness of relief schemes

degree turned to business due to the lack of lucrative job opportunities. Business was considered the best avenue for earning decent income and supporting a family, especially for those with lower education levels. Participants highlighted the potential for growth through hard work in business, a sentiment not necessarily shared regarding salaried positions, which were viewed as static.

Seed money and a viable, marketable idea were seen as essential prerequisites for starting a business. The initial investment varied, ranging from PKR 10,000 to 8–10 lac (USD 33– 3,282), depending on the industry and available capital (e.g., inherited businesses with existing supplies or a shop). Initial business investments ranged from PKR 10,000 to 8–10 lac (USD 33–3,282), depending on industry and available capital (e.g., inherited businesses or existing supplies). Funding sources included borrowing from family or peers (interest-free) and personal savings. Many also utilized a Rotating Credit and Savings Association (ROSCA), known as a "committee" system in Pakistan, where a group contributes monthly shares, and a recipient is selected monthly through a lottery system (Ardener, 1964).

Other key needs included securing a suitable location, a challenge in densely populated urban areas, while effectively marketing to attract customers. This required a delicate balance between costs and customer accessibility. Purchasing necessary supplies and equipment, along with reserves for managing initial lean months without guaranteed returns, was also emphasized. Many owners spoke of their faith in God, believing that hard work and persistence would yield future success, serving as a sustaining force in perseverance. Mentorship or seeking support beyond a small circle was uncommon.

9.3.1.2 Planning vs. Flowing – Low Expectations for Business Growth

Participants collectively recognized the difficulty in definitively assessing a business's success, acknowledging the inherent cycles of growth, stalling, and occasional decline. While most participants experienced challenges only with the onset of COVID-19, they expressed overall satisfaction with the current state of their businesses.

Planning appeared to be an unstructured process across all 30 MSEs. Business owners were content with their (pre-COVID) earnings and sales, but could not articulate any concrete growth plans. They would expand their business if funding were available but lacked a clear vision on expansion specifics in terms of supplies, number of employees, or anticipated profits. Many of them tied the success of their business to divine providence and believed their "*rizq* (sustenance) is in Allah's hands." Critical factors for success were location, customer base, time and energy invested by the business owner, hard work, quality products, interpersonal skills, and limited competition. Owners did not mention the need for marketing beyond building a strong customer network through friendly customer service. Planning and marketing remained traditional, with little focus on business models, targets, and minimal reliance on online platforms.

9.3.1.3 Hiring and Retention Processes – Reliance on Informal Social Networks

Owners hire employees based on word-of-mouth and through personal networks. They see no use in hiring through social media, newspaper ads, or any recruitment agency. No formal HR department exists for hiring purposes and personal references are preferred, as it is easier to trust the employee and is seen as a safer investment. Majority of participants do not conduct reference checks, require résumés or any other type of documentation, nor are formal written contracts used. The average monthly salary range given to employees is PKR 8,000–PKR 15,000 (USD 26–49) with some businesses like tailoring offering commission-based payments based on outputs.

Findings indicate a pattern of low employee retention (3–6 months), influenced by the nature of the job and industry. For example, food shop owners noted that waiters or dishwashers tend to leave within weeks, as they are paid daily wages or find other higher paying positions. Employees who have good relationships with employers, who are trusted, or who are the sole breadwinners tend to stay longer. Other business owners cited retention problems related to seasonal migration or employees relocating for better job opportunities and lower living costs. In skill-based businesses such as tailoring or cooking, employees may leave after one year to start their own businesses once learning enough about the craft from the employer.

9.3.1.4 Difficulties Accessing and Navigating through Formal Structures and Facilitation

Participants showed hesitancy in discussing sensitive topics such as business registration, taxation, and bank account information. While there were mixed opinions on the benefits of registering their businesses, the general inclination was toward not registering. Micro businesses like tailoring shops, small general stores, and food/drink establishments remained unregistered with government entities such as the Federal Board of Revenue (FBR) or the Securities and Exchange Commission of Pakistan (SECP). However, the four registered businesses (construction company, pharmacy, retail shop, and salon) emphasized the importance of registration to avoid issues with government or law enforcement authorities, especially during transportation of goods. They mentioned benefits such as prevention of supply confiscation by FBR or police and tax relief, though specific amounts and the impact on savings were not detailed. Registered MSEs reported no discernible benefits other than legal protection.

In contrast, unregistered MSEs believed registration would lead to increased taxation, auditing issues, and potential bribery of taxation officers. A pharmacy owner shared the general perception that registration leads to bureaucratic entanglements, reflecting widespread distrust and frustration with the government. Many business owners expressed a preference for risking detection at a later stage rather than choosing to register upfront. The inefficiency of government agencies fosters the belief that operating without registration in small setups would go unnoticed. A salon owner disclosed that, despite legally registering his business, proper procedures are not followed by the government. He mentioned paying the Capital Development Authority (CDA)[2] PKR 5,000–6,000 (USD 16–20) monthly to renew his salon license but could not specify the purpose of this payment. This suggests a potential off-the-books arrangement between CDA officials and the owner, with the funds potentially not reaching government coffers.

Majority of the enterprise owners do not have bank accounts nor feel the need to open one. Some business owners felt the process for opening a bank account is complex, time consuming for low-literate people, and that there is too much paperwork; most low-income and micro and small-scale businesses do not have the know-how to navigate through these processes. Majority of MSEs conduct transactions in cash only, further reducing their need to open a bank account. Further, many business owners shared they only earn enough to meet monthly expense needs and have no extra money to be put in a bank. MSE owners also do not prefer using banks for loans, mainly due to high interest rates (which they cite as un-Islamic), complicated paperwork, and a long verification process. Many believe banks exhibit bias against the low-literate and low-income classes, making it unlikely for them to secure large loans (PKR 100,000 (USD 328) and above) without significant assets.

9.3.2 Economic Impact of COVID-19 on MSEs

COVID-19 significantly impacted MSEs, with owners reporting a 50–70% reduction in sales, primarily due to lockdowns, transport restrictions, low sales, customer loss, and disrupted supply chains. The resulting unpredictability and uncertainty created challenges that MSEs were ill prepared to manage. Even after lockdowns were lifted, restarting businesses at pre-COVID levels proved difficult due to decreased consumption, lack of customers, low sales and supply, and trade and transport issues. Both demand and supply-side issues hampered recovery. Business owners generally maintained existing practices, incorporating safety protocols, but did not change business models or shift to online platforms. The inability to adapt was attributed to entrenched "traditional business practices" and a lack of resources for change, including limited internet and digital access in low-income areas.

Businesses that were considered "non-essential" suffered more than others, as they could not open their shops. Other businesses like grocery, meat, and dairy shops managed to survive, as they were allowed to remain open with limited store timings. Fixed expenses like rent were a major issue, as shopkeepers had to pay rent despite market closure and promised government relief in rent and utilities.

Transport closure and shorter business hours also impacted businesses negatively. Small construction companies struggled to procure and transport materials, with inter-province travel either completely closed or heavily restricted. Grocery and dairy shops storing frozen and refrigerated items incurred losses from expired products and high utility bills to keep coolers running. Even after the lockdown was lifted, businesses had to operate within limited hours. This particularly impacted merchandise shops, usually busier in the evening, resulting in a loss of customers due to the government-imposed 6 p.m. curfew.

9.3.3 Coping Strategies in the Face of Financial Declines

Overall, micro and small business owners did not make any significant changes in their business operations, other than implementing safety protocols, and were essentially managing day by day with no explicit long-term plan. Some MSEs attempted to adapt by offering delivery or home services, but police patrolling posed challenges. For instance, a barber faced shutdowns during home visits as police searched his bag. Others opened their shops after curfew hours, quickly closing gates or shutters when spotting patrolling police. A tailor expressed interest in moving his business online but lacked digital expertise and the necessary devices (laptop or smartphone) to do so.

Businesses made significant employee reductions or implemented salary cuts (averaging around 50%). Some employees stayed despite knowing they wouldn't receive salaries, while others left voluntarily, anticipating a return when conditions improved. Many business owners took loans from family or friends to cover expenses during the lockdown. For those with existing loans before COVID-19, repaying installments became even more challenging due to business closures.

Participants had limited awareness of government support, and none received aid or business relief. The prevailing sentiments toward the government were disappointment, anger, and frustration, with a belief that more assistance, including tax relief and interest-free loans, should have been provided. While some knew about the Ehsaas Emergency Cash Program,[3] none applied or received benefits. The Kamyab Jawan Program[4] (loans for entrepreneurs) and bank loans were not utilized by any of the participants. Monetary support primarily came through personal networks, with participants noting the overall difficulty in borrowing and lending money, both before and after COVID-19.

9.4 Discussion

COVID-19 had a widespread impact on MSEs, revealing their lack of resources and know-how for adaptation. Faced with lockdowns and disruptions in supplies, customers, and services, MSEs adopted informal survival strategies, including clandestine operations, employee layoffs, and improvised home services. Perceived government assistance did not align with their needs, and the choice between compliance with lockdown measures and sustaining livelihoods was equally risky due to capital constraints and an unprotected legal status. The study findings align with previous studies on the effect of COVID-19 on Pakistani enterprises (Aftab et al., 2021; Seth et al., 2020; Shafi et al., 2020), but uniquely focuses on unregistered MSEs. Studies from India (Banu & Suresh, 2020; Behera et al., 2020; Ramaswamy, 2020), Bangladesh (Hossain, 2021; Kader & Pattanayak, 2020), South Africa (Anaç et al., 2022; Khambule, 2022; Price, 2020), and Thailand (Komin et al., 2021) also reflect similar vulnerabilities of MSEs in the informal economy and the lack of proper policy and planning specific to the needs of these businesses. Thus, government support schemes for businesses across the region are missing the most in need.

Micro and small businesses were generally lean to begin with and post COVID-19 their marginal reserves took massive setbacks. The study underscores the informal and casual nature of these businesses, revealing a slow growth trajectory for MSEs in Pakistan. The majority focus on survival rather than growth, constrained by limited access or willingness to take capital, low savings, and a lack of proper planning and business forecasting. Structural and individual-level barriers impede optimal business expansion. Table 9.3 summarizes the main barriers and recommendations to help MSEs better mitigate economic shocks and facilitate their financial inclusion.

9.4.1 Barriers to Entrepreneurial Resilience

9.4.1.1 Weak Institutional Environment

Due to perceived institutional neglect across socio-economic domains, many enterprise owners see no value in formal registration. Those who do register encounter confusing policies and procedures among regulating bodies, lacking support

Table 9.3 Barriers and recommendations to improve MSE resilience to economic shocks

Barriers to entrepreneurial resilience for informal MSEs	*Recommendations to better facilitate informal MSEs*
• Weak individual motivation and institutional environment • Distrust of financial institutions and hesitancy toward digitization • No formal or informal safety nets • Poor digital literacy and marketing skills for business expansion	• Ease the loan process and develop tailored schemes for MSEs • Educate business owners on financial schemes tailored to their needs • Create opportunities for training and business development • Incentivize formal registration

to navigate the complexities. Conflicting interests among government and regulatory workers, prone to exploitation and bribery, further discourage institutional improvement to better serve MSEs. Findings also challenge the stereotype of informal sector participants as deliberate tax evaders, suggesting that many enter this sector inadvertently due to a lack of opportunities or guidance on the benefits of the formal economy. Operating informally is more a consequence of limited options and lack of guidance than a deliberate choice.

Pakistan's unemployment rate in 2021 was 6.3% (4.5 million people), with higher unemployment among educated youth facing a "jobless graduate" phenomenon (PBS, 2021). The minimum wage is PKR 32,000 (USD 105) monthly, making it challenging for sole earners to meet expenses or save. The lower end of the job market lacks structure, hindering career advancement. Despite the unpredictability of business, it offers a chance for some financial respite. Amidst distrust in the government's commitment to uphold the "social contract" (Rousseau, 1968) and create productive employment opportunities, citizens may turn to informal means for a livelihood, reflecting a global trend where 81% of enterprises operate informally (OECD, 2019). The onus for pushing people into informality lies with the government and the available enabling environment, or lack thereof, for its citizens.

Despite the government's efforts to promote business development, such as establishing SMEDA in 1998, MSEs remain overlooked. SMEDA's focus tends to favor larger businesses in the formal sector (ILO and SMEDA, 2002). Further, bank schemes for micro business loans typically target small and medium enterprises, further neglecting micro enterprises. Considering there is no standardized definition of MSEs across Pakistan (Jassim & Khawar, 2018), it is no wonder that MSEs are left in the shadows of policy discussions and government programs surrounding business development.

Without formal support systems and resources, faith then becomes the invisible hand of hope in trying times. In struggling environments, business owners may attribute their difficulties to a larger divine plan, believing that means will emerge to overcome tough times. In expressing their faith, MSE owners do not exhibit a sense of impending doom or panic about future planning, potentially explaining the absence of planning and adopting new behaviors in response to the pandemic. However, they do display resilient behaviors like flexibility, perseverance, and optimism (de Vries & Shields, 2006). These behaviors inadvertently become assets for entrepreneurs in the informal sector. Despite the odds being stacked against them, they nevertheless persevere.

9.4.1.2 Distrust of Financial Institutions and Poor Financial Inclusion

Most participants avoid government and bank loans due to anticipated difficulties in accessing funds, red tape, and a lack of trust in the government's loan forgiveness in case of non-payment. MSEs prefer low or non-interest loans with simple terms, but the complicated criteria for loan eligibility, including guarantors and collateral, pose challenges. Loan requirements for a small loan are nearly the same as for a multi-million-rupee loan. This exclusionary approach by banks and financial institutions overlooks a significant group of enterprises that could potentially contribute to economic revitalization with proper investment. Additionally, the voices and concerns of MSEs led by women are often overlooked by government economic planners (Safavian & Haq, 2013).

Financial inclusion is already low across South Asia, with Pakistan ranking among the region's lowest in terms of bank account ownership (Malik et al., 2021). Despite Pakistan's National Financial Inclusion Strategy (SBP, 2015) setting a target of 50% financial inclusion by 2020, only 30% of the population is considered financially included with 81% lacking a bank account (Karandaaz, 2023). To encourage this population to open bank accounts, banks should simplify the application process as suggested by Malik et al. (2020b) in their study on savings behaviors in low-income communities in India. The fee structure for depositing and withdrawing money may also be revised to encourage a shift toward digital banking and mobile money use rather than cash transactions only.

9.4.1.3 Poor Digital Literacy and Hesitancy toward Digitization

In addition to financial constraints, another reason informal MSEs struggle with expansion is the inability to cross the digitization threshold and market to newer customers. Internet usage in Pakistan varies 21 –52% of the population, with no clear statistics on owners of computers or laptops (Kemp, 2023). MSEs interviewed showed no indication of using online platforms or digital banking apps for business operations, citing a lack of technical skills. However, there has been a post-COVID-19 increase in mobile money wallet usage (Khan & Jaffar, 2021). Registered users of mobile money accounts in Pakistan increased from 9% at the start of the initial lockdown (March 2020) to 16% by the end of 2020 (FII, 2021), indicating potential for digitization growth with the right environment and equipping citizens with the knowledge and skills required to enter the digital realm.

9.4.2 Facilitating MSEs to Better Mitigate Economic Shocks

To foster resilience among MSEs, addressing key barriers is crucial. This includes building trust in financial institutions, promoting formal borrowing for financial inclusion, providing digital skills and tools for marketing, and encouraging a culture of realistic business planning prioritizing growth. Tailored policies from governments and financial institutions are essential to support MSEs in navigating post-COVID challenges and preventing their further marginalization.

Despite the federal government's approval of a stimulus relief package (Ehsaan Emergency Cash Program and Ehsas Ration Program) aimed at supporting households during the pandemic, the amount fell short of compensating for lost income and covering essential monthly household needs. The implementation faced challenges related to eligibility criteria and monitoring, resulting in the exclusion of many households from receiving benefits. However, the swift rollout of the program, within 10 days after the lockdown, utilizing existing socio-economic databases, suggests that well-planned and adequately budgeted digital social protection programs can be successful with enough political will.

9.4.2.1 Easing the Loan Process

MSEs in Pakistan need simplified access to government and financial support. Tailored financing solutions, adapted to the needs of low-literacy or less technology-savvy business owners and catered to enterprise size and sector, should be implemented. Community outreach programs, in collaboration with local NGOs, can inform business owners about financing options, addressing barriers such as complex application processes and unclear eligibility criteria. Financial institutions should create flexible payment plans, considering the challenges faced by MSEs, to build trust and facilitate support. These recommendations have also been echoed by Malik et al. (2020a).

Enterprise owners were forced to dip into scarce savings, and even then, most still faced significant losses. The survey by Pakistan Microfinance Network (2020) in May 2020 revealed that only 6% of enterprises could financially sustain their businesses for the next six months. While the Punjab government offered tax relief, it only benefited registered businesses. The State Bank of Pakistan's Debt Relief Scheme also excluded unregistered MSEs. To address this, establishing fast-track lending hubs through local NGOs could assist MSEs in navigating application processes, building their capacity, and qualifying for various schemes.

9.4.2.2 Creating Opportunities for Training and Business Development

Business owners typically evolved organically, lacking formal enterprise training or vocational education. The study reveals a lack of risk management strategies among MSEs to navigate crises effectively. These enterprises lacked knowledge on handling sudden disruptions, rebuilding businesses, or retooling skills to adapt to changes. There's a pressing need for community training to build resilience, providing entrepreneurs with tools to respond, adapt, and adjust to crises effectively. Research by Haider et al. (2017) in Punjab highlights the positive impact of training on MSE growth and performance and ability to meet household expenses compared to those who do not receive training.

Government-sponsored business development training should not only focus on technical skills but also train participants on creativity, agility, technology use, and coping strategies (i.e., building entrepreneurial resilience). Modules should emphasize the benefits of digital adoption, raising awareness about the benefits of online platforms. If MSEs were facilitated in utilizing digital channels perhaps many would not be forced to shut down.

9.4.2.3 Incentivizing Formal Registration

Majority of unregistered MSEs fear the registration process and do not see any utility. Awareness campaigns and social protection programs should better incentivize this process and focus on what MSEs could gain from registration rather than how they would be penalized for being unregistered. For example, incentives for business and tax registration could be included as part of lending packages to encourage unregistered businesses to formalize as part of their loan process. The current taxation policies for large businesses and MSEs need to be revisited.

9.5 Conclusion

There is no doubt that MSEs in Pakistan are vulnerable to and ill prepared for shocks, and COVID-19 only aggravated their plight. The shockwaves felt from this pandemic revealed many gaps in Pakistan's institutional structures, including deficiencies in social protection measures, planning processes, and crisis mitigation. Support from government programs missed out on the informal MSEs that operate below the radar in many low-income areas and industrial zones, underscoring a lack of connectivity with civil society which could have been utilized for access and outreach. Furthermore, there is no planning to address these urgent gaps in the national (or provincial) economic plans for the inclusion of MSEs for revitalization of the economy. Informal MSEs require incentivization for formalization and capacity building, necessitating strategic business planning and a shift toward digitization. Economic recovery demands tailored financial and taxation policies to foster growth, build MSE trust in government engagement, and enhance productivity nationwide.

9.6 Limitations

This study has several limitations. First, it relies on enterprise owners' perspectives, introducing self-reporting biases such as selective memory or exaggeration. Second, the sample comprises only male-owned businesses, excluding the female perspective. Research involving small-scale female entrepreneurs would offer insights into gender-specific challenges during COVID-19. The study is geographically limited to Islamabad and Rawalpindi, relatively better-off areas. Additionally, it focuses on businesses still operating during the study, overlooking those forced to shut down, which could represent a more vulnerable subset. Lastly, the evolving context of COVID-19 in Pakistan should be considered, as the study examines a specific three-month post-lockdown period, and findings are contextualized within this timeframe.

Acknowledgments

Funding for this research and project came from the Foundation Open Society Institute (FOSI) grant number OR2020-71381 to the Principal Investigator, Dr. Ayesha Khan, affiliated with the non-profit NGO Akhter Hameed Khan Foundation (AHK-F), Pakistan. AHKF is a non-profit working on women's economic empowerment and enterprise building in poor urban communities of Pakistan. The research reflected in this paper does not in any way represent or reflect the granting agency or implementation organization's views, conflict of interest, or influence. The views are solely based on research findings and the research team interpretation.

Conflict of Interest

The authors declare that they have no known competing financial interests or personal relationships that could have appeared to influence the work reported in this paper.

Notes

1 MSEs and MSE/business owners may be used interchangeably in the Findings and Discussion sections.
2 The CDA is a government entity responsible for providing municipal services for the capital city (Islamabad) of Pakistan.
3 Ehsas Program was enacted by Prime Minister Imran Khan in April 2020 for COVID-19 relief in which a one-time sum of PKR 12,000 (USD 39) was dispersed to citizens identified through the National Socioeconomic Database.
4 Kamyab Jawan – Youth Entrepreneurship Scheme was launched by Prime Minister Imran Khan in 2019 to provide subsidized financing for young entrepreneurs and businesses between the age group of 21 and 45 years.

References

Aftab, M., Field, E., Garlick, R., Khan, L., Subramanian, N., & Vyborny, K. (2021). *A Tentative Story of Resilience: The Impact of COVID-19 on the Pakistani Labour Market*. PEDL C-19 Note [online] Centre for Economic Policy Research. Available at https://pedl.cepr.org/publications/tentative-story-resilience-impact-covid-19-pakistani-labour-market.

Afzal, A., Mirza, N., & Arshad, F. (2019). Conditional vs unconditional cash transfers: A study of poverty demographics in Pakistan. *Ekonomska Istrazivanja-Economic Research, 32*(1), 33663383. https://doi.org/10.1080/1331677x.2019.1661006.

Anaç, N., Egger, E. M., Jones, S., Santos, R., & Warren-Rodriguez, A. (2022). *The impact of COVID-19 on urban informal workers in Maputo*. Helsinki: United Nations University World Institute for Development Economics Research.

Ardener, S. (1964). The comparative study of rotating credit associations. *The Journal of the Royal Anthropological Institute of Great Britain and Ireland, 94*(2), 201–229. https://doi.org/10.2307/2844382.

Banu, S., & Suresh, B. (2020). COVID-19 and its impact on micro, small and medium enterprises in India. *Mukt Shabd Journal, 9*(X), 606–617.

Behera, M., Mishra, S., Mohapatra, N., & Behera, A. R. (2020). COVID-19 pandemic and micro, small and medium enterprises (MSMEs): Policy response for revival. *SEDME (Small Enterprises Development, Management & Extension Journal), 47*(3), 213–228. https://doi.org/10.1177/09708464211037485.

Chen, M. A. (2012). *The Informal Economy: Definitions, Theories and Policies*. WIEGO Working Paper No 1 [online] Women in Informal Employment: Globalizing and Organizing (WIEGO). Available at https://www.wiego.org/sites/default/files/publications/files/Chen_WIEGO_WP1.pdf.

CIA World Factbook (2017). "Country Comparisons - Labor Force". [online] Central Intelligence Agency. Available at https://www.cia.gov/the-world-factbook/field/labor-force/country-comparison/.

Çiçek, D., & Elgin, C. (2010). Cyclicality of fiscal policy and the shadow economy. *Empirical Economics, 41*(3), 725–737. https://doi.org/10.1007/s00181-010-0409-0.

de Vries, H., & Shields, M. (2006). Towards a theory of entrepreneurial resilience: A case study analysis of New Zealand SME owner operators. *New Zealand Journal of Applied Business Research (NZJABR)*, *5*(1), 33–43.

Financial Inclusion Insights (2021). Pakistan COVID-19 Impact Study Survey Report 2020. Available at https://kantarpublic.com/articles/previous-financial-inclusion-index-reports.

Haider, S. H., Asad, M., Fatima, M., & Zain Ul Abidin, R. (2017). Microfinance and performance of micro and small enterprises: Does training have an impact. *Journal of Entrepreneurship and Business Innovation*, *4*(1), 1. https://doi.org/10.5296/jebi.v4i1.10566.

Handa, S., Daidone, S., Peterman, A., Davis, B., Pereira, A., Palermo, T., & Yablonski, J. (2018). Myth-busting? Confronting six common perceptions about unconditional cash transfers as a poverty reduction strategy in Africa. *The World Bank Research Observer*, *33*(2), 259–298. https://doi.org/10.1093/wbro/lky003.

HÉTFA (2020). Female entrepreneurs in the time of COVID-19: 1 hour less for business, 2 hours more for family. HÉTFA Research Institute. [online] Available at https://hetfa.eu/wp-content/uploads/2020/06/HETFA_female-entrepreneurs_COVID.pdf.

Hossain, M. I. (2021). COVID-19 impacts on employment and livelihood of marginal people in Bangladesh: Lessons learned and way forward. *South Asian Survey*, *28*(1), 57–71. https://doi.org/10.1177/0971523121995072.

International Labour Organization (ILO) (2018). *Women and men in the informal economy: A statistical picture*. Geneva: International Labour Office. Available at https://www.ilo.org/publications/women-and-men-informal-economy-statistical-picture-third-edition.

International Labour Organization (ILO), Small and Medium Enterprise Development Authority of Pakistan (SMEDA) (2002). *Creating a Conducive Policy Environment for Micro, Small and Medium-Sized Enterprises in Pakistan*. International Labour Organization. Available at https://www.ilo.org/empent/Publications/WCMS_100985/lang–en/index.htm.

International Monetary Fund (2019). *World economic outlook, April 2019: Growth slowdown, precarious recovery*. International Monetary Fund. Available at https://www.imf.org/en/Publications/WEO/Issues/2019/03/28/world-economic-outlook-april-2019.

Jassim, J., & Khawar, M. (2018) *Defining Micro, Very Small & Small Enterprises: Moving Towards a Standard Definition-Continuum*. Pakistan Microfinance Network. Available at https://www.pmn.org.pk/publications/Defining%20Micro,%20Very%20Small%20&%20Small%20Enterprises.pdf.

Kader, A. W., & Pattanayak, M. (2020), *Business Pulse Survey: Impact of COVID-19 on MSMEs in Bangladesh*. International Finance Corporation. Available at https://www.ifc.org/wps/wcm/connect/region__ext_content/ifc_external_corporate_site/south+asia/resources/business+pulse+survey+-+impact+of+covid-19+on+msmes+in+bangladesh.-

Karandaaz (2023). Karandaaz Financial Inclusion Survey. Available at https://karandaaz-main.wpenginepowered.com/wp-content/uploads/2023/02/Karandaaz-Financial-Inclusion-Survey-2.pdf.

Kemp, S. (2023). Digital 2023: Pakistan. Kepios. Available at https://datareportal.com/reports/digital-2023-pakistan.

Khambule, I. (2022). COVID-19 and the informal economy in a small-town in South Africa: Governance implications in the post-COVID era. *Cogent Social Sciences*, *8*(1), 2078528. https://doi.org/10.1080/23311886.2022.2078528.

Khan, I., & Jaffar, K. H. (2021). Searching for the binding constraint to digital financial inclusion in Pakistan: A decision tree approach. *CGD Policy Paper*, *218*. Available at https://www.cgdev.org/publication/searching-binding-constraint-digital-financial-inclusion-pakistan-decision-tree-approach.

Komin, W., Thepparp, R., Subsing, B., & Engstrom, D. (2021). Covid-19 and its impact on informal sector workers: A case study of Thailand. *Asia Pacific Journal of Social Work and Development*, *31*(1–2), 80–88. https://doi.org/10.1080/02185385.2020.1832564.

Lone, T., Shakeel, M., & Bischler, J. (2020) Towards shock-responsive social protection: lessons from the COVID-19 response in Pakistan [Research Report]. Oxford Policy

Management. Available at https://www.opml.co.uk/files/Publications/A2241-maintains/maintains-covid-19-srsp-responses-pakistan-country-case-study-final-2.pdf.

Malik, F. A., Yadav, D. K., Adam, H., & Omrane, A. (2020a). The urban poor and their financial behavior: A case study of slum dwellers in Lucknow (India). In *Sustainable entrepreneurship, renewable energy-based projects, and digitalization* (pp. 305–315). CRC Press.

Malik, F. A., Yadav, D. K., & Ismail, A. (2020b). Purpose of savings and its determinants in case of destitute population an empirical analysis of slum dwellers. *International Journal of Social, Political and Economic Research*, *7*(3), 499–517.

Malik, F. A., Yadav, D. K., Lone, N. A., & Adam, H. (2021). An investigation into the dynamics of financial inclusion in south Asian countries. *Pakistan Economic and Social Review*, *59*(2), 231.

Manolova, T. S., Brush, C. G., Edelman, L. F., & Elam, A. (2020). Pivoting to stay the course: How women entrepreneurs take advantage of opportunities created by the COVID-19 pandemic. *International Small Business Journal: Researching Entrepreneurship*, *38*(6), 481–491. https://doi.org/10.1177/0266242620949136.

Moeen, M. S. et al. (2020) *COVID-19: Estimating impact on the economy and poverty in Pakistan: Using SAM multiplier model*. Washington: International Food Policy Research Institute. https://doi.org/10.2499/p15738coll2.134244.

Nicola, M., Alsafi, Z., Sohrabi, C., Kerwan, A., Al-Jabir, A., Iosifidis, C., Agha, M., & Agha, R. (2020). The socio-economic implications of the coronavirus and COVID-19 pandemic: A review. *International Journal of Surgery*, *78*(78), 185–193. https://doi.org/10.1016/j.ijsu.2020.04.018.

OECD (2019). *Tackling vulnerability in the informal economy*. Development Centre Studies. Paris: OECD. https://doi.org/10.1787/939b7bcd-en.

Pakistan Bureau of Statistics (PBS) (2021). Labour Force Survey 2020-2021 (Annual Report). Government of Pakistan. Available at https://www.pbs.gov.pk/publication/labour-force-survey-2020-21-annual-report.

Pakistan Microfinance Network (2020) *The Impact of Coronavirus on Micro & Small Enterprises (MSEs)*. [online] Available at https://pmn.org.pk/wp-content/uploads/2020/06/Impact-of-Coronavirus-on-MSEs.pdf.

Price, R. A. (2020). *Impacts of COVID-19 regulatory measures on small-scale and informal trade in Zimbabwe*. K4D Helpdesk Report 815-816. Brighton: Institute of Development Studies.

Ramaswamy, K. V. (2020). Impact of COVID-19: Micro, small and medium enterprises in India, pandemic shock of COVID-19 and policy response: A Bird's eye view. *KIEP visiting scholars program*, No. 2: Business and Industry, pp. 159–171.

Rousseau, J. J. (1968). The social contract (M. Cranston, Trans.). *Harmondworth*. London: Penguin. (Original work published 1762.)

Safavian, M., & Haq, A. (2013). *Are Pakistan's women entrepreneurs being served by the microfinance sector?* The World Bank. https://doi.org/10.1596/978-0-8213-9833-3

Seth, N. J., Ganaie, M. A., & Zafar, F. (2020). *Survey Report: Impact of COVID-19 on SMEs*. Small and Medium Enterprises Development Authority. Available at https://smeda.org/phocadownload/Research_Publications/SMEDA%20Survey%20Report%20-%20COVID-19%20Impact%20on%20SMEs%20reduce.pdf.

Shafi, M., Liu, J., & Ren, W. (2020). Impact of COVID-19 pandemic on micro, small, and medium-sized enterprises operating in Pakistan. *Research in Globalization*, *2*(1), 100018. https://doi.org/10.1016/j.resglo.2020.100018.

Shah, Y., Liu, Y., Shah, F., & Shah, F. (2020). Challenges of small- and medium-sized businesses in Pakistan due to COVID-19 pandemic. *R-Economy*, *6*(3), 222–226. https://doi.org/10.15826/recon.2020.6.3.019.

Shaikh, H. (2019, May 23). How can we protect contract and informal workers in Pakistan? *Dawn News*. Available at https://www.dawn.com/news/1484090

State Bank of Pakistan (SBP) (2015). National Financial Inclusion Strategy – Government's 100-days Agenda. Available at https://www.finance.gov.pk/NFIS.pdf.

Suri, H. (2011). Purposeful sampling in qualitative research synthesis. *Qualitative Research Journal, 11*(2), 63–75. https://doi.org/10.3316/qrj1102063.
The World Bank (2020). *World Development Indicators; GDP per capita (current US$) – Pakistan.* [online] The World Bank Group. Available at https://data.worldbank.org/indicator/NY.GDP.PCAP.CD?locations=PK.
The World Bank (2021). *Widespread Informality Likely to Slow Recovery from COVID-19 in Developing Economies.* Press ReleaseAvailable at https://www.worldbank.org/en/news/press-release/2021/05/11/widespread-informality-likely-to-slow-recovery-from-covid-19-in-developing-economies.
Webb, A., McQuaid, R., & Rand, S. (2020). Employment in the informal economy: Implications of the COVID-19 pandemic. *International Journal of Sociology and Social Policy, 40*(9/10), 1005–1019. https://doi.org/10.1108/IJSSP-08-2020-0371
Williams, C. C., & Horodnic, I. A. (2016). An institutional theory of the informal economy: Some lessons from the United Kingdom. *International Journal of Social Economics, 43*(7), 722–738. https://doi.org/10.1108/IJSE-12-2014-0256.

10 Complaint Handling Strategies and Customer Advocacy in the Nigerian Banking Sector

Itai H. Muktar, Ufual E. Daniel, and Okorie E. Uchechukwu

10.1 Introduction

Generally, customer advocacy in businesses has been of great interest to business owners, entrepreneurs, government institutions and non-governmental organisations. While extant literature has been inundated with various forms of customer attraction strategies, little has been done in the area of complaints handling and customer advocacy. Customer advocacy is very key in the banking sector because of the competitive nature of the environment under which they operate. The survival and success of any business can only be assured through an effective customer advocacy. Customer advocacy is regarded as important because it has become increasingly difficult for firms to assume that there exists an unlimited customer base (Olonade et al., 2021; Wu & Cheng, 2017).

It is important to address the challenges relating to decline of customer advocacy as a result of the increasing customers' complaints in Nigeria banking sector. Dewitt et al. (2007) posited that complaints by customers are consequences of service concern during banking transactions. When customers complain, employees insinuate, in many instances, that complaining might not be suitable within the particular circumstances (Atalik, 2007). Bank customers can typically be divided into three groups when it comes to their complaining behaviour (Kim & Lynn, 2012). First, those that do not complain to the service provider, but rather to their friends and family and in this way, spread negative word-of-mouth (WOM) about the services. The second group is third-party response complainers who prefer to complain to regulators or take legal action. The third group refers to the voice response complainers who inform the service providers where the service concern was experienced about their dissatisfaction (Kim & Lynn, 2012).

The effective handling of complaints is seen as critical, since complaints that are not correctly handled will not solve problems within the service business and will only grow into bigger problems (Ufua et al., 2018). Aigboje and Itai (2023) are of the opinion that complaint handling is essential to building a competitive service business and customer advocacy. It was in the quest to stern complaints and control the arbitrary bank charges, Central Bank of Nigeria (CBN) in 2012 established the Consumer Protection Department. In its circular referenced FPR/DIR/GEN/01/020 dated August 16, 2011, the CBN compelled the commercial banks to establish

DOI: 10.4324/9781032655185-14

consumer help desks to address complaint management, among others. Banks were also mandated to capture complaints received during the financial year especially those that are related to excess charges on their annual financial report. The CBN publication (2015) recorded over 6,000 complaints relating to illegal bank charges, and the banks were compelled to refund over N6.2 billion to affected customers.

As a result, the implication of this research gap in relevant literature necessitates the conduct of empirical work to ascertain the impact of complaint handling strategies on customers' advocacy in Nigerian banking sector as a departure from previous studies which have regional arrangements. Hence, the main objective of this study sets to measure the effect of complaint handling strategies on customer advocacy in Nigerian banking sector in order to give answer to the following proposed research questions as:

i How does complaint handling strategy affect customer satisfaction in Nigerian banking sector?
ii To what extent does compensation strategy impact on customer's positive WOM in Nigerian banking sector?

10.2 Literature Review

Customer complaints are signs of customer calling for help as a result of dissatisfactions with the service provider as portrayed in the literature as a negative feedback (Steven et al., 2012). The reason why customers take the pains to complain is that they only want value for what they were denied by the service provider. If an organisation clearly resolves the concern of a customer, then the individual would respond by doing business with the organisation continuously in future. This customer could then recommend the organisation to others.

According to Ekiz and Huseyin (2017), an apology in this context is the offering of a genuine regret to a client; it is the most effective procedure in compliant handing and service recovery. They defined apology as an emotional exchange offered by a service provider in resolving a customer's concern who had suffered a service failure. Boshoff and Leong (1998) documented the relationship between apology and service recovery, they provided that an apology has a resilient outcome on service recovery satisfaction. Also, in the study of Johnston and Fern (2017), they stated that an apology plays an important role in a customer's advocacy with a bank's service recovery strategy (Rosenmayer et al., 2018). Furthermore, effective complaint handling can have dramatic impacts on customers' advocacy rate; achieve secondary satisfaction and customers' loyalty (Tax & Brown, 2000)). From a service provider's perspective, handling customers' complaints embodies an advantage and an opportunity to build a pleasant relationship and satisfaction of customer experience rather than unresolved concern (Berry & Parasuraman, 2011). Every service provider should consider customers' complaints as valuable gifts from customers (Ateke & Kalu, 2016).

Estelami (2000) refers to compensation as replacements, reimbursements or discount by a service provider or an organisation to a customer who has suffered a service failure. Therefore, compensation symbolises a tangible value in the form of a financial or monetary payment. Also, Davidow (2000, 2003) used the word compensation to describe benefits or outcomes by a service provider to address a service complaint. The benefits may include more than the product purchase price, it may cover added cost, and the customer had suffered. In a wider sense, compensation, similarly, includes intangible consequences that can be well thought-out to be emotional benefit. This is because a product or service failure frequently involves social loss, for example, loss of self-esteem. Social loss can be redeemed by an apology, which is an intangible outcome that comforts and restores social equity and esteem (Ufua et al., 2020). Mattila and Patterson (2016), in line with others, consider apology as a method of compensation.

According to Bonifield and Cole (2008), the characteristics of complaint handling using compensation strategy include the following: (i) It increases future purchase intentions. (ii) It enhances the customer's tendency towards complaining to the service provider when faced with future service failures complaints to the organisation as it has previously revealed its intention and ability to resolve the concern of the customer. (iii) It increases positive WOM of the customer. (iv) It reduces the possibility of customers complaining to others. (v) It reduces negative WOM communication. Furthermore, in Grewal et al. (2008), the advantage of recovery compensation strategy is to restore the equity of the relationship between a service provider and a customer.

Customer advocacy starts with positive memorable experiences and ends with WOM marketing. Customer advocacy is very important in the company's efforts to satisfy existing and get new customers. The information received by a satisfied customer is more convincing than that delivered by the business organisation. Customer advocacy has duality relationship between a company and a customer. On the side of the company the relationship must be honest, trust worthy and transparent whilst the customers will reciprocate with product or service purchases, enduring loyalty and most especially inform others about the firm of its services or products. Advocacy is the willingness of the customer to provide strong recommendations and say positive WOM to other consumers on behalf of a products or service supplier (Hill et al., 2006). According to Swanson and Kelley (2011), they explained that WOM is the act of informing others about one's customer experience of a product and service of an organisation. WOM engagement is extremely dependable and facilitates customers' intentions to make future purchase of products and services as well as provide customer insights into a service provider (Maxham & Netemever,2002). Similarly, in Maxham (2014), customers who received fair and excellent responses on their service failure from the service provider would engage others in positive WOM experience.

In their study Atake and Kalu (2016) complaint handling and post-complaint satisfaction of customers in Port Harcourt, Nigeria. The study found that complaint handling and post-complaint satisfaction have a positive and significant correlation; as all the dimensions of complaint handling considered in the study were found to have strong positive links with post-complaint satisfaction. In the same vein, Oranusi and Mojekeh (2019) researched on the effect of service recovery on customer retention in selected commercial banks in Onitsha, Anambra State Nigeria. The results showed that service recovery has a significant positive effect on customer retention and advocacy in selected banks. Equally, in their work (Ebere et al., 2020), on electronic banking and customers' satisfaction: evidence from some selected deposit money banks in Nigeria. The study found out a positive relationship between electronic banking and customers resolved complaints.

Awa, Ogwo and Ukoha (2015) carried out a study on service recovery and competitive positioning: The moderation effect of technical efficiency. The study's findings were limited by its domain – competitive positioning instead of customers' satisfaction and retention. In their study, Awa, Nwobu and Igwe (2021) on service failure handling and resilience, that empathy was most critical covariance with agility, followed by compensation with anticipatory ability; attentive will facilitate positive WOM. Osagie et al. (2021) researched on E-service quality and customer satisfaction in deposit money banks, the study revealed that a significant relationship exists between customisation and advocacy for deposits money bank. This study hypothesises thus:

H_{01}: There is no significant relationship between complaints handling strategy and customer satisfaction.

H_{02}: Compensation strategy has no significant effect on a customer's positive WOM.

10.3 Methodology

This study adopted survey research design. A sample of 520 customers of banks in Nigeria has been chosen from a population of 4,800,000. The sample size for the study was arrived at using Krejcie and Morgan (1970). A multiple sampling method was adopted for the study.

Data were collected through the physical distribution of structured questionnaire. The questionnaire items were adapted from previous studies based on the similarities and peculiarities with the current study (Awa, Nwobu & Igwe, 2021; Chueh et al., 2014; Kim & Lynn, 2012; Wu & Cheng, 2017).

10.3.1 Demographic Characteristics

The main respondents were the bank customers who registered for bank verification number (BVN) in Lagos State, Nigeria. The choice of bank customers is based on the premise that they have full and adequate knowledge about the service experience of the banks. The employees of the banks were not used to avoid element of bias.

10.3.1.1 Validity of Instrument

The research instrument was subjected to expert opinion. Average Variance Extracted (AVE) > 0.5 was treated as additional evidence of convergent validity, the

Table 10.1 Validity statistics

S/N	*Variables*	*Number of items*	*AVE*	*Composite reliability*
1	Complaints handling	6	0.809	0.949
2	Compensation	6	0.984	0.921
	Customers advocacy			
1	Customers satisfaction	6	0.852	0.992

construct validity of all variables involved in the study was established through Exploratory Factor Analysis using varimax extraction method as indicated in the validity table (Table 10.1).

Reliability test was conducted to ascertain whether the variables of the study measured consistently the factors intended. For the purpose of this study internal consistency measure using Cronbach's Alpha was adopted for assessing reliability of all the variables (Bryman & Bell, 2011). In addition, it is conducted to reduce errors and give stable results of the data collection. The reliability for each of these variables is accepted at a threshold of 0.7 and above. Table 10.2 shows respective Cronbach's Alpha reliability coefficients for the variables.

The data analysis of this research was descriptive and inferential analysis. The descriptive analysis was done using percentage distribution, mean and standard deviation arranged in tables. The inferential analysis was carried out using Pearson's Product Moment Correlation analysis to test the hypothesis one (1) to determine the degree of association between dependent and independent variables. Multiple regression was used to test hypotheses two (2).

Statistical Program for Social Sciences (SPSS) version 24 was used to analyse data by use of both descriptive and inferential statistics. The two hypotheses of the study were tested using Pearson product-moment correlation coefficient and simple regression. The response rate of 88.09% for this study was considered enough for data analysis and interpretation.

Table 10.3 shows the descriptive statistics of respondent's responses on complaints handling strategy. The study sought to establish the extent of the respondents'

Table 10.2 Cronbach's alpha for all variables

S/N	*Variables*	*Number of items*	*Cronbach's Alpha value*
A			
1	Complaint's handling	6	0.89
2	Compensation	6	0.90
	Customer advocacy		
1	Customers satisfaction	6	0.79
2	Positive WOM	6	0.85

Table 10.3 Descriptive analysis of complaint handling strategy

Items	*Strongly disagree*	*Disagree*	*Partially disagree*	*Partially agree*	*Agree*	*Strongly agree*	*Mean*	*Standard deviation*
Complain handling strategy	*Freq.* %	*Freq.* %	*Freq.* %	*Freq.* %	*Freq.* %	*Freq.* %		
My complaint was handled in a timely manner	22 4.8%	31 6.8%	46 10.0%	130 28.4%	122 26.6%	107 23.4%	4.35	1.372
My bank's complaints handling process is simple and not complicated	19 4.1%	31 6.8%	60 13.1%	128 27.9%	149 32.5%	71 15.5%	4.24	1.290
After a service failure, I was satisfied with immediate apology	20 4.4%	39 8.5%	40 8.7%	130 28.4%	169 36.9%	60 13.1%	4.24	1.288
After a service failure, I was satisfied with the immediate explanations and response	19 4.2%	45 9.8%	43 9.4%	138 30.2%	173 37.9%	39 8.5%	4.13	1.252
After a service failure, I was satisfied with the bank's immediate resolution	23 5.0%	36 7.9%	54 11.8%	176 38.4%	112 24.5%	57 12.4%	4.07	1.275

Source: Field Survey (2022).

agreements or disagreements with statements on customer satisfaction. The responses were rated on a Likert scale and the results presented in Table 10.4.

Table 10.4 shows the descriptive statistics of respondents' responses on customer satisfaction.

Relating Tables 10.3 and 10.4 together, the pattern of increase in complaints handling strategy is same as that of customer satisfaction. The finding reveals that complaints were handled in a timely manner in the selected banks. The finding also reveals that after a service failure, customers were satisfied with immediate apology and explanations. Furthermore, finding reveals the banks treat customers fairly well and meet their service expectations. In addition, finding indicates that customers are satisfied with the services they received from their banks. These findings provide answer to the research question three and enable the researcher to achieve objective three.

To test the hypothesis one, Pearson's product-moment correlation coefficient (*r*) was used. The data for complaints handling strategy and customer satisfaction were generated by adding responses of all items for each of the variables as

Table 10.4 Descriptive analysis of customer satisfaction

Items	*Strongly disagree*	*Disagree*	*Partially disagree*	*Partially agree*	*Agree*	*Strongly agree*	*Mean*	*Standard deviation*
Customer satisfaction	*Freq.* %	*Freq.* %	*Freq.* %	*Freq.* %	*Freq.* %	*Freq.* %		
My bank meet my service expectations	18 3.9%	16 3.5%	53 11.6%	113 24.7%	161 35.2%	97 21.2%	4.47	1.261
My bank services exceed my expectations	48 10.5%	18 3.9%	79 17.2%	95 20.7%	132 28.8%	86 18.8%	4.10	1.519
My bank treats me fairly	13 2.8%	26 5.7%	42 9.2%	110 24.0%	181 39.5%	86 18.8%	4.48	1.222
I am proud of my relationship with my bank	20 4.4%	26 5.7%	58 12.7%	146 31.9%	163 35.6%	45 9.8%	4.18	1.211
My experiences with my bank is always been good	72 15.7%	36 7.9%	27 5.9%	136 29.7%	130 28.4%	57 12.4%	3.84	1.597
I am satisfied with the services I received from my bank	19 4.1%	31 6.8%	38 8.3%	159 34.7%	157 34.3%	54 11.8%	4.24	1.220

indicated on Tables 10.3 and 10.4, respectively. The results of the regression are presented in Table 10.5.

Table 10.5 shows the Pearson's product-moment correlation coefficient between complaints handling strategy and customer satisfaction. The result revealed that complaints handling strategy has a positive and significant relationship with customer satisfaction (r = .768*, ρ = .000). This reveals that any positive change in complaints handling strategy on customer satisfaction would lead to a higher level of customer satisfaction. Based on this finding, the null hypothesis (H_{01}) which

Table 10.5 Pearson's product-moment correlation coefficient relationship between complaints handling strategy and customer satisfaction

Correlations			
		Complaints' handling strategy	*Customers satisfaction*
Complaints handling strategy	Pearson correlation	1	.768*
	Sig. (2-tailed)		.000
	N	458	458
Customers satisfaction	Pearson correlation	.768*	1
	Sig. (2-tailed)	.000	
	N	458	458

* Correlation is significant at the 0.01 level (2-tailed).

Table 10.6 Descriptive analysis of compensation strategy

Items	*Strongly disagree*	*Disagree*	*Partially disagree*	*Partially agree*	*Agree*	*Strongly agree*	*Mean*	*Standard deviation*
Compensation strategy	*Freq.* %	*Freq.* %	*Freq.* %	*Freq.* %	*Freq.* %	*Freq.* %		
I get compensation according to my expectation	130 28.4%	66 14.4%	77 16.8%	75 16.4%	76 16.6%	34 7.4%	3.01	1.668
Compared to what I expected, the compensation is fair	117 25.5%	93 20.3%	71 15.5%	55 12.0%	76 16.6%	46 10.0%	3.04	1.708
I did get compensation I deserved	94 20.5%	96 21.0%	95 20.7%	43 9.4%	109 23.8%	21 4.6%	3.09	1.577
I am satisfied with the bank's promise to offer compensation	63 13.8%	105 22.9%	104 22.7%	79 17.2%	83 18.1%	24 5.2%	3.19	1.455
The compensation is satisfactory	111 24.2%	84 18.3%	108 23.6%	59 12.9%	79 17.2%	17 3.7%	2.92	1.518
The speed of compensation is good	86 18.8%	134 29.3%	94 20.5%	55 12.0%	78 17.0%	11 2.4%	2.86	1.431
Grand mean								

states that there is no significant relationship between complaints handling strategy and customer satisfaction is rejected.

Table 10.6 gives results of the descriptive statistics of respondent's responses on compensation strategy. The study requested respondents to rate the extent to which they agree with the statements on positive WOM. The results are given in Table 10.7.

Table 10.7 provides results of the descriptive statistics of respondent's responses on positive WOM.

Relating Tables 10.6 and 10.7 together, compensation strategy and positive WOM do not have the same pattern of increase. The finding reveals that customers do not get compensation according to their expectations. Furthermore, the findings indicate that the compensation is not satisfactory. However, there is positive WOM among the respondents. The finding reveals that when customers' friends were looking for a bank, they were properly referred and recommended. This provides answer to the research question two and enables the researcher to achieve objective two as well.

To test hypothesis two, the researcher used linear regression analysis. The data for compensation strategy and customer's positive word of mouth were formed by summing responses of all items for each of the variables. The results of the regression are presented in Table 10.8.

Table 10.7 Descriptive analysis of positive word of mouth

Items	*Strongly disagree*	*Disagree*	*Partially disagree*	*Partially agree*	*Agree*	*Strongly agree*	*Mean*	*Standard deviation*
Positive word of mouth	*Freq.* %	*Freq.* %	*Freq.* %	*Freq.* %	*Freq.* %	*Freq.* %		
When I experience good services with my bank, I inform others	14 3.1%	16 3.5%	33 7.2%	101 22.1%	166 36.2%	128 27.9%	4.69	1.224
When my friends were looking for a bank I referred them to my bank	17 3.7%	13 2.8%	37 8.1%	70 15.3%	222 48.5%	99 21.6%	4.67	1.198
I had recommended my banks to my friends	20 4.4%	8 1.7%	31 6.8%	103 22.5%	213 46.5%	83 18.1%	4.59	1.171
I had spread positive WOM concerning my bank	12 2.6%	22 4.8%	30 6.6%	119 26.0%	207 45.3%	67 14.7%	4.51	1.132
I say positive things about my bank to my colleagues and other people	11 2.4%	12 2.6%	41 9.0%	128 27.9%	183 40.0%	83 18.1%	4.55	1.112
I will always promote my bank services	17 3.7%	9 2.0%	36 7.9%	108 23.6%	169 36.9%	119 26.0%	4.66	1.212
Grand mean								

Table 10.8 Regression analysis for influence of compensation strategy on customer's positive word of mouth

Coefficients[a]					
Model	*Unstandardised coefficients*		*Standardised coefficients*	*t*	*Sig.*
	B	*Standard error*	*Beta*		
1 (Constant)	22.436	.643		34.908	.000
R = 0.386;	$R^2 = 0.149$;		$F_{(1,456)} = 79.504$, $p < 0.05$		

[a] Dependent variable: Customers positive word of mouth.

Table 10.8 illustrates regression analysis of compensation strategy on customer's positive WOM. From Table 10.6, compensation strategy has positive and significant influence on customer's positive WOM in Lagos State (β = .288, t = 8.916, p = 0.000). The result further shows that there is a positive linear relationship between compensation strategy and customer's positive WOM of selected banks. This is shown by a correlation (R) coefficient of 0.386. In addition, 14.9% of the variations in customer's positive WOM are explained by compensation strategy, while 85.1% remains unexplained by the regression model. Overall, the explanatory power of the model was considered statistically significant with the F ratio output of the model reporting a p-value of .000 ($F_{(1,456)} = 79.504$, $p < 0.05$). The regression model explaining the variance in customer's positive WOM brought about by compensation strategy was stated as follows:

$$PWM = 22.436 + 0.288COS \qquad \text{eq. (10.1)}$$

where

PWM = Positive word of mouth
COS = Compensation strategy

According to the regression equation (10.1), taking compensation strategy constant at zero, customer's positive WOM was 22.436. From the model, the unstandardised coefficient of compensation strategy was 0.288, which denotes that a unit increase in compensation strategy would lead to 0.288-unit increase in customer's positive WOM. The significant value is less than 0.05. Therefore, the null hypothesis four (H_{02}) which states that compensation strategy has no significant influence on a customer's positive WOM is hereby rejected.

10.4 Results and Discussions

The finding of hypothesis one states that there is a significant relationship between complaints handling strategy and customer satisfaction. The result agreed with the study of previous studies (Ateke & Kalu, 2016; Oranusi & Mojekeh, 2019). From the results, 78.4% of the respondents agreed that their complaints were handled in a timely manner, majority of the respondents agreed that bank's complaints handling process is simple and not complicated. Those who agreed that after a service failure, they were satisfied with immediate apology from their banks are 78.4% which shows that on the average the respondents partially agreed to the statement with a mean of 4.24 and a standard deviation of 1.288. This is supported by Ebere et al. (2020) that there is a positive relationship between service satisfaction in electronic banking and customers resolved complaints in deposit money banks in Nigeria. Based on the findings and its supporting literature, the study therefore rejects the null hypotheses (H_{01}) which states that there is no significant relationship between complaints handling strategy and customer satisfaction.

The result of hypothesis two revealed that compensation strategy has a significant influence on a customer's positive WOM. The finding is supported by the previous researchers such as Hart and Chigbu (2020), Vázquez-Casielles, Iglesias and Varela-Neira (2011), Chang, Wu, and Hsu, (2013), Ufua et al. (2021), and Lee, Singh, and Chan (2011). Hart and Chigbu (2020) found that compensation with anticipatory ability; attentive will facilitate positive WOM. Chang,Wu, and Hsu, (2013) found that in terms of reward approaches, intrinsic compensation (for example, apologising and providing reasonable explanations) and economic compensation (for example, providing product discounts or refunds) is shown to be more effective than product replacement. Finding also reveals that a majority of the respondents agreed with the statements in the positive WOM scale. Additionally, the standard deviation of 1.175 indicates that the responses were varied. In the study, those who agreed that they say positive things about their banks to their colleagues and other people are 86.2% as indicated by a mean of 4.55 and a standard deviation of 1.112. Those who agreed that they would always promote their banks services are 86.5% with a mean of 4.66 and a standard deviation of 1.212. Based on the findings and its extant supporting literature, the study, therefore, rejects the null hypotheses (H_{02}) which states that states compensation strategy has no significant influence on a customer's positive WOM.

10.5 Policy Implications

This study will help managers identify the key complaints handling strategies that can aid the maximisation of overall customers' satisfaction, modelling, designing frameworks and policies that can be used to improve customer's positive WOM and fast response to global competition. The results of the study provide information on how the banks in Nigeria can improve their overall customers' advocacy through complaints handling strategies initiatives.

10.6 Conclusion

There is no significant relationship between complaints handling strategy and customer satisfaction. The result of hypothesis one shows that there is a significant relationship between complaints handling strategy and customer satisfaction. The result revealed that complaints handling strategy has a positive and significant relationship with customer satisfaction ($r = .768^{**}$, $\rho = .000$). Any positive change in complaints handling strategy on customer satisfaction would lead to higher level of customer satisfaction. Based on the findings and its supporting literature, the study, therefore, rejects the null hypotheses.

The last hypothesis: Compensation strategy has no significant influence on a customer's positive WOM. Compensation strategy has a positive and significant influence on customer's positive WOM in Lagos State ($\beta = .288$, $t = 8.916$, $p = 0.000$). The result further shows that there is a positive linear relationship between compensation strategy and customer's positive WOM of selected banks. This is shown by a correlation (R) coefficient of 0.386. In addition, 14.9% of the variations in customer's positive WOM are explained by compensation strategy, while 85.1% remains unexplained by the regression model. Overall, the explanatory power of the model was considered statistically significant with the F ratio output of the model reporting a p-value of .000 ($F_{(1,456)} = 79.504$, $p < 0.05$). Therefore, the null hypothesis two (H_{02}) which states that compensation strategy has no significant influence on a customer's positive WOM is hereby rejected.

Conflict of Interest

Authors declare no conflict of interest.

Dataset

This manuscript has no associated dataset.

References

Aigboje, P., & Itai, M. (2023). Quality management effect: An exploratory study on market share of SMEs manufacturing companies in Port Harcourt and Aba, Nigeria. *International Journal of Business & Entrepreneurship Research, 14*(10), 104–112.

Atalik, O. (2007). Customer complaints about airline service: A preliminary study of Turkish frequent flyers. *Management Research News, 30*(6), 409–419. doi.org/10.1108/01409170710751908

Ateke, B., & Kalu, S. E. (2016). Complaint handling and post-complaint satisfaction of customers of eateries in Port Harcourt, Nigeria. *International Journal of Research in Business Studies and Management, 3*(12), 16–26. ijrbsm.ijrsset.org/papers/v3-i12/3.pdf

Awa, H, Nwobu, C, & Igwe, S. (2021). Service failure handling and resilience amongst airlines in Nigeria. *Cogent Business & Management, 8*(1). doi: 10.1080/23311975.2021.1892924

Awa, O., & Ukoha (2016). Correlates of justice encounter in service recovery and word-of-mouth publicity. *Cogent Business and Management Journal, 1*(1). doi.org/10.1080/23311975.2016.1179613

Berry, L., & Parasuraman, A. (2011). *Marketing services: Competing through quality*. New York: The Free Press.

Boshoff, C. & Leong, J. (1998). Empowerment, attribution and apologising as dimensions of service recovery an experimental study. *International Journal of Service Industry Management, 9*(1), 24–47. doi.org/10.1108/09564239810199932

Bryman, A., & Bell, E. (2011). *Business research methods* (3rd ed.). New York. Oxford: University Press Inc.

Central Bank of Nigeria (CBN), (2016). Circular on alleged excess, illegal charges by deposit money Banks. cbn.gov.ng/Out/2016/CCD/CBN_Press_Statement_Bank-charges.pdf

Chang, H., Wu, H., & Hsu, Y. (2013). Integrating a mobile augmented reality activity to contextualize student learning of a socio scientific issue. *British Journal of Educational Technology, 44*, 95–99. doi.org/10.1111/j.1467-8535.2012.01379.

Chueh, T., Wang, J., & Liao, H. (2014). Effects of service recovery on customer satisfaction and relationship retention in catering industry. *Journal of Anthropologist, 17*(3), 857–863.

Davidow, M. (2000). The bottom line impact of organizational responses to customer complaints. *Journal of Hospitality and Tourism Research, 24*(4), 473–490. doi/10.1177/109634800002400404

Davidow, M. (2003). Organizational responses to customer complaints: What works and what doesn't. *Journal of Service Research, 5*(3), 225–250. doi.10.1177/1094670502238917

Ebere, C., Fagbola, L., Jolayemi, L., & Balogun, A. (2020) Electronic banking and customers' satisfaction: Evidence from some selected deposit money banks in Nigeria. *Acta Universitatis Danubius OEconomica, 16*(2), 363–374.

Ekiz, H., & Huseyin, A. (2017). Measuring the impacts of organizational responses: A case of Northern Cyprus hotels. *Managing Global Transitions: International Research Journal, 5*(3), 271–287.

Estelami, H. (2000). Competitive and procedural determinants of delight and disappointment in consumer complaint outcomes. *Journal of Service Research, 2*, 285–300.

Grewal, D. Roggeveen, A. & Tsiros, M. (2008). The effects of compensation on repurchase intentions in service recovery. *Journal of Retailing 84(4),* 424–434. ssrn.com/abstract=2763115

Hill, S., Provost, F., & Volinsky, C. (2006). Network based marketing: Identifying likely adopters via consumer networks. *Statistical Sciences, 21*(2), 256–276.

Johnston, R., & Fern, A. (2017). Service recovery strategies for single and double deviation scenarios. *The Service Industries Journal, 12*(2), 69–82.

Kim, J., & Lynn, J. (2012). Classification of Asian complainers in restaurant services. *Asia Pacific Journal of Tourism Research, 12*(4), 365–375. doi.org/10.1080/10941660701761035

Krejcie, R. V., & Morgan, D. W. (1970). Determining sample size for research activities. *Educational and Psychological Measurement*. doi: 10.13140/RG.2.2.11445.19687

Lee, M; Singh. N, & Chan S, W, (2011). Service failures and recovery actions in the hotel industry: A text-mining approach. *Journal of Vacation Marketing, 17*(3). doi.10.1177/1356766711409182

Mattila, A., E., & Patterson, P. G. (2004). The impact of culture on consumers' perceptions of service recovery efforts. *Journal of Retailing, 80*(3), 196–206. doi.org/10.1016/j.jretai.2004.08.001

Maxham, J. (2014). Service recovery's influence on consumer satisfaction, positive word-of-mouth, and purchase intentions. *Journal of Business Research, 54*, 11–24.

Maxham, J. & Netemeyer, R. (2002). A longitudinal study of complaining customers' evaluations of multiple service failures and recovery efforts. *Journal of Marketing, 4*, 57–71. dx.doi.org/10.1509/jmkg.66.4.57.18512

Olonade, O. Y., Busari, D. A., Egharevba, M. E., George, T. O., & Adetunde, C. O. (2021). Factors Underlying the Success of Megamalls Over Small Shop Retailing in Ibadan Metropolis. Waseas transactions on environment and development. doi: 10.37394/232015.2021.17.103

Oranusi, I., & Mojekeh, M. O. (2019). Effect of service recovery on customer retention in selected commercial banks in Onitsha, Anambra State. *International Journal of Business & Law Research, 7*(3), 83–90.

Osagie, L. U., John, C. A., Geraldine, Egondu, U., & Ogemdi, N. E. (2021). E-service quality and customer satisfaction in deposit money banks. *International Journal of Marketing and Communication Studies, 5*(1), 1–19.

Rosenmayer, A., Mc-Quilken, L., Robertson, N., & Ogden, S. (2018). Omni-channel service failures and recoveries: Refined typologies using Facebook complaints. *Journal of Services Marketing, 32*(3), 269–285. doi.10.1108/JSM-04-2017-0117

Steven, A. B., Dong, Y., & Dresner, M., (2012). Linkages between customer service, customer satisfaction and performance in the airline industry: Investigation of non-linearity and moderating effects. *Transportation Research, Part E 48(4)*, 743–754. doi.10.1016/j.tre.2011.12.006

Swanson, S., & Kelley, S. (2011). Attributions and outcomes of the service recovery process. *Journal of Marketing Theory and Practice, 9*(4), 50–65.

Tax, S. & Brown, S. (2000). Service recovery: Research insights and practices. doi.org/10.4135/9781452231327.n19

Ufua, D. E., Ibidunni, A. S., Papadopoulos, T., Matthew, O. A., Khatoon, R., & Agboola, M. G. (2021). Implementing just-in-time inventory management to address contextual operational issues: A case study of a commercial livestock farm in southern Nigeria. *The TQM Journal*. doi.10.1108/TQM-09-2021-0268

Ufua, D. E., Papadopoulos, T., & Midgley, G. (2018). Systemic lean intervention: Enhancing lean with community operational research. *European Journal of Operational Research, 268*(3), 1134–1148.

Ufua, D. E., Salau, O. P., Ikpefan, O., Dirisu, J. I., & Okoli, E. E. (2020). Addressing operational complexities through re-inventing leadership style: A systemic leadership intervention. *Heliyon, 6*(7), e04270.

Wu, H. C., & Cheng, C. C. (2017). What drives green advocacy? A case study of leisure farms in Taiwan. *Journal of Hospitality and Tourism Management, 33*, 103–112.

Vázquez-Casielles, R., Iglesias, V. & Varela-Neira, C. (2012). Service recovery, satisfaction and behaviour intentions: Analysis of compensation and social comparison communication strategies. *The Service Industry Journal, 32*(1) https://doi.org/10.1080/02642069.2010.511187

11 Financial Inclusion and Its Implications for Cocoa Production in the Southwest Region of Cameroon

Norbert Ngoongeh Ngwang and Mary-Juliet Bime-Egwu

11.1 Introduction

The role of financial inclusion as a foundation for the economic development of most economies is common knowledge (Amoah et al., 2020; Li et al., 2023; Mhlanga et al., 2020; Ozili et al., 2023). Globally, about 1.7 billion people (representing 31% of people aged 15 years and above) are reported to be financially excluded, and about half of this population include poor-women households in rural areas (World Bank, 2022). Let alone, the vulnerable group such as beggars and slum dwellers rather opt for the informal banking sector despite its expensive rates (Malik et al., 2020). The United Nations in its 17 sustainable development goals (SDGs) identified the relevance of financial inclusion by including it as a major focus in 8 of these SDGs, where it enhances, for example, poverty eradication, and zero hunger, food security, and sustainable agriculture (IFAD, 2016; World Bank, 2022). Low production, truncated income, poverty, and inequality are typical issues farmers experience due to a plethora of factors, among which is financial exclusion (Adeola & Evans, 2017; Akanbi et al., 2020; Fowowe, 2020). Financial exclusion is more pronounced in African and Asian countries (Abubakar et al., 2020). About 25% of Africans are caught in the web of financial exclusion (World Bank, 2022), and Cameroon is one of those countries with low financial inclusion, where only about 40% (urban areas) and 17% (rural areas) had access to formal financial services (FFSs) in 2019 (Doh, 2020).

Financial inclusion's relevance is quite visible in the agricultural sector. Globally, cocoa producers fell short in the credit they sought by about USD[1,2] 150 billion, which had impeding dangers on sustainability in the sector (Bonnieux, 2019). Cocoa is an important export crop that is most traded worldwide and contributes enormously to the growth of all the economies that grow it (Suh & Molua, 2022). As of the 2021–2022 cocoa season, a total of 5.1 million metric tons of cocoa were produced worldwide (ICCO, 2022) by about 50 million smallholder farmers (Bonnieux, 2019). About 77% of the cocoa contribution comes from Africa alone, chiefly from West Africa, located in the tropical region (10°N and 10°S of the equator) (ICCO, 2019). In Africa, about 70% of the total population is involved in cocoa production, which contributes about 40% to its Gross Domestic Product (GDP) (Ozil, 2018). However, cocoa production and its value chain face sustainability

DOI: 10.4324/9781032655185-15

issues, and poverty remains widespread among its producers (Fountain & Hütz-Adams, 2015). This is seen when production continues to fall primarily because cocoa producers are excluded from FFSs (Adeola & Evans, 2017; Akanbi et al., 2020; Fowowe, 2020; Vercillo et al., 2015).

Cameroon is a major cocoa-producing country, accounting for 4.6% of global production. Despite being placed at the fifth position behind Ivory Coast, Ghana, Indonesia, and Nigeria with respective global contribution of 39.8%, 21.1%, 9.8%, and 5.5% (ICCO, 2023), Cameroon is faced with the issue of low production (Essougong et al., 2020; Ngwang & Meliko, 2021; Suh et al., 2020). About 292,471 tons of cocoa were produced nationally during the 2020–2021 season by six main regions out of the 10: the Center (43.6%), the Southwest (31.6%), the Littoral (13.5%), the South (5.2%), the East (3.1%), and the West (2.9%) (BIC, 2021).

The Southwest Region (SWR) used to be at the top in terms of cocoa contribution in the nation but no longer, after the emergence of the socio-political crisis[3] that began in 2016 (BIC, 2021). This crisis further exacerbated the level of financial exclusion, where most financial institutions were shut down and others relocated to urban areas and other regions, leading to several related issues that impeded cocoa production in the region. Some of these issues are untimely credit services with unaffordable terms and conditions (Martey et al., 2015), lack of technical assistance, lack of access to finance, and inefficient use of inputs and technology (Mukete et al., 2018), lack of collateral security, distant formal financial institutions, and low income (Ngwang & Bime, 2023). Access to finance could considerably enhance cocoa production in the region. Demirgüç-Kunt et al. (2018) and Olaniyi (2017) emphasized the need for financial inclusion in order to enhance cocoa production, poverty reduction, and social inclusiveness. Relatedly, Suh et al. (2020) show that financial incentives such as premiums support farmers and promote the production of safe and quality cocoa beans, improving their livelihoods.

In all, what is suggested in this study is a low level of financial inclusion (Omar & Inaba, 2020) that is further influencing the already low level of cocoa production in Cameroon and the SWR in particular (BIC, 2021; Mukete et al., 2018). Drawing from other SSA countries, Cameroon falls below the average condition when considering variables like number of bank branches accessible to every group of 1,000 adults, account ownership, number of financial institutions, and formal savings (Ilunguana et al., 2020). No study known to this researcher is seeking the implications of financial inclusion for cocoa production in Cameroon. Considering that financial inclusion varies across countries (Ozili, 2020), this study attempts to examine the pioneering effect of financial inclusion on cocoa production in Cameroon. Thus, this study has three objectives: (1) to assess the implication of financial inclusion for cocoa production in the SWR of Cameroon; (2) to examine the level of implication through the decomposed results by gender, land ownership, and scale of production; and (3) to identify the major constraints to cocoa production in the area. This paper is further structured according to the following sections: method and data (Section 11.2), results and discussion (Section 11.3), and conclusion and recommendations (Section 11.4).

11.2 Method and Data

11.2.1 Study Area

Cameroon, classified as a low-middle-income country, has a total population of about 27.2 million people (World Bank, 2021) and is made up of 10 administrative regions, including the SWR which is the study area. It is an important cocoa-growing region and is ranked second in the nation after the Centre region in terms of cocoa bean contribution (BIC, 2021). The region consists of about 1,553,300 inhabitants with varying ethnic groups (City Population, 2020). Cocoa production affects the lives of about 79,893 farmers who cultivate a total surface area of about 211,148.5 ha with about 2–3 ha on average per farmer in the region (MINADER, 2021). The region has a longer duration of the rainy season (seven months), accompanied by high humidity of usually above 60%, temperatures ranging from 23°C and 28°C and rich volcanic soils that promote the cultivation of cocoa and other crops like palms, rubber, tea, cassava, yams, cocoyams, maize, egusi, groundnuts, pepper, and plantains (DDARD, 2020). With a surface area of about 25,410 km^2, the SWR is geographically positioned within latitude 2° and longitude 6° N, which is just above the equator (Chambon & Mokoko, 2015) with six administrative divisions (Manyu, Lebialem, Koupe-Manengouba, Ndian, Meme, and Fako).

11.2.2 Sampling and Data Collection

Primary data was obtained for the study through stratified multistage sampling technique. In the first stage, purposive sampling was applied to select the main cocoa-producing divisions in the SWR (Meme, Manyu, Koupe-Manengouba, and Fako) based on their percentage contribution to cocoa output in the region. The second stage purposefully selected four areas from each of the four divisions (Konye, Mamfe, Tombel, and Buea, respectively) due to accessibility. In the third stage, 400 respondents (100 from each area) were randomly selected, in line with the Cochran (1963) equation for large populations, thus, 380 respondents were valid for analysis.

11.2.3 Analytical Framework

The Cobb-Douglas production function (CDPF) has remained among the top-used production functions in social sciences. It has been widely used in empirical studies (Khatun & Afroze, 2016; Suh & Molua, 2022) to estimate the coefficient of inputs, their marginal productivities, factor shares in total output and degree of returns to scale. The CDPF is widely used due to its applicability and simplicity as it can be linearized and easily estimated using the ordinary least square (OLS) technique. Thus, the CDPF was used in this study to examine the significance of financial inclusion for cocoa production in the SWR of Cameroon.

An indicator of financial inclusion was determined and its implication on production derived. The decomposed results by gender, land ownership, and scale

Table 11.1 Variables used to construct the financial inclusion indicator (Findex)

Variable	*Modality*	*Nature*
Access: Do you own an account at any formal financial institution (FFI)?	{1 = Yes; 0 = No}	Dummy
Use: Have you borrowed money from any FFI before?	{1 = Yes; 0 = No}	Dummy
Quality: Have you saved in any FFI before?	{1 = Yes; 0 = No}	Dummy

of production are further obtained. Since financial inclusion is one of the key-determining factors according to this study, a financial inclusion indicator was developed and captured as Findex. The construction of index in empirical studies has gained ground over the years (Mohammed et al., 2020; Peprah et al., 2020). Primarily, two methods are trendy; the principal component analysis (PCA) and the multiple correspondence analysis (MCA). They mainly differ in that PCA is construed on continuous variables and MCA on dummy variables. Moreover, MCA is non-parametric and not subject to assumptions of normality and linearity (Aslan et al., 2017). Since the financial inclusion variables considered in this study are dichotomous (Table 11.1), the MCA was chosen, considering the variables access to FFSs (account ownership), use of FFSs (access to loans), and quality of FFSs (savings) as the main dimensions of financial inclusion (Fowowe, 2020; Fowowe & Folarin, 2019; Soumaré et al., 2016). In other to obtain this, a set of synthetic variables as well as their modalities are selected on a matrix of indicators (Table 11.1).

11.2.4 Empirical Model

Implicitly, the CDPF could be expressed as follows (Suh & Molua, 2022):

$$Q = f\left(Ls, Lb\right) = ALs^{\beta 1} Lb^{\beta 2} \varepsilon^{\mu} \tag{11.1}$$

where Q, the production level (cocoa output in kg); A, the constant term (efficiency parameter); Ls, land size (ha) under cultivation; Lb, labor (days); ε, the base of natural logarithm; μ, stochastic disturbance term; and β, coefficient of the respective exogenous variables.

Equation (11.1) is further linearized by applying logarithm on either side of the equation as follows:

$$\ln Q = \ln A + \beta 1 \ln Ls + \beta 2 \ln Lb + \mu \tag{11.2}$$

Based on production theory, it is feasible to include more variables (financial inclusion, traditional inputs, and socio-economic) in the augmented CDPF model as follows:

$$\begin{aligned} \ln Q = {} & \beta 0 + \beta 1 \ln Findex + \beta 2 \ln Pt + \beta 3 \ln Ls + \beta 4 \ln Lb + \beta 5 \ln Ft \\ & + \beta 6 \ln Ag + \beta 7 \ln Hs + \beta 8 Po + \beta 9 El + \mu \end{aligned} \tag{11.3}$$

where Findex is the financial inclusion indicator; Pt, pesticide cost (FCFA); Ls, land size; Lb, labor; Ft, fertilizer (kg); Ag, age (years); Hs, household size; Po, primary occupation; El, education level; lnA equal $\beta 0$ (Equation 11.1); and $\beta 1$ to $\beta 9$ are coefficients of the respective variables.

11.3 Results and Discussion

11.3.1 Descriptive Statistics on Cocoa-Producing Variables

Concerning cocoa production, the mean annual quantity of cocoa that a farmer could harvest was about 1,289 kg (1.3 tons). Several factors influenced the level of cocoa output (Table 11.2).

First, the Findex with a mean of –1.58e–08 and standard deviation (SD) of 1 revealed a low level of financial inclusion of about 1.6%. Limited access to credit and savings greatly hinder cocoa production. Averagely, the farmers spent about 164,740 FCFA on pesticides. Pest attack is a threat to cocoa output especially cocoa black pod disease which is very prominent due to longer duration of the rainy season in the production cycle (Wessel & Quist-Wessel, 2015). Hence, how much the producers invest in pest management determines their yield. Moreover, the 164,740 FCFA spent on pesticides on a mean land size of 2.6 ha is insufficient for the whole year. For the effective management of cocoa farms against pests, pesticides consume about 20% of the total cost (Ngwang & Meliko, 2021). Therefore, producers must equally engage in proper pest and disease control measures such as good agricultural practices (GAPs).

Also, the mean number of annual labor days was found to be 73.3 days. Likewise, the mean household (HH) size was five members per HH with about 80% of HH heads involved full-time in cocoa production. All these parameters contributed to a proper labor source. Hence, as a major cost element, labor must be easily accessed and properly managed in order to guarantee high levels of cocoa production.

Table 11.2 Descriptive statistics on cocoa-producing variables

Variables	*Mean*	*SD*	*Minimum*	*Maximum*
Quantity harvested in kg	1,289.0	1,396.4	186	13,000
Findex	–1.58e–08	1.0	–2.0	0.6
Pesticide cost in FCFA	164,739.6	180,596.3	26,500	1,581,600
Land size in ha	2.6	2.6	0.5	18.5
Labor days	73.3	76.6	10	510
Transportation cost in FCFA	73,256.8	92,790.8	7,500	925,000
Age in years	40.8	11.6	18	67
Household size	5.1	1.9	2	13
Full-time farmer	0.8	0.4	0	1
Above primary education	0.3	0.4	0	1
N	380			

Source: Authors' computation from survey data (2021).

Table 11.3 Multiple correspondence analysis of financial inclusion dimensions

Dimension	*Principal inertia*	*Percent*	*Cumulative percent*
dim 1	0.8537	85.37	85.37
dim 2	0.1068	10.68	96.05
dim 3	0.0395	3.95	100.00
Total	1	100.00	

Source: Authors' computation from survey data (2021).

Moreover, the farmers spent, on average, about 73,255 FCFA on transportation. This is tied up to the distant farms and the poor road infrastructure. Consequently, investing in farm-to-market roads is beneficial. Likewise, education will enable the producers to embrace new techniques of production and a consequent increase in yields. However, only about 30% of the respondents obtained formal education above the primary level. This contributed negatively to farm output.

Theoretically, access to, use, and quality of FFSs enhance the production level of farmers (Akanbi et al., 2020) with positive indications on farm income and financial inclusion. The results of the MCA's first stage as presented in Table 11.3 (on account of the principal inertia) showed that the first instrument/dimension (access to FFSs) is a major driver of financial inclusion as it accounts for up to 85.37%. Access to FFSs is a proxy for the use of FFSs (Chaia et al., 2009) where financial inclusion is not only limited to the creation of a bank account (Malik & Yadav, 2022).

11.3.2 Implications of Financial Inclusion for Cocoa Production

11.3.2.1 General Estimates on the Implication of Financial Inclusion for Cocoa Production

Financial inclusion was revealed to have a significant positive ($P < 0.01$) implication for cocoa production (Table 11.4). The greater the level of financial inclusion, the higher the level of production by about 26% increase in cocoa output. Osabohien et al. (2020) and Taise (2013) equally revealed that financial inclusion through access to credit can cause yields and income to increase to an extent of three times above those without access. Thus, financial inclusion measures could boost production and guarantee sustainability in the cocoa sector.

Likewise, a larger farmland could result in higher cocoa yields. Statistically significant at 1%, an additional hectare of farmland could lead to about 67% increase in output. According to Teryomenko (2008), farm size indeed has a significant positive effect on agricultural production but could only increase up to a certain size of land (e.g., 120 ha for cereals) due to the non-linear relationship. Hence, farmers should be encouraged to expand their farms through relaxed tenure systems. Similarly, an increase in the number of labor days has the possibility of

Table 11.4 Implications of financial inclusion for cocoa production

Variable	*Coefficient*	*Standard value*	*Significance*	*Hypothesis*
Financial inclusion (Findex)	0.2556***	0.0500	$P \leq 0.000$	Accepted
Pesticide cost (FCFA)	−0.0007	0.0480	$P \leq 0.988$	Not accepted
Land size (ha)	0.6735***	0.0625	$P \leq 0.000$	Accepted
Labor (days)	0.1512***	0.0479	$P \leq 0.002$	Accepted
Transportation cost (FCFA)	0.1734***	0.0278	$P \leq 0.000$	Accepted
Age (years)	−0.0201	0.0431	$P \leq 0.641$	Not accepted
Household size	−0.0822***	0.0302	$P \leq 0.007$	Accepted
Full-time farmer	0.0019	0.0119	$P \leq 0.872$	Not accepted
Above primary education	0.0053	0.0123	$P \leq 0.664$	Not accepted
Constant	1.8345***	0.2618	0.000	
Adjusted R^2	0.94			
F-value (9, 370)	676.29			
Prob > F	0.0000			
N	380			

Note: *** $P < 0.01$.

Source: Authors' computation from survey data (2021).

increasing output significantly by about 15%. This finding is consistent with that of Akanbi et al. (2020) to the case of Uganda. Mulie (2014) further asserted that cocoa production is labor-intensive and more labor could be accessed through hiring. Financial inclusion could enhance the payment of hired labor.

An increase in transportation cost was revealed to significantly enhance cocoa production. If transportation costs increased by a franc, the level of production increased by about 17%. This could be because the farms are further away from homes and/or market with bad roads (especially during the rainy season) and usually entails transportation by bike. Similarly, Kassali et al. (2009) noted that the distance of the farm is directly proportional to the technical efficiency of food farmers. Hence, the construction of farm-to-market roads is eminent.

Generally, a larger family size requires more labor and, hence, more output (Teryomenko, 2008). However, the results revealed that a larger HH size rather causes a fall in the production level by about 8%. This was because most of the HH members were children and/or students and did not fully commit themselves to cocoa production. As a result, most of the farmers (57.9%) hired labor in the cause of production.

The primary occupation of farmers and their education level also had an impact on the production level of cocoa producers in the area. Farmers who were involved full-time in farming and those with an education level above the primary level (i.e., secondary and tertiary education) had a positive relationship with cocoa production. If the number of full-time farmers increased and the level of education rose, output was bound to increase as well although not statistically significant. Moving forward, Kassali et al. (2009) emphasized the need for extension services and a higher level of experience as a way of enhancing the producers' knowledge on proper agronomic practices.

11.3.2.2 Implications of Financial Inclusion for Cocoa Production by Gender and Land Ownership

Irrespective of gender and the nature of land ownership, financial inclusion exhibited a positive and statistically significant relationship (P < 0.05) with cocoa production (Table 11.5). Female producers observed a higher level in production by about 43.8% when compared to their male counterparts (25.6%). Likewise, landowners had a higher output of about 30.8% when compared to 28.6% for those who leased land. Based on these findings, financial inclusion results in higher cocoa production for female farmers and land owners. Thus, women should be included in the financial mainstream and encouraged as well to actively pick up roles in cocoa production where just about 5% of women interviewed were currently involved. Also, farmers should be encouraged to own land through relaxed tenure systems. Land serves as collateral and will enable producers to participate fully in the financial market, thus, improving production.

Table 11.5 Implications of financial inclusion for cocoa production by gender and land ownership

	Gender		*Land ownership*	
Variable	*Male*	*Female*	*Owned land*	*Leased land*
Financial inclusion indicator	0.2561***	0.4383**	0.3083***	0.2856***
	(0.0501)	(0.1637)	(0.0547)	(0.0934)
Pesticide cost	0.0045	0.6107	0.0059	−0.0445
	(0.0476)	(0.4282)	(0.0639)	(0.0734)
Land size	0.6791***	−0.5742	0.2514**	0.8103***
	(0.0624)	(0.3319)	(0.1015)	(0.0922)
Labor days	0.1629***	−0.2107	0.5509***	0.0789
	(0.0476)	(0.4972)	(0.0963)	(0.0623)
Transportation cost	0.1511***	1.0470***	0.1753***	0.1292**
	(0.0279)	(0.1039)	(0.0299)	(0.0548)
Age	−0.0292	−0.2700	0.0048	−0.1067
	(0.0427)	(0.2632)	(0.0468)	(0.0824)
Household size	−0.0663**	−0.0963	−0.0961***	−0.0630
	(0.0308)	(0.1093)	(0.0324)	(0.0562)
Full-time farmer	0.0000	(omitted)	−0.0097	0.0278
	(0.0118)		(0.0128)	(0.0227)
Above primary education	0.0045	(omitted)	0.0023	−0.0082
	(0.0121)		(0.0127)	(0.0242)
Constant	1.8965***	−3.9868**	1.2189***	2.4519***
	(0.2610)	(1.5627)	(0.3286)	(0.4298)
Adjusted R^2	0.94	0.97	0.97	0.90
F-value	676.37	72.69	675.71	167.42
Prob > F	0.0000	0.0000	0.0000	0.0000
N	362	18	220	160

Note: *** P < 0.01, ** P < 0.05. Values in parentheses are the standard values.

Source: Authors' computation from survey data (2021).

11.3.2.3 Implications of Financial Inclusion for Cocoa Production by Scale of Production and Production Constraints

In line with Fule (2013), the scale of production was classified into three groups: small-scale ($x \leq 2$ ha), medium-scale (2 ha $< x <$ 5 ha), and large-scale ($x \geq$ 5ha), to ascertain if financial inclusion had any effect. Majority of the farmers (62.1%) operated on a small-scale and the rest, medium-scale (27.1%), and large-scale (10.8%). Consequently, the greater the farmland the fewer the number of farmers. This confirmed the poor land tenure system in the region and the difficulties faced in acquiring more land. On account of the adjusted R^2 and F-ratio, the results generally proved statistically significant. The variables considered (Findex, pesticide cost, labor days, transportation cost, age, HH size, primary occupation, and education level) accounted for over 50% of cocoa production in the study area (Table 11.6).

The results of this study exposed that irrespective of the scale of production, financial inclusion still has a significant effect ($P < 0.05$) on cocoa production. That is, higher levels of financial inclusion result in increased cocoa production, irrespective of the farm size. Akudugu (2016) also found out that access to formal credit increases agricultural productivity by about 10% in Ghana. However, those who produce on a small-scale had a higher tendency of being more productive by about 35.6% than the large-scale (31.0%) and medium-scale farmers (15.1%) (Table 11.6). The study suggests that the small-scale farmers were more productive because of proper management and proficiency in managing smaller farms. Hence, due to the limited farm size by many farmers, small-scale farmers can be included

Table 11.6 Implications of financial inclusion for cocoa production by the scale of production

	Small-scale ($x \leq$ 2ha)		*Medium-scale (2ha $< x <$ 5ha)*		*Large-scale ($x \geq$ 5 ha)*	
Variable	*Coefficient*	*Standard value*	*Coefficient*	*Standard value*	*Coefficient*	*Standard value*
Financial inclusion	0.3562***	0.0894	0.1507**	0.0669	0.3095**	0.1225
Pesticide cost	0.3300***	0.0573	0.0101	0.0890	0.0923	0.1908
Labor days	0.3769***	0.0586	0.3518***	0.1130	0.5172***	0.1614
Transportation cost	0.2043***	0.0385	0.5083***	0.0603	0.2776**	0.1245
Age	−0.0519	0.0682	0.0373	0.0735	0.3822***	0.1214
Household size	−0.0537	0.0528	−0.1398***	0.04263	−0.1319*	0.0718
Full-time farmer	0.0205	0.0213	−0.0012	0.0174	−0.0265	0.0250
Above primary education	0.0109	0.0208	0.0282*	0.0167	0.0444	0.0335
Constant	−0.1859	0.2708	0.0153	0.3461	−0.1555	0.4626
Adjusted R^2	0.74		0.79		0.93	
F-value (8, 227)	83.60		F(8, 94) 50.32		F(8, 32)70.23	
Prob > F	0.0000		0.0000		0.0000	
N	236		103		41	

Note: *** $P < 0.01$, ** $P < 0.05$, * $P < 0.1$.

Source: Authors' computation from survey data (2021).

in the formal financial market to boost their performance. Should larger farmlands be considered, the producers need to consider appropriate planting distance, management of pests and diseases, and obtain adequate infrastructures on drying facilities and road networks.

In the case of more farmlands, additional labor is also required. The findings further revealed that an additional labor day was more productive for large-scale farmers contributing about 51.7% of output when compared to the small-scale producers with just 37.7%. It is common sense that additional land will require more labor force. Elsewhere (Eastern Uganda), Akanbi et al. (2020) also observed that labor has a significant positive effect on productivity.

The study further revealed the major constraints on cocoa production: inadequate credit (26.3%), unsuitable pricing (23.4%), inadequate land (16.6%), and the socio-political instability in the area (15.8%), confirming the place of financial inclusion for credit purposes.

11.4 Conclusion and Recommendations

Utilizing the CDPF model, we show a significant positive association between financial inclusion and cocoa production by about 26%. The other variables that were statistically significant in influencing cocoa production were land size, labor days, transportation cost, and HH size. Moreover, financial inclusion generally proved to have a significant positive implication on cocoa production irrespective of gender, type of land ownership, and the scale of production. However, female producers and those who owned the land they cultivated obtained a higher level of production than their male counterparts and those who leased land by about 18.2% and 2.2%, respectively. Additionally, those who produced on a small-scale ($x \leq 2$ha) had a higher tendency of being more productive by about 20.5% than medium-scale, and 4.6% than the large-scale farmers.

It is imperative that, financial inclusion initiatives like establishment of more formal financial institutions is embraced. The government could promote this through sound policies like tax relief and subsidies for financial institutions. Also, women's inclusion in the financial mainstream and participation in the cocoa sector should be encouraged. The universal thought is that, empowering women implies empowering the nation. Moving forward, there is a need for the government to revisit its land policy so as to increase farmers' access to cheap land in synergy with the local authorities. Also, land documents could serve collateral for loans.

For the purpose of further research, this study can be expanded to other communities to make valid conclusions for the SWR which of course would require funding. Also, it could be extended to other regions to identify if the contexts matter and as well to other crops of food security relevance such as maize, oil palm, plantains, etc.

Acknowledgment

The authors are grateful to the College of Technology for the encouragement and for providing an enabling environment to be able to carry out this research.

Author's Contribution

Norbert Ngoongeh Ngwang did the conceptualization, engaged in the study's questionnaire design, methodology, investigation and data curation, formal analysis, writing of original draft, visualization and compilation of the of the article. Mary-Juliet Bime-Egwu also involved in the conceptualization and data curation, provided the resources, supervision, likewise reviewed and edited the work.

Conflict of Interest

The authors declare that they have no known competing financial interests or personal relationships that could have appeared to influence the work reported in this paper.

Funding

This research did not have any external funding.

Notes

1 Throughout this report, the terms "USD" and "FCFA", respectively, stand for the United States Dollar, Franc Communauté Financière d'Afrique ("Financial Community of Africa").
2 Exchange rate at USD 1 = 601.7 FCFA (https://www.forbes.com/advisor/money-transfer/currency-converter/usd-xaf/. Accessed 23 June 2023).
3 "The current crisis in Cameroon's Northwest and Southwest regions is the latest (and most severe and intense) iteration of a conflict characterized by a linguistic fault line – a legacy of colonialism – that signifies deeper grievances of alienated identity and perceptions of structural inequality" (World Bank, 2021, p. 9).

References

Abubakar, A. M., Daneji, B. A., Muhammed, A. I., & Chekene, I. A. (2020). Driving faster financial inclusion in developing nations. *Technology Audit and Production Reserves*. https://doi.org/10.15587/2706-5448.2020.201120.

Adeola, O., & Evans, O. (2017). The impact of microfinance on financial inclusion in Nigeria. *The Journal of Developing Areas*, *51*(4), 193–206.

Akanbi, A., Olayide, O., & Agabalinda, C. (2020). Effects of financial inclusion on smallholder farmers' productivity in Busoga Region of Eastern Uganda. MDP-IFAD Research Report, Project for Financial Inclusion in Rural Areas (PROFIRA) Ministry of Finance, Planning and Economic Development, Kampala, Uganda. http://dx.doi.org/10.13140/RG.2.2.18381.59362

Akudugu, M. A. (2016). Agricultural productivity, credit and farm size nexus in Africa: A case study of Ghana. *Agricultural Finance Review*, *76*(2), 288–308.

Amoah, A., Korle, K., & Asiama, R. K. (2020). Mobile money as a financial inclusion instrument: What are the determinants? *International Journal of Social Economics*, *47*(10), 1283–1297.

Aslan, G., Deléchat, C., Newiak, M. M., & Yang, M. F. (2017). Inequality in financial inclusion and income inequality. Washington: International Monetary Fund.

BIC (2021). Business in Cameroon, Cocoa: 2020 – 2021 has been a record-breaking season, the NCCB says. https://www.businessincameroon.com/agriculture/2308-11813-cocoa-2020-2021-has-been-a-record-breaking-season-the-nccb-says.

Bonnieux, G. (2019). Access to finance for cocoa farmers. Access to Finance Working Group. Swiss Platform for Sustainable Cocoa. https://www.kakaoplattform.ch/fileadmin/redaktion/dokumente/news/Access_to_finance_for_cocoa_Swiss_Platform_for_Sustainable_Cocoa_June_2019.pdf

Chaia, A., Dalal, A., Goland, T., Gonzalez, M. J., Morduch, J., & Schiff, R. (2012). Half the world is unbanked. https://doi.org/10.7551/mitpress/9517.003.0003

Chambon, B., & Mokoko, S. G. (2015). Determinants in the choice of perennial crops in diversified production systems of rubber growers in South-Western Cameroon. *Economics and Ecology of Diversification*, 225–237. https://doi.org/10.1007/978-94-017-7294-5_10.

City Population (2020). Cameroon Cities Population. Accessed at https://www.citypopulation.de/en/cameroon/cities/.

Cochran, W. G. (1963). *Sampling techniques* (2nd ed.). New York: John Wiley & Sons.

DDARD (2020). *The divisional delegation of agriculture and rural development*. MINADER: Report for the South West Region.

Demirgüç-Kunt, A., Klapper, L., Singer, D., Ansar, S., & Hess, J. (2018). *The global findex database 2017: Measuring financial inclusion and the fintech revolution*. Washington: World Bank Group.

Doh, E. T. (2020). The impact of innovation on financial inclusion case of the financial sector of Cameroon. *International Journal of Economics and Business Management*, *6*(4), 26–39.

Essougong, K. U. P., Slingerland, M., Mathé, S. *et al.* (2020). Farmers' Perceptions as a Driver of Agricultural Practices: Understanding Soil Fertility Management Practices in Cocoa Agroforestry Systems in Cameroon. *Human Ecology*, *48*, 709–720. https://doi.org/10.1007/s10745-020-00190-0

Fountain, A. C., & Hütz-Adams, F. (2015). Cocoa Barometer 2015. http://www.cocoabarometer.org/Cocoa_Barometer/Download_files/Cocoa%20Barometer%202015%20.pdf.

Fowowe, B. (2020). The effects of financial inclusion on agricultural productivity in Nigeria. *Journal of Economics and Development*, *22*(1), 61–79. https://doi.org/10.1108/JED-11-2019-0059.

Fowowe, B., & Folarin, E. O. (2019). The effects of fragility and financial inequalities on inclusive growth in African countries. *Review of Development Economics*, *23*, 1141–1176.

Fule, C. B. (2013). Small-scale versus large-scale cocoa farming in Cameroon; Which farm type is more ready for the future? MSc thesis in the Department of Agricultural Food and Environmental Policy Analysis (AFEPA), Uppsala, Sweden.

Hunguana, H., Fall, A. S., Yitamben, G., Goases, M., Gwarinda, S., & Trust, G. M. (2020). Women's Financial Inclusion in Cameroon. Final Report © 2020, New Faces New Voices (Graca Machel Trust). Accessed at https://idl-bnc-idrc.dspacedirect.org/bitstream/handle/10625/59154/59308.pdf.

ICCO (2019). International Cocoa Organization cocoa facts and figures. Accessed at https://www.kakaoplattform.ch/about-cocoa/cocoa-facts-and-figures.

ICCO (2022). International Cocoa Organization on quarterly bulletin of cocoa statistics. Accessed at https://www.icco.org/november-2022-quarterly-bulletin-of-cocoa-statistics/.

ICCO (2023). Cocoa market report. Accessed at https://www.icco.org/wp-content/uploads/ICCO-Monthly-Cocoa-Market-Report-April-2023.pdf

IFAD (2016). Rural finance: Sustainable and inclusive financing for rural transformation. Inclusive Rural Financial Services Policy and Technical Advisory Division IFAD. Accessed at https://www.ifad.org/documents/38714170/39150184/Rural+finance.pdf/ef7080b0-3bd5-4a7f-8830-ac1fbfb07d4b?t=1505147487000 www.ifad.org/topic/overview/tags/rural_finance.

Kassali, R., Ayanwale, A. B., & Williams, S. B. (2009). Farm location and determinants of agricultural productivity in the Oke-Ogun Area of Oyo State, Nigeria. *Journal of Sustainable Development in Africa*, *11*(2), 1–19.

Khatun, T., & Afroze, S. (2016). Relationship between real GDP and labour & capital by applying the Cobb-Douglas production function: A comparative analysis among selected Asian countries. *Journal of Business Studies*, *37*(1), 113–129.

Li, Z., Hasan, M. M., & Lu, Z. (2023). Studying financial inclusion, energy poverty, and economic development of South Asian countries. *Environmental Science and Pollution Research*, *30*, 30644–30655. https://doi.org/10.1007/s11356-022-24209-9.

Malik, F. A., & Yadav, D. K. (2022). Impact of recent financial inclusion schemes on status of financial inclusion in India: Secondary data analysis. In *Financial inclusion schemes in India*. Singapore: Springer. https://doi.org/10.1007/978-981-19-1316-7_3.

Malik, F. A., Yadav, D. K., Adam, H., & Omrane, A. (2020). The urban poor and their financial behavior. In *Sustainable entrepreneurship, renewable energy-based projects, and digitalization*. Oxfordshire: Taylor & Francis. https://doi.org/10.1201/9781003097921.

Martey, E., Wiredu, A. N., Etwire, P. M. & Kuwornu, J. K. M. (2019). The impact of credit on the technical efficiency of maize-producing households in Northern Ghana. *Agricultural Finance Review*, *79*(3), 304–322. https://doi.org/10.1108/AFR-05-2018-0041

Mhlanga, D., Henry, D. S., & Moloi, T. (2020). Financial inclusion and poverty alleviation among smallholder farmers in Zimbabwe. *Eurasian Journal of Economics and Finance*, *8*(3), 168–182. https://doi.org/10.15604/ejef.2020.08.03.004.

MINADER (2021). Annual Report for the Ministry of Agriculture and Rural Development, South West Regional Delegation, Chief of Service, SS (unpublished).

Mohammed, F., Barrowclough, M. J., Kibler, M. L., & Boerngen, M. A. (2020). Measuring usage of formal financial services as a proxy for financial inclusion: A case of agricultural households in Ghana. *Agricultural Finance Review*, *80*(4), 471–489. https://doi.org/10.1108/AFR-09-2019-0096

Mukete, N., Zhou, L., Mukete, B., & Bobyeg, P. (2018). Cocoa production in Cameroon: A socioeconomic and technical efficiency perspective. *International Journal of Agricultural Economics*, *3*(1), 1–8. https://doi.org/10.11648/j.ijae.20180301.11.

Mulie, H. (2014). The determinants of profit efficiency of coffee producing and marketing cooperatives (the case study of sidama coffee farmers' union). *Journal of Economics and Sustainable Development*, *5*(7), 125–137. https://core.ac.uk/download/pdf/234646339.pdf

Ngwang, N. N., & Bime, M. J. E. (2023). Drivers of financial inclusion among cocoa producers in the Southwest Region of Cameroon. *Finance & Economics Review*, *5*(1), 1–13. https://doi.org/10.38157/fer.v5i1.525.

Ngwang, N. N., & Meliko, M. O. (2021). Profitability analysis of smallholder cocoa production in South West Region of Cameroon. *African Journal of Agricultural Research*, *17*(7), 991–997. https://doi.org/10.5897/AJAR2021.15452.

Olaniyi, E. (2017). Back to the land: The impact of financial inclusion on agriculture in Nigeria. *Iranian Economic Review*, *21*(4), 885–903. https://ier.ut.ac.ir/article_64086_74016617c9b22d98af659d586409eaff.pdf

Omar, A., & Inaba, K. (2020). Does financial inclusion reduce poverty and income inequality in developing countries? A panel data analysis. *Journal of Economic Structures*, *9*, 37.

Osabohien, R., Adeleye, N., & Alwis, T. (2020). Agro-financing and food production in Nigeria. *Journal of Business and Economics*, *6*(5). https://doi.org/10.1016/j.heliyon.2020.e04001.

Ozili, P. K. (2018). Impact of digital finance on financial inclusion and stability. *Borsa Instanbul Review*, *18*(4), 329–340. Accessed at http://http//www.elsevier.com/journals/borsa-istanbul-review/2214-8450

Ozili, P. K. (2020): Financial inclusion research around the world: A review. *Forum for Social Economics*, *50*(4), 457–479. https://doi.org/10.1080/07360932.2020.1715238.

Ozili, P. K., Lay, S. H., & Syed, A. A. (2023). Impact of financial inclusion on economic growth in secular and religious countries. *Journal of Financial Regulation and Compliance*, *31*(4), 420–444. Accessed at https://doi.org/10.1108/JFRC-08-2022-0093.

Peprah, J. A., Koomson, I., Sebu, J., & Chei, B. (2020). Improving productivity among smallholder farmers in Ghana: Does financial inclusion matter? *Agricultural Finance Review*. https://doi.org/10.1108/AFR-12-2019-0132.

Soumaré, I., Tchana, T. F., & Kengne, T. M. (2016). Analysis of the determinants of financial inclusion in Central and West Africa. *Transnational Corporations Review*, *8*(4), 231–249. https://doi.org/10.1080/19186444.2016.1265763. https://www.sciencedirect.com/science/article/pii/S1925209924001669

Suh, N. N., & Molua, E. L. (2022). Cocoa production under climate variability and farm management challenges: Some farmers' perspective. *Journal of Agriculture and Food Research*. https://doi.org/10.1016/j.jafr.2022.100282.

Suh, N. N., F. Njimanted, G., & Thalut, N. (2020). Effect of farmers' management practices on safety and quality standards of cocoa production: A structural equation modeling approach. *Cogent Food & Agriculture*, *6*(1), 1844848. https://doi.org/10.1080/23311932.2020.1844848.

Tasie, C. M. (2013). Effects of International Fund for Agricultural Development (IFAD) credit supply on rural farmers in Rivers State, Nigeria. *Journal of Development and Agricultural Economics*, *5*(5), 186–191. http://dx.doi.org/10.5897/JDAE12.062

Teryomenko, H. (2008). Farm size and determinants of agricultural productivity in Ukraine. A thesis submitted in partial fulfillment of the requirements for the degree of Master of Arts in Economics. http://www.kse.org.ua/uploads/file/library/2008/batalina.pdf.

Vercillo, S., Kuuire, V. Z., Armah, F. A., & Luginaah, I. (2015). Does the new Alliance for food security and nutrition impose biotechnology on smallholder farmers in Africa? *Global Bioethics*, *26*(1), 1–13. https://www.tandfonline.com/doi/pdf/10.1080/11287462.2014.1002294?needAccess=true.

Wessel, M., & Quist-Wessel, P. M. F. (2015). Cocoa production in West Africa, a review and analysis of recent developments. *NJAS – Wageningen Journal of Life Sciences*, *74-75*, 1–7. https://doi.org/10.1016/j.njas.2015.09.001

World Bank (2021). The Socio-Political Crisis in the Northwest and Southwest Regions of Cameroon: Assessing the Economic and Social Impacts. International Bank for Reconstruction and Development/The World Bank: Washington, DC 20433. Accessed at https://documents1.worldbank.org/curated/en/795921624338364910/pdf/The-Socio-Political-Crisis-in-the-Northwest-and-Southwest-Regions-of-Cameroon-Assessing-the-Economic-and-Social-Impacts.pdf.

World Bank (2022). Financial Inclusion: Financial inclusion is a key enabler to reducing poverty and boosting prosperity. Accessed at https://www.worldbank.org/en/topic/financialinclusion/overview#1.

Part V

Women's Empowerment and Financial Inclusion

12 Women's Empowerment, Gender Inequality, and Financial Inclusion

Evidence from a Developing Country

Daisy Mui Hung Keen and Aizza Anwar

12.1 Introduction

A well-functioning monetary system facilitates the rapid expansion of any economy. This applies to both established economies and those still in their developing stages. A country's economic growth and development are greatly aided by its sound financial infrastructure, mainly due to financial inclusion (FI) (Sharma, 2016; Van et al., 2021). More people can improve their living standards when more individuals have access to financial resources and opportunities for economic growth (Arora & Sarker, 2023). This is why FI is so significant. Governments, academics, and the general public have increased interest in FI, described as the readiness of numerous "financial products and services." This curiosity stems from the realization that significant regional and global disparities in access to formal financial services pose obstacles to global economic growth and development (Arora & Sarker, 2023). Inequalities in people's ability to obtain and use bank assets and liabilities are what we mean when discussing "financial inclusion gaps" (Cabeza-García et al., 2019). There is not nearly enough research on FI as a facet of financial development from the perspective of women empowerment and gender inequality that can be found in the relevant literature (Saluja et al., 2023).

Women's economic independence rises as they take advantage of FI programs. Women can increase their income and self-sufficiency with the help of these programs (Ben Mahjoub & Amara, 2020). There is consensus in the academic literature that closing the gender gap in FI is crucial for empowering women economically, socially, and for national development (Ghosh & Vinod, 2017). In developing countries, the lack of access to financial services is seen as a significant barrier to fostering economic growth, gender equality, women empowerment, and job creation. According to a report, 70% of the world's female population lives in extreme poverty because industrialized and underdeveloped countries have different economic prospects (Chant, 2006). Empowering women is "to embrace women's perspectives, make an effort to find them and improve women's status through education, awareness, literacy, and training" (Bayeh, 2016). Women's empowerment aims to help women feel confident in their abilities and assert their leadership roles by capitalizing on their strengths (Ben Mahjoub & Amara, 2020). Gender equality

DOI: 10.4324/9781032655185-17

isn't only about giving women the respect they deserve but also about giving them the same opportunities men do (Baqutayan, 2020).

The Sustainable Development Aims (SDGs) are an approach to global development that includes the reduction of inequality as well as gender equality. However, the financial industry appears to be swayed regarding FI for these admirable goals (Ohiomu & Ogbeide-Osaretin, 2019). Policymakers in many countries see FI as the key to economic and women empowerment and the solution to improving the quality of living (Ozili, 2021). Therefore, this study's overarching goal is to contribute to efforts in Malaysia toward achieving gender parity and women empowerment. It contributes to the Sustainable Development Agenda to achieve gender equity. The Manifesto of the Government of Malaysia reflects the fundamental principles and imperatives of the 2030 Agenda and SDGs, to which Malaysia is fully committed. This research aligns with Malaysia Shared Prosperity Vision 2030 (fair and equitable distribution), Sustainable Development Goal 5 (gender equality), and Sustainable Development Goal 8 (sustainable decent work).

Thus, the study aims to identify who is responsible for paid jobs and household responsibilities and determine the extent to which each gender contributes to unpaid and paid labor. Moreover, the study intends to understand Malaysian couples' perception of the government's initiative for gender equality. The rest of this chapter is structured as follows. The chapter's following section will provide a more in-depth analysis of the relevant literature. In Section 12.3, we detail our research methods. Section 12.4 presents the results and data analysis strategies, while Section 12.5 provides commentary. Finally, a conclusion and policy implications section is presented.

12.2 Literature Review

12.2.1 Women's Empowerment, Gender Equality, and Financial Inclusion

Gender equality can mean many things depending on the culture. In some societies, it simply indicates that they have equal opportunities to advance their education. It is because while some countries have made great strides toward gender equality, others are still fighting for women to have the same rights as men. Therefore, people's goals when they demand gender equality depend on the cultural context in which the demand is made. Because of how culturally distinctive these phenomena are, gender equality research has gotten surprisingly little attention up to this point (Siddiqi, 2021). Gender disparities persist in the labor market, with significant discrimination in access to paid employment, unequal distribution of care and household duties, and bias in public decision-making (Baqutayan, 2020).

A broader range of financial services is required for female entrepreneurs to expand their businesses and contribute to economic growth and job creation in order for women to achieve full financial empowerment (Cabeza-García et al., 2019). UN Women and the World Bank found that women are poorer than men between 20 and 34. Divorce, separation, and widowhood hurt women more than men. Divorced women are twice as poor as men in the 18–49 age range. It needs to be changed because women are a significant part of the economy. Women FI is crucial for women to exercise their economic autonomy and assist nations in improving in terms of gender equality, in addition to combating poverty, boosting productivity, and fostering sustainable growth (Cabeza-García et al., 2019).

12.2.2 Gender Equality and Financial Inclusion in Malaysia

Malaysia ranks 103 on the list of 146 countries included in the Global Gender Gap Index 2022 (UNDP, 2023). In order to begin establishing a culture of equality for both women and men in Malaysia, it is necessary to disrupt the norms by altering the stereotyping such as only role women play is in household. Researchers should, therefore, consider how to equip women to realize their full capability in all aspects of society: economy, politics, culture, and family (Lee & Choong, 2020). Existing studies on gender empowerment in Malaysia have identified several key factors in influencing the proportion of women in the labor force: educational attainment, age dependency ratio, Gross Domestic Product (GDP), and fertility rate (Wei & Cinn, 2021). A notable example is the microfinance organization Amanah Ikhtiar Malaysia (AIM), which has significantly impacted the economic independence of Malaysian Muslim women. The findings demonstrate that women's access to microcredit through AIM increased gender equality (Al-Shami et al., 2016). This access has enabled women could start micro and small businesses, generating income to support their families (Sanmugam et al., 2023).

Evidence revealed that women in these places have greater talents to aid to tourism industry (Janjua et al., 2023). Women's perceived efficacy in society and the economy is bolstered by the opportunities afforded by increased social capital and access to financial resources (self-efficacy) (McNamara et al., 2021). Women business owners' social capital is stronger than ever, making it easier for them to access funding. When women have confidence in themselves, they are more likely to achieve their goals, which benefits society and the economy (Kamberidou, 2020). A study in Peninsular Malaysia, 157 female company owners were interviewed using a cross-sectional methodology. This study discovered that gains in social capital, financial capability, and self-efficacy increased women's empowerment in social entrepreneurial projects in Peninsular Malaysia. Because social enterprise development projects increase social capital and economic independence, public and private entities should emphasize those initiatives (Sabri et al., 2022).

A recent study examined the extent to which parents as well as the location of the family's residence (rural versus urban) influenced the division of labor in Malay households. Both mothers and fathers were interviewed from a random sample of 100 Malay families living in rural and urban peninsular Malaysia. The results in both rural and urban settings highlight that mothers spend more time than fathers on housework, laundry, child care, and meal preparation. Fathers in urban areas spent more time caring for their children and going grocery shopping than their rural counterparts, but both parents in urban families shared the responsibility of budgeting. In urban settings, moms and fathers shared childcare responsibilities less unequally than in rural areas. While mothers did the most of the work around the house, men in urban regions put in more time with children and other household chores than their rural counterparts. The research findings are significant because they shed insight into the modern patterns of parental engagement in household labor, including childcare in understudied Malay households in the setting of rapid urbanization and a multiethnic social context (Hossain & Madon, 2022). Although the SDGs have helped advance gender equality and women's empowerment, including providing girls and boys with equal access to primary education, women and girls still face discrimination and violence on a global scale.

12.3 Methodology

A research paradigm serves as the foundation for all scientific investigations (Mackenzie & Knipe, 2006). As a result, the methodology behind this study is based on positivist principles (O'Leary, 2017). The study used a cross-sectional survey design to collect data at one point in time (Frey, 2018). Before taking part in this online survey, the respondents were provided with information regarding the research, informed consent, the anticipated amount of time needed to finish the study, and the researcher's contact details (Kee et al., 2023). This online survey employed a method known as purposive sampling, which targeted married couples with children who lived in households where both housework and childcare responsibilities were shared. It was requested of the respondents that they supply information regarding their demographics as well as their job situation throughout the pandemic. The demographic information includes the ages, ethnicities, levels of education attained, and monthly incomes of both couple members.

This project is the first study in Malaysia to gather data from dual-earner couples more clearly to test whether gender differences exist within the same relationships and context. This project will employ purposive sampling. To be eligible as the participant in this project, both parents must:

1 have at least one child,
2 in a marital relationship, and
3 dual-earners in urban cities.

The respondents to the online poll were questioned about the typical number of hours that they spend each week on (1) paid job, (2) housekeeping, and (3) childcare responsibilities. Meal preparation, dishwashing, laundry, ironing, house cleaning, shopping for food, paying bills, gardening, and putting waste away are examples of chores that fall under the category of "housework." Childcare entails activities such as feeding, bathing, dressing, calming, carrying, telling stories, reading, assisting children in learning, having conversations with children, instructing, putting children to bed, playing games, and overseeing games. The instrument has been put through substantial preliminary research to ensure its validity and reliability.

12.4 Results

The data were collected from Malaysian youth; out of 1191 respondents, 563 (47%) were males, and 628 (53%) were female. The majority of respondents, 351 (29.47%), are from the age group 41–50; 331 (27.79%) are from the age group 50 years old and above; 207 (17.38%) participants are from the age group of 31–40; 166 (13.94%) respondents are from the age group of 26–30 years old; 132 (11.08%) respondents are from the age group of 21–25 years old. Only four (0.34%) participants are from the age group of 19–20 years old, as shown in Table 12.1.

Out of 1191, the majority 855 (71.85%) of participants, live in Urban areas, whereas 335 (28.15%) of respondents live in rural areas. The vast majority of respondents, 335 (28.15%), have only one child; 326 survey participants (27.37%) have two children, while 305 respondents (25.61%) have three children. Only 31 people (2.61%) have six or more children. Figure 12.1 highlights the education qualifications of participants. Most participants, 470 (39.5%), have bachelor's degrees; 351 (29.5%) of participants have a high school degree; 19.16% of respondents have diplomas and only 1% reported no formal education.

The participants' respective fields of employment are illustrated in Figure 12.2. The results reported that out of 1191 respondents, 538 respondents (45.21%) work in a private organization, 328 (27.56%) respondents worked for the government, 275 respondents (23.11%) are self-employed and only 39 (3.28%) reported they are unemployed.

In addition, respondents were asked about their annual income. The 423 (35.52%) females and 307 (25.78%) males indicated annual earnings of RM 50,000 or less.

Table 12.1 Demographic profile

	Frequency	*Percentage*
Gender		
Male	563	47
Female	628	53
Age		
19–20 years	4	0.34
21–25 years	132	11.08
26–30 years	166	13.94
31–40 years	207	17.38
41–50 years	351	29.47
50 and above	331	27.79
Number of Children		
One child	335	28.13
Two children	326	27.37
Three children	305	25.61
Four children	150	12.59
Five children	44	3.69
Six and more children	31	
Location		
Urban area	885	71.85
Rural area	335	28.15

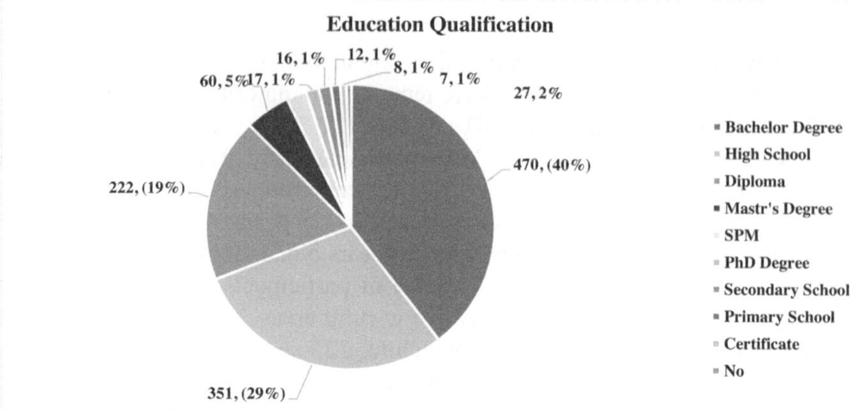

Figure 12.1 Education qualification

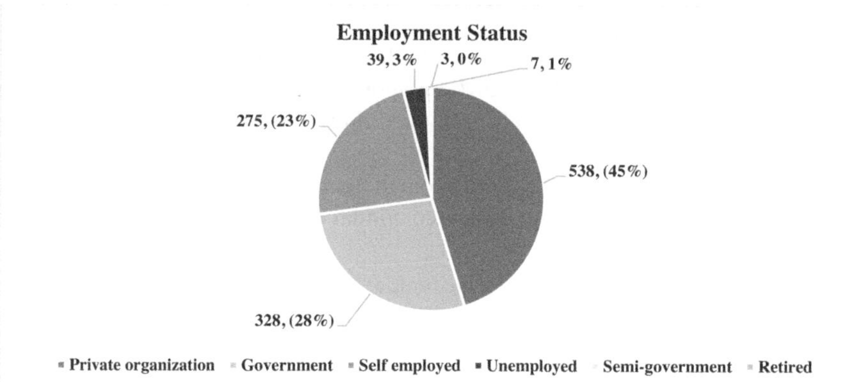

Figure 12.2 Employment status

The 155 (13.1%) female respondents and 165 (13.85%) male participants reported earning between RM 50,001 and RM 100,000 per year; 37 female and 69 male respondents earn between RM 100,000 and RM 200,000 annually. Only 8 females and 10 males make RM 200,000 to RM 300,000; 5 females and 12 males make more than RM 300,000 every year, as depicted in Table 12.2.

The respondents were further inquired about their current employment status. Figure 12.3 shows that most respondents 1039 (87%) have full-time employment; 107 (2%) participants have part-time employment. The rest of the respondents are either retired or self-employed. Few participants reported that they are unemployed, too.

The respondents were inquired about who is more participating in paid work. It involves receiving wages, salaries, fees, commissions, or other financial compensation. It entails doing work, selling services, or making items for money. Figure 12.4

Table 12.2 Annual income

Annual income	*Female-frequency*	*Percentage*	*Male-frequency*	*Percentage*
RM 50,000 and below	423	35.52	307	25.78
RM 50,001 – RM 100,000	155	13.10	165	13.85
RM 100,001 – RM 200,000	37	3.0	69	5.70
RM 200,000 – RM 300,000	8	0.67	10	0.83
More than 300,000	5	0.42	12	1.01

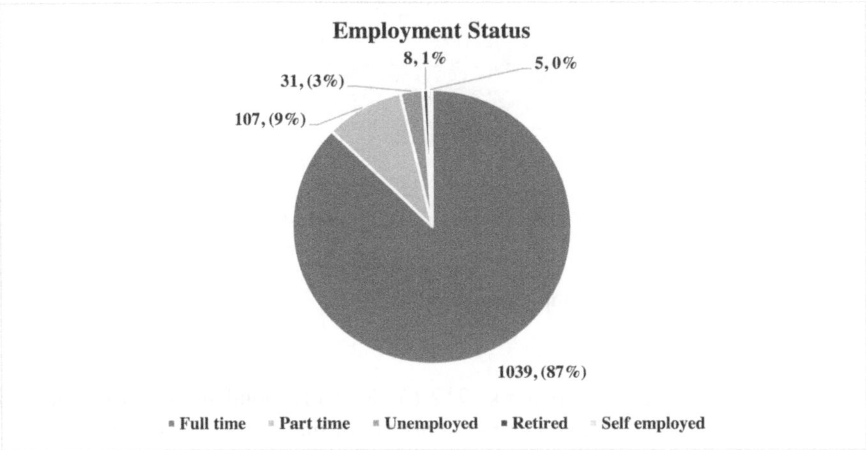

Figure 12.3 Current employment status

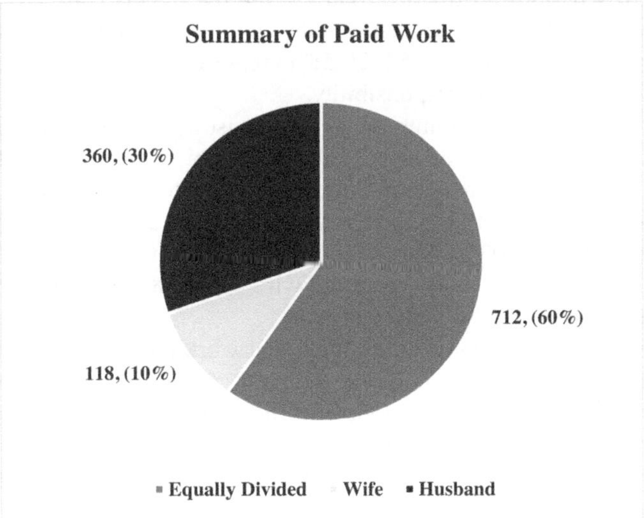

Figure 12.4 Summary of paid work

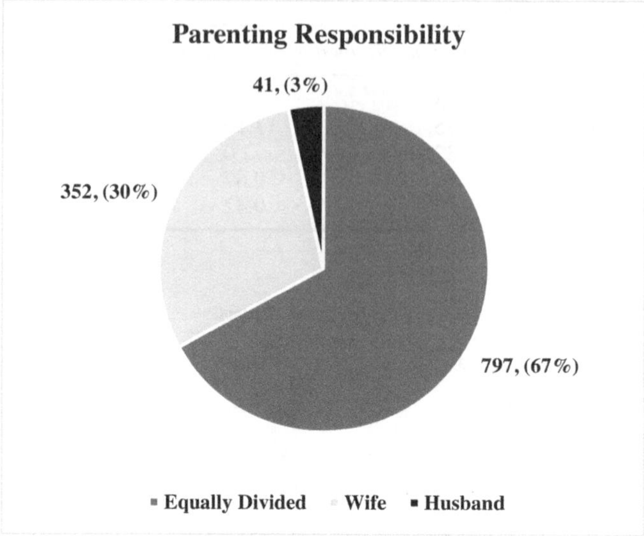

Figure 12.5 Summary of parenting responsibility

shows which participant paid work; 712 (59.83%) respondents reported that it is equally divided; 360 (30.25%) respondents claim that their husband takes care of paid work; 118 (9.92%) participants reported that wives participate in paid work.

Figure 12.5 shows that the respondents were further inquired about parenting responsibilities, such as feeding, calming, carrying, supporting children in learning, having discussions, instructing, putting, and overseeing.

The majority, 797 (66.97%) respondents, claimed it is equally divided between husband and wife. In contrast, 352 (29.58%) reported that the wife is the one who is responsible for parenting responsibility.

Figure 12.6 shows the summary of the housework task division. The term "housework task division" describes the process by which household members divide up the numerous tasks and duties that need to be completed around the house; 618 (51.93%) participants reported that wives are responsible for housework, whereas 524 (44.03%) respondents claimed that it is equally divided among household members such as husband and wife. Only 48 respondents claimed that husbands are responsible for housework.

The 748 (62.91%) respondents claimed that workload is equally disturbed between husband and wife, as shown in Figure 12.7. The workload summary in a household setting provides an overview of the various duties and responsibilities that need to be handled. It promotes order and harmony within in the home by ensuring that each member contribute their fair share to both maintenance and entertainment tasks. However, out of 1,190 participants, only 263 (22.12%) reported that their husband is responsible for managing the workload, while only 178 respondents (14.97%) stated that the wife bears this responsibility.

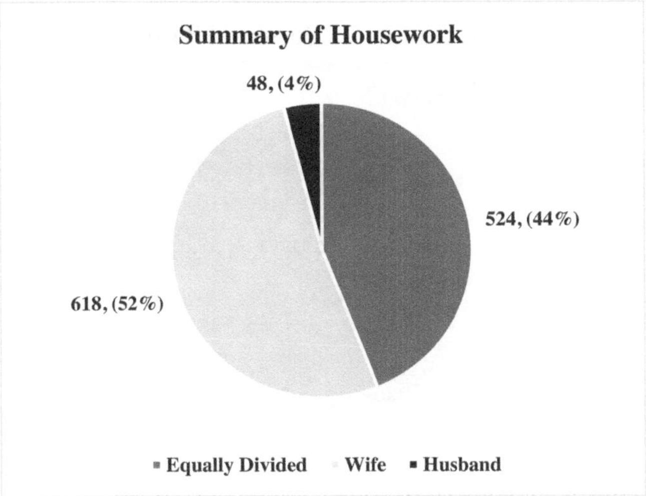

Figure 12.6 Summary of housework

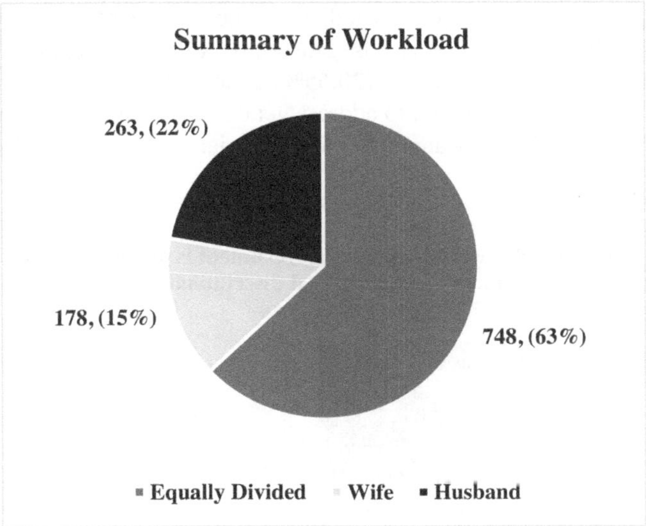

Figure 12.7 Summary of workload

The respondents were asked about their personal time to determine whether it is equally distributed or if the husband or wife gets more time. Figure 12.8 shows that 883 (74.2%) participants reported that it is equally distributed between husband and wife. However, 173 (14.54) respondents claimed that wife takes more personal time, while 134 (11.26%) indicated that the husband takes more personal time.

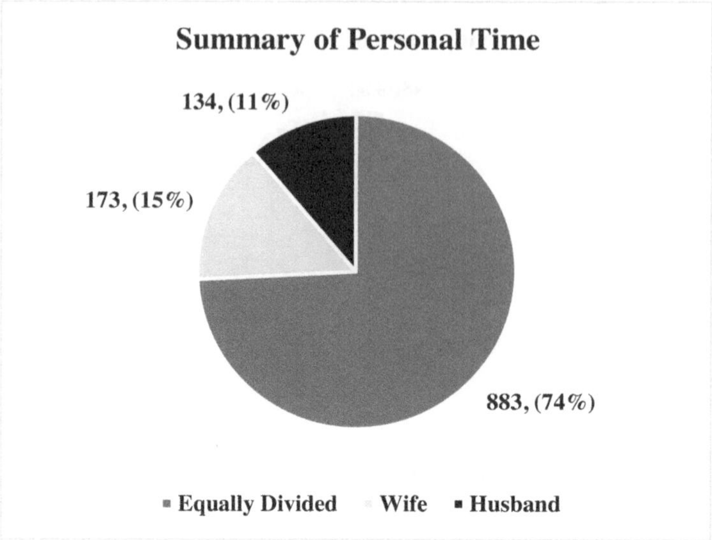

Figure 12.8 Summary of personal time

The respondents were inquired whether they believe the Malaysian government is doing enough to address gender-based discrimination; 555 (46.48%) respondents reported that they are not sure, 633 (30.65%) claimed that they do not believe that the government is doing enough to address gender-based discrimination in Malaysia. Only 273 (22.86%) indicated that the Malaysian government is doing enough, as shown in Figure 12.9.

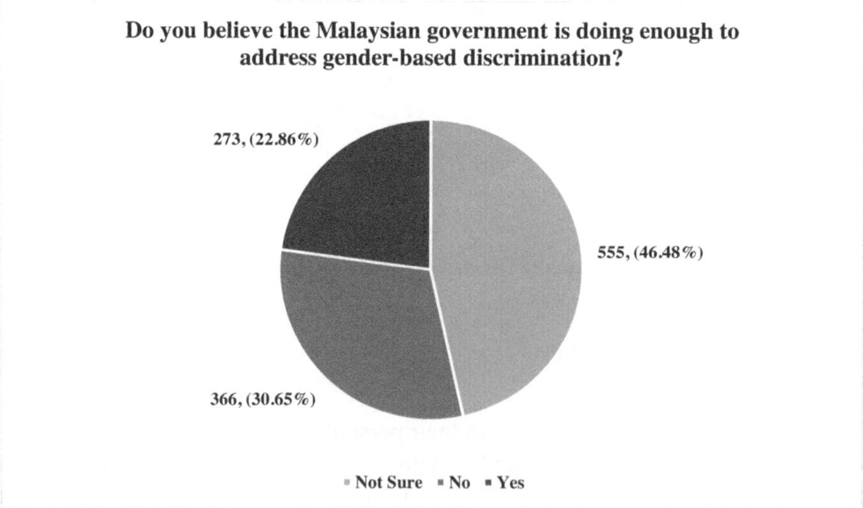

Figure 12.9 Satisfy with government actions

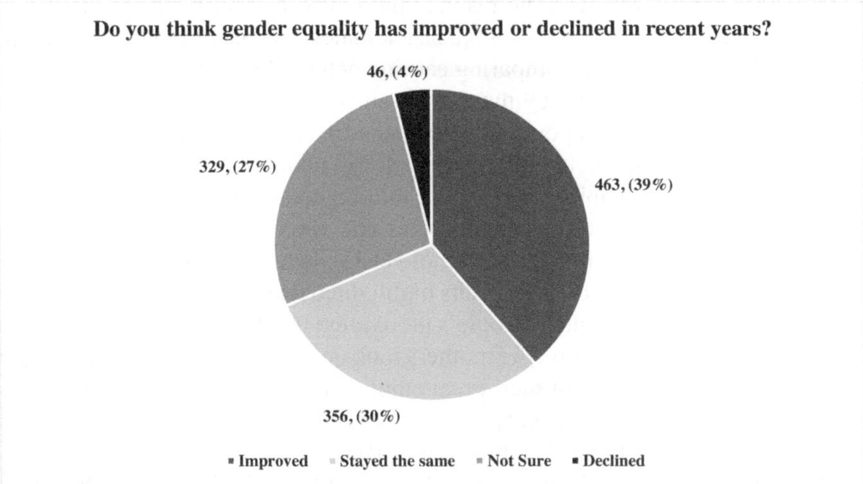

Figure 12.10 Satisfy with Malaysian government

The participants were asked whether they believe gender equality has improved or declined recently. The 463 (38.78%) claimed it has improved, whereas 356 (29.82%) reported it stayed the same, 329 (27.55%) reported it is the same, and 46 (3.85%) said it has declined over the years as shown in Figure 12.10.

12.5 Discussion

The majority of the literature focuses on the theoretical and conceptual development of FI and inclusive growth in the context of developed economies, with only a few studies emphasizing the necessity for study in developing countries (Malik et al., 2020; Malik & Yadav, 2022a, 2022b). According to the data, women devote more of their time to unpaid domestic labor during COVID-19 and spend more time than males caring for children and performing housework-related tasks (Boo, 2021). The findings highlight the need for emerging markets to address gender inequality, improve the enforcement of laws protecting women, and ensure women's empowerment and equality.

The present study collected data from 1191 participants; 53% were women and 47% were men.

Respondents were inquired about their annual earnings to determine who is earning more. Previous research has shown that those with higher earning potential have better access to financial services, ensuring FI. Ghosh and Vinod (2017) determined that families led by women are, on average, less likely to have access to formal finance than households led by men. This difference was found when comparing the two types of households. As a direct result, families led by women take out cash loans at a rate 20% lower than those headed by men. The study results reported that 423 (35.52%) female and 307 (25.78%) male annual earnings were

RM 50,000 or less. However, the results highlighted that husbands fall under the higher earning bracket than wives, such as 5 females, whereas 12 males make more than RM 300,000 yearly. In comparing earning potential between RM 100,000 and RM 200,000, 37 females and 69 males earn annually. It indicated that most of the household is financially supported by men because of access to financial services.

Moreover, Malaysian couples were questioned about their involvement in paid work, parenting responsibility, and household-related chores. Firstly, the participants were inquired about household chores and workload. The results indicated that 52% wife are responsible for household tasks; 44% suggested that it is equally divided among the members. The results highlighted that the wife is responsible for household chores. It can reduce people's motivation to take part in FI. The findings aligned with the existing study; the mothers took on greater mental work during the pandemic. They also spoke of their great emotional labor as they worked to maintain everyone's safety and serenity. They had to divide the work at home, which stressed and frustrated them (Hjálmsdóttir & Bjarnadóttir, 2021).

The respondents were further asked about workload distribution, such as tasks related to home maintenance; 63% of respondents claimed that the workload is equally distributed between husband and wife, whereas 22% reported that the husband is responsible. The results here imply that men are not taking the lead in home related. It can reduce people's motivation to take part in FI. The respondents were asked who takes on the more significant amount of parental responsibilities, such as considering the child's health, safety, and overall growth and development; 67% claimed it is equally divided between husband and wife, whereas 30% indicated it is the wife responsibility. The results suggest that either wife is responsible for child care and development or it is equally divided. The men are not actively participating in parental responsibility. Concerning the respondents' leisure activities and their personal time, questions were posed to determine how it is distributed between husband and wife; 74.2% of participants reported that it is equally distributed between husband and wife. These results are promising because having the option of personal time would ensure that both husband and wife have a good, healthy relationship.

According to existing literature in Malaysia, mothers in both rural and urban settings were found to devote more time to housework, laundry, child care, and meal preparation than fathers. In contrast, males in both settings were found to devote more time to maintenance and food buying. Fathers in urban areas spent more time caring for their children and going grocery shopping than their rural counterparts, but both parents in urban families shared the responsibility of budgeting. In urban settings, moms and fathers share childcare responsibilities less unequally than in rural areas. While mothers did most of the work around the house, men in urban regions spent more time with children and other household chores than their rural counterparts. These results shed light on the modern way of parental engagement, particularly relevant in light of the increasing urbanization and multiethnic nature of the social setting in which these families live (Hossain & Madon, 2022). The father's sense of self, socioeconomic status, and social support were analyzed to determine their impact on the father's decision to participate in household chores in both rural and urban households in Bangladesh. Forty mothers and 40 fathers from rural and urban nuclear households participated in the research. Research shows that regardless of location, mothers spend more time than fathers doing housework and meal preparation. However, parents spent about the same amount of time caring for the home's infrastructure. Rural dads spent more hours scrubbing toilets and mopping floors than their metropolitan counterparts. Dads spent the least amount of time on meal preparation in urban and rural settings. Rural dads' involvement in upkeep was affected favorably by extra-family support and negatively by institutional support. Fathers' participation in housework was negatively impacted by fathers' income, children, and self-presentation and favorably affected by fathers' family support (Hossain, 2018).

The participants were also inquired about paid work, such as a job requiring a person to exert physical or mental effort to earn money; 60% reported that paid work is equally divided; 30% claimed that husbands are responsible for paid work. The results suggest that both husband and wife contribute equally in most households. The salary statistics highlighted that husbands fall under the high earning bracket. In particular, closing the gender gap in financial participation leads to greater economic growth and improved health and social conditions (Cabeza-García et al., 2019).

The study also tries to inquire about government actions. Therefore, the respondents were asked about Malaysian government and gender-based discrimination; 555 (46.48%) respondents reported that they are unsure, and 633 (30.65%) claimed they do not believe that the government is doing enough to address gender-based discrimination in Malaysia. Only 273 (22.86%) indicated that the Malaysian government is doing enough. The participants were asked whether they believe gender equality has improved or declined recently. The 463 (38.78%) claimed it has improved, whereas 356 (29.82%) reported it stayed the same; 329 (27.55%) reported it is the same, and 46 (3.85%) said it has declined over the years. Several initiatives have been undertaken to raise and maintain the number of women participating in the workforce.

12.6 Policy Implications

Policymakers and financial sector representatives must understand the economy as a whole. Governments and development agencies worldwide must rethink the rhetoric of equality and empowerment in the workplace. Consider how words like "balance," "diversity," and "inclusion" are used to avoid acknowledging the structural injustices that afflict the society and keep people from looking within to solve these problems (Yoong, 2022). The government around the globe recognizes the importance of gender equality for FI and it is trying to increase financial literacy (Güngen, 2018). The financial institutions have more inclination toward men (Mouna & Jarboui, 2022). The provision of financial services to all segments of society has elevated FI to a policy position of critical importance in the pursuit of inclusive growth in the context of the Sustainable Development Goals (SDGs) (Kara et al., 2021). Thus, the Malaysian government and policymakers should also focus on the development of new financial products and services by advocating the importance of women empowerment for FI. As a direct consequence, governments contribute to women's empowerment.

The main focus of state-level efforts to implement the FI strategy was formulating, adapting, and drafting relevant policies. Financial literacy and education should be the policy's primary focus to create gender equality people in a changing economy. The importance of financial literacy education has been brought to light in recent years by multiple state agencies. Many of these groups are partnerships between businesses and non-governmental organizations. Women, college students, the unemployed, and people living in rural areas are disproportionately likely to lack financial knowledge and services. Educating specific populations about financial products helps them improve their knowledge and skill sets and allows them to participate more effectively in the economy of society. The correlation suggests that higher education levels positively correlate with women staying in the workforce. Increased literacy and high school completion rates have been linked to faster growth in human capital. As a result, employers can hire a larger pool of qualified women for skilled and semi-skilled positions (Wei & Cinn, 2021).

The literature has highlighted that educated people are more inclined to use digital financial services than less educated people (Mouna & Jarboui, 2022). Therefore, it is advised that policymakers make it easier for women to access finance in order to safeguard them against financial exclusion. It is achievable by giving them access to opportunities at the grassroots level, such as educational institutions. In addition, the government can play a role by making it simple for women to obtain bank accounts. Policymakers in underdeveloped nations need to keep in mind that FI is a crucial step toward a cashless economy. Therefore, additional work is needed to build an atmosphere that is conducive to digital transformation before the government invests in Information and Communication Technology (ICT) infrastructure. Finally, effective use of government ICT systems will contribute to a reduction in the growth of bureaucracy. The Twelfth Malaysia Plan (2021-2025) aims to introduce suitable social policies to further raise female labor force participation rate to 60%.

12.7 Conclusion

Many emerging markets' economies are fast expanding. In developing nations, however, gender imbalance in FI persists. The study collected data from Malaysian married couples in which both partners work for a living. According to the findings, wives are more responsible for unpaid domestic activities such as cleaning, parenting, and household maintenance. Furthermore, annual income statistics show that husbands earn more than wives. Thus, based on the research and results, the husband has better access to financial resources and inclusion than the wife. It emphasizes Malaysia's lack of female empowerment and gender equality. Furthermore, it contributes to the economy's financial inclusiveness. This research is consistent with Malaysia's Shared Prosperity Vision 2030 (fair and equitable distribution), SDG 5 (gender equality), and SDG 8 (sustainable decent work). Inequality is a main policy goal in Malaysia, as well as a topic of study that is both timely and critical at the moment.

Conflict of Interest

The authors declare no conflict of interest.

Funding

This research was funded by grant number: 304/PMGT/6501311/P165. The funding source did not play a role in the study design, the collection, analysis, and interpretation of data, the writing of the report, or the decision to submit this chapter for publication.

References

Al-Shami, S. S. A., Razali, M. M., Majid, I., Rozelan, A., & Rashid, N. (2016). The effect of microfinance on women's empowerment: Evidence from Malaysia. *Asian Journal of Women's Studies*, *22*(3), 318–337. https://doi.org/10.1080/12259276.2016.1205378.

Arora, R. U., & Sarker, T. (2023). Financing for sustainable development goals (SDGs) in the era of COVID-19 and beyond. *The European Journal of Development Research*, *35*(1), 1–19. https://doi.org/10.1057/s41287-022-00571-9.

Baqutayan, S. M. S. (2020). Women empowerment is needed to boost gender equality in Malaysia. *Current Research Journal of Social Sciences and Humanities*, *3*(1), 95–107. https://doi.org/10.12944/CRJSSH.3.1.09.

Bayeh, E. (2016). The role of empowering women and achieving gender equality to the sustainable development of Ethiopia. *Pacific Science Review B: Humanities and Social Sciences*, *2*(1), 37–42. https://doi.org/10.1016/j.psrb.2016.09.013.

Ben Mahjoub, L., & Amara, I. (2020). The impact of cultural factors on shareholder governance and environmental sustainability: An international context. *World Journal of Science, Technology and Sustainable Development*, *17*(4), 367–385. https://doi.org/10.1108/WJSTSD-06-2020-0060.

Boo, H. S. (2021). Unpaid domestic work and gender inequality in the time of COVID-19 in Malaysia. *Pertanika Journal of Social Sciences and Humanities*, *29*(3). https://doi.org/10.47836/pjssh.29.3.16.

Cabeza-García, L., Del Brio, E. B., & Oscanoa-Victorio, M. L. (2019). Female financial inclusion and its impacts on inclusive economic development. *Women's Studies International Forum*, *77*, 102300. https://doi.org/10.1016/j.wsif.2019.102300.

Chant, S. (2006). Re-thinking the 'Feminization of Poverty' in relation to aggregate gender indices. *Journal of Human Development*, *7*(2), 201–220. https://doi.org/10.1080/14649880600768538.

Frey, B. B. (2018). The SAGE encyclopedia of educational research, measurement, and evaluation. *The SAGE encyclopedia of educational research, measurement, and evaluation*. Thousand Oaks: Sage. https://doi.org/10.4135/9781506326139.

Ghosh, S., & Vinod, D. (2017). What constrains financial inclusion for women? Evidence from Indian micro data. *World Development*, *92*, 60–81. https://doi.org/10.1016/j.worlddev.2016.11.011.

Güngen, A. R. (2018). Financial inclusion and policy-making: Strategy, campaigns and microcredit a la Turca. *New Political Economy*, *23*(3), 331–347. https://doi.org/10.1080/13563467.2017.1349091.

Hjálmsdóttir, A., & Bjarnadóttir, V. S. (2021). 'I have turned into a foreman here at home': Families and work–life balance in times of COVID-19 in a gender equality paradise. *Gender, Work and Organization, 28*(1). https://doi.org/10.1111/gwao.12552.

Hossain, Z. (2018). The division of domestic labor between mothers and fathers in rural and urban families in Bangladesh. *Journal of Behavioral & Social Sciences, 5*(1), 1–14.

Hossain, Z., & Madon, Z. (2022). Distribution of household labor between mothers and fathers in rural and urban Malaysia. *Journal of Comparative Family Studies, 52*(4), pp. 569–595. https://doi.org/10.3138/jcfs.52.4.03.

Janjua, Z.u.A., Krishnapillai, G. and Rehman, M. (2023), "Importance of the sustainability tourism marketing practices: an insight from rural community-based homestays in Malaysia", Journal of Hospitality and Tourism Insights, Vol. 6 No. 2, pp. 575–594. https://doi.org/10.1108/JHTI-10-2021-0274.

Kamberidou, I. (2020). 'Distinguished' women entrepreneurs in the digital economy and the multitasking whirlpool. *Journal of Innovation and Entrepreneurship, 9*(1), 3. https://doi.org/10.1186/s13731-020-0114-y.

Kara, A., Zhou, H., & Zhou, Y. (2021). Achieving the United Nations' sustainable development goals through financial inclusion: A systematic literature review of access to finance across the globe. *International Review of Financial Analysis, 77*, 101833. https://doi.org/10.1016/j.irfa.2021.101833.

Kee, D. M. H., Anwar, A., Gwee, S. L., & Ijaz, M. F. (2023). Impact of acquisition of digital skills on perceived employability of youth: Mediating role of course quality. *Information, 14*(1), 42. https://doi.org/10.3390/info14010042.

Lee, H.-A., & Choong, C. (2020). Inequality in Malaysia empirical questions, structural changes, gender aspects. *Southeast Asian Economies, 36*(3), 329–354. https://doi.org/10.1355/ae36-3d.

Mackenzie, N., & Knipe, S. (2006). Research dilemmas: *Paradigms, Methods and Methodology, Issues in Educational Research, 16*(2), 193–205.

Malik, F. A., & Yadav, D. K. (2022a). Financial inclusion schemes and changing socio economic status of poorest of the poor. In *Financial inclusion schemes in India* (pp. 109–130). Singapore: Springer Nature Singapore. https://doi.org/10.1007/978-981-19-1316-7_5.

Malik, F. A., & Yadav, D. K. (2022b). Impact of recent financial inclusion schemes on status of financial inclusion in India: Secondary data analysis. *Financial inclusion schemes in India* (pp. 37–51). Singapore: Springer Nature Singapore. https://doi.org/10.1007/978-981-19-1316-7_3.

Malik, F. A., Yadav, D. K., Adam, H., & Omrane, A. (2020). The urban poor and their financial behavior. In *Sustainable entrepreneurship, renewable energy-based projects, and digitalization* (pp. 305–315). Boca Raton: CRC Press. https://doi.org/10.1201/9781003097921-17.

McNamara, K. E., Clissold, R., & Westoby, R. (2021). Women's capabilities in disaster recovery and resilience must be acknowledged, utilized and supported. *Journal of Gender Studies, 30*(1), 119–125. https://doi.org/10.1080/09589236.2020.1801397.

Mouna, A., & Jarboui, A. (2022). Understanding the link between government cashless policy, digital financial services and socio-demographic characteristics in the MENA countries. *International Journal of Sociology and Social Policy, 42*(5/6), 416–433. https://doi.org/10.1108/IJSSP-12-2020-0544.

O'Leary, Z. (2017), *The essential guide to doing your research project, SAGE publications* (3rd ed., Vol. 26). London: Sage.

Ohiomu, S., & Ogbeide-Osaretin, E. N. (2019). Financial inclusion and gender inequality reduction: Evidence from Sub-Saharan Africa. *The Indian Economic Journal, 67*(3–4), 367–372. https://doi.org/10.1177/0019466220946411.

Ozili, P. K. (2021). Financial inclusion research around the world: A review. *Forum for Social Economics, 50*(4), 457–479. https://doi.org/10.1080/07360932.2020.1715238.

Sabri, M. F., Wahab, R., Mahdzan, N. S., Magli, A. S., & Rahim, H. A. (2022). Mediating effect of financial behaviour on the relationship between perceived financial wellbeing and its factors among low-income young adults in Malaysia. *Frontiers in Psychology*, *13*, 858630 https://doi.org/10.3389/fpsyg.2022.858630

Saluja, O. B., Singh, P., & Kumar, H. (2023). Barriers and interventions on the way to empower women through financial inclusion: A 2 decades systematic review (2000–2020). *Humanities and Social Sciences Communications*, *10*(1), 1–19. https://doi.org/10.1057/s41599-023-01640-y.

Sanmugam, N., Ismail, H. H., & Azizan, M. (2023). Between goddess or homemaker: A review of the portrayal of women in Malaysia ESL textbook. *Creative Education*, *14*(06), 1269–1283. https://doi.org/10.4236/ce.2023.146081.

Sharma, D. (2016). Nexus between financial inclusion and economic growth. *Journal of Financial Economic Policy*, *8*(1), 13–36. https://doi.org/10.1108/JFEP-01-2015-0004.

Siddiqi, N. (2021). Gender inequality as a social construction in India: A phenomenological enquiry. *Women's Studies International Forum*, *86*, 102472. https://doi.org/10.1016/j.wsif.2021.102472.

UNDP (2023). Gender Equality. *UNDP*. Available at https://www.undp.org/malaysia/gender-equality. Accessed 31 August 2023.

Van, L.T.-H., Vo, A. T., Nguyen, N. T., & Vo, D. H. (2021). Financial inclusion and economic GROWTH: An international evidence. *Emerging Markets Finance and Trade*, *57*(1), 239–263. https://doi.org/10.1080/1540496X.2019.1697672.

Wei, L.C., & Cinn, L. Y. (2021). A research on female labour force participation in Malaysia. *Conference on Management, Business, Innovation, Education, and Social Science*, *1*(1), 50–69.

Yoong, M. (2022). Women's empowerment, employment and exclusion. Discourses in economic competitiveness initiatives in Malaysia. *Globalisation, geopolitics, and gender in professional communication* (pp. 85–105). New York: Routledge. https://doi.org/10.4324/9781003159674-5.

13 Predicting the Indian Housewife's Intention to Adopt Mobile Banking Services

Jyoti Shukla, Rachit Ranjan, Alok Tewari, Nitesh Thakur, and Vimal Chandra Verma

13.1 Introduction

Financial security is a major concern of the female population in the developing countries. In terms of income, education, ownership, and other criteria, women continue to have less economic clout than men. This has a negative impact on women's health, opportunities for education and employment, and even their level of control – or lack thereof – over their own lives and decisions (Van Eeden-Moorefield et al., 2007). The housewives are a major but frequently ignored demographic at the centre of India's vibrant sociocultural scene. Indian housewives have always been seen as the foundations of family stability and the caretakers of the home, and they have contributed much to society (Nathawat & Mathur, 1993). However, their contributions have frequently been restricted to the domestic sphere, making it difficult for them to freely access and manage financial resources. To address gender financial inequities, empower women's financial decision-making, and comprehend cultural nuances influencing their usage patterns, it is critical to study m-banking uptake among Indian housewives. Gained knowledge can be used to develop inclusive policies, close financial service disparities, advance gender equality, and advance India's economy.

The banking industry in the country has experienced a major technological transition that has ushered in the unheard-of era of m-banking. According to Kumar et al. (2020) the landscape is set for a revolutionary change in how financial services are accessed and used, with the growth of smartphones and the internet reaching even the most remote regions of the country. M-banking is revolutionary as it is putting ease, accessibility, and financial empowerment at the fingertips of millions of Indian women as smartphones become more widely used across the country (Chawla & Joshi, 2017).

There is still a significant gender gap in India despite the country's steadily rising use of m-banking, particularly among women who usually take the lead in managing household finances (Priya et al., 2018). The industry needs a thorough understanding of the reason(s) behind this slower-than-expected growth in order to increase these consumption rates. Recently, several significant scholarly studies have been published (e.g., Chawla & Joshi, 2017; Kumar et al., 2020; Souiden et al., 2021; Suhartanto et al., 2020) that address the intention to utilize m-banking services from the perspective of technological adoption. Nevertheless, there hasn't been an empirically comprehensive

DOI: 10.4324/9781032655185-18

attempt to compile the findings and identify the factors that most clearly explain why Indian housewives are drawn to using this technology. Thus, the goal of this research is to identify the antecedents of m-banking adoption by Indian housewives.

The Technology Acceptance Model (TAM) is probably the most well known and widely accepted model among all the models that have been frequently used to describe the phenomenon of technology adoption through research (Davis, 1989; Venkatesh & Bala, 2008; Venkatesh et al., 2016). However, due to the complexity of technology adoption process, research on the adoption of m-banking is still needed, according to the literature. Furthermore, research has documented the ways in which core human values shape behaviour (Mathur et al., 2021). Studies have specifically shown how important it is for people to be adaptable when it comes to using technology (Tewari et al., 2023). Prior studies (Alalwan et al., 2018; Nathawat & Mathur, 1993) have highlighted housewives' concerns over risk, or perceived risk (PR), when using m-banking services. Furthermore, it has been found that a major element influencing users' intention to use m-banking is PR. By taking a close look at the variables influencing behavioural intention (BI) of Indian housewives towards m-banking adoption, governments and financial institutions may create focused campaigns to remove obstacles and boost involvement in the digital banking sector, thereby advancing financial inclusion for women in India.

13.1.1 Rationale of the Study

Financial inclusion has been the focus area of India government for quite some and has consequently gained much scholarly attention (see Malik & Yadav, 2022). M-banking is thought to be one of the important means by which financial inclusion can be achieved. However, the use of m-banking by Indian housewives (a major segment of Indian demography) is not well understood. Their particular financial obligations and limitations demand a focused analysis. The adoption factors crucial for m-banking will be shown by this study, promoting gender equality and financial inclusion. The results will facilitate the m-banking industry to integrate services with the particular demands of housewives.

The following sections make up the research document. The literature research on m-banking services and the conceptual framework for this project are presented in Section 13.2. The methodologies employed are described in Section 13.3 along with the data, variables, and meta-analytical techniques used. The study's findings are presented in Section 13.4 after this. Discussion on overall findings is presented in Section 13.5 whereas contributions are discussed in Section 13.6. Section 13.7 is concerned with the drawbacks and recommendations for further study.

13.2 Literature Review

13.2.1 M-banking in India

In the financial services sector, mobile banking, often known as m-banking, has changed the game by enabling the user to conduct financial transactions using a mobile phone (Suhartanto et al., 2020). Scholars and professionals have closely observed m-banking adoption and the ways in which people from different demographic backgrounds, including housewives, wish to use it (Malaquias & Hwang, 2019).

Owusu Kwateng et al. (2019) state in their research that m-banking is a result of technological improvements, especially the spread of smartphones and the expansion of internet connectivity. The creation of user-friendly applications that let users execute a variety of financial activities from the convenience of their mobile devices has been made easier as a result of this convergence. Researchers have drawn attention to the rapid uptake of m-banking services due to the technological convergence, which has changed the traditional banking model by facilitating more accessibility and convenience (Flavián et al., 2006).

Senyo and Osabutey (2020) highlight the advantages of m-banking for expanding financial inclusion. M-banking has made it possible for people to undertake financial transactions without access to traditional banking infrastructure, particularly in developing nations like India and Africa. According to studies, m-banking fosters economic empowerment by giving previously disadvantaged individuals access to savings accounts, credit, and insurance services.

13.2.2 Indian Housewives

Due to the lack of previous studies on technology adoption among this demographic segment, Indian housewives were chosen as the research subject. They are also among the categories that are sceptic about technology-based financial services, which could hinder the adoption of digital banks (Shaikh & Karjaluoto, 2015). All Indian housewives who utilize online banking make up the study's population.

13.2.3 Theoretical Framework

To better understand user behaviour in relation to the adoption of new technology, the scientific literature has developed a number of purposeful models and behavioural choice theories during the past 40 years. In particular, this study makes use of the TAM model, one of several attitudinal models and theories having roots in social psychology. We have chosen to use TAM because it aligns with our research goals and has a proven track record of being a useful method for analysing online consumer behaviour (Davis, 1989). Numerous disciplines have extensively examined and used TAM's value in predicting future customer behaviour (Chawla & Joshi, 2017; Liaw, 2008; Venkatesh et al., 2016). The TAM model was created to identify the factors that contribute to an organization's information systems' success and their ability to meet workplace demands, and to predict how adoption and use of new IT-related services and systems is affected by various factors. Theory of Reasoned Action provided the foundational concepts and principles around which TAM was built (Venkatesh & Davis, 2000).

Within the context of the TAM, two factors – perceived usefulness (PU) and perceived ease of use (PEU) – are critical in predicting the intention to embrace a specific technology. Venkatesh et al. (2016) define PU as a belief that a specific technology will enhance the ability to perform tasks successfully. Venkatesh and Bala (2008) define PEU as an individual's estimate of how easy it would be to use a specific piece of technology. It's crucial to remember that numerous studies have shown that PU is the most accurate measure of use intention. Two variables that are employed as independent variables to test our hypothesis are PU and PEU.

In addition to PU and PEU, we have found three more factors that predict Indian housewives' propensity to adopt m-banking services: PR; openness to change, OC; and social influence, SI (Tewari et al., 2023).

13.2.4 Hypotheses Development

13.2.4.1 PU and BI to Adopt m-banking

PU is described by Davis (1989) as an individual's opinion of how utilizing a certain technology could enhance their performance in the workplace. This implies that a service that the user finds helpful will probably improve productivity, job performance, and the overall worth and efficacy of the employment.

Previous research on technology adoption has demonstrated the construct's validity and dependability (Priya et al., 2018). PU and perceived value (PV) in technology are closely related concepts (Venkatesh et al., 2023). PV in technology includes an assessment of the advantages above the cost of purchase. When people think m-banking offers substantial benefits, they are more inclined to utilize it; conversely, when they think it offers only little benefits, they are less receptive of the technology.

Individuals use PU as a criterion to assess if using m-banking services in their everyday lives has any positive effects on them. According to studies on information system adoption, a system is not seen favorably if it does not successfully help users do their jobs. One of the reasons people choose m-banking over conventional in-person bank visits is that it can save them time and money (Jeong & Yoon, 2013). In decision-making, the idea of PU is important since it suggests that a system is beneficial when users believe that using it improves their performance, effectiveness, and satisfaction (Suhartanto & Leo, 2018).

Therefore, we hypothesize

H1: PU positively influences housewives' BI towards m-banking adoption.

13.2.4.2 PEU and BI to Adopt m-banking

Another important component of TAM is PEU, which expresses a user's perception of how easy and convenient utilizing technology is (Ratten, 2015). Simple, easy-to-use technology, like mobile services, is perceived by individual clients as less scary because it is less complicated and burdensome to operate.

How rapidly new technologies are adopted in the banking industry depends in large part on their accessibility (Ramayah et al., 2003). Certain financial services, particularly websites, might be challenging to access on mobile devices due to their limitations, such as limited screens and keyboards. Providing a user-friendly interface is essential to promoting the uptake of m-banking solutions. This includes, as Jamshidi and Hussin (2016) emphasize, unambiguous instructions, conspicuous navigation options, relevant material, attractive visuals, functional features, intelligible symbols, and instructive error messages. In summary, it is expected that PEU and BI will positively correlate. This brings us to our second hypothesis.

H2: PEU positively influences BI towards m-banking adoption.

13.2.4.3 SI and BI to Adopt m-banking

Venkatesh et al. (2003) say that SI evaluates how much a person believes that other people are deciding whether or not to adopt a technology. SI refers to how much a user's behaviour alters as a result of using technology while being influenced by others. When using an e-wallet, Yang et al. (2021) talk about the influence of SI. When they see other people acting in certain ways, people often assume that those actions are also reasonable. Teo et al. (2012) speak about how people rely on social influence to boost their intention to use technology. Based on this discussion, it is hypothesized:

H3: SI positively influences BI towards m-banking adoption.

13.2.4.4 OC and BI to Adopt m-banking

OC entails having an open mind, being creative, being willing to take risks, and being open to trying new things. Schwartz (1992) asserts that this feature helps people to pursue their emotional and intellectual interests along unanticipated and untried paths. Numerous earlier studies have broadly embraced the idea of being open to change or prepared to accept it. Kruse et al. (2019) claim that OC directly alters behavioural intention, i.e., it significantly affects people's propensities to act in a particular way. Additionally, it has been discovered that OC affects customers' tendency to buy novel and unorthodox goods (Tewari et al., 2022). Thus, we formulate following hypothesis:

H4: OC positively influences BI towards m-banking adoption

13.2.4.5 PR and BI to Adopt m-banking

Featherman and Pavlou (2003) state that one aspect of PR for customers utilizing m-banking services is the potential for losses or adverse outcomes. Concerns regarding PR significantly impede users' intentions to utilize m-banking services, according to research conducted by Curran and Meuter (2007). This is particularly crucial, according to Kesharwani and Singh Bisht (2012) and Thi et al. (2023), because m-banking is characterized by inherent uncertainties, intangibility, unpredictability, and ambiguity in addition to the absence of a human intermediary. In light of this conversation, the following hypothesis has been put forth:

H5: PR negatively influences BI towards m-banking adoption.

The conceptual model is shown in Figure 13.1.

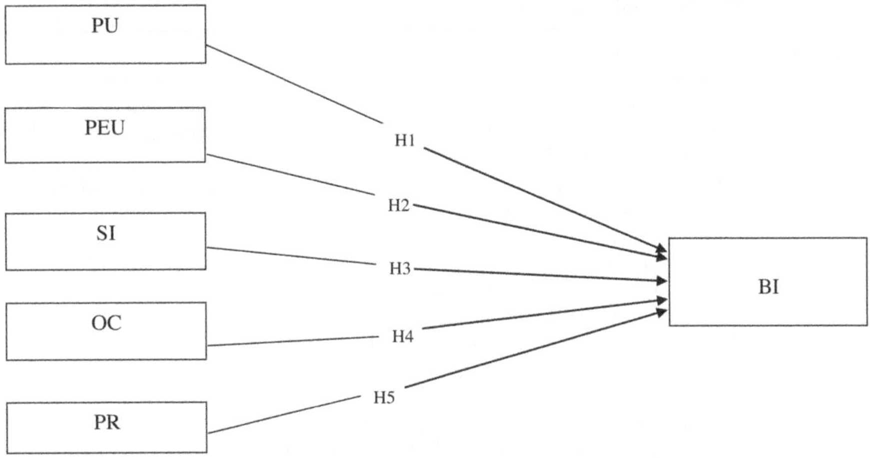

Figure 13.1 The proposed conceptual model

13.3 Methodology

13.3.1 Questionnaire Development

We employed the already developed and tested measuring scales from earlier studies. The four scale items for PU and PEU were derived from Suhartanto et al. (2020); Venkatesh et al. (2016) and modified as per the context of our study, i.e. m-banking services adoption. Three items have been adapted from Tewari et al. (2023) to assess SI. The six items to assess OC have been derived from Schwartz (1992). For PR, four items have been adapted from Featherman and Pavlou (2003). Four items for BI were adapted from Wu and Wang (2005); Venkatesh et al. (2003). A "7-point Likert scale" was used to measure the items where "1 denotes strongly disagree" whereas "7 denotes strongly agree". Table 13.1 shows the constructs and measurement items along with the source.

13.3.2 Data Collection

Indian housewives are the subject of this study. A pilot survey with 30 housewives was undertaken to guarantee questionnaire clarity and internal consistency. Following this, a total of 350 housewives were approached using a convenience sampling technique and their responses were collected using a self-administered questionnaire after obtaining their informed consent. Data collection was carried out from February 2023 to April 2023 in northern Indian cities of New Delhi and Lucknow. A total of 293 replies were received out of which 269 questionnaires were judged appropriate for study after omitting the incomplete ones. The study's 25 measurement items meant that the sample size was greater than the 250 needed

Table 13.1 Constructs and their items

Construct	*Measurement items*	*Source*
PU	Four items including "It helps in my everyday life" "It is flexible in use"	Suhartanto et al. (2020); Venkatesh et al. (2016)
PEU	Four items including "It is not difficult to learn" " It has clear feature"	Suhartanto et al. (2020); Venkatesh et al. (2016)
SI	Three items including "People who are important to me think that I should use m-banking services" "People who influence my behaviour think that I should use m-banking services"	Tewari et al. (2023)
OC	Six items including "Thinking up new ideas and being creative is important to me. I like to do things in my own original way" "I think it is important to do lots of different things in life. I always look for new things to try"	Schwartz (1992)
PR	Four items including "I think using m-banking services puts my privacy at risk" "Using mobile services involves more financial risk"	Featherman and Pavlou (2003)
BI	Four items including "Assuming I have access to online classes for learning, I intend to use it" "Given that I have access to online classes for learning I predict that I would use it"	Wu and Wang (2005); Venkatesh et al. (2003)

for structural equation modelling (as per 10:1 rule suggested by Kline, 2011). The sample demographics are shown in Table 13.2.

13.4 Data Analysis

Statistical package for social sciences (SPSS) and Analysis of Moment Structures (AMOS) softwares were used for analysis of data. Skewness and kurtosis indices were calculated for checking the normality of the data. The indices were within the acceptable range (±3 and ±10 for skewness and kurtosis, respectively) suggesting the data to be normal (Kline, 2011).

13.4.1 Measurement Model

The measurement model was found to have an excellent fit as per Confirmatory factor analysis (CFA) as shown by the following values: CMIN/df = 1.488 (Chi-square minimum); CFI = 0.964 (Comparative fit index); SRMR = 0.046 (Standardized root mean squared residual); RMSEA = 0.043 (Root mean square error of

Table 13.2 Sample demographics

Variable	*Category*	*Number*	*Percentage*
Age	18–27	78	29.00
	28–37	90	33.46
	38–47	67	24.91
	48 and above	34	12.64
Education	No formal education	27	10.04
	Below matriculation	49	18.22
	Matriculation/higher secondary	95	35.32
	Other technical course	29	10.78
	Graduation and above	69	25.65
Family income	Below 100,000	36	13.38
	100,000–500,000	126	46.84
	500,000–1,000,000	84	31.23
	1,000,000 and above	23	8.55

approximation). The reliability and validity estimates for the constructs were well above the acceptable threshold. The composite reliability values were above 0.7 for all the subscales. The AVE values were above 0.5 demonstrating good convergent validity. The discriminant validity was assessed by comparing square root of average variance extracted (AVE) with factor correlations and the values for the former were greater than that of latter for all the constructs (see Table 13.3) which satisfied the criterion suggested by Fornell and Larcker (1981).

13.4.2 Method Bias

Harman's single factor method was used to check for method bias. The single factor accounted for 27.51% (less than 50%) of the total variance which confirmed the absence of method bias.

13.4.3 Structural Model and Path Analysis

CFA was carried out on the structural model which provided the following fit statistics: CMIN/df = 1.488; CFI = 0.964; SRMR = 0.046; RMSEA = 0.043. These

Table 13.3 Reliability and validity

	CR	*AVE*	*PEU*	*PR*	*OC*	*PU*	*BI*	*SI*
PEU	0.896	0.682	**0.826**					
PR	0.865	0.617	–0.43	**0.785**				
OC	0.897	0.592	0.266	–0.38	**0.769**			
PU	0.824	0.54	0.173	–0.079	0.161	**0.735**		
BI	0.892	0.673	0.567	–0.601	0.493	0.377	**0.82**	
SI	0.791	0.56	0.249	–0.231	–0.058	0.095	0.347	**0.748**

Diagonal values represent sq. root of AVE.

PEU = perceived ease of use; PR = perceived risk; OC = openness to change; PU = perceived usefulness; BI = behavioural intention; SI = social influence measures suggest that the model fit is excellent. The model explained 64% variance in BI.

Path analysis revealed that all the factors significantly impacted behavioural intention. The effect of PU ($\beta = 0.244$, $p < 0.001$), PEU ($\beta = 0.266$, $p < 0.001$), SI ($\beta = 0.200$, $p < 0.001$), OC ($\beta = 0.274$, $p < 0.001$), and PR ($\beta = -0.318$, $p < 0.001$) on BI was statistically significant. Thus, all the hypotheses (H1–H5) were supported.

13.5 Discussion

The purpose of this study is to determine the characteristics that impact Indian housewives' inclination to use m-banking, an important but little-researched subject in the country. Considering the dearth of studies in similar settings, it was useful to look at the factors of PU, PEU, SI, OC, and PR in the context of BI to adopt m-banking services.

Our findings confirm past research that emphasized that PU has a positive effect on BI. When women believe m-banking will help them better manage their finances and make decisions, they are more inclined to utilize it. This is in line with the fundamental principle of the TAM, which underlines the significance of perceived technological advantages.

It also becomes clear that PEU is a significant component affecting BI. Adoption is frequently prompted by a simple and smooth user experience (Venkatesh & Bala, 2008). Housewives will be more inclined to adopt m-banking if they believe it to be simple and user-friendly, which is in line with studies that stress the importance of usability (Davis, 1989). It has been surprisingly found that PEU appears to have slightly more of an effect on BI than PU, indicating that while appreciating the utility is important, an intuitive and user-friendly design may be even more crucial for this group of people.

Similar to the findings of Tewari et al. (2023), SI has a significant impact on BI. Housewives' opinions might be affected by interpersonal encounters, peer advice, and familial direction. This highlights how crucial a role social networks play in influencing people's views towards embracing new technology.

Among Indian housewives, OC has a strong effect on BI. The concept of innovation adoption as a whole is aligned with the readiness to accept new practices (Rogers, 2003). Higher OC housewives are more likely to embrace cutting-edge technologies like m-banking, which supports their favourable BI.

PR has the biggest negative impact on BI. The considerable negative influence that PR has on Indian housewives' behavioural intentions to utilize m-banking may have a number of root factors. Given how frequently cybercrimes and data breaches happen, these housewives could be worried about the security of their financial information and transactions. The lack of confidence a person has in m-banking systems, their lack of technological know-how, and their fear of making expensive mistakes can all have an impact on how risky they perceive situations to be. Due to these alleged concerns, Indian housewives may be reluctant to use m-banking, choosing prudence instead.

13.6 Implication

13.6.1 Theoretical Implication

The following are some key theoretical implications of our research:

Extension of the TAM: In the context of Indian housewives' adoption of m-banking, the study expands the TAM by integrating other variables like SI, OC, and PR. This update broadens the TAM's scope of application and highlights its versatility in a range of demographic and cultural contexts.

This research advances theories about how technology adoption occurs in various sociocultural contexts by shedding light on the interactions between gender dynamics and technical choices.

The study offers theoretical insights into the financial empowerment of women by examining factors affecting housewives' use of m-banking. This is consistent with more general conversations about gender studies and the agency of women in their homes and communities.

The study's findings can help behavioural economics theories by shedding light on the thought processes that drive people's acceptance or opposition to technology. Topics from behavioural economics like aversion to loss, information processing, and decision-making biases interact with elements like PU, PEU, and PR.

It may be useful to analyse the factors influencing housewives' early adoption of m-banking services to develop theories of innovation diffusion. It can be useful in understanding how innovators and early adopters fit within a certain population.

The lack of study on housewives' use of technology in developing countries, in particular, presents an opportunity to help establish new theoretical frameworks that accurately represent the unique challenges and potential in these situations.

13.6.2 Practical Implication

Several useful conclusions may be derived from the study's insightful findings to guide various stakeholders' plans, initiatives, and actions.

Creating user-friendly and straightforward m-banking apps should be a top priority for financial institutions and developers. A user-friendly interface is essential, as shown by PEU's considerable effect. This design strategy would improve Indian housewives' adoption experiences by catering to their unique demands and level of technological knowledge.

Hold seminars and educational programmes to raise housewives' digital literacy levels, with an emphasis on helping them comprehend the advantages of m-banking. Given that PU has a positive impact, it is critical to inform housewives of the benefits of utilizing m-banking for money management so that they will be more likely to adopt.

Work together with family, friends, and peers to raise knowledge of and favourable attitudes of m-banking. Given the important role that SI plays, using social networks can aid in creating an atmosphere where housewives are more likely to adopt m-banking because of referrals from reliable sources.

Tailor outreach programmes and marketing campaigns to emphasize m-banking's advantages for effective money management and adjusting to new technological developments. OC is significantly important. It can be helpful to target housewives with communications that emphasize how m-banking fits with their willingness to adopt new practices.

Financial institutions should keep highlighting and informing the public about the robust security measures put in place for m-banking platforms. Preserving confidence through strong security measures is still crucial. Concerns about the hazards of conducting business online might be allayed by clear data protection communication.

Develop comprehensive strategies for encouraging the use of m-banking by using a holistic approach that integrates the results relating to PU, PEU, SI, OC, and PR. Each element has a distinct role in the choice to adopt. These findings may be used to create a complex strategy that targets several aspects of adoption.

Constantly keep an eye on how Indian housewives' attitudes and behaviours are evolving regarding the use of m-banking, and adjust methods as necessary. The shifting effects of variables like PEU and PR suggest that as technology advances and attitudes change, methods may need to be modified over time.

Encourage a climate where housewives actively participate in the digital economy by rewarding them for utilizing m-banking with incentives and other forms of recognition. It is necessary to provide a compelling atmosphere where the advantages and simplicity of m-banking are accentuated in order to increase BI.

The use of m-banking among Indian housewives may be considerably increased by incorporating these practical consequences into the goals and actions of financial institutions, educational institutions, and legislators. The results of above study provide useful information that fills the gap between theoretical comprehension and practical application.

13.6.3 Policy Implication

The study's findings can have significant policy implications. In addition to boosting financial inclusion, these findings are crucial in encouraging Indian housewives to embrace m-banking, a market that has received little attention. The Ministry of Women and Child Development and the Ministry of Electronics and Information Technology should play a major role in the establishment of Digital Literacy Programmes, which are first and foremost essential. Given the importance of PEU and OC in the adoption process, these programmes should concentrate on improving technological expertise and usability for m-banking apps.

Social influence campaigns can make use of the favourable impact of family, friends, and peers to encourage the use of m-banking. These campaigns are backed by government organizations like the Ministry of Communications and Information Technology. Regulating agencies like the Reserve Bank of India (RBI) and the Ministry of Finance must implement strict security controls and promote clear information about data protection in order to reduce the PR barrier. This will increase customer trust.

The Ministry of Women and Child Development's incentive programmes, developed in partnership with financial institutions, can encourage Indian housewives to utilize m-banking to participate in the digital economy. Governmental organizations, academic institutions, and research organizations should combine their research and data-gathering activities to better understand the particular requirements of this group.

Last but not least, financial institutions should implement the holistic strategy development under the direction of regulatory agencies, taking into account elements like PU, PER, SI, PR, and OC. These policy implications work together to close the adoption gap for m-banking, advancing financial inclusion and the wider digital revolution. Effective implementation and monitoring call for cooperation between these parties. Governmental organizations, academic institutions, and research organizations should combine their research and data-gathering activities to better understand the particular requirements of this group.

13.7 Conclusion and Future Research Directions

Our research sheds great light on the influence of PU, PEU, SI, OC, and PR on BI, i.e., intention of housewives to adopt m-banking. The research does have certain restrictions, though. First of all, because non-probability sampling was used, the results might not be generalizable. Additionally, the research is geographically restricted to northern India, which restricts the applicability of the findings to other areas. It's also crucial to keep in mind that the study only examines intention, not actual usage behaviour. This model might be expanded in future studies to look at how housewives really use mobile devices.

Declaration of Conflict of Interests

The authors declare no potential conflict of interest.

Acknowledgement

Special thanks to Dr. Sushil Pande for his invaluable guidance and support throughout this research. Dr. Pande's insights and mentorship greatly contributed to the success of this study.

Funding

This research was conducted without external funding or financial support.

References

Alalwan, A. A., Dwivedi, Y. K., Rana, N. P., & Algharabat, R. (2018). Examining factors influencing Jordanian customers' intentions and adoption of internet banking: Extending UTAUT2 with risk. *Journal of Retailing and Consumer Services*, *40*, 125–138. https://doi.org/https://doi.org/10.1016/j.jretconser.2017.08.026.

Chawla, D., & Joshi, H. (2017). Consumer perspectives about mobile banking adoption in India – A cluster analysis. *International Journal of Bank Marketing*, *35*(4), 616–636. https://doi.org/10.1108/IJBM-03-2016-0037.

Curran, J. M., & Meuter, M. L. (2007). Encouraging existing customers to switch to self-service technologies: Put a little fun in their lives. *Journal of Marketing Theory and Practice*, *15*(4), 283–298. https://doi.org/10.2753/MTP1069-6679150401.

Davis, F. D. (1989). Perceived usefulness, perceived ease of use, and user acceptance of information technology. *MIS Quarterly*, *13*(3), 319–340.

Featherman, M. S., & Pavlou, P. A. (2003). Predicting e-services adoption: A perceived risk facets perspective. *International Journal of Human-Computer Studies*, *59*(4), 451–474. https://doi.org/10.1016/S1071-5819(03)00111-3.

Flavián, C., Guinalíu, M., & Torres, E. (2006). How bricks-and-mortar attributes affect online banking adoption. *International Journal of Bank Marketing*, *24*(6), 406–423. https://doi.org/10.1108/02652320610701735.

Jamshidi, D., & Hussin, N. (2016). Forecasting patronage factors of Islamic credit card as a new e-commerce banking service. *Journal of Islamic Marketing*, *7*(4), 378–404. https://doi.org/10.1108/JIMA-07-2014-0050.

Kesharwani, A., & Singh Bisht, S. (2012). The impact of trust and perceived risk on internet banking adoption in India. *International Journal of Bank Marketing*, *30*(4), 303–322. https://doi.org/10.1108/02652321211236923.

Kline, R. B. (2011). *Principles and practice of structural equation modeling*. New York: Guildford Press.

Kruse, P., Wach, D., Costa, S., & Moriano, J. A. (2019). Values matter, don't they? – Combining theory of planned behavior and personal values as predictors of social entrepreneurial intention. *Journal of Social Entrepreneurship*, *10*(1), 55–83. https://doi.org/10.1080/19420676.2018.1541003.

Kumar, A., Dhingra, S., Batra, V., & Purohit, H. (2020). A framework of Mobile Banking adoption in India. *Journal of Open Innovation: Technology, Market, and Complexity*, *6*(2), 40. https://doi.org/https://doi.org/10.3390/joitmc6020040.

Liaw, S. S. (2008). Investigating students' perceived satisfaction, behavioral intention, and effectiveness of e-learning: A case study of the Blackboard system. *Computers and Education*, *51*(2), 864–873. https://doi.org/10.1016/j.compedu.2007.09.005.

Malaquias, R. F., & Hwang, Y. (2019). Mobile banking use: A comparative study with Brazilian and U.S. participants. *International Journal of Information Management*, *44*, 132–140. https://doi.org/https://doi.org/10.1016/j.ijinfomgt.2018.10.004.

Malik, F. A., & Yadav, D. K. (2022). *Financial inclusion schemes in India*. Berlin: Springer. https://doi.org/10.1007/978-981-19-1316-7.

Mathur, S., Tewari, A., & Singh, A. (2021). Modeling the factors affecting online purchase intention: The mediating effect of consumer's attitude towards user-generated content. *Journal of Marketing Communications*. https://doi.org/10.1080/13527266.2021.1936126.

Nathawat, S. S., & Mathur, A. (1993). Marital adjustment and subjective well-being in Indian-educated housewives and working women. *The Journal of Psychology*, *127*(3), 353–358. https://doi.org/10.1080/00223980.1993.9915570.

Owusu Kwateng, K., Osei Atiemo, K. A., & Appiah, C. (2019). Acceptance and use of mobile banking: An application of UTAUT2. *Journal of Enterprise Information Management*, *32*(1), 118–151. https://doi.org/10.1108/JEIM-03-2018-0055.

Priya, R., Gandhi, A. V., & Shaikh, A. (2018). Mobile banking adoption in an emerging economy: An empirical analysis of young Indian consumers. *Benchmarking*, *25*(2), 743–762. https://doi.org/10.1108/BIJ-01-2016-0009.

Ratten, V. (2015). International consumer attitudes toward cloud computing: A social cognitive theory and technology acceptance model perspective. *Thunderbird International Business Review*, *57*(3), 217–228. https://doi.org/https://doi.org/10.1002/tie.21692.

Schwartz, S. H. (1992). Universals in the content and structure of values: Theoretical advances and empirical tests in 20 countries. In *Advances in Experimental Social*

Psychology (M. P. Zanna Ed., Vol. 25, pp. 1–65). Academic Press. https://doi.org/10.1016/S0065-2601(08)60281-6.

Senyo, P. K., & Osabutey, E. L. C. (2020). Unearthing antecedents to financial inclusion through FinTech innovations. *Technovation, 98*, 102155.https://doi.org/https://doi.org/10.1016/j.technovation.2020.102155.

Souiden, N., Ladhari, R., & Chaouali, W. (2021). Mobile banking adoption: A systematic review. *International Journal of Bank Marketing, 39*(2), 214–241. https://doi.org/10.1108/IJBM-04-2020-0182.

Suhartanto, D., Dean, D., Ismail, T. A. T., & Sundari, R. (2020). Mobile banking adoption in Islamic banks: Integrating TAM model and religiosity-intention model. *Journal of Islamic Marketing, 11*(6), 1405–1418. https://doi.org/10.1108/JIMA-05-2019-0096.

Teo, A., Tan, G. W., Cheah, C., Ooi, K., & Yew, K. (2012). Can the demographic and subjective norms influence the adoption of mobile banking? *International Journal of Mobile Communications, 10*(6), 578–597. https://doi.org/10.1504/IJMC.2012.049757.

Tewari, A., Mathur, S., Srivastava, S., & Gangwar, D. (2022). Examining the role of receptivity to green communication, altruism and openness to change on young consumers' intention to purchase green apparel: A multi-analytical approach. *Journal of Retailing and Consumer Services, 66*(June 2021), 102938. https://doi.org/10.1016/j.jretconser.2022.102938.

Tewari, A., Singh, R., Mathur, S., & Pande, S. (2023). A modified UTAUT framework to predict students' intention to adopt online learning: Moderating role of openness to change. *International Journal of Information and Learning Technology, 40*(2), 130–147. https://doi.org/10.1108/IJILT-04-2022-0093.

Thi, H. P., Tran, Q. N., La, L. G., Doan, H. M., & Vu, T. D. (2023). Factors motivating students' intention to accept online learning in emerging countries: The case study of Vietnam. *Journal of Applied Research in Higher Education, 15*(2), 324–341. https://doi.org/10.1108/JARHE-05-2021-0191.

Van Eeden-Moorefield, B., Pasley, K., Dolan, E. M., & Engel, M. (2007). From divorce to remarriage. *Journal of Divorce & Remarriage, 47*(3–4), 21–42. https://doi.org/10.1300/J087v47n03_02.

Venkatesh, V., & Bala, H. (2008). Technology acceptance model 3 and a research agenda on interventions. *Decision Sciences, 39*(2), 273–315. https://doi.org/10.1111/J.1540-5915.2008.00192.X.

Venkatesh, V., & Davis, F. D. (2000). A theoretical extension of the technology acceptance model: Four longitudinal field studies. *Management Science, 46*(2), 186–204. https://doi.org/10.1287/mnsc.46.2.186.11926.

14 Analysis of Economic Development of Financial Inclusion and Women Empowerment

Namita Verma, Akash Bag, Lalit Mohan Pant, and Nupur Kumari

14.1 Introduction

> There is no tool for development more effective than women empowerment.
>
> Mr Kofi Annan

The previous UN general secretary made this declaration in response to the concern that gender equality is an obstacle to economic inclusion as well as to international development. He also mentioned the significance of a "Inclusive Financial Sector" to ensure that there is no economic disparity based on gender. When it comes to the advancement and welfare of society, financial inclusion can be seen as a crucial indicator in the modern world. For many nations, particularly the G20 countries, offering a financial service that is affordable for everyone has emerged as a fundamental objective. The G20 countries also stressed the importance of financial inclusion as a tool for achieving gender equality and other achievable objectives (George & Thomachan, 2018). Women's empowerment is a strategy that focuses on shifting the balance of power in favour of the female gender. This current article delves into the dimensions of the several aspects of women empowerment, starting from social, economic, and till political aspects too.

According to "World Bank data from Findex, since 2011", 1.2 billion adults have had access to a variety of financial services, which was close to one third of the 1.7 billion people who were still without a bank account. Financial inclusion was viewed as one of the key pillars of global success during the G20 conference that was held in 2010. Seven of the 17 sustainable development goals have been linked to financial inclusion as a facilitator (Siddik, 2017). The World Bank views financial inclusion as being essential to boosting prosperity through the eradication of poverty. More than 60 nations have started specialised national strategies since 2010 with the aim of achieving universal financial inclusion.

14.1.1 What Is Financial Inclusion

Financial inclusion makes sure the delivery of the basic banking facilities at an affordable and nominal price to the vast sections of a particular country, specially

DOI: 10.4324/9781032655185-19

a developing one. It caters to the disadvantaged people who belong to the low-income groups (Ojo, 2022). These financial services may include to the basic access of saving, credit, insurance, having a valid bank account, etc. In the terms of a feminine gender, this financial inclusion helps them in their development be it be socially or economically. It is evident that the basic access to the financial facilities through the financial inclusion has an impact directly on the social and financial empowerment of the feminine gender which eventually leads to a comprehensive development in their lives (Arnold & Gammage, 2019).

Financial inclusion ensures that all people have access to a range of financial services, understand how to use them, and can do so totally independently. These services will include a straightforward, no-frills bank account for sending and receiving payments from others, money transfer capabilities, small-dollar loans, overdraft protection, and insurance. Financial inclusion was defined as the process of ensuring that vulnerable groups, such as weaker sections and low-income groups, have access to financial services and timely and adequate credit where needed at an affordable cost by a committee on financial inclusion that was established in India and was headed by Dr. C. Rangarajan in 2008 (Ghosh, 2022). In April 2005, Y. V. Reddy used the term "financial inclusion" for the first time in an Indian context. Despite the fact that the United Nations introduced the idea of financial inclusion in the early 2000s, the sad reality, according to the former United Nations secretary general Kofi Annan, is that the majority of the world's poor still don't have access to even the most basic financial services, such as savings, credit, or insurance (Bhatia & Singh, 2019). Later, Queen Maxima of the Netherlands was named UNSGSA (short for United Nations Special Advocate for Inclusive Finance for Development), a position placed inside the United Nations Development Programme, by United Nations Secretary-General Ban Ki-Moon (Table 14.1).

14.1.2 Importance of Financial Inclusion in Feminine Gender

Women empowerment is an approach which will eventually transform the power relations in the favour of the feminine gender which will lead to a better gender equality. This will enable the females to make their own independent life choices, which in the meantime will improve their well-being and quality of life. Women empowerment and gender equality, both are important for global progress and it can be developed through providing an affordable financial facility to women.

Table 14.1 Abbreviation list

Abbreviation	*Full form*
UNDP	United Nations Development Programme
IMF	International Monetary Fund
GDP	Gross Domestic Product
NGOs	Non-Governmental Organisations
SDGs	Sustainable Development Goals

After the persuasion of the G20 which happened in the year of 2014, financial services were applied to major sections of the society, and the timeline between 2011 to 2014, we can witness an upward trend regarding the number of the first-time account holders (Sharma & Changkakati, 2022). Despite this financial inclusion there was a gender gap for accessing to the basic banking services. This resulted in social exclusion and gender disparity which was widespread especially in the developing countries as compared to the developed countries (Arnold & Gammage, 2019).

In the words of Noble Laureate Amartya Sen, "Poverty is not merely lowness of income, but deprivation of basic capabilities" (Nechad, A., 2021). Though accomplishment of complete financial inclusion will not only determine the issues regarding the financial structure but also will annul the conditions created by social exclusion (Rangarajan Committee, 2008). Thus, the inclusive financial model became a system for the developing countries to attain the formative targets. Forming a mechanism through which to attain women empowerment with the help of financial services is a rigorous way to achieve sustainable growth (Kim, 2022).

14.1.3 Scenario of Financial Inclusion in India

Financial inclusion takes together the unbanked and the people who are not included in any banking financial system, to give them the scope to access the financial tools for the sake of creating an economically larger opportunity. In the year of 2015, the Reserve Bank of India gave the definition of what is means regarding the term of "Financial Inclusion". While expressing its views it stated that it is a procedure for making sure that proper financial tools and services which are required by the weaker sections of the society including the low-income groups, are provided at a nominal cost in a fare way. Financial exclusion is a notion to worry about be it be for the developing nation, as well as the developed nations (Pal & Gupta, 2023). Despite being a developed nation, the financial system has not been able to include everyone into the system.

In the context of India, after the LPG model period in 1991, they witnessed a humongous increase as far as the number of bank branches is concerned. It gradually grew not only in urban areas, but also in the semi urban and rural areas too. Despite this havoc expansion there was a section of people who still were in need of basic financial products.

According to the data by RBI, 25.1-cr account holders were using banking in mobile around 2018 and the amount of transaction with mobile banking technology has crossed 3047 billion in the fiscal years of 2018–19. Currently there are several financial inclusive plans such as PMJDY, PMSBY, etc. which encourages the backward people to open zero balance bank accounts and have several insurance options. These government schemes have tried to fill in the gaps of financial inclusion, and eventually these government steps have filled up 55% women account holder's share (Fouejieu et al., 2020).

According to the Global Findex database, 20% of Indian adults do have an active savings account through which they do their regular transactions. The access of small amounts of loans are only of 7%, as far as the Indian adult market is considered, which is eventually more regrettable (Kazemikhasragh & Buoni Pineda, 2022).

Women empowerment has got an increased amount of attention in the last several decades, which eventually has enhanced not only the financial condition for women, but also has improved their health conditions and also, they presently do take part in the decision-making. Empowering is a multilayered idea and having a bank account provides a certain financial improvement for the feminine gender.

14.1.4 Women Empowerment in Bangladesh

Developing countries are facing an issue regarding the fact of gender inequality, which is an obstacle in their way towards a comprehensive development. Nowadays empowerment of the feminine gender is being considered as a mark of a developing society. Bangladesh is being considered now a days as a developing nation, but until now it used to be considered to be an economy which was evidently rural in its nature. Sixty-six per cent citizens of this country still live in the rural areas which creates a sense of vulnerability for those women who live in those isolated areas. Among 144 countries, Bangladeshis ranked 75th in the Gender Gap Index released in 2015 by the World Economic Forum (Andriamahery & Qamruzzaman, 2022).

A new initiative of providing micro credits has been started in Bangladesh. It is being offered so as to generate a certain amount of income and this will eventually help in the process of decreasing poverty and increase security of food and women empowerment by increasing the development of economy. It is a way through which people in rural areas can participate in the income-generating activities which are very much necessary or making sure that they have a working capital when they need any kind of financial assistance. Providing microcredit, an investment without any collateral, to poverty-stricken females enables them to accomplish the necessary empowering projects (Lee & Huruta, 2022). This will curtail the lack of loans problem which these poor females will not be getting from any traditional or systematic banking system. Mainly the poor women work for the benefit of some other people or some other organisation, be it be financial organisation or an industrial organisation. The main aim of the micro credit schemes is that they will gradually improve the lifestyle of these poor female simply by including them into any financial system (Asad et al., 2020). These borrowers are significantly influenced by the micro credit schemes in the fields of education, regarding their household expenses and assets. These schemes have also tremendously impacted the incomes of the household, production of crops, rising employment in the fields of agricultural as well as rural sectors. This kind of scheme support will also improve the self-confidence and self-esteem, and thus help them feel empowered. This will eventually impact in their decision-making, and also in the fields of planning a family, their children's marriage, any kind of transaction regarding their property and most importantly in the field of education regarding their daughters.

14.2 Literature Review

14.2.1 Financial Inclusion and Women's Empowerment Nexus

A crucial nexus in the area of socioeconomic growth is the interconnectedness of economic inclusion as well as women's empowerment. Financial integration, which is defined as the availability and use of official banking services by people and businesses, has become an effective tool for promoting women's empowerment on a number of fronts (Razak & Asutay, 2022). The literature review digs into the theoretical foundations and empirical data that help to explain this complicated connection in this part. Theoretical frameworks have emphasised how removing conventional gender norms and giving women the means to have more influence over their life can help women become more empowered. Women can manage their finances, make investments in their children's health and academic success, and take part more actively in the economy when they have better access to financial institutions (Abdelghaffar et al., 2023). Financial inclusion serves as a bridge for both of these elements, which are both included in the premise of women's empowerment. Furthermore, research shows that women who are financially independent are better positioned to participate in decision-making processes in their communities and homes.

The theoretical assertions are strongly supported by empirical studies. Access to credit and retirement savings has been associated with a rise in the participation of women in business ownership and income-generating endeavours. The capacity to invest and save helps women become more resilient and take advantage of possibilities for socioeconomic growth. Additionally, it has been demonstrated that financial inclusion increases women's bargaining power inside households by enabling them to advocate for themselves and negotiate other resources (Antonijević et al., 2022; Figure 14.1).

The research does, however, agree that there are still problems. Women's complete involvement in financial institutions may be hampered by gender-specific

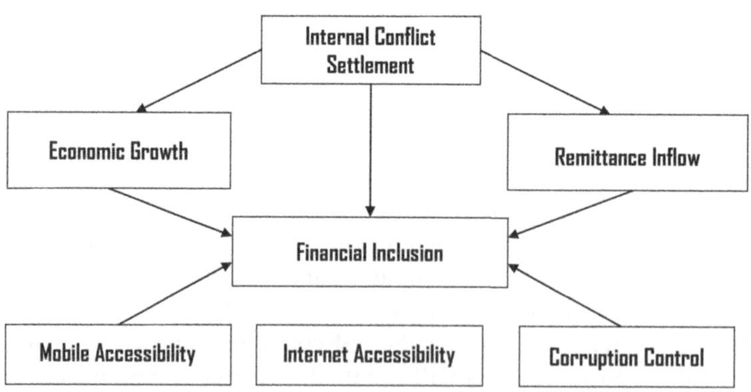

Figure 14.1 Financial inclusion

Source: Self-developed

impediments such low financial literacy, social conventions, and discriminatory practices (Reshi, 2023). Therefore, removing these obstacles is necessary for financial inclusion campaigns in order to provide fair access and substantial empowerment.

14.2.2 Impact of Financial Inclusion on Women's Socioeconomic Advancement

A key component of the larger conversation about gender equality as well as economic growth is how financial participation affects women's economic success. The empirical data that illustrate how better access to financial resources affects many aspects of women's lives and ultimately aids in their socioeconomic advancement are examined in this portion of the literature study. Studies from various contexts constantly highlight the monetary inclusion's beneficial effects for women's political agency. Significant improvements in women's earnings-generating endeavours and entrepreneurship have been associated with increased opportunities for savings accounts, credit options, and insurance options (Atakli & Agbenyo, 2020). Women who have access to finance are better able to invest in enterprises that will generate revenue, grow already-existing ones, or pursue career development, all of which will improve their financial chances. Financial inclusion is also essential for improving women's resilience to financial hardship. Their total economic stability and well-being are influenced by their capacity to put money aside for unanticipated events or to make investments in their education and healthcare. When women have traditionally been excluded from official financial systems, this element becomes especially important (Shah & Ali, 2022).

The literature also emphasises how women's economic empowerment has a domino effect on larger societal dimensions. Women who are more economically independent typically devote a bigger percentage of their pay checks to providing for their families' health and education, which promotes the growth of human capital. This intergenerational effect promotes long-term environmentally friendly growth in addition to ending the perpetuation of poverty. It's crucial to recognise that the effectiveness of financial inclusion depends on how accessible and acceptable financial goods and amenities are. Women's effective participation may be hampered by gender prejudices that exist inside financial organisations and products (Adegbite & Machethe, 2020) Additionally, according to the literature, the effects of being financially included may change depending on contextual elements including cultural norms, physical location, and socioeconomic levels (Figure 14.2).

14.2.3 Policies and Initiatives for Women's Financial Inclusion

Women's monetary inclusion programmes and efforts are now widely recognised as essential tactics for advancing gender equality while promoting economic growth. This part of the overview of the literature looks at the many initiatives that governments, banking organisations, and international organisations have put in place to

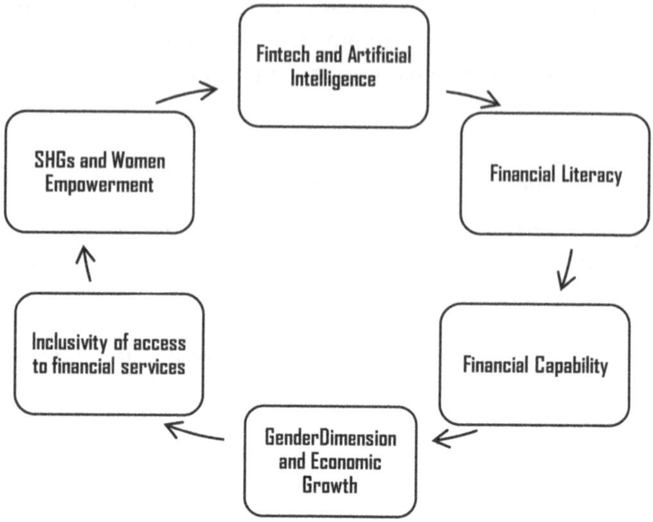

Figure 14.2 Socioeconomic impact of financial inclusion

Source: Self-developed

address the particular difficulties that women encounter when trying to access and take advantage of the formal system of finance (Al Hakim et al., 2022). Politicians and governments are aware of the need for focused actions to narrow the gender access gap in the financial sector. Regulations that facilitate the distribution of financial assistance and goods that take gender into account are frequently included in national regulations. These regulations could include light collateral requirements, lenient identification standards, and steps to improve women's monetary literacy and educational achievement (Bhatia & Singh, 2019). Traditional and online financial institutions have launched cutting-edge products designed to satisfy the specific financial demands of women. For instance, microfinance organisations have been crucial in helping women business owners who would not otherwise have access to traditional banking facilities obtain small loans. A revolution in the financial industry, online banking services allow women to obtain monetary services across mobile devices and break down geographical restrictions (Figure 14.3).

Through joint initiatives, international organisations and development organisations have contributed by contributing to the female economic empowerment. Equality-responsive financial systems are essential, as stressed by initiatives like the World Bank's Equality Strategy along with the World Bank's feminist empowerment Principles. Increasing data collecting, exchanging best practices, and amplifying the contributions of women in influencing financial policies are all goals of multilateral cooperation (Sakyi-Nyarko et al., 2022). The literature does, however, also highlight the difficulties in turning these principles into useful results. Women's desire to use official banking services is impacted by gender conventions and prejudices that continue to influence financial behaviours (Kemal, 2019). Broader

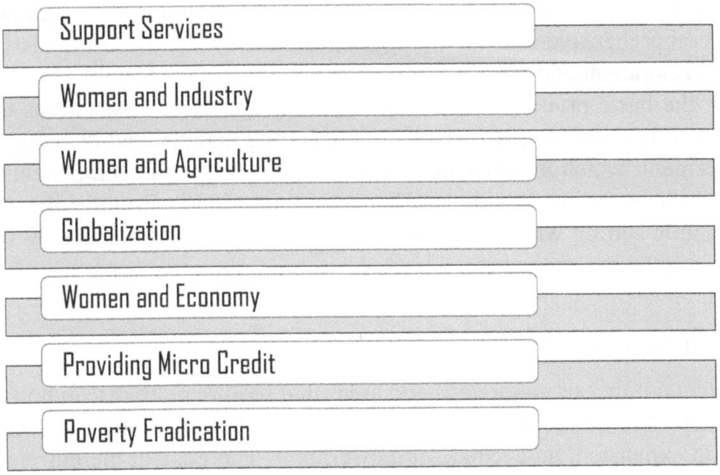

Figure 14.3 Policies

Source: Kemal (2019)

structural inequities, a lack of awareness, and poor knowledge of finance can further limit the beneficial effects of policies.

14.2.4 Measuring the Link between Financial Inclusion, Economic Growth, and Women's Empowerment

Researchers have made an effort to measure the complex interactions between financial accessibility, economic expansion, and female empowerment. The methods and procedures used to quantify and analyse the correlations between these three crucial factors are covered in this portion of the literature review, offering light on the mechanisms through which monetary inclusion affects both economic growth and female empowerment (Leight et al., 2022). Statistical methods are frequently used in quantitative investigations to establish an empirical relationship between financial integration and economic expansion. To find correlations, causal connections, and potential feedback loops, this research frequently use cross-country skiing analyses, data from panels regressions, including econometric modelling (Ozili, 2021). To determine the strength of the connection, indicators including increased gross domestic product (GDP), rate of savings, lending penetration, and access to institutional financial services are typically utilised.

However, the literature recognises that precise and context-specific aspects of empowering women may be missed by quantitative assessments. To probe deeper into the everyday lives of women and the effects of financial participation on their agency, power to make decisions, and economic standing, qualitative research approaches, such as case studies, conversations, and discussions in focus groups, are used. Mixed-methods techniques are becoming more popular as they provide a more thorough understanding of the complex processes at work (O'Brien et al., 2022).

These techniques combine quantitative information with qualitative knowledge to offer a comprehensive understanding of how money inclusion affects both economic development and female empowerment. This method enables researchers to pinpoint the basic processes that underlie the quantitative associations they have found. Data limitations, particularly in developing nations, and the complexity of empowerment, which includes financial, political, and social components, present difficulties in assessing these links (Bhatia & Singh, 2019). Establishing attribution in a dynamic setting where numerous factors interplay simultaneously is another challenge faced by researchers.

14.2.5 Literature Gap

There are a number of major gaps and areas that require more research in the enormous body of literature addressing the connection between financial accessibility, economic expansion, and female empowerment. The gaps in the current body of knowledge are examined in the following part of the literature review, showing the chances for further investigation to advance our knowledge of this intricate connection. First off, there is a paucity of research that explores the fundamental mechanisms as well as causal pathways linking financial inclusion, economic expansion, and female empowerment, despite the fact that multiple studies have found connections between these factors. The existing research frequently focuses on statistical correlations without fully exploring how increased access to monetary services affects women's autonomy, decision-making, as well as socioeconomic position in concrete ways. Future studies should use qualitative techniques to investigate women's lived experiences and reveal the complex ways that financial inclusion affects women's empowerment. Furthermore, the majority of studies have concentrated on how women can access traditional financial products like credit and savings. However, the literature frequently neglects the wider range of money-related products and services, which include insurance coverage, possibilities for investment, especially digital financial instruments, that are essential to female empowerment (Duvendack & Mader, 2020). A more complete picture regarding the way financial inclusion affects women's economic trajectory could be obtained by examining the use and impact of these frequently overlooked financial instruments.

Concerning the connection between economic expansion, women empowerment, and financial accessibility, the researchers have identified some literature gaps that are essential to be closed. The research topic critically focuses on several areas such as socioeconomic development, gender equality, and policymaking. Hence, it is essential to link these factors to formulate evidence-based policies. A comprehensive understanding of access to financial understanding and its impacts on socioeconomic standing, women empowerment, and decision-making is essential to be discussed to establish effective strategies to promote economic growth. Moreover, in order to provide insights about gender equality it is essential to bridge those gaps. By conducting this study, the impacts of financial inclusion on women's empowerment can be identified which can be used in future research to develop informed policies and initiatives for women's empowerment and fostering gender equality in financial decision-making. In addition to that, it is also essential to close the literature gap for socioeconomic development. A comprehensive understanding needs to be provided of various financial services and instruments that directly influence women's empowerment. Thus, this research paper can significantly contribute towards the increased participation of women in economic activities as well as driving economic growth and development.

14.3 Research Methodology

This research intends to thoroughly examine the complex interplay between financial participation, economic growth, and women being empowered. To do this, the research will be guided by the research into interpretivism philosophical thought, allowing for a thorough examination of subjective perceptions of being financially included and its effect on women's empowerment. In order to give a thorough overview of the literature, policies, as well as initiatives already in place, a design based on descriptive statistics will be used. This strategy fits with the goals of the study, which include evaluating how well we currently understand the relationships between economic development, financial inclusion, along with women's empowerment (Duvendack & Mader, 2020). Discovering the social realities along with meanings that people create within their surroundings is emphasised by interpretivism. Given the intricacy of the topic, using an interpretivist stance will allow for a more thorough investigation of how the inclusion of money affects women's empowerment. Given that women's experiences with monetary autonomy fluctuate by their societal, cultural, as well as economic origins, this ideology promotes the examination of all viewpoints. The goal of this research is to map out the present level of knowledge on the topic, which is a good fit for the method of descriptive research. This design entails gathering and examining already-existing data, guidelines, and activities concerning money inclusion, economic expansion, and women being empowered. The research seeks to offer a thorough overview of the current landscape by summarising and classifying the literature relevant policies. Using a deductive research strategy, hypotheses are derived from accepted ideas and evaluated against empirical facts. The validity of current theories about the effects of financial participation on female autonomy and economic expansion will be evaluated in this research using the deductive method. The research will analyse the literature and government regulations, comparing empirical data to theoretical hypotheses, and improving or changing these hypotheses as necessary. The research will rely on supplementary information gathered from reliable sources such as scholarly publications, reports from global organisations including the Bank for International Settlements the UNDP, the International Finance Corporation (IMF), and other pertinent organisations (Bhatia & Singh, 2019). A useful source for knowledge will be the international Findex database, which provides information on economic integration trends. To get a variety of viewpoints on the subject, academic journals, advocacy organisations, and research organisations will also be surveyed. This strategy is consistent with the investigation's deductive strategy and enables the comparison of current concepts and models with empirical data.

Care will be made to ensure that the appropriate credit is given when attributing specific sources, information, or examples in order to uphold the confidentiality of intellectual property and recognise the work of authors along with researchers. In the event that direct quotations or excerpts are used, accurate reference and referencing shall be upheld. Any private knowledge or information that might be used to identify specific people or entities will be handled with the utmost discretion. Researchers will take care to maintain participants' along with stakeholders' confidentiality by not revealing private or confidential data. As secondary information from reliable sources makes up the majority of the research, measures will be taken to abide by the data usage policies and restrictions established by the data suppliers. Any restrictions on the use, distribution, or reproduction of data will be honoured. Researchers will work towards a fair and impartial depiction of findings in order to guarantee the ethical the viewpoints (Park & Mercado, 2021). When highlighting the effects of economic inclusion as well as women's empowerment, this involves avoiding any kind of prejudice, stereotyping, or misunderstanding of culture.

14.4 Results and Discussions

14.4.1 Theme 1: Unveiling the Nexus: Financial Inclusion and Women's Empowerment

The chapter "Unveiling the power source Nexus: Financial Participation and Women's Empowerment" explores this relationship thematically, showing how these two vital factors profoundly interact. This theme reveals the ways whereby financial inclusion operates as a catalyst promoting women's empowerment through a detailed assessment of philosophical frameworks as well as empirical discoveries. Data on a global scale from the Global Findex database of the World Bank emphasises the importance of monetary inclusion in influencing women's agency and financial choice-making. Approximately 1.7 billion women worldwide do not have access to traditional banking services since they are not banked. This information demonstrates how gender differences in financial access still exist, highlighting the critical need for governmental initiatives to close these inequalities. A fuller knowledge of women's experiences can be gained from the qualitative insights acquired from interviews along with narratives (Koomson et al., 2020). These stories demonstrate how giving women the ability to control their financial lives through access to monetary services motivates them. For instance, microfinance programmes in India have given rural women the ability to start and maintain small companies, improving their standing in the communities where they live.

Additionally, the subject highlights how important financial inclusion is in breaking long-standing gender conventions. Research across Sub-Saharan Africa demonstrates how women are empowered to resist patriarchal institutions by having access to financial amenities and amplifying their perspectives in domestic and societal concerns. But this subject also highlights ongoing difficulties. Despite advancements, women continue to face challenges like low financial literacy as well as cultural hurdles. In Pakistan, for instance, cultural norms that limit women's mobility as well as autonomy continue to prevent them from participating in official financial systems (Malik et al., n.d.).

14.4.2 Theme 2: Empowering Socioeconomic Progress: Financial Inclusion Impact on Women

A revolutionary journey propelled by better access to financial resources is revealed by the theme of promoting women's socioeconomic advancement through financial inclusion. Significantly positive changes are being noticed in income creation, financial resilience, and the development of human capital as more women are given the chance to interact with conventional financial systems (Malik & Yadav, 2022).

14.4.2.1 Income Generation and Entrepreneurship

Empirical studies highlight the significant influence of economic empowerment on female business ownership and earning opportunities. The International Findex database shows that women's involvement in businesses that generate revenue has significantly increased in nations where access to formalised monetary services has become easier for women (Baber, 2020). Women who were previously denied access to credit markets have since been able to obtain loans and make investments, increasing their level of economic independence. By encouraging the creation and growth of women-owned companies, this access to money boosts local economies while also promoting personal empowerment.

14.4.2.2 Financial Resilience and Security

In order to increase women's financial stability and resilience, having financial resources is essential. According to studies, women who have access to deposit accounts as well as insurance solutions are better prepared to deal with shocks as well as uncertainties in the economy. In areas where women have historically had trouble saving, increased financial access has resulted in higher savings rates, protecting against unforeseen costs (Malik et al., 2021). Women can preserve stability and safeguard the welfare of their family by having access to loans in times of need.

14.4.2.3 Education and Human Capital

Increased financial inclusion leads to investments in feminine human capital growth and educational opportunities. An extensive analysis of the literature reveals a strong correlation between women's availability of financial products and services and higher spending in learning and skill-development initiatives. The development of a trained and confident female workforce as a result of this movement ultimately benefits economies as a whole (Duvendack & Mader, 2020). For instance, research shows that higher percentages of females enrolling in school have been seen in nations where women are empowered to make savings and investments, advancing the goal of equal opportunity in education.

14.4.3 Theme 3: Advancing Equity: Policies and Initiatives for Inclusive Financial Inclusion

This topical area digs into the world of laws and programmes designed to advance equitable financial inclusion, with a specific emphasis on women. The goal is to assess how well different methods and tactics work to close the gender gap regarding money access and support for women's financial independence. Three major subthemes underlying this theme stand out:

14.4.3.1 Policy Frameworks and Reforms

This subtheme examines how regulatory changes and policy changes can help to foster an environment that supports financial empowerment of women. It entails evaluating how governments and pertinent authorities have handled prejudices and barriers that are specific to gender in the financial systems (Bhatia & Singh, 2019). Understanding how legal and legislative developments, such as lowering collateral demands or recognising property rights for females, have affected access to regulated financial services for women can be learned through analysing the effects of these changes.

14.4.3.2 Innovative Financial Products

This subtheme examines the effects of cutting-edge financial solutions and goods created specifically to meet the unique demands of women. We'll assess gender-sensitive financial products like microloans, investments, insurance that takes into account the different stages of a woman's life, and more. It will be evaluated to what extent these goods help women minimise risks, save money, and engage in economic activity (Malik et al., 2020). Additionally, an examination of how much these products enable women to develop monetary resiliency and make educated financial choices would shed light on their efficacy.

14.4.3.3 Financial Literacy and Education

This subtheme explores the value of financial literacy programmes in empowering women with the information and abilities they need to interact with formal financial institutions. It will be determined how well women comprehend financial principles, banking practices, and investment prospects as a result of educational programmes (Cicchiello et al., 2021). The research will also examine the relationship between increased financial literacy and women's trust when handling their finances, enhancing their total economic agency.

14.4.4 Theme 4: Pathways and Dynamics: Understanding Financial Inclusion Links to Empowerment

The topic of "Pathways especially Dynamics: Recognising Financial Participation's Link to Development" explores the complex relationships that exist between financial accessibility, economic development, and empowerment for women. The goal of this theme is to understand the complex dynamics as well as mechanisms that influence how these important variables interact.

14.4.4.1 Quantitative Correlations and Empirical Relationships

An examination of empirical correlation along with quantitative linkages takes the stage throughout this theme. The results of multiple studies will be combined to show statistical correlations between economic expansion, financial wellness, and other aspects of female empowerment (Duvendack & Mader, 2020). Such associations will provide information about the magnitude and character of the connections, laying the groundwork for quantitative analysis of the possible effects of being financially included on female empowerment.

14.4.4.2 Causal Mechanisms

This subtheme dives more deeply into the causal threads that link the inclusion of money to empowerment for women along with economic growth. In order to provide women more agency as well as power over decisions, it aims to identify the mechanism through which improved access to financial products and services promotes economic growth (Hendriks, 2019). The research tries to pinpoint crucial intervention points that can be pursued through legislation and initiatives by closely examining these systems.

14.4.4.3 Longitudinal and Comparative Approaches

It is crucial to comprehend how things function across time and in various circumstances. Studies that follow movements and advances over a prolonged period of time, known as longitudinal research, can highlight patterns, variations, and the changing nature of the connections between financial literacy, economic development, as well as empowerment for women (Baber, 2020). On the contrary hand, comparative research can shed light on how various economic, cultural, as well as policy environments influence how the relationships turn out.

14.5 Policy Implications

14.5.1 Conclusion

14.5.1.1 Critical Analysis of Findings

The research examined the many facets of how financial inclusion affects women's empowerment and how that affects growth in the economy. Empirical studies have confirmed links between monetary inclusion and feminine economic advancement, but the underlying causes of these relationships are still unclear. According to the report, financial inclusion serves as a catalyst by giving women the resources they need to increase their agency, make investments in their health and academic achievement, and take part in activities that generate income. The necessity for tailored strategies to attain equal results was nevertheless underscored by local variations and various levels economic empowerment.

14.5.1.2 Summary of Achievements

The research was successful in combining various viewpoints and empirical data across this investigation to reveal the complex connections between financial inclusion, the empowerment of women, as well as economic progress. The research highlighted the importance of financial innovations and policy changes in closing gender gaps, but it also brought to light problems caused by cultural norms, data shortages, and practical difficulties. The research has advanced knowledge of how financial literacy can promote gender equality along with environmentally friendly growth by providing a comprehensive assessment of the situation.

14.5.1.3 Recommendations

Several suggestions are made for governments, banking institutions, and organisations working to improve the well-being of women by means of financial inclusion on the basis of the insights acquired. It is crucial to have a framework for policy that is gender-conscious, removes regulatory obstacles, and supports inclusive financial institutions. Second, specialised financial products that respond to the various demands and preferences of women should be created and promoted. Third, it's crucial to provide women with thorough financial literacy programmes that provide them the information and skills they need to understand how financial institutions work. Lastly, in order to promote comprehensive transformation and guarantee the significant impact of economic inclusion, cooperation between governance, financial institutions, especially civil society is essential.

14.5.1.4 Future Work

Although this research has uncovered many of the complexity of financial inclusion's effects, there are still many directions for future study. Richer insights could be gained through a thorough analysis of the cultural and environmental elements that influence the relationship between financial autonomy and women's empowerment. Additionally, worldwide comparisons as well as longitudinal studies that track developments over time might offer a more dynamic knowledge of these linkages. There is room for more research in the areas of marginalised women's experiences and the contribution of technology to financial empowerment.

After analysing the economic development with focusing on financial inclusion and women empowerment, it is revealed that there are some significant interconnections between them and there are several potential for mutual reinforcement. Through this research it is quite evident that empowering the feminine gender and promoting financial inclusion to them are some of the most important drivers of a sustainable economic growth and also of social progress. This conclusion will summarise the key elements from the analysis and will underscore the importance of these two factors in the shaping of a prosperous and comprehensive society.

Financial inclusion, which is defined as the basic access to and the very use of affordable and appropriate financial services, is very much crucial component of the economic development. The research shows that when the population which is marginalised, especially women, gain access to formal financial systems, they also become more and more capable to participate in the daily economic activities. This kind of increased participation leads to greater amounts of savings, investments and entrepreneurship, which eventually results in enhanced economic growth and also reduces income inequality in any given country.

Advancement of the financial inclusion system and women empowerment are not only moral compulsions but they are also powerful drivers of any country's economic development. By merging these elements into basic framework of policy making and developmental agendas, societies can unleash their full economic potential and also can create more profitable and equitable and prosperous future for all of the mankind.

References

Abdelghaffar, R. A., Emam, H. A., & Samak, N. A. (2023). Financial inclusion and human development: Is there a nexus? *Journal of Humanities and Applied Social Sciences*, *5*(3), 163–177. https://www.emerald.com/insight/content/doi/10.1108/jhass-11-2021-0178/full/html.

Adegbite, O. O., & Machethe, C. L. (2020). Bridging the financial inclusion gender gap in smallholder agriculture in Nigeria: An untapped potential for sustainable development. *World Development*, *127*, 104755. https://repository.up.ac.za/bitstream/handle/2263/73912/Adegbite_Bridging_2020.pdf?sequence=1.

Al Hakim, G., Bastian, B. L., Ng, P. Y., & Wood, B. P. (2022). Women's empowerment as an outcome of NGO projects: Is the current approach sustainable? *Administrative Sciences*, *12*(2), 62. https://www.mdpi.com/2076-3387/12/2/62.

Andriamahery, A., & Qamruzzaman, M. (2022). Do access to finance, technical know-how, and financial literacy offer women empowerment through women's entrepreneurial development? *Frontiers in Psychology*, *12*, 776844. https://drive.google.com/file/d/1bnU2KHnUW7rz0vaY_qIak3J1-2zDF6Jt/view.

Antonijević, M., Ljumović, I., & Ivanović, Đ. (2022). Is there a gender gap in financial inclusion worldwide? *Journal of Women's Entrepreneurship and Education*, (1-2), 79–96. http://ebooks.ien.bg.ac.rs/1829/1/1404-Article%20Text-6126-1-10-20220712.pdf.

Arnold, J., & Gammage, S. (2019). Gender and financial inclusion: The critical role for holistic programming. *Development in Practice*, *29*(8), 965–973. https://www.tandfonline.com/doi/pdf/10.1080/09614524.2019.1651251.

Asad, A., Hameed, W. U., Irfan, M., Jiang, J., & Naveed, R. T. (2020). The contribution of microfinance institutes in women-empowerment and role of vulnerability. *Revisita Argentina Clínica Psicologica*, *29*, 223–238. https://revistaclinicapsicologica.com/data-cms/articles/oldissue/20200929112358pm.pdf.

Atakli, B. A., & Agbenyo, W. (2020). Nexus between financial inclusion, gender and agriculture productivity in Ghana. *Theoretical Economics Letters*, *10*(03), 545. https://www.scirp.org/html/8-1502098_100757.htm.

Baber, H. (2020). Financial inclusion and FinTech: A comparative research of countries following Islamic finance and conventional finance. *Qualitative Research in*

Financial Markets, *12*(1), 24–42. https://www.researchgate.net/profile/Hasnan-Baber/publication/337237425_Financial_inclusion_and_FinTech_A_comparative_study_of_countries_following_Islamic_finance_and_conventional_finance/links/5e265c6592851c89c9b5a824/Financial-inclusion-and-FinTech-A-comparative-study-of-countries-following-Islamic-finance-and-conventional-finance.pdf.

Bhatia, S., & Singh, S. (2019). Empowering women through financial inclusion: A research of urban slum. *Vikalpa*, *44*(4), 182–197. https://journals.sagepub.com/doi/pdf/10.1177/0256090919897809.

Cicchiello, A. F., Kazemikhasragh, A., Monferrá, S., & Girón, A. (2021). Financial inclusion and development in the least developed countries in Asia and Africa. *Journal of Innovation and Entrepreneurship*, *10*(1), 1–13. https://innovation-entrepreneurship.springeropen.com/articles/10.1186/s13731-021-00190-4.

Duvendack, M., & Mader, P. (2020). Impact of financial inclusion in low-and middle-income countries: A systematic review of reviews. *Journal of Economic Surveys*, *34*(3), 594–629. https://ueaeprints.uea.ac.uk/id/eprint/74530/1/Accepted_Manuscript.pdf.

Fouejieu, A., Sahay, R., Cihak, M., & Chen, S. (2020). Financial inclusion and inequality: A cross-country analysis. *The Journal of International Trade & Economic Development*, *29*(8), 1018–1048. https://www.tandfonline.com/doi/abs/10.1080/09638199.2020.1785532.

George, B., & Thomachan, K. T. (2018). Financial inclusion and women empowerment: A gender perspective. *International Journal of Research - Granthaalayah*, *6*(5), 229–237.

Ghosh, S. (2022). Political empowerment of women and financial inclusion: Is there a link? *Social Sciences & Humanities Open*, *5*(1), 100267. https://www.sciencedirect.com/science/article/pii/S2590291122000213.

Hendriks, S. (2019). The role of financial inclusion in driving women's economic empowerment. *Development in Practice*, *29*(8), 1029–1038. https://www.tandfonline.com/doi/pdf/10.1080/09614524.2019.1660308.

Kazemikhasragh, A., & Buoni Pineda, M. V. (2022). Financial inclusion and education: An empirical research of financial inclusion in the face of the pandemic emergency due to Covid-19 in Latin America and the Caribbean. *Review of Development Economics*, *26*(3), 1785–1797. https://www.ncbi.nlm.nih.gov/pmc/articles/PMC9115501/.

Kemal, A. A. (2019). Mobile banking in the government-to-person payment sector for financial inclusion in Pakistan. *Information Technology for Development*, *25*(3), 475–502. https://arro.anglia.ac.uk/id/eprint/702628/1/Kemal_2018.pdf.

Kim, K. (2022). Assessing the impact of mobile money on improving the financial inclusion of Nairobi women. *Journal of Gender Studies*, *31*(3), 306–322. https://www.tandfonline.com/doi/pdf/10.1080/09589236.2021.1884536.

Koomson, I., Villano, R. A., & Hadley, D. (2020). Effect of financial inclusion on poverty and vulnerability to poverty: Evidence using a multidimensional measure of financial inclusion. *Social Indicators Research*, *149*(2), 613–639. https://www.researchgate.net/profile/Isaac-Koomson-2/publication/338982531_Effect_of_Financial_Inclusion_on_Poverty_and_Vulnerability_to_Poverty_Evidence_Using_a_Multi-Dimensional_Measure_of_Financial_Inclusion/links/5e3c8dc792851c7f7f2326d3/Effect-of-Financial-Inclusion-on-Poverty-and-Vulnerability-to-Poverty-Evidence-Using-a-Multi-Dimensional-Measure-of-Financial-Inclusion.pdf.

Lee, C. W., & Huruta, A. D. (2022). Green microfinance and women's empowerment: Why does financial literacy matter? *Sustainability*, *14*(5), 3130. https://www.mdpi.com/2071-1050/14/5/3130.

Leight, J., Pedehombga, A., Ganaba, R., & Gelli, A. (2022). Women's empowerment, maternal depression, and stress: Evidence from rural Burkina Faso. *SSM-Mental Health*, *2*, 100160. https://www.sciencedirect.com/science/article/pii/S2666560322001001.

Malik, F. A., & Yadav, D. K. (2022). *Financial inclusion schemes in India*. Springer. https://www.researchgate.net/profile/Devendra-Yadav-14/publication/365852147_financial_inclusion_ebook/links/6386ff848e63c56dae46800b/financial-inclusion-ebook.pdf.

Malik, F. A., Yadav, D. K., Adam, H., & Omrane, A. (n.d.). *The Urban Poor and Their Financial Behavior*. https://www.researchgate.net/profile/Firdous-Ahmad-Malik/publication/346784990_The_Urban_Poor_and_their_Financial_Behaviour_A_Case_Study_Of_Slum-Dwellers_In_Lucknow_India/links/60374bd192851c4ed5954da6/The-Urban-Poor-and-their-Financial-Behaviour-A-Case-Study-Of-Slum-Dwellers-In-Lucknow-India.pdf.

Malik, F. A., Yadav, D. K., Adam, H., & Omrane, A. (2020). The urban poor and their financial behavior: A case research of slum dwellers in Lucknow (India). In *Sustainable entrepreneurship, renewable energy-based projects, and digitalization* (pp. 305–315). CRC Press. https://www.taylorfrancis.com/chapters/edit/10.1201/9781003097921-17/urban-poor-financial-behavior-firdous-ahmad-malik-yadav-hebatallah-adam-amina-omrane.

Malik, F. A., Yadav, D. K., Lone, N. A., & Adam, H. (2021). An investigation into the dynamics of financial inclusion in south Asian countries. *Pakistan Economic and Social Review, 59*(2), 231. https://www.researchgate.net/profile/Naveed-Lone/publication/358396214_AN_INVESTIGATION_INTO_THE_DYNAMICS_OF_FINANCIAL_INCLUSION_IN_SOUTH_ASIAN_COUNTRIES/links/61ffeb6ca7d76d0f08c5a3ef/AN-INVESTIGATION-INTO-THE-DYNAMICS-OF-FINANCIAL-INCLUSION-IN-SOUTH-ASIAN-COUNTRIES.pdf.

O'Brien, C., Leavens, L., Ndiaye, C., & Traoré, D. (2022). Women's empowerment, income, and nutrition in a food processing value chain development project in Touba, Senegal. *International Journal of Environmental Research and Public Health, 19*(15), 9526. https://www.mdpi.com/1660-4601/19/15/9526/pdf.

Nechad, A. (2021). Rethinking poverty analysis, towards a multidimensional approach to deprivation. *Journal of Economic and Social Development*, *8*(2), 9–20.

Ojo, T. A. (2022). Digital financial inclusion for women in the fourth industrial revolution: A key towards achieving sustainable development goal 5. *Africa Review*, *14*(1), 98–123. https://www.researchgate.net/profile/Tinuade-Ojo/publication/352825690_Digital_Financial_Inclusion_for_Women_in_the_Fourth_Industrial_Revolution_A_Key_towards_Achieving_Sustainable_Development_Goal_5/links/6232e25c069a350c8b944734/Digital-Financial-Inclusion-for-Women-in-the-Fourth-Industrial-Revolution-A-Key-towards-Achieving-Sustainable-Development-Goal-5.pdf.

Ozili, P. K. (2021). Financial inclusion research around the world: A review. *Forum for Social Economics*, *50*(4), 457–479. https://mpra.ub.uni-muenchen.de/101809/1/mpra_paper_101809.pdf.

Pal, M., & Gupta, H. (2023). Sustainable women empowerment at the bottom of the pyramid through credit access. *Equality, Diversity and Inclusion: An International Journal*, *42*(1), 157–171. http://gnanaganga.inflibnet.ac.in:8080/jspui/bitstream/123456789/581/1/10-1108_EDI-02-2022-0028.pdf.

Park, C. Y., & Mercado, R. V. (2021). Financial inclusion: New measurement and cross-country impact assessment 1. In *Financial inclusion in Asia and beyond* (pp. 98–128). Routledge. https://www.econstor.eu/bitstream/10419/203379/1/1016259859.pdf.

Rangarajan, C. (2008). Report of the Committee on Financial Inclusion. Ministry of Finance, Government of India.

Razak, A. A., & Asutay, M. (2022). Financial inclusion and economic well-being: Evidence from Islamic Pawnbroking (Ar-Rahn) in Malaysia. *Research in International Business and Finance*, *59*, 101557. https://durham-repository.worktribe.com/preview/1239704/33917.pdf

Reshi, I. A. (2023). Women's self-help groups-role in poverty nexus and empowerment. *International Journal of Economic, Business, Accounting, Agriculture Management and Sharia Administration (IJEBAS)*, *3*(1), 79–84. http://radjapublika.com/index.php/IJEBAS/article/download/659/528.

Sakyi-Nyarko, C., Ahmad, A. H., & Green, C. J. (2022). The gender-differential effect of financial inclusion on household financial resilience. *The Journal of Development Studies*, *58*(4), 692–712. https://www.tandfonline.com/doi/pdf/10.1080/00220388.2021.2013467.

Shah, S. M., & Ali, A. (2022). A survey on financial inclusion: Theoretical and empirical literature review. *Journal of Policy Research, 8*(4), 310–330. https://jprpk.com/index.php/jpr/article/download/172/242.

Sharma, U., & Changkakati, B. (2022). Dimensions of global financial inclusion and their impact on the achievement of the United Nations Development Goals. *Borsa Istanbul Review, 22*(6), 1238–1250. https://www.sciencedirect.com/science/article/pii/S2214845022000631.

Siddik, M. N. A. (2017). Does financial inclusion promote women empowerment? Evidence from Bangladesh. *Applied Economics and Finance*, *4*(4), 169–177.

15 Leveraging Fintech Services to Drive Financial Inclusion among Women in Development and Emerging Markets

A Case Study in Malaysia

Hong Liang, Daisy Mui Hung Kee, and Siti Rohaida Mohamad Zainal

15.1 Introduction

Over the last decade, there have been significant advancements in technology and the widespread adoption of digital financial services (DFS), including mobile and internet-based financial transactions. This trend accelerated even further during the COVID-19 crisis. The integration of individuals, households, and businesses into this system becomes particularly vital for achieving the goal of inclusive finance, preventing them from being excluded from the traditional financial sector (Sahay et al., 2022). Consequently, the ongoing evolution of monetary innovation, known as FinTech, is reshaping conventional financial services and holds the potential to impact broader social and economic considerations. Fintech is the practice of harnessing technology to supply financial services, including innovations that improve and automate service delivery. Technological developments, changes in client behavior, and regulatory constraints are all drivers of fintech development (Olowookere, 2019). One of the key goals of implementing such technology is to make commercial operations more convenient.

In Malaysia, the embrace of financial technology (fintech) is reshaping the business landscape, offering tools that enhance the ease of doing business. The digital payments sector has experienced rapid growth, surpassing US$10 billion in transactions, and e-wallet usage has become ubiquitous among more than 40 million users. Fintech-powered lending has infused approximately US$284 million into Small and Medium Enterprises (SMEs), catalyzing growth by providing faster access to capital. The momentum behind digital banking and neobanks is rising, simplifying financial management for businesses and users alike. Additionally, blockchain technology is anticipated to elevate supply chain transparency and cross-border transactions. Initiatives utilizing regulatory technology (Regtech) are expected to guarantee regulatory adherence while slashing compliance expenses by as much as 40%. Data analytics and AI-driven insights have contributed to a 20% increase in productivity, while the Compound Annual Growth Rate (CAGR) of 18.7% in InsurTech underscores its role in offering tailor-made insurance coverage. E-commerce transactions have surged to US$6.5 billion, facilitated by FinTech-enabled marketplaces, and initiatives like the Regulatory Sandbox underscore the

DOI: 10.4324/9781032655185-20

government's commitment to fostering innovation. Inclusivity is also on the rise as FinTech expands financial education and access. Collectively, these trends underscore the pivotal role that FinTech plays in propelling business ease and growth across Malaysia. Consequently, the number of fintech businesses offering payment solutions has surged.

According to the World Bank, 1.7 billion people do not have access to bank accounts (Anderloni & Vandone, 2007). The majority of these unbanked people live in seven developing and emerging economies: Bangladesh, China, India, Pakistan, Indonesia, Nigeria, and Mexico. Non-bank account holders refer to the adult population excluded from financial services due to their limited participation in the formal financial system. In essence, this means that many individuals lack bank accounts and do not utilize services provided by financial institutions.

The global outbreak of COVID-19 has underscored the necessity for collaboration between governments and financial institutions to bridge the gap in inclusive finance and ensure that a greater number of individuals have access to affordable financial services. While a considerable amount of research has focused on inclusive finance, particularly concerning traditional face-to-face banking operations, limited attention has been directed toward digital inclusive finance, particularly within developing countries and emerging markets (Ozili, 2018). Despite these advances, the gender gap in financial inclusivity remains. Globally, 65% of women have bank accounts, a figure lower than the 72% of men (Demirguc-Kunt et al., 2018). Obstacles such as distance from the nearest bank, inadequate documentation for account creation, and socioeconomic and cultural barriers hinder women's access to financial institutions (Murata & Sioson, 2018). Thus, improved usability and accessibility of fintech have the potential to surmount these obstacles and economically empower women (Sioson & Kim, 2019).

Given these gaps in the existing literature, this study aims to address the following question: How can fintech services promote financial inclusivity in Malaysia? The subsequent sections delve into the intricate connections and implications between fintech and inclusive finance. The third section investigates women's perceptions and expectations regarding bank and fintech service offerings. The fourth segment examines the barriers to fintech's role in promoting inclusive finance, focusing on Malaysia's financial inclusion and fintech landscape. Recommendations for enhancing the role of fintech in fostering financial inclusion are provided in the fifth part. The sixth section analyzes the broader lessons derived from the Malaysian case study, applicable to other developing countries and emerging economies. Lastly, this study concludes by summarizing key insights and suggesting directions for future research.

15.2 Literature Review

In recent years, governments across the globe have enacted legislation aimed at alleviating poverty and improving the living conditions of their residents. Financial inclusion has emerged as a critical avenue for reducing poverty and fostering inclusive growth (Sahoo et al., 2017). As a consequence, it is essential to briefly explore the institutional theories that underpin the discussions in this study.

15.2.1 Institutional Theory

Applying institutional theory to discussions surrounding inclusive finance provides a focused and insightful perspective. This theoretical framework offers a structured approach to understanding the crucial role of functional institutions in driving inclusive finance while also suggesting strategies to address financial exclusion in emerging economies. It emphasizes how economic behaviors, whether by individuals or corporations, are influenced by the institutional framework within which they operate (Ohnesorge, 2007). This lens unveils how Malaysia's institutional structure can restrict property rights, access to financial services, and related opportunities, thus impeding financial inclusion. Fundamentally, the theory asserts that supportive institutions are integral to economic growth and poverty reduction. Notably, examples like the UK, where functional institutions correlate with reduced levels of financial exclusion, further underscore this correlation. The Kempson and Collard framework (2012) aims to facilitate universal access to suitable financial products, building confidence and competence in using financial services for everyday needs. However, in developing and emerging economies, institutional gaps present challenges. These gaps signify weak institutions that struggle to operate effectively (Khanna & Palepu, 1997). Within the institutional theory framework, it is argued that Malaysia's context contributes to its financial exclusion challenges, stemming from inadequate political and socioeconomic institutional arrangements that exacerbate disparities in inclusive finance.

15.2.2 The Concept of Financial Inclusion

Defining financial inclusion is pivotal within the literature as it underpins equitable economic growth and the reduction of disparities. This concept ensures that a diverse range of financial services is accessible to all individuals and communities, regardless of their economic status or geographic location. A clear definition enables researchers and policymakers to gauge exclusion levels across various groups, identify barriers to financial access, and devise targeted solutions. A well-defined understanding of financial inclusion forms the basis for tracking progress, designing effective interventions, and assessing policies to enhance financial access, encourage savings, facilitate credit availability, and promote responsible financial behavior (Gupta & Kanungo, 2022). Ultimately, a well-established definition of financial inclusion is central to driving inclusive economic progress and building resilient and participatory financial systems. However, the global average of Inclusive finance remains below 50.0%, with particularly acute issues in developing and emerging markets (Ardic et al., 2011). The global aim is to eliminate all barriers, including those related to education, gender, age, irregular income, regulation, and geographical location, that hinder billions of individuals worldwide from accessing and utilizing financial services, collectively affecting their livelihoods.

Inclusive finance refers to the provision and availability of financial services to all individuals, particularly those from low-income, marginalized, and underserved segments of society (Ozili, 2018). It can also be described as an individual's capacity to easily access formal financial institutions and services, such as savings and account services (Zins & Weill, 2016). These financial services encompass investments, loans, fund management, asset management, and various other financial products provided by fintech firms (Kama & Adigun, 2013). It is important to note that financial inclusivity is viewed as a fundamental right, akin to social welfare, improved living standards, and a means of strengthening a nation's adult population, especially those with low incomes. Consequently, social activists, human rights advocates, and other stakeholders consider inclusive finance a fundamental right for all citizens, as it embodies principles of justice and equality.

On the other hand, financial exclusion pertains to the challenges individuals face in easily accessing formal financial products and services. Mohan (2006) emphasizes that fostering an environment conducive to financial inclusivity can yield numerous benefits for consumers, regulatory bodies, and the overall economic framework. For instance, loans from financial institutions can serve diverse purposes, ranging from facilitating small remittances to enabling credit-based purchases. Financial exclusion is a process whereby individuals encounter barriers in accessing and utilizing financial services and products that align with their needs within mainstream markets, hindering their seamless engagement in societal activities (European Commission, 2008). This lack of access can trigger a series of limitations, constraining both individual and communal financial growth opportunities.

The Center for Financial Inclusion (CFI) provides a comprehensive definition of inclusive finance, characterizing it as a state where all adults with access to financial services are also able to avail a comprehensive range of high-quality financial offerings delivered affordably, conveniently, and with dignity (Gardeva, 2010). This implies that diverse providers within a country offer financial products tailored to the needs of a wide spectrum of individuals, including marginalized groups such as the impoverished, disabled, and rural communities (Gardeva, 2010). For instance, microfinance institutions providing small loans to entrepreneurs in underserved regions exemplify endeavors toward financial inclusivity.

15.2.3 Financial Technology

The evolution of fintech is inherently linked to advancements in enabling technology. Leong (2018) categorize fintech into three stages. The first stage, Fintech 1.0, marked the emergence of "financial globalization." This era introduced significant enabling technologies like transatlantic communication cables and large-scale computer systems. These technologies paved the way for fintech products such as Society for Worldwide Interbank Financial Telecommunications (SWIFT) and Automated Teller Machine (ATMs). The establishment of credit card systems in the 1950s marked a transition from cash-based transactions to digital methods. This era culminated with the rise of electronic trading platforms like National Association of Securities Dealers Automated Quotations (NASDAQ), which set the stage for modern financial markets. Fintech 2.0 witnessed the shift from analog to digital, resulting in traditional financial institutions entering the scene. During the 1980s, centralized banking systems and Internet banking began to take root, digitizing the internal operations of banks and customer interactions. By the turn of the century, banks had fully embraced digital operations, both internally and in their interactions with clients. The global financial crisis of 2008 marked the end of this era.

Conversely, the rise of additional digital technologies has heralded the third stage, Fintech 3.0. With the global financial crisis transitioning from a crisis to the norm, a paradigm shift occurred, paving the way for a new era in the financial industry – Fintech 3.0. The widespread adoption of smartphones, connecting millions worldwide to the Internet, further accelerates this transformation. Mirjam (2021) noted that smartphones now serve as the main gateway for internet access and utilizing a range of financial services.

Fintech, as described as bridges current Internet technologies with banking industry innovations. On the other hand, Hung and Luo (2016) outline five attributes that influence fintech market elements: participants, added value, regulations, strategies, and scope. Puschmann (2017) characterizes fintech as an industry-wide or industry-specific incremental or disruptive innovation driven by the evolution of information technology, leading to the creation of new intra- or inter-organizational models, labor, products, processes, and systems (Puschmann, 2017). Software-based tools assist businesses and their consumers in conducting, surviving, and enhancing their financial interactions (Leong, 2018). It encompasses opportunities to lower the cost of providing financial services and enhance financial inclusivity.

15.2.4 The Interlink between Financial Growth and Financial Inclusion

The finance growth is positively related to the theory of financial inclusion. When financial services are accessible, individuals and businesses can save, invest, and manage their finances more effectively. By striving for financial inclusion, policymakers and financial institutions work to ensure that a broader cross section of society can participate in and benefit from the financial sector's growth. This includes traditionally underserved populations, such as low-income individuals, women, and rural communities. Also, fintech innovation and DFS have become powerful tools for achieving financial inclusion by leveraging technology. Technology can make financial services more accessible and affordable, aligning with finance growth by expanding the reach of financial institutions and services (Xi & Wang, 2023). As more people and businesses gain access to financial services, they can better manage their finances, invest in businesses and education, and participate in economic activities, all of which can promote economic growth as postulated by finance growth (Zhang, 2023). In conclusion, the relationship between Finance Growth and the Theory of Financial Inclusion lies in the fact that financial progress, coupled with measures and strategies promoting financial inclusion, has the potential to propel economic growth and development. The two concepts work together to create a more inclusive and prosperous financial ecosystem.

15.3 The Roles of Fintech Services among Women

Malaysia is a diverse country with a population that includes various ethnic and demographic groups. The demographic division of women in Malaysia is based on ethnicity, and the three main ethnic groups are Malay (Bumiputera): The majority of the population in Malaysia is Malay, and Malay women make up a significant portion of the female population; Chinese: The Chinese population in Malaysia includes Chinese Malaysian women; Indian: The Indian population in Malaysia includes Indian Malaysian women. There are the three largest ethnic groups, and there is also a smaller population of indigenous peoples (Orang Asli) in Malaysia. The demographic division of women in Malaysia includes women from different ethnic backgrounds, each with its own cultural, linguistic, and religious diversity.

The dynamics shaping women's perspectives on fintech services and traditional banking are intricate, rooted in the interplay between financial requirements, technological advancements, and societal norms. Fintech enterprises, with their emphasis on convenience and accessibility, have introduced transformative tools capable of alleviating gender-based financial discrepancies (Beck, 2020). For instance, microfinance apps extend the means for women in developing regions to access credit and govern their finances, enabling investments in businesses and education. However, the digital divide persists as a formidable challenge, with disparities in digital literacy constraining women's meaningful engagement with these platforms.

Furthermore, a noteworthy trajectory involves banks increasingly acknowledging women's distinct financial requisites and undertaking measures to address them (OECD, 2012). This recognition surfaces prominently within the realm of female entrepreneurship. Historical impediments have historically hindered women entrepreneurs from accessing credit, stemming from factors encompassing gender biases and a dearth of collateral. To circumvent these barriers, certain banks are introducing tailor-made loan products, especially catering to women-owned businesses (Chowdhury et al., 2018). These financial instruments might proffer more adaptable terms, diminished interest rates, and mitigated collateral prerequisites, thus facilitating unobstructed access to funding. By configuring financial products that align with the needs of women entrepreneurs, banks are effectually flattening the playing field and nurturing economic prosperity through amplified women-led enterprises.

Moreover, specialized financial literacy initiatives are surging to the forefront as potent tools for fostering women's efficacy in financial decision-making (Andriamahery & Qamruzzaman, 2022). Addressing areas like budgeting, investment strategies, retirement planning, and risk assessment, these initiatives aim to embolden women's financial assurance and autonomy. This empowerment gains amplified significance within contexts where women are traditionally marginalized from financial dialogues or decision-making proceedings (Park et al., 2021). Hence, the endeavors undertaken by banks to recognize and cater to women's specific financial necessities epitomize a commitment to inclusivity and gender parity within the financial realm.

However, entrenched societal perceptions and historical biases can significantly mold women's attitudes toward both fintech and traditional banking. Stereotypes that correlate technological prowess with masculinity might deter some women from embracing fintech solutions to their full potential, even if these platforms could significantly enhance their financial autonomy (Fintech Circle, 2023).

Mitigating such barriers mandates not only cultivating gender diversity within the fintech sector but also disseminating information that underscores the inclusivity and advantages of these tools for all. Therefore, the interactions women have with both fintech and traditional banking embody nuanced reflections of their diverse needs, technological acumen, and cultural milieu. Attaining genuine financial inclusion demands a comprehensive approach that acknowledges the potency of fintech innovations while addressing digital divides and ensuring that conventional banking services are tailored to the distinct financial aspirations of women.

15.4 Obstacles Faced by Fintech

The landscape of financial inclusion in Malaysia presents a complex tapestry that interweaves both notable advancements and areas ripe for enhancement. On the one hand, the nation has made remarkable strides in propelling financial access and services (Feyen et al., 2022). The advent of digital banking platforms such as Maybank2u and CIMB Clicks has empowered urban residents to effortlessly engage in transactions and oversee their financial affairs online. Moreover, initiatives like the e-Tunai Rakyat program, which orchestrated direct cash transfers via e-wallets for eligible citizens, stand as a testament to the government's commitment to nurturing digital financial inclusion.

Nonetheless, within the Malaysian context, despite overall headway in financial inclusivity, there persist entrenched challenges that particularly reverberate within rural and remote enclaves (Heng & Tok, 2022). In East Malaysia, encompassing regions like Sabah and Sarawak, communities grapple with substantial impediments in accessing formal financial services, largely attributable to their geographical isolation and underdeveloped infrastructures. These regions often lack ready access to physical bank branches or ATMs, severely limiting avenues for conventional banking activities. This geographical disparity thus amplifies financial exclusion, preventing individuals from readily accessing services like savings accounts, loans, and other indispensable financial tools that their urban counterparts take for granted (1). Consequently, residents of these underserved areas are compelled to resort to informal financial networks like rotating savings and credit associations (ROSCAs) or moneylenders to fulfill their financial needs. The stark deficiency of consumer protections and regulatory oversight in these informal systems leaves individuals susceptible to exploitative practices and uncertain financial outcomes.

Addressing these obstacles necessitates initiatives to extend financial services to remote regions through mobile banking units, digital financial platforms, and agent banking models. These endeavors hinge upon technology as a conduit to bridge the geographical divide and furnish marginalized communities with rudimentary banking services.

Notably, despite Malaysia's collective endeavors to advance financial inclusivity, significant gender disparities persist (De Luna-Martinez, 2017). Women, particularly those dwelling in rural areas, continue to grapple with hurdles that hinder their access to formal financial services and digital financial tools. In response, Malaysia has initiated targeted measures to fortify women's economic empowerment.

Among these initiatives is the Women Entrepreneurs Financing Plan, a program designed to furnish women entrepreneurs with specialized financial support and training. Acknowledging that women often encounter unique challenges in accessing credit and capital, especially when initiating or expanding businesses, this initiative not only bridges the gender gap in entrepreneurship but also uplifts women's economic autonomy.

Furthermore, the "MyRINGGIT" financial literacy program by Malaysia's National Bank endeavors to impart women with essential financial skills and knowledge (Othman et al., 2022). By nurturing women's financial competence and confidence, "MyRINGGIT" is committed to cultivating a more inclusive financial ecosystem where women emerge as proactive participants and informed decision-makers. In essence, Malaysia's pursuits toward narrowing the gender gap in financial inclusion are underscored by deliberate endeavors tailored to address the pronounced challenges faced by women, particularly in rural settings (Ozili et al., 2022). Malaysia, in this trajectory, propels itself toward a financial landscape that ensures women's equitable access to financial services and empowers them to make astute financial choices.

The potential of fintech to augment financial inclusion is undeniably immense, yet a constellation of challenges obstruct its realization. Foremost among these is the formidable digital divide, a barrier that thwarts the application of fintech to promote financial inclusivity (Ghosh & Günther, 2017). The digital divide encapsulates the unequal access to digital technologies and the Internet, disproportionately affecting marginalized demographics, particularly those residing in rural and low-income enclaves. Fintech's capacity to offer convenient financial services through mobile applications and online platforms is hampered when individuals lack access to requisite technologies and dependable internet connectivity. In rural contexts, the absence of rudimentary technological infrastructure erects barriers to the effective utilization of fintech services. Even if residents in these regions own smartphones, the gradual or intermittent nature of their internet connections poses hurdles to seamless transactions. Consequently, this not only curtails their capacity to avail financial services but also undermines the potential benefits of fintech in terms of cost-effectiveness and efficiency.

Moreover, the obstacle of digital literacy looms large, amplifying the challenges that fintech faces in propelling financial inclusion (Noviyanti et al., 2022). Even if marginalized cohorts access technology, they may lack the skills and knowledge requisite for navigating fintech platforms adeptly. In the absence of foundational comprehension of these technologies, individuals might find themselves excluded from the dividends of fintech, exacerbating existing financial disparities. Inadequate regulation could furnish fintech solutions with the potential to incubate fraudulent activities, data breaches, and the misuse of personal information (Younas et al., 2022). This undermines public trust and confidence in these platforms, posing a challenge that, if mishandled, could compromise fintech's long-term viability.

Moreover, the challenge of financial exclusion assumes multifaceted dimensions that become even more intricate due to the interplay of socioeconomic factors and cultural norms. Within certain communities, especially those comprising older individuals or those with limited exposure to technology, there exists a palpable resistance to embrace fintech solutions (Ojo, 2022). Older generations, for instance, might display hesitancy toward fintech adoption due to apprehensions about the security of digital transactions. Cultural norms, too, hold significant sway. In societies that venerate face-to-face interactions, traditional modes of financial transactions afford a sense of comfort and trust. The preference for tangible currency is deeply ingrained in many cultural contexts, embodying a palpable and tactile representation of wealth. Among older generations, especially, the handling of physical money symbolizes financial security, rendering the transition to digital currencies and online transactions a formidable endeavor.

In essence, the challenge of financial inclusion presents itself as an intricate tapestry woven from multiple threads of barriers, necessitating a multifaceted approach that considers socioeconomic complexities and cultural variances. As Malaysia's journey toward comprehensive financial inclusion progresses, a nuanced strategy must address the digital divide, enhance digital literacy, refine regulatory frameworks, and navigate the intricate interplay of cultural norms and technological innovations (Asongu & Kodila-Tedika, 2017). The assimilation of these manifold strands within a comprehensive framework is pivotal to heralding a financial landscape that extends its benefits equitably across all strata of society. Figure 15.1 indicates the elements of obstacles faced by FinTech.

15.5 Recommendations

The recommendations aimed at harnessing the potential of fintech to bolster financial inclusivity in Malaysia encompass a range of multifaceted strategies,

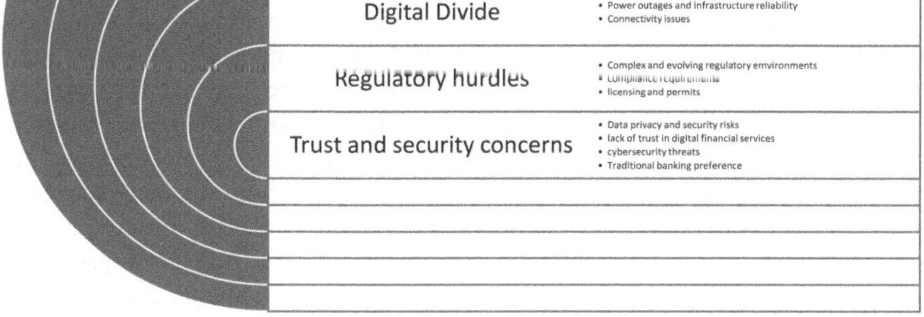

Figure 15.1 Key challenges in the fintech landscape

Source: Developed by researchers.

encompassing technology integration, regulatory enhancements, and targeted community engagement.

Firstly, the imperative lies in the expansion of digital infrastructure within rural and underserved areas. Intensified efforts to enhance internet connectivity and facilitate affordable smartphone accessibility serve as pivotal bridges across the digital divide. This endeavor facilitates the integration of remote populations into the realm of fintech services. Moreover, a pertinent strategy involves crafting locally relevant fintech solutions that resonate with language preferences and cultural nuances. This localized approach not only bolsters user engagement but also enhances the propensity for fintech adoption within these communities.

Secondly, a paramount emphasis should be placed on cultivating digital literacy. Robust training programs that acquaint individuals with fintech platforms are indispensable, as they engender a sense of confidence in utilizing DFS. This pedagogical approach must span all demographic strata, encompassing the elderly and those with limited exposure to technology. Collaborative partnerships between fintech enterprises, educational institutions, and community organizations serve as conduits for the effective execution of these transformative educational initiatives. Complementary to this, robust education and awareness campaigns stand as linchpins. By meticulously outlining the convenience and efficacy of these tools while underscoring their user-friendly interfaces, the campaign effectively addresses concerns and fosters adoption.

Moreover, user interface design should incorporate elements of familiarity, streamlining the transition from conventional methodologies. Incorporating features that replicate face-to-face interactions or mirror the tangible exchange of currency within digital transactions can seamlessly amalgamate cultural norms with technological advancements. As such, surmounting the multifaceted barriers entrenched by socioeconomic factors and cultural traditions necessitates a nuanced strategy that acknowledges legacy practices while introducing the merits of fintech.

Thirdly, regulatory frameworks must exhibit agility and a proclivity toward fostering innovation, all while safeguarding the interests of consumers. Regulatory paradigms should strike a harmonious balance, nurturing the coexistence of fintech with traditional financial methodologies. Collaborative synergies between regulators and industry stakeholders can culminate in the formulation of robust benchmarks for data security, cybersecurity, and consumer rights. Moreover, tailored financial literacy initiatives that target the concerns and preferences of the elderly or women in rural domains can markedly enhance their comfort level with fintech adoption. Pioneering initiatives such as the Women Entrepreneur Financing Program and comprehensive financial literacy drives can empower women economically and equip them with the acumen to make judicious financial decisions.

In essence, cultivating financial inclusivity within Malaysia through the catalytic instrument of fintech demands a comprehensive approach encompassing infrastructural amplification, pedagogical empowerment, regulatory astuteness, and finely targeted interventions. The convergence of these strategies presents Malaysia with an unparalleled opportunity to harness the transformational potential of fintech, ensuring equitable access to financial services and opportunities across all echelons of society. By embracing the plurality of perspectives and tailoring solutions accordingly, fintech stands poised to illuminate a path toward financial systems characterized by inclusivity, enriching the lives of all citizens.

15.6 Lessons Learned for the Emerging Market

This study delves into Malaysia as a case study, revealing insightful observations and exemplifications that underscore the pivotal role of fintech in propelling financial inclusivity across developing and emerging economies, particularly in contexts characterized by intricate institutional landscapes. The significance of financial inclusion in addressing pressing global concerns, as enunciated in the Sustainable Development Goals (SDGs), is paramount, with poverty eradication by 2030 being a primary focus (Wood et al., 2018). Fintech emerges as a potent means to combat poverty, mitigate health vulnerabilities, curb criminality, and alleviate illiteracy by rendering financial services accessible. To illustrate, consider the plight of farmers without access to digital payment services. Their inability to transact digitally may lead to fears of theft, compelling them to swiftly deplete their earnings instead of securing them. Consequently, pivotal objectives such as funding children's education and ensuring the retirement well-being of seniors are jeopardized.

Furthermore, the drive for bolstering financial inclusion can potentially augment the overall volume of financial assets. This emphasis on inclusivity, alongside strategic prioritization and implementation of initiatives geared toward nurturing the financial sector's growth, can catalyze significant financial transformation and digitization. This transformation is particularly consequential in developing and emerging economies, where novel streams of capital can be harnessed (Zhong & Yoong, 2021).

However, as previously highlighted, the stark reality persists that approximately 1.7 billion individuals remain excluded from financial systems and services, with a substantial portion of this demographic hailing from developing nations and emerging markets. For developing and burgeoning market economies, the gateway to heightened financial inclusion lies in harnessing fintech to surmount the barriers impeding access to financial services. This endeavor maximizes the prospects of these nations aligning with the United Nations' 2030 Sustainable Development Goals, painting a promising trajectory toward a more equitable and inclusive financial landscape.

15.7 Conclusion

This book chapter looks into a compelling narrative that highlights the ongoing economic exclusion faced by a notable segment of Malaysian. The absence of established banks in many rural areas exacerbates this disparity. However, a ray of hope emerges through fintech, which has the potential to bridge these gaps by reducing the cost barriers associated with providing financial services. With a favorable ecosystem and a well-designed regulatory framework, fintech is poised to play a crucial role in enhancing financial inclusion, not only in Malaysia but also in other developing and emerging economies.

The global consensus on the centrality of inclusive finance in promoting financial stability and driving economic progress is evident. Within this framework, fintech's catalytic role becomes even more pronounced, with the potential to catalyze both financial stability and economic growth. This symbiotic relationship aligns seamlessly with Malaysia's context as a burgeoning emergent market, aligning with its aspirations intricately linked to the United Nations Sustainable Development Goal 2030.

It is essential to highlight the understudied nature of gender-inclusive finance in developing countries and emerging markets. The lack of empirical research in this domain emphasizes an unexplored frontier that calls for comprehensive exploration. As the discussion concludes, the need for proactive scholarly inquiry becomes evident, driven by the urgency to address the conspicuous lack of data and insights that could reshape financial inclusion paradigms in the years ahead.

References

Anderloni, L., & Vandone, D. (2007). Financial services provision and prevention of financial exclusion. *Report by the Director-General for Employment, Social Affairs and Equal Opportunities, European Commission, Brussels*. https://air.unimi.it/handle/2434/44241

Andriamahery, A., & Qamruzzaman, M. (2022). Do access to finance, technical know-how, and financial literacy offer women empowerment through women's entrepreneurial development? *Frontiers in Psychology, 12*. https://doi.org/10.3389/fpsyg.2021.776844.

Ardic, O. P., Heimann, M., & Mylenko, N. (2011). Access to financial services and the financial inclusion agenda around the world: a cross-country analysis with a new data set (Policy Research working paper No. WPS 5537). World Bank. https://openknowledge.worldbank.org/bitstream/handle/10986/3310/WPS5537.pdf?sequence51&isAllowed5y.

Asongu, S. A., & Kodila-Tedika, O. (2017). Institutions and poverty: A critical comment based on evolving currents and debates. *Social Indicators Research, 139*(1), 99–117. https://doi.org/10.1007/s11205-017-1709-y.

Beck, T. (2020, July 29). Fintech and Financial Inclusion: Opportunities and pitfalls. *Asian Development Bank.* https://www.adb.org/publications/fintech-financial-inclusion-opportunities-pitfalls.

Chowdhury, T. Y., Yeasmin, A., & Ahmed, Z. (2018). Perception of women entrepreneurs to accessing bank credit. *Journal of Global Entrepreneurship Research, 8*(1). https://doi.org/10.1186/s40497-018-0119-1.

De la Cuesta-Gonzalez, M., Paredes-Gazquez, J., Ruza, C., & Fernández-Olit, B. (2021). The relationship between vulnerable financial consumers and banking institutions. A qualitative study in Spain. *Geoforum, 119*, 163–176. https://doi.org/10.1016/j.geoforum.2021.01.006.

De Luna-Martinez, J. (2017). *Financial inclusion in Malaysia: Distilling Lessons for other countries.* Open Knowledge Repository. https://openknowledge.worldbank.org/entities/publication/73ae9c35-f706-5ff4-a3d1-0f414e8d8bcf/full.

Demirguc-Kunt, A., Klapper, L., Singer, D., Ansar, S., & Hess, J. (2018). *The Global Findex Database 2017: Measuring Financial Inclusion and the Fintech Revolution.* https://doi.org/10.1596/978-1-4648-1259-0.

Demirguc-Kunt, A., Klapper, L., Singer, D., & Van Oudheusden, P. (2015). The Global Findex Database 2014: Measuring Financial Inclusion around the World. In *World Bank policy research working paper*. https://doi.org/10.1596/1813-9450-7255

Feyen, E., Heffernan, R. R., Natarajan, H., Saal, M., & Sarkar, A. (2022). *World Bank Group Global Market SurveyFintech and the Future of Finance Flagship Technical Note.* https://doi.org/10.1596/37364.

Fintech Circle (2023, March 14). *Why women are core to a fintech future. Fintech Circle.* https://fintechcircle.com/insights/why-women-are-core-to-a-fintech-future-2/.

Gardeva, A. (2010). *A vision for full financial inclusion.* Center for Financial Inclusion. https://www.centerforfinancialinclusion.org/a-vision-for-full-financial-inclusion

Ghosh, S., & Günther, M. K. (2017). Financial inclusion through public works program: Does gender-based violence make a difference? *Gender Issues*, *35*(3), 254–286. https://doi.org/10.1007/s12147-017-9202-0.

Gupta, S., & Kanungo, R. P. (2022). Financial inclusion through digitalisation: Economic viability for the bottom of the Pyramid (bop) segment. *Journal of Business Research, 148*, 262–276. https://doi.org/10.1016/j.jbusres.2022.04.070.

Heng, D., & Tok, Y. W. (2022). Fintech: Financial inclusion or exclusion? *IMF Working Papers, 2022*(080), 1. https://doi.org/10.5089/9798400208645.001.

Hung, J.-L., & Luo, B. (2016). FinTech in Taiwan: A case study of a bank's strategic planning for an investment in a fintech company. *Financial Innovation*, *2*(1). https://doi.org/10.1186/s40854-016-0037-6.

Kama, U., & Adigun, M. (2013). *Financial inclusion in Nigeria: Issues and challenges.* https://www.cbn.gov.ng/Out/2014/RSD/Occasional%20Paper%20No.%2045%20Issues%20and%20Challenges.pdf.

Kempson, E., & Collard, S. (2012). *Developing a vision for financial inclusion.* Bristol: University of Bristol for Friends Provident Foundation.

Khanna, T., & Palepu, K. G. (1997). Why focused strategies may be wrong for emerging markets. *Harvard Business Review*, *75*(4), 41–48. https://dialnet.unirioja.es/servlet/articulo?codigo=425098.

Mirjam, J. (2021). *Evolution of Fintech: the 5 key eras.* https://www.e-zigurat.com/innovation-school/blog/evolution-of-fintech/.

Mohan, R. (2006). *Economic growth, financial deepening and financial inclusion' address at the annual bankers* Conference 2006, Hyderabad. https://www.bis.org/review/r061121e.pdf.

Murata, A., & Sioson, E. P. (2018). *Financial literacy programs for remittances. Migration and remittances for development in Asia.* Manila: ADB-World Bank Co-Publication.

Noviyanti, S., Mulyadi, D., & Hari Sandi, S. P. (2022). The effect of financial literacy towards financial management behavior of MSME: A study on MSME administrators in Karawang regency. *Proceedings of the 20th Malaysia Indonesia International Conference on Economics, Management and Accounting.* https://doi.org/10.5220/0010599100002900.

OECD (2012). In *OECD eBooks.* https://doi.org/10.1787/entrepreneur_aag-2012-en.

Ohnesorge, J. K. (2007). Developing development theory: Law and development orthodoxies and the Northeast Asian experience. *University of Pennsylvania Journal of International Law*, *28*(2), 219. http://law.wisc.edu/m/dzfwz/developing_development_theory_upjiel.pdf.

Ojo, T. A. (2022). Financial inclusion and women empowerment in BRICS countries: Perspectives on India and South Africa. In *International political economy series* (pp. 175–203). https://doi.org/10.1007/978-3-030-97397-1_10.

Olowookere, D. (2019). *Role of fintech in accelerating financial inclusion in Nigeria.* Business Post Nigeria. https://businesspost.ng/featureoped/role-of-fintech-in-accelerating-financial-inclusion-in-nigeria/.

Othman, I. W., Mokhtar, S., & Esa, M. S. (2022). The stages of national education system operation: Issues, rationale, and challenges for the Ministry of Education Malaysia (MOE) in facing post-pandemic norms of COVID-19. *International Journal of Education, Psychology and Counseling*, *7*(47), 616–638. https://doi.org/10.35631/ijepc.747048.

Ozili, P. K. (2018). Impact of digital finance on financial inclusion and stability. *Borsa Istanbul Review*, *18*(4), 329–340. https://doi.org/10.1016/j.bir.2017.12.003.

Ozili, P. K., Ademiju, A., & Rachid, S. (2022). Impact of financial inclusion on economic growth: Review of existing literature and directions for future research. *International Journal of Social Economics.* https://doi.org/10.1108/ijse-05-2022-0339.

Park, C. M., Kraus, A. D., Dai, Y., Fantry, C., Block, T., Kelder, B., Howard, K. A., & Solberg, V. S. (2021). Empowering women in finance through developing girls' financial literacy skills in the United States. *Behavioral Sciences*, *11*(12), 176. https://doi.org/10.3390/bs11120176.

Puschmann, T. (2017). Fintech. *Business & Information Systems Engineering*, *59*(1), 69–76. https://doi.org/10.1007/s12599-017-0464-6.

Sahay, R., Ogawa, S., Khera, P., & Ng, S. (2022). Is digital financial inclusion unlocking growth? *IMF Working Paper*, *2021*(167), 1. https://doi.org/10.5089/9781513584669.001.

Sahoo, A. K., Pradhan, B. B., & Sahu, N. C. (2017). Determinants of financial inclusion in tribal districts of Odisha: An empirical investigation. *Social Change*, *47*(1), 45–64. https://doi.org/10.1177/0049085716683072.

Sioson, E. P., & Kim, C. J. (2019). Closing the Gender Gap in Financial Inclusion through Fintech. *Asian Development Bank*, 2019(3). https://www.adb.org/sites/default/files/publication/498956/adbi-pb2019-3.pdf

Wood, S. C., Jones, S. K., Johnson, J. A., Brauman, K. A., Chaplin-Kramer, R., Fremier, A. K., Girvetz, E. H., Gordon, L., Kappel, C. V., Mandle, L., Mulligan, M., O'Farrell, P. J., Smith, W. K., Willemen, L., Zhang, W., & DeClerck, F. (2018). Distilling the role of ecosystem services in the sustainable development goals. *Ecosystem Services*, *29*, 70–82. https://doi.org/10.1016/j.ecoser.2017.10.010.

Xi, W., & Wang, Y. (2023). *Digital financial inclusion and quality of economic growth. Heliyon*, *9*(9). https://doi.org/10.1016/j.heliyon.2023.e19731.

Younas, Z. I., Qureshi, A., & Al-Faryan, M. A. S. (2022). Financial inclusion, the shadow economy and economic growth in developing economies. *Structural Change and Economic Dynamics*, *62*, 613–621. https://doi.org/10.1016/j.strueco.2022.03.011.

Zhang, Z. (2023). *The Economic Growth Effects of Digital Financial Inclusion: Evidence from Rural China.* https://doi.org/10.2139/ssrn.4476182.

Zhong, E., & Yoong, R. (2021, February 25). *Fintech in responsible financing. Responsible Business.* https://www.responsiblebusiness.com/channels/sustainable-finance-news/fintech-in-responsible-financing/#!

Zins, A., & Weill, L. (2016). The determinants of financial inclusion in Africa. *Review of Development Finance*, *6*(1), 46–57. https://doi.org/10.1016/j.rdf.2016.05.001

Part VI

Financial Inclusion Awareness and Policy Implications

16 An Empirical Analysis of the Awareness of Financial Inclusion and Policy Implications

Ch Sudipta Kishore Nanda, Priti Gupta, Mazharunnisa, and Samiya Mubeen

16.1 Introduction

Financial inclusion has become a very critical goal for policymakers all over world in the quickly changing global economy of recent times. The phrase "financial inclusion" generally refers to the idea which financial goods as well as services should be accessible to all other people, especially those from a very underserved and marginalised groups. It includes different of services, such as banking, credit, protection, as well as savings, all of which are very necessary for people along with enterprises to fully engage inside economic activity. A proven method for a very advancing social as well as economic progress, reducing total poverty, and fostering inclusive growth is to increase proper financial inclusion.

Financial inclusion is becoming very important, yet despite this, there are still many gaps in the availability of financial products as well as services that prevent it from being fully realised. The degree to which people are very much aware of the advantages along with possibilities provided by financial services is a critical aspect that influences financial inclusion. Without sufficient knowledge, people risk remaining outside the official financial system and losing out on its benefits (Koomson et al., 2020). Therefore, it is essential for policymakers to comprehend financial inclusion awareness and its ramifications in order to develop efficient strategies that close existing gaps and advance inclusive financial systems. Financial inclusion awareness refers to people's knowledge of their comprehension of financial services including banking, credit, insurance coverage, and savings, along with their capacity to successfully access and make use of these services.

The study intends to offer useful information on the level of awareness among people regarding being financially included through an extensive literature review and additional information evaluation. The study will incorporate many views and empirical data on the issue of financial awareness by looking at an extensive selection of literature sources. The study also aims to explore potential policy intervention areas in addition to evaluating the existing state of financial literacy awareness. The study seeks to suggest relevant policy suggestions by analysing empirical data and synthesising the results. Policymakers can create more effective targeted initiatives by studying the factors that affect awareness and taking

DOI: 10.4324/9781032655185-22

into account the socioeconomic context in which monetary inclusion happens. The study recognises the value of taking into account the many different characteristics, including wealth, schooling, occupation, and where one lives, that affect awareness degrees. To identify important variables and their effects, these parameters will be compared to economic awareness.

Lack of knowledge frequently causes people to turn to informal and uncontrolled financial options, which can be expensive, dangerous, and ineffective in addressing their financial requirements (Malik et al., n.d.). For lawmakers and other interested parties to develop successful tactics and approaches to close the awareness gap and advance inclusive financial systems, it is essential to understand the awareness of financial equality and its implications.

This study objective is to undertake an empirical examination of financial inclusion understanding and its political consequences: To determine how well-informed people are about financial inclusion and the services that go along with it, such as finance, credit, assurance, and savings; to pinpoint the major determinants of awareness levels, such as socioeconomic traits, educational background, and location; to investigate how people's financial behaviour and decision-making processes are affected by their awareness of financial inclusion; to evaluate the findings' effects on policy and make suggestions on how to successfully raise awareness regarding and promote financial equality. An approach centred around analysing secondary data will be used to accomplish the goals of this study (Hsu et al., 2021). Third-party data, which will be used in this investigation for evaluation and comprehension, is pre-existing information gathered by other scholars or organisations.

16.2 Literature Review

16.2.1 Awareness Levels of Financial Inclusion

Individuals' knowledge, comprehension, and identification of the idea of financial inclusion as well as the numerous financial services and possibilities available to them are referred to as their awareness stages of financial inclusion. It includes their knowledge of formal financial tools including banking services, credit alternatives, insurance policies, savings plans, and other ways to save money. As discussed by Omar and Inaba (2020), understanding how well-informed people are about being financially included and if they are capable of making wise financial decisions and effectively interacting with formal financial institutions depends on looking at awareness levels. As defined Morgan and Long (2020), these studies assess people's financial well-being knowledge, attitudes, and behaviours using survey information and qualitative methodologies.

As influenced by Senyo and Osabutey (2020), access to knowledge, exposure to monetary services, and the capacity to comprehend and use the regulated financial system are all significantly influenced by socioeconomic characteristics. To measure awareness, different study uses different survey tools and procedures, making it challenging to compare study results. Furthermore, actual comprehension and

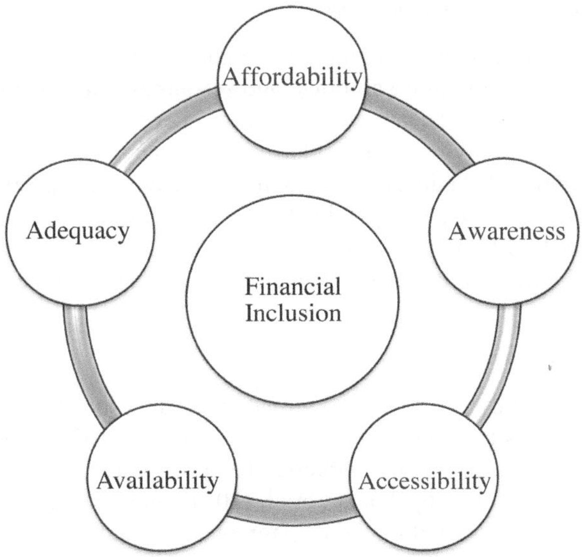

Figure 16.1 Financial inclusion

Source: Self-developed

knowledge may not necessarily match what oneself reports on awareness. As stated by Van et al. (2021), to obtain a more precise picture regarding consciousness levels, study in the future should concentrate on creating standardised measurement instruments and investigating cutting-edge techniques, such as behavioural trials and observation studies.

Programmes for financial education and awareness should be ongoing and updated to reflect changing socioeconomic conditions, technology developments, and financial environments. As explained by Demir et al. (2022), regular analysis and assessment appropriate awareness campaigns can shed light on their efficacy and aid in the development of plans for ongoing development (Figure 16.1).

16.2.2 Policy Interventions to Enhance Awareness

The strategic actions and initiatives taken by policymakers, regulatory agencies, financial companies, and other players to advance and improve the public's knowledge and comprehension of financial inclusion are referred to as actions taken to enhance awareness. As stated by Ozili (2021), by bridging the knowledge gap between different population segments, especially underserved and marginalised communities, these interventions hope to enable people to make wise financial decisions and interact with institutional financial systems.

To raise public awareness of financial inclusion, a number of policy measures have been identified and put into practice.

16.2.2.1 Financial Education Initiatives

Initiatives to promote financial literacy are a core type of policy intervention. By giving people the information, abilities, and resources required to make wise financial decisions, these projects seek to increase people's financial literacy. They include a variety of activities like workshops, seminars, training courses, and instructional resources that address financial literacy, savings, budgeting, and managing one's credit. As explained by Tripathi et al. (2022), to reach a large audience and accommodate different ways of learning, financial literacy can be provided through schools, charitable organisations, workplaces, and internet platforms.

16.2.2.2 Capacity Building Programmes

In order to successfully spread information on monetary inclusion, capacity development programmes concentrate on improving the knowledge and abilities of intermediaries, such as community workers, educators, and frontline staff at financial institutions. As mentioned by Trianto et al. (2021), these programmes offer these intermediates instruction and materials, empowering them to serve as facilitators as well as educators in their own neighbourhoods.

16.2.2.3 Technology-Driven Solutions

Innovative opportunities to raise awareness of the importance of financial inclusion are provided by technological breakthroughs. Websites, applications for smartphones, and online resources are used by government agencies to engage people and distribute financial education materials. Financial information may be made available, convenient, and interesting with the help of technology-driven solutions that can offer personalised and interactive educational opportunities (Malik & Yadav, 2022).

16.2.2.4 Evaluation and Monitoring

Strong assessment and monitoring systems should be used in conjunction with policy actions to increase awareness. Stakeholders as well as policymakers can identify areas for development and make based on study adjustments while continuously assessing the interventions' performance and impact. As discussed by Erlando et al. (2020), to monitor changes in consciousness levels, knowledge, as well as financial behaviour, evaluation frameworks might include methods that are qualitative as well as quantitative, which includes as focus group discussions, interviews, surveys, and even behavioural experiments.

16.2.2.5 Collaboration and Stakeholder Engagement

Collaboration and stakeholder involvement are essential for the implementation of effective policy initiatives that increase awareness. To develop and carry out coordinated awareness efforts, policymakers should collaborate closely with financial

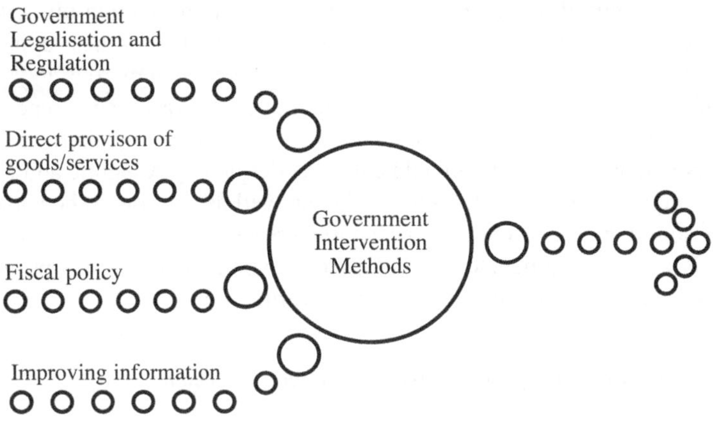

Figure 16.2 Policy intervention

Source: Self-developed

companies, regulatory authorities, community organisations, academia, including advocacy groups for consumers. As stated by Le et al. (2019), collaboration encourages the sharing of best practices, the mobilisation of resources, and the transfer of knowledge (Figure 16.2).

16.2.3 Implications of Awareness on Financial Behaviour

The effects and outcomes that people's awareness of being financially included have on their economic decision-making, behaviour, and participation with formal banking services are referred to as the implications of being aware on financial behaviour. Policymakers, businesses, and organisations working to promote financial inclusion must understand the consequences in order to establish ties between knowledge and actual economic results. As explained by Ahmad et al. (2020), stakeholders can develop targeted efforts and approaches to improve financial literacy, encourage good financial habits, and boost people's use of official banking services by looking at the effects of understanding on financial behaviour.

The tendency for more informed as well as accountable monetary choices to follow from increasing levels of knowledge of financial inclusion is a significant conclusion. As discussed by Goyal and Kumar (2021), additionally, they are more likely to practise financial planning, budgeting, saving, regulate spending and goal-setting, which enhances financial stability over the long run.

According to study, people with greater amounts of knowledge are more inclined to participate in institutional savings systems, have financial accounts, and be able to access credit. As stated by Ozili (2020), they additionally are more likely to use mobile payment systems and online banking, as well as embracing technology advancements that promote financial inclusion.

Designing focused treatments that meet the unique needs and obstacles faced by various demographic segments requires an understanding of these dynamics. As mentioned by Aldieri et al. (2019), in conclusion, there are numerous and important effects of awareness on the way people spend money. By raising awareness, people can make better financial decisions, become more financially literate, and have better personal and societal financial health. As defined by Adegbite and Machethe (2020), to equip people with the knowledge as well as the comprehension needed to make sound financial choices, policymakers as well as stakeholders should place a high priority on developing comprehensive financial literacy programmes, awareness campaigns, and easily available information outlets.

16.2.4 Factors Influencing Awareness on Financial Inclusion and Policy Implications

Individuals' knowledge, comprehension, and recognition of the concept of financial inclusion and its accompanying services are shaped by a variety of factors, which are referred to as factors impacting awareness of financial inclusion. Socioeconomic factors have a big impact on how much people are aware of financial inclusion. Another significant variable affecting awareness of being financially included is educational background. As explained by Lee et al. (2022), knowledge of finances, which is closely related to awareness and combined high school graduation have been found to have a favourable relationship. Financial inclusion awareness is also influenced by social and cultural conventions. For instance, in some backgrounds, there can be an appreciation for informal saving strategies or mistrust of official financial organisations, which would result in a lack of understanding and use of official banking services (Malik et al., 2021).

Due to the absence of exposure to official financial institutions and restricted access to monetary education programmes, this may lead to lower understanding levels. As defined by Campedelli et al. (2021), for increasing knowledge and fostering economic mobility across all regions, it is essential to address regional discrepancies and guarantee equal distribution of financial services and data.

16.2.4.1 Policy Implications

The factors affecting public perception of financial inclusion have a big impact on how inclusive systems of finance are promoted from a policy standpoint. Following are some significant policy ramifications gleaned from the literature.

16.2.4.2 Targeted Awareness Campaigns

Campaigns for raising awareness that are specifically tailored to the requirements, cultural quirks, and socioeconomic traits of various demographic groups should be developed by policymakers. As stated by Schuetz and Venkatesh (2020), for these efforts to efficiently reach and inspire the target audience, a variety of methods of communication as well as messages should be used.

16.2.4.3 Evaluating and Monitoring

It is essential to continuously review and monitor awareness-raising efforts in order to determine their efficacy and make the necessary corrections. As defined by Xie et al. (2021), to assess the effectiveness of awareness campaigns, follow changes in public awareness over time, and pinpoint areas that need more attention, policymakers should set up effective monitoring methods.

16.2.4.4 Tailoring Policies to Marginalised Groups

The special problems that women, minorities, and those with low socioeconomic status – all groups who are marginalised and underprivileged –face should be the focus of policy responses. The knowledge gap among these communities can be closed with the use of customised techniques, focused interventions, and inclusive legislation (Malik et al., 2020).

16.3 Methodology

A study of secondary data will be done to determine how knowledge of financial inclusion relates to different socioeconomic traits. In pertinent datasets, this analysis will assist in finding patterns and relationships that can be used to infer people's levels of awareness.

Secondary data will be gathered by the study from reliable sources such as government publications, financial institutions, including surveys across the nation. Data on monetary inclusion indicators, understanding levels, and socioeconomic factors including income, schooling, gender, and geography will all be included. To determine potential policy implications, conclusions from the literature study and supplementary data analysis are going to be employed. The study will highlight knowledge gaps and barriers to monetary integration and offer focused solutions in the form of plans and activities.

The consequences for policy will be created in collaboration with decision-makers, financial industry stakeholders, and subject-matter experts. The objective is to offer practical suggestions that help improve programmes for financial inclusion and advance a more open and responsible financial system (Mikalef & Gupta, 2021). In the end, this study aims to support continuing initiatives to encourage financial inclusion and build a more sustainable and accessible financial system.

16.4 Results and Discussions

16.4.1 Access to Financial Services

The literature upon financial inclusion emphasises the importance of access to financial services, which have a significant impact on people's economic well-being and chances for progress in society. Access to formal monetary services like banking, credit, protection, and savings that is both inexpensive and convenient is essential for fostering financial inclusion and lowering poverty.

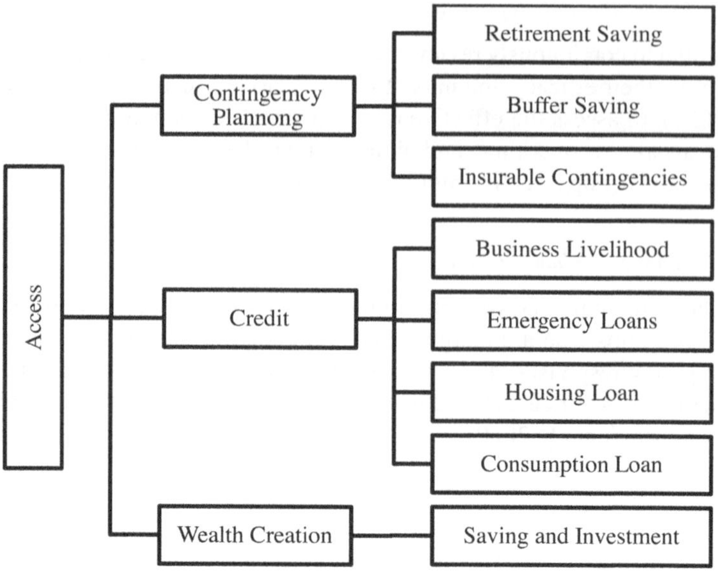

Figure 16.3 Financial services

Source: Self-developed

Expanding both traditional and online access to financial products and services is crucial, as shown by case studies and actual data. Physical access refers to the presence of financial service providers, such as banks, in close proximity to people, especially those living in rural or underserved areas. Insufficient physical infrastructure makes it difficult for people to easily access financial institutions in many developing nations (Lashitew et al., 2019).

Despite the fact that technology can make access easier, there are still issues with digital literacy, communication, and affordability that must be resolved. To guarantee that people are able to profit fully from online banking services, efforts must be made to bridge the digital gap through construction of infrastructure and digital literacy programmes (Figure 16.3). Additionally, accessibility to financial services goes beyond the availability of both electronic and physical infrastructure. Additionally, it entails removing obstacles relating to cost, documentation requirements, and unfair practices (Murshed, 2020).

16.4.2 Financial Literacy and Education

In order to encourage financial inclusion and provide people the power to make intelligent financial choices, financial knowledge and instruction are vital. It entails giving people the information, abilities, and resources they need to efficiently manage their personal finances. Understanding financial ideas, setting up a budget, saving money, investing, and having access to financial services and goods are all included in the concept of financial literacy. Raising understanding of the advantages and risks of financial goods and services is a crucial component of financial literacy. Many people, especially those from underprivileged and marginalised groups, are uninformed about the range of financial possibilities and lack basic financial literacy. Initiatives for financial education seek to accurately close this gap through giving people relevant and further easily accessible knowledge that aids in directly navigating the complexity of the financial world. The major goals of the entire monetary education courses usually include knowledge acquisition, the development of different practical skills, and the encouragement of sound financial practices (Sahay et al., 2020). These programmes could be made available in a different of ways, including training sessions, online classes, instructional campaigns, and digital tools.

16.4.3 Understanding of Financial Inclusion and Its Political Consequences

This study has adopted a secondary data analysis approach to provide a comprehensive understanding of financial inclusion and its political consequences. Regarding secondary data, thematic data analysis has been employed to identify various themes and patterns to generate valuable findings about the study topic. However, the aim of adopting the thematic analysis was critically focused on gaining adequate insights into the significant relationship between understanding financial inclusion and its political consequences. Moreover, the study has reviewed many sources including industry reports, existing literature, journal papers, and other datasets to identify various themes and patterns that have been recurring to provide a better understanding of the relationship.

Based on the thematic analysis, the study has identified that the understanding of financial inclusion has a multifaceted nature. According to the data, financial inclusion is not equally distributed, it varies significantly based on different socioeconomic backgrounds, demographic groups, and regions (Ahmad et al., 2020). This multifaceted nature of variation of financial inclusion is essential to understand for policymakers to improve the overall effectiveness and impacts of different financial inclusion policies. Apart from that, the thematic analysis has also identified a crucial relationship between financial inclusion and its political consequences. It has been identified that individuals who are well aware of finance are more likely to be active politically (Van et al., 2021). Hence, it can be said that a better understanding of financial inclusion leads to positive political consequences.

Moreover, using thematic analysis, the study also gathers crucial insights about the significant role of financial institutions in shaping the understanding of financial inclusion. The analysis has highlighted that the current practices of financial institutions have a direct influence on the perception of financial inclusion among individuals (Senyo & Osabutey, 2020). Responsible and inclusive practices need to be adopted by financial institutions to provide adequate awareness about financial inclusion to their customers. Furthermore, the thematic analysis has also identified the significance of various government policies to promote the understanding of financial inclusion. Effective regulations and supportive policies need to be implemented to enhance the overall understanding of financial inclusion people and maintain continuous engagement (Ozili, 2021).

16.4.4 Policy and Regulatory Framework

The necessity of a supporting policy and regulatory environment in increasing financial inclusion is one of the major themes that emerge throughout the case literature and academic study. The development of an environment that fosters safeguarding consumers, competition, and innovation depends critically on the design and implementation of a regulatory framework.

16.4.4.1 Enabling Access and Market Entry

By removing pointless impediments to market entrance, the policy as well as regulatory framework must prioritise making financial services more accessible. This includes expediting the application process for licences, lowering start-up capital requirements, and promoting competition among the providers of financial services.

16.4.4.2 Consumer Protection

An essential part of the policy as well as regulatory structures is consumer protection. It entails setting guidelines and requirements to protect consumers' interests, especially those of people from disadvantaged and marginalised groups. This involves taking steps to ensure fairness, openness, and disclosure of the terms and circumstances pertaining to financial services and goods. To handle consumer complaints and preserve public confidence in the financial system, strong supervision from regulators, enforcement, and restitution procedures are necessary.

16.4.4.3 Financial Product Suitability and Disclosure

The goal of legislative and regulatory structures should be to make sure that financial services and goods are appropriate for the requirements and preferences of consumers. This entails supporting transparent pricing, opposing predatory lending, and promoting ethical lending practices (Nuryyev et al., 2020).

16.4.4.4 Proportionate Regulation

The broad range of financial service companies and their target consumer categories should be taken into account under an effective legislative and regulatory framework, which should use a proportionate approach. According to their dimensions, complexity, and risk profile, various institution types, including conventional financial institutions, microfinance organisations, and fintech companies, may require various regulatory methods. This strategy guarantees that rules are not too onerous for smaller institutions, supporting their involvement in financial inclusion initiatives.

16.4.4.5 Digital Financial Services and Innovation

Policymakers must support innovation and the growth of online financial services in light of the swift development of the internet. This entails establishing a legislative environment that is favourable to the development of fintech start-ups, electronic payment systems, and mobile banking applications. By removing physical obstacles, lowering the price of transactions, and reaching marginalised people, embracing internet financial services can dramatically improve financial inclusion.

16.4.4.6 Coordination and Collaboration

The coordination and collaboration of essential players, such as government agencies, banking organisations, technological companies, and consumer advocacy groups, should be made easier by the policy as well as regulatory framework. Regular communication, information sharing, and collaboration can promote innovation, improve the effectiveness of policy, and quickly handle new threats and issues (Figure 16.4).

16.4.5 Financial Inclusion and Sustainable Development

Sustainable development with financial inclusion is interwoven ideas that support one another. The three main pillars of sustainable development are financial, social, and environmental. By enabling people, especially those from marginalised and poor areas, to fully participate in economic activity, access necessary services, and develop resilience towards shocks and vulnerabilities, financial inclusion supports each of these elements.

16.4.5.1 Economic Dimension

Increasing financial inclusion is essential for boosting economic growth and eradicating poverty. Financial inclusion enables people to save, invest, and build wealth

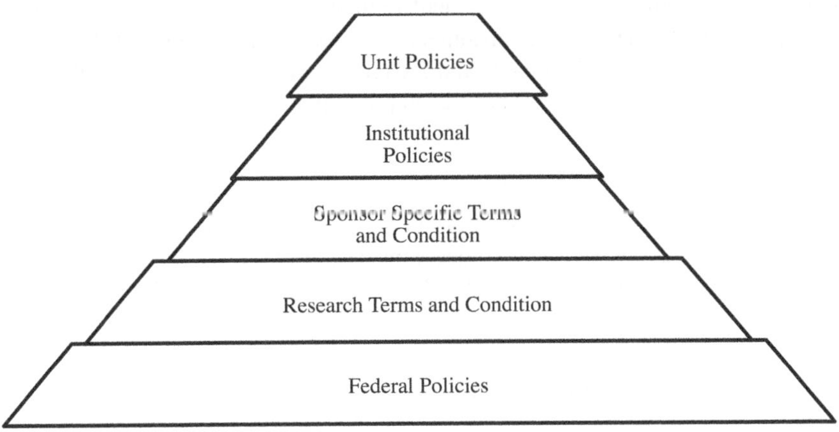

Figure 16.4 Regulatory framework

Source: Self-developed

by giving them access to official financial resources including banking, credit, insurance coverage, and savings.

Financial inclusion encourages inclusive finance, which guarantees that the advantages of economic progress are distributed fairly across all societal groups (Khan et al., 2020).

16.4.5.2 Social Dimension

The social and economic health of people and communities is profoundly impacted by financial inclusion. The ability to manage risks, deal with situations of emergency, and improve one's quality of life is improved when people have access to financial services. It makes it possible for them to spend money on things like healthcare, schools, housing, and other necessities, so enhancing their total social welfare.

16.4.5.3 Environmental Dimension

Environmental sustainability can be advanced by promoting financial inclusion. Access to financial products and services makes it easier for people and companies to invest in energy sources that are renewable, practise sustainable agriculture, and adopt other green practices.

16.5 Policy Implications

Prioritising and implementing a number of crucial policy initiatives are necessary for policymakers to fully realise the potential of economic inclusion for equitable development.

16.5.1 Enabling Regulatory Environment

Governments should create a benevolent regulatory environment that encourages creativity, competitiveness, and consumer safety. Regulations should strike a balance between fostering equitable finance and the requirement for financial stability, making sure that the right safeguards have been put in place without limiting innovation.

16.5.2 Financial Literacy and Education

Financial literacy programmes must be funded if people are to have the knowledge and abilities to make wise financial decisions (Kaur et al., 2021). Targeting people who are vulnerable and underserved will enable them to successfully navigate the financial world.

16.5.3 Infrastructure and Technology

In order to increase access to financial products and services, especially to distant and underdeveloped regions, governments ought to invest in enhancing physical and digital infrastructure. In particular, this entails encouraging the growth of agent banking relationships, mobile banking applications, and steady internet connectivity.

16.5.4 Public-Private Partnerships

For financial inclusion plans to be implemented successfully, cooperation between governments, banking institutions, vendors of technology, and civil society organisations is essential. Public-private collaborations can take advantage of each sector's advantages and assets to promote innovation, expansion, and sustainability.

16.6 Conclusion

A quantitative examination of financial inclusion consciousness and its policy consequences has been done in this study. The study has provided insight into the present situation of the financial inclusion conversation, identified key factors impacting awareness, and investigated the connection between social and economic background and knowledge of monetary inclusion by synthesising a thorough literature review and carrying out secondary data analysis. The results have important policy implications and offer useful information on the efficacy of current policies and programmes for financial services stakeholders. The study has brought to light the significance of ensuring that people from disadvantaged and marginalised groups have access to a variety of financial services, such as banking, credit, health coverage, and savings. It has emphasised the need of financial education and literacy in enabling people to make wise financial decisions and successfully negotiate the financial landscape (Gutiérrez-Romero & Ahamed, 2021).

According to study on public perceptions of the inclusion of money and its political ramifications, there are a number of areas that have room for additional investigation and development. Future study in the following areas could be taken into consideration:

In-depth Analysis of Socioeconomic Factors: Future study can go deeper into specific elements including income levels, schooling, profession, and geographical region. This study focused on the relationship amongst socioeconomic indicators and knowledge of financial inclusion. For policymakers to develop deeper knowledge and focused policies, it is important for them to comprehend how these factors affect awareness of as well as access to financial services.

Impact Assessment of Financial Inclusion Programmes: Future studies could concentrate on assessing the success of particular financial inclusion initiatives and programmes. Impact assessments can be used to find the programmes' strengths, flaws, and potential trouble areas, which can then be used to inform the creation and execution of new initiatives.

Behavioural Aspects of Financial Inclusion: Future studies may find success by examining the behavioural components of financial inclusion (Hu et al., 2019). Understanding the opinions, convictions, and processes for making decisions in relation to being financially included can be a useful starting point for developing interventions that successfully raise awareness and drive behavioural change.

Role of Technology and Innovation: Exploring the impact of the internet of things, fintech developments, and new inventions in fostering financial inclusion is essential given how quickly technology is developing. Future studies can concentrate on comprehending the possible advantages, difficulties, and policy ramifications of using technology to increase knowledge and accessibility to financial services.

References

Adegbite, O. O., & Machethe, C. L. (2020). Bridging the financial inclusion gender gap in smallholder agriculture in Nigeria: An untapped potential for sustainable development. *World Development*, *127*, 104755. https://repository.up.ac.za/bitstream/handle/2263/73912/Adegbite_Bridging_2020.pdf?sequence=1.

Ahmad, F., Widén, G., & Huvila, I. (2020). The impact of workplace information literacy on organizational innovation: An empirical study. *International Journal of Information Management*, *51*, 102041. https://fardapaper.ir/mohavaha/uploads/2020/07/Fardapaper-The-impact-of-workplace-information-literacy-on-organizational-innovation-An-empirical-study.pdf.

Aldieri, L., Carlucci, F., Vinci, C. P., & Yigitcanlar, T. (2019). Environmental innovation, knowledge spillovers and policy implications: A systematic review of the economic effects literature. *Journal of Cleaner Production*, *239*, 118051. https://eprints.qut.edu.au/132202/1/eprints.pdf.

Campedelli, G. M., Aziani, A., & Favarin, S. (2021). Exploring the immediate effects of COVID-19 containment policies on crime: An empirical analysis of the short-term aftermath in Los Angeles. *American Journal of Criminal Justice*, *46*(5), 704–727. http://m.growingscience.com/uscm/Vol10/uscm_2021_123.pdf.

Demir, A., Pesqué-Cela, V., Altunbas, Y., & Murinde, V. (2022). Fintech, financial inclusion and income inequality: A quantile regression approach. *The European Journal of Finance*, *28*(1), 86–107. https://www.tandfonline.com/doi/pdf/10.1080/1351847X.2020.1772335.

Erlando, A., Riyanto, F. D., & Masakazu, S. (2020). Financial inclusion, economic growth, and poverty alleviation: Evidence from eastern Indonesia. *Heliyon*, *6*(10). https://www.cell.com/heliyon/pdf/S2405-8440(20)32078-8.pdf.

Goyal, K., & Kumar, S. (2021). Financial literacy: A systematic review and bibliometric analysis. *International Journal of Consumer Studies*, *45*(1), 80–105. https://www.thestraughtergroup.org/wp-content/uploads/2022/09/A-Systemic-Review-of-Financial-Literacy.pdf.

Gutiérrez-Romero, R., & Ahamed, M. (2021). COVID-19 response needs to broaden financial inclusion to curb the rise in poverty. *World Development*, *138*, 105229. https://www.ncbi.nlm.nih.gov/pmc/articles/PMC7580698/.

Hsu, C. C., Quang-Thanh, N., Chien, F., Li, L., & Mohsin, M. (2021). Evaluating green innovation and performance of financial development: Mediating concerns of environmental regulation. *Environmental Science and Pollution Study*, *28*(40), 57386–57397. https://mpra.ub.uni-muenchen.de/109671/1/MPRA_paper_109671.pdf.

Hu, Z., Ding, S., Li, S., Chen, L., & Yang, S. (2019). Adoption intention of fintech services for bank users: An empirical examination with an extended technology acceptance model. *Symmetry*, *11*(3), 340. https://www.mdpi.com/2073-8994/11/3/340/pdf.

Kaur, S. J., Ali, L., Hassan, M. K., & Al-Emran, M. (2021). Adoption of digital banking channels in an emerging economy: Exploring the role of in-branch efforts. *Journal of Financial Services Marketing*, *26*, 107–121. https://link.springer.com/article/10.1057/s41264-020-00082-w.

Khan, K., Zhao, H., Zhang, H., Yang, H., Shah, M. H., & Jahanger, A. (2020). The impact of COVID-19 pandemic on stock markets: An empirical analysis of world major stock indices. *The Journal of Asian Finance, Economics and Business*, *7*(7), 463–474. https://pdfs.semanticscholar.org/435f/e3e8f910a1f1161dfd934cfc2ff0c1a6edba.pdf.

Koomson, I., Villano, R. A., & Hadley, D. (2020). Effect of financial inclusion on poverty and vulnerability to poverty: Evidence using a multidimensional measure of financial inclusion. *Social Indicators Study*, *149*(2), 613–639. https://www.studygate.net/profile/Isaac-Koomson-2/publication/338982531_Effect_of_Financial_Inclusion_on_Poverty_and_Vulnerability_to_Poverty_Evidence_Using_a_Multi-Dimensional_Measure_of_Financial_Inclusion/links/5e3c8dc792851c7f7f2326d3/Effect-of-Financial-Inclusion-on-Poverty-and-Vulnerability-to-Poverty-Evidence-Using-a-Multi-Dimensional-Measure-of-Financial-Inclusion.pdf.

Lashitew, A. A., van Tulder, R., & Liasse, Y. (2019). Mobile phones for financial inclusion: What explains the diffusion of mobile money innovations? *Study Policy*, *48*(5), 1201–1215. https://www.studygate.net/profile/Addisu-Lashitew-2/publication/330716526_Mobile_Phones_for_Financial_Inclusion_What_Explains_the_Diffusion_of_Mobile_Money_Innovations/links/5c50bf1a92851c22a398d279/Mobile-Phones-for-Financial-Inclusion-What-Explains-the-Diffusion-of-Mobile-Money-Innovations.pdf.

Le, T. H., Chuc, A. T., & Taghizadeh-Hesary, F. (2019). Financial inclusion and its impact on financial efficiency and sustainability: Empirical evidence from Asia. *Borsa Istanbul Review*, *19*(4), 310–322. https://www.sciencedirect.com/science/article/pii/S2214845019301267.

Lee, K., Azmi, N., Hanaysha, J., Alzoubi, H., & Alshurideh, M. (2022). The effect of digital supply chain on organizational performance: An empirical study in Malaysia manufacturing industry. *Uncertain Supply Chain Management*, *10*(2), 495–510. http://m.growingscience.com/uscm/Vol10/uscm_2021_123.pdf.

Malik, F. A., & Yadav, D. K. (2022). *Financial inclusion schemes in India*. Springer. https://www.studygate.net/profile/Devendra-Yadav-14/publication/365852147_financial_inclusion_ebook/links/6386ff848e63c56dae46800b/financial-inclusion-ebook.pdf.

Malik, F. A., Yadav, D. K., Adam, H., & Omrane, A. (n.d.). *The Urban Poor and Their Financial Behavior*. https://www.studygate.net/profile/Firdous-Ahmad-Malik/publication/346784990_The_Urban_Poor_and_their_Financial_Behaviour_A_Case_Study_Of_Slum-Dwellers_In_Lucknow_India/links/60374bd192851c4ed5954da6/The-Urban-Poor-and-their-Financial-Behaviour-A-Case-Study-Of-Slum-Dwellers-In-Lucknow-India.pdf.

Malik, F. A., Yadav, D. K., Adam, H., & Omrane, A. (2020). *The urban poor and their financial behavior: A case study of slum dwellers in Lucknow (India)*. In Sustainable entrepreneurship, renewable energy-based projects, and digitalization (pp. 305–315). CRC Press. https://www.taylorfrancis.com/chapters/edit/10.1201/9781003097921-17/urban-poor-financial-behavior-firdous-ahmad-malik-yadav-hebatallah-adam-amina-omrane.

Malik, F. A., Yadav, D. K., Lone, N. A., & Adam, H. (2021). *An investigation into the dynamics of financial inclusion in south Asian countries. Pakistan Economic and Social Review*, *59*(2), 231. https://www.studygate.net/profile/Naveed-Lone/publication/358396214_AN_INVESTIGATION_INTO_THE_DYNAMICS_OF_FINANCIAL_INCLUSION_IN_SOUTH_ASIAN_COUNTRIES/links/61ffeb6ca7d76d0f08c5a3ef/AN-INVESTIGATION-INTO-THE-DYNAMICS-OF-FINANCIAL-INCLUSION-IN-SOUTH-ASIAN-COUNTRIES.pdf.

Mikalef, P., & Gupta, M. (2021). Artificial intelligence capability: Conceptualization, measurement calibration, and empirical study on its impact on organizational creativity and firm performance. *Information & Management*, *58*(3), 103434. https://www.sciencedirect.com/science/article/pii/S0378720621000082.

Morgan, P. J., & Long, T. Q. (2020). Financial literacy, financial inclusion, and savings behavior in Laos. *Journal of Asian Economics*, *68*, 101197. https://www.studygate.net/profile/Long-Trinh-6/publication/341066558_Financial_Literacy_Financial_Inclusion_and_Savings_Behavior_in_Laos/links/5f10373ea6fdcc3ed70b6f58/Financial-Literacy-Financial-Inclusion-and-Savings-Behavior-in-Laos.pdf.

Murshed, M. (2020). An empirical analysis of the non-linear impacts of ICT-trade openness on renewable energy transition, energy efficiency, clean cooking fuel access and environmental sustainability in South Asia. *Environmental Science and Pollution Study*, *27*(29), 36254–36281. https://link.springer.com/article/10.1007/s11356-020-09497-3.

Nuryyev, G., Wang, Y. P., Achyldurdyyeva, J., Jaw, B. S., Yeh, Y. S., Lin, H. T., & Wu, L. F. (2020). Blockchain technology adoption behavior and sustainability of the business in tourism and hospitality SMEs: An empirical study. *Sustainability*, *12*(3), 1256. https://www.mdpi.com/2071-1050/12/3/1256/pdf.

Omar, M. A., & Inaba, K. (2020). Does financial inclusion reduce poverty and income inequality in developing countries? A panel data analysis. *Journal of Economic Structures*, *9*(1), 37. https://link.springer.com/article/10.1186/s40008-020-00214-4.

Ozili, P. K. (2020). Theories of financial inclusion. In *Uncertainty and challenges in contemporary economic behaviour* (pp. 89–115). Emerald Publishing Limited. https://mpra.ub.uni-muenchen.de/104257/1/MPRA_paper_104257.pdf.

Ozili, P. K. (2021, October). Financial inclusion study around the world: A review. *Forum for Social Economics*, *50*(4), 457–479. https://mpra.ub.uni-muenchen.de/101809/1/mpra_paper_101809.pdf.

Sahay, M. R., von Allmen, M. U. E., Lahreche, M. A., Khera, P., Ogawa, M. S., Bazarbash, M., & Beaton, M. K. (2020). *The promise of fintech: Financial inclusion in the post COVID-19 era*. International Monetary Fund. https://www.elibrary.imf.org/downloadpdf/journals/087/2020/009/087.2020.issue-009-en.pdf.

Schuetz, S., & Venkatesh, V. (2020). Blockchain, adoption, and financial inclusion in India: Study opportunities. *International Journal of Information Management*, *52*, 101936. https://link.springer.com/article/10.1007/s12103-020-09578-6.

Senyo, P. K., & Osabutey, E. L. (2020). Unearthing antecedents to financial inclusion through FinTech innovations. *Technovation*, *98*, 102155. https://eprints.soton.ac.uk/441492/1/Technovation_Manuscript_R2_2020_Clean.pdf.

Trianto, B., Barus, E. E., Sabiu, T. T., & Annisa, S. T. E. I. S. I. (2021). Relationship between Islamic financial literacy, Islamic financial inclusion and business performance: Evidence from culinary cluster of creative economy. *Jurnal Ekonomi dan Bisnis Islam*, *6*(1), 19–38. https://www.studygate.net/profile/Budi-Trianto/publication/351744217_Relationship_Between_Islamic_Financial_Literacy_Islamic_Financial_Inclusion_And_Business_Performance_Evidence_From_Culinary_Cluster_Of_Creative_Economy/links/60a71d6f45851522bc06fa33/Relationship-Between-Islamic-Financial-Literacy-Islamic-Financial-Inclusion-And-Business-Performance-Evidence-From-Culinary-Cluster-Of-Creative-Economy.pdf.

Tripathi, S., Chaubey, A., & Goel, I. (2022). An empirical analysis of potential Central bank digital currency adoption procedure by Indian government and its implications. *Sachetas*, *1*(1), 32–38. https://www.studygate.net/profile/Shivam-Tripathi-11/publication/359929177_AN_EMPIRICAL_ANALYSIS_OF_POTENTIAL_CENTRAL_BANK_DIGITAL_CURRENCY_ADOPTION_PROCEDURE_BY_INDIAN_GOVERNMENT_AND_ITS_IMPLICATIONS/links/6256f09f4173a21a0d0f8e53/AN-EMPIRICAL-ANALYSIS-OF-POTENTIAL-CENTRAL-BANK-DIGITAL-CURRENCY-ADOPTION-PROCEDURE-BY-INDIAN-GOVERNMENT-AND-ITS-IMPLICATIONS.pdf.

Van, L. T. H., Vo, A. T., Nguyen, N. T., & Vo, D. H. (2021). Financial inclusion and economic growth: An international evidence. *Emerging Markets Finance and Trade*, *57*(1), 239–263. https://mpra.ub.uni-muenchen.de/103282/7/MPRA_paper_103282.pdf.

Xie, R., Fu, W., Yao, S., & Zhang, Q. (2021). Effects of financial agglomeration on green total factor productivity in Chinese cities: Insights from an empirical spatial Durbin model. *Energy Economics*, *101*, 105449. https://www.qzgeog.com/publication/p2021-xie-financial/p2021-xie-financial.pdf.

17 Examining the Determinants of Savings in Post-Reform India

Aamir Ahmad Teeli and Saima Nazir

17.1 Introduction

The economic trajectory of a nation is significantly influenced by savings. It provides the capital required for investments, promoting the growth of infrastructure and technology, and facilitating future economic development. Higher savings demonstrate that a larger proportion of the nation's revenue is going toward constructive endeavors which in turn may result in long-term sustainable economic growth.

Savings are a critical driver of economic growth and financial stability, making it imperative to identify the key elements that impact savings behavior. By examining these determinants, we can provide policymakers with valuable insights into how to encourage higher savings rates and thereby enhance capital accumulation for investments, which, in turn, supports economic development. This study is particularly relevant in the context of India, where a growing economy and a large population create a unique set of challenges and opportunities related to savings, making it important to uncover the specific factors that affect savings in this country.

The conventional economic wisdom held that raising domestic savings is necessary to hasten economic expansion (Lewis, 1955). Samuelson and Modigliani (1966), for instance, investigated how various savings behaviors promoted economic growth. According to Solow's (1970) neoclassical model, rising savings have a greater positive impact on production than rising investment. The Harrod-Domar models, however, advocated that investment is crucial to promote economic growth.

The relationship between savings and growth is well established through empirical literature as well. A high saving rate is not only associated with long-term economic growth (Jangili, 2011), but it also serves as a catalyst for higher investment due to the increasing availability of capital (Ang & Sen, 2011). Therefore, a high national saving rate is considered to be crucial for promoting economic growth (Ribaj & Mexhuani, 2021).

There is diversity in the economic growth of countries across the world, and this diversity can be attributed to variation in their levels of savings (Khan & Sarker, 2016). The low level of domestic savings keeps the growth rates low (Adelakun, 2015;

DOI: 10.4324/9781032655185-23

Adewuyi et al., 2010; Epaphra, 2014; Nwachukwu, 2012; Touny, 2008), as there is a positive relation between the level of savings and economic growth (Chaturvedi et al., 2009). A rise in domestic savings can result in the internal accumulation of capital, which can be employed to finance profitable investments. This reduces a country's reliance on foreign funding, shielding it from external shocks (Ribaj & Mexhuani, 2021). In fact, in comparison to growth obtained through the use of borrowed money, domestic savings-based growth is more sustainable (Patra et al., 2017). Therefore, to understand the complexities of a country's economic landscape, it is crucial to comprehend the factors that affect savings.

Following its economic reforms, India has undergone a tremendous economic change (Patra et al., 2017), moving from an agrarian-based economy to one that is characterized by industry, urbanization, and technological breakthroughs. Savings play a bigger part in this shift since they have an impact on the nation's economic growth. India's gross domestic savings (GDS as % of Gross National Income) grew from 21% between 1983 and 1991 to 33.7% between 2008 and 2020 exhibiting an upward trend (World Bank).

Although there are many studies on the factors that affect savings around the world, the particular situation in India calls for a distinct analysis. The distinctive demographic makeup, cultural variety, political climate, and economic disparities of the nation all play a role in the intricate interaction of variables that affect saving behavior (Bhatia & Tyagi, 2018; Filipiak et al., 2017; Jain & Goli, 2022; Malik et al., 2020). This study examines the factors that influence savings in India in great detail in an effort to fill a vacuum in the literature.

The rest of the study is structured as follows: The existing literature on the subject of gross saving is reviewed in Section 17.2, and Section 17.3 discusses the concerns connected to data and methodology for the empirical exercise done in the study. In Section 17.4, empirical findings that evaluate the contribution of several factors to gross savings in India are examined, and Section 17.5 exhibits the conclusion of the study with policy implications.

17.2 Review of Literature

Numerous factors that affect a nation's savings have been discovered in the literature. The hypothesis of absolute income developed by Keynes (1936) propounds the relationship between savings, consumption, and income claiming that savings and consumption rise at increasing and decreasing rates in response to an increase in current disposable income, respectively. According to the life-cycle hypothesis advocated by Ando and Modigliani (1963), as workers' income rises as a result of their higher productivity, the proportion of their savings also rises, illustrating a positive relationship between income and savings. Various growth theories have emphasized the significance of savings in fostering economic growth. The Harrod-Domar growth model asserts that an economy's growth rate is positively correlated with its savings ratio but negatively correlated with its capital-output ratio. The economic growth theory advocated by Solow (1956) suggests that higher savings rates precede economic growth. This means that when the savings rate rises, investment rises as well, which eventually results in economic growth. Empirical evidence also supports the close connections between savings and economic growth from a global perspective, which is in line with theoretical projections. It has been noted that nations with fast-growing economies, including Brazil, China, Egypt, India, Indonesia, Japan, and Malaysia also have high rates of savings (Bashir et al., 2015; Khan et al., 2017, 2018; Mowafy & Ela, 2020; Narayan, 2005; Samantaraya & Patra, 2014; Teeli et al., 2023).

Financial inclusion, which entails offering financial services to underprivileged and marginalized sections of the population in an economy, is another element that influences a nation's savings. Financial inclusion promotes household savings that can be invested in financial assets, leading to capital formation in a country (Ahmad Malik & Yadav, 2022a; Shrestha & Nursamsu, 2021). Ouma et al. (2017) establish that ease of access to financial services through mobile phones promotes household savings among the low-income groups in sub-Saharan Africa. Savings are encouraged both at the individual and national levels thanks to the expanded access to financial services provided by a variety of cutting-edge financial products and instruments (Ahmad & Wongsurawat, 2023; Ahmad Malik & Yadav, 2022b; Azimova & Mollaahmetoglu, 2017: Malik & Yadav, 2022; Malik et al., 2021). However, the study carried out in Ghana by Ansong et al. (2011) revealed that easy access to finance through innovative products stimulates withdrawals rather than savings which resulted in a drop in financial savings in the short run.

There is much discussion surrounding how interest rates affect savings. According to Ando and Modigliani's (1963) life-cycle hypothesis, higher interest rates may encourage households to save more money as they aim to maximize their lifetime utility. Two effects can be separated out of the real interest rate's overall impact on savings. According to the substitution effect, a higher interest rate would make the current price of spending more expensive than the future price, favoring savings. The income effect on the other hand shows that if a household is a net lender, a rise in interest rates will result in a higher lifetime income, which will lead to higher consumption and lower savings. As a result, it is anticipated that the interest rate will only increase the savings ratio when the substitution effect outweighs the income effect. Since the substitution effect is anticipated to outweigh the income effect significantly in developing nations with underdeveloped financial markets, the real interest rate is projected to have a net positive effect on domestic savings. However, the benefits of an increase in interest rates are generally diminished by complexity and distortions in the real and financial aspects of the economy, and as a result, the increase in domestic savings may not have the desired effect (Abou El-Seoud, 2014). The study by Gupta (1987) revealed that real interest rates influence savings rates favorably in Asia but not in Latin America. Similarly, studies by Desroches and Francis (2010), Khan and Sarker (2016), and Ogaki et al. (1996) demonstrated the beneficial effects of interest rates on savings. However, studies by Agrawal et al. (2009), Gleizer (1991), Khatkhate (1988), Nagawa et al. (2020), Ogwumike and Ofoegbu (2012), and Salahuddin and Islam (2008) failed to discover any conclusive evidence of an impact of interest rates on savings leaving the topic up to debate.

Money loses purchasing power as a result of inflation, which may affect how much people save. Savings can be discouraged by high inflation rates because people try to avoid holding on to money that is depreciating in value. Studies by Aleemi et al. (2015), Dash and Kumar (2018), Premik and Stanisławska (2017), and von Ungern-Sternberg (1981), among others, provide empirical evidence in support of the idea that inflation has a negative effect on the rate of savings, but Ariç (2015) and Heer and Süssmuth (2009) could not find any evidence to support this claim.

Other factors that have been highlighted in the literature to affect savings in economies include the current account deficit, trade openness, financial development, money supply, public finances, real disposable income growth, and the aged-dependency ratio (Baharumshah & Thanoon, 2003; Bayar, 2014; Duran et al., 2017; Hondroyiannis, 2006; Horioka & Terada-Hagiwara, 2012; Narayan & Siyabi, 2005; Seraphin & Cesar, 2023). In the Indian context, Agrawal et al. (2010), Ang (2009), Athukorala and Sen (2004), Samantaraya and Patra (2014), and Yadav et al. (2018) are some of the studies that have investigated savings functions to look at the factors that influence savings in the country.

Thus it is evident that the literature is ambiguous regarding the determinants affecting savings in an economy. Therefore, it is important to do additional economic research in this area to identify the variables influencing savings in India so that appropriate savings-promoting policies can be developed.

17.3 Data and Methodology

The current study is based on annual time series data for the period of 1991–2022. Data for the study was obtained from the Reserve Bank of India (RBI) database on the Indian economy, World Bank database, and International financial statistics database of IMF. The data was specifically obtained on variables: saving bank accounts (SBA) per 1000 of population, credit bank accounts (CBA) per 1000 of population, scheduled commercial bank branches (BB) per 1000 population, banking personnel (BE) per 1000 of population, volume of credits (CRE), volume of deposits (DEP), gross savings, real rate of interest, inflation (CPI), and gross domestic product (GDP) per capita.

Since financial inclusion is a multifaceted term, it can be assessed by creating a composite index using a number of different variables. Following Lenka (2022), the study uses principal component index (PCA), which calls for input variables to have a comparable scale of measurement, and therefore, variables are standardized to zero mean and unit variance. Since the index indicators are in different units, the following standardization method has been employed to standardize them:

$$z = \left(X - M\right)/SD$$

where z = standardized value of the input variable; X = actual value of the input variable; M = mean value of the series; SD = standard deviation of the series.

The index is composed of six input variables, viz. SBA per 1000 of population, CBA per 1000 of population, scheduled commercial BB per 1000 population, BE per 1000 of population, CRE, and DEP. The financial inclusion index (FII) can be expressed as follows using the PCA procedure:

$$FII_i = w_{1i}SBA_i + w_{2i}CBA_i + w_{3i}BB_i + w_{4i}BE_i + w_{5i}CRE_i + w_{6i}DEP_i$$

where FII_i is the financial inclusion index of ith year, and w_1, w_2, w_3, ... are the respective weights of factors (indicators) included.

17.3.1 Autoregressive Distributed Lag Model

Autoregressive Distributed Lag (ARDL) is a statistical technique that is used in modeling the variables that are stationary at I(0) or I(1) or a combination of both. In such a situation applying simple cointegration becomes impossible. Pesaran and Shin (1995) and Pesaran and Shin. (1996) proposed ARDL approach of cointegration or bound procedure for analyzing the long-run relationship between the variables which are either level stationary or stationary of first difference or combination of both. Here autoregressive refers to gaps in the dependent variable and distributed lags refer to lags in the independent variable. In economic analysis, ARDL (Pesaran et al.,, 1999; Pesaran et al., 2001), the Granger (1981), Engle and Granger (1987), Johansen and Juselius (1990) cointegration techniques have popularly become the methods for estimating long-run relationships between the variables that are non-stationary as it is simple to apply and easy to interpret and involves just a single equation. ARDL cointegration technique does not require pretests for unit roots unlike other techniques (Nkoro & Uko, 2016). However, it is necessary to carry unit root tests in order to avoid the model crash, in case any of the variables comes out to be I(2). So ARDL model is used to determine the relationship between the variables that are having different order of integration (Pesaran et al., 1999; Pesaran et al., 2001), while the issue of variables having different lags is also sorted out in ARDL technique. The issue of variables having different optimal lags can be dealt with easily while using ARDL, which is impossible to take into account in case of cointegration, which makes ARDL superior to its alternatives (Duasa, 2007). Before applying this statistical method one must make sure that none of the variables is I(2). The basic equation of ARDL can be represented as:

$$y_t = \beta_0 + \beta_1 y_{t-1} + \ldots\ldots + \beta p y_{t-m} + \alpha_0 x_t + \alpha_1 x_{t-1} + \alpha_2 x_{t-2} + \ldots\ldots\ldots + \alpha_q x_{t-n} + \varepsilon_t$$

In the above basic regression function of the ARDL model, m and n refer to the time periods (lags), ε_t is the disturbance term (white noise), β's refers to short-run coefficients, and α's refers to long-run coefficients.

17.3.2 Model Specification

The study is carried out while using the classic gap model developed by OKUN (1962), given as:

$$GS_t = \alpha + \beta_1 FI_t + \beta_2 RR_t + \beta_3 INF_t + \beta_4 PCI_t + \varepsilon_t$$

where GS represents rate of growth of gross savings, FI represents financial inclusion, RR represents real rate of interest, INF represents inflation rate consumer prices, PCI represents per capita income, β's represents the respective coefficients, and Et represents the error term in time period t.

17.4 Empirical Analysis

17.4.1 Unit Root Results

While attempting any econometric analysis, it is imperative to test the stationary nature of underlying variables. For the said purpose augmented dickey fuller test is used (ADF) is used. The results of unit root test presented in Table 17.1 revealed that GDP per capita and inflation are stationary at level while rest of the variables are stationary at first difference.

Keeping in view the results of unit root test which evidenced variables being a combination of I(0) and I(1), ARDL seems to be the optimal choice for model estimation. ARDL involves a whole series of steps and tests that one needs to go through while applying this statistical technique. Bound test is an extension of ARDL modeling which is applied in order to know whether the long-run relationship between the variables exists or not. The bounds test is proposed by Pesaran et al. (2001). This technique uses T- and F-statistic for the said purpose. The long-run relationship is said to exist when the value of F-statistic is greater than the upper bond value. If the F-statistic value comes out to be in between the lower bound and upper bound, the result of the inference is inconclusive and depends on whether the underlying variables are I(0) or I(1). Bound test F-Statistic procedure will be invalid if any variable is I(2) (Chigusiwa et al., 2011). However, according to Narayan (2005), the procedure of Pesaran et al. (2001) is applicable only in situations when the sample size is large. Hence Narayan (2005) developed a procedure for the examination of long-run relationship existence for the small sample size ranging between 30 and 80 observations. Bounds test results presented in Table 17.2 provided sufficient evidence that there exists a long-run relationship between the underlying variables as the F-statistic is greater than upper bond values at 5% level of significance leading to the rejection of null hypothesis.

Table 17.1 Unit root results

Variable	*Level*	*First difference*	*Remark*
Gross savings	−1.569	−2.981**	I(1)
Financial inclusion index	4.897	−4.484*	I(1)
GDP per capita	−5.546*	−7.001*	I(0)
Real rate of interest	−2.593	−7.556*	I(1)
Inflation (CPI)	−6.640*	−8.980*	I(0)

Note: * and ** represent 1% and 5% levels of significance, respectively.

Table 17.2 Bounds test results

F-statistic	*Significance level*	*Lower bond I(0)*	*Upper bond I(1)*	*Null hypothesis*
10.34	10%	2.2	3.09	Rejected
	5%	2.56	3.49	
	1%	3.29	4.37	

Source: Authors' calculation.

17.4.2 Long-Run Results

The long-run results are presented in Table 17.3. After evidenced by bounds test results that there exists a long-run relationship among the variables under consideration, the long-run form of equation is estimated. Long-run results presented in the table reveal that financial inclusion, GDP per capita, and real rate of interest have a positive impact on gross savings with coefficients of 1.36, 0.40, and 0.90, respectively, while inflation has a negative impact on gross savings with a coefficient of −1.42. The findings are in line with the results of Adelakun (2015), Adewuyi et al. (2010), Epaphra (2014), Nwachukwu (2012), and Touny (2008) in the case of GDP per capita, Gupta (1987), Desroches and Francis (2010), Khan and Sarker (2016), and Ogaki et al. (1996) in case of real rate of interest, and Burgess and Pande (2005) and Demirgüç-Kunt and Klapper (2012) in case of financial inclusion.

17.4.3 Short-Run Results

Short-run estimation presented in Table 17.4, almost in line with long-run results, reveals that financial inclusion has a positive association with growth rate of savings, where 1% increase in financial inclusion increases savings by 2.09, GDP per capita has a positive but insignificant impact while real rate of interest and inflation have negative impacts on gross savings in the short run, showing that 1% increase in real rate of interest and inflation decreases gross savings by –0.33 and –0.24, respectively.

Error correction results show a statistically significant association between the study's variables and the lagged error correction representation (ECMt 1), pointing to a possible relationship between them. The rate of transition from short-run disequilibrium to long-run equilibrium is shown by the coefficient of –0.27. Accordingly, adjustments are rectified by 0.27% annually. A bigger error term causes

Table 17.3 Long-run estimates

Variable	*Coefficient*	*Standard error*	*t-statistic*	*Probability*
FI	*1.36*	*0.46*	*–5.65*	*0.000*
RR	*0.90*	*0.34*	*–6.50*	*0.000*
INF	*–1.42*	*0.28*	*–5.03*	*0.000*
PCI	*0.40*	*0.20*	*–3.08*	*0.036*

Source: Authors' calculations.

Table 17.4 ECM and short-run estimates

Variable	*Coefficient*	*Standard error*	*t-statistic*	*Probability*
DFI	2.09	0.538	5.52	0.000
DRR	–0.33	0.058	–5.69	0.000
DINF	–0.24	0.053	–4.54	0.000
DPCI	0.05	0.054	1.01	0.320
Coint Eq. (–1)	–0.27	0.031	–8.80	0.000
R-Square		Adjusted R-Square		
0.97		0.96		

Source: Authors' calculations.

economies to regain equilibrium more quickly. The change in dependent variable can be described by the independent variables in 96% of cases, with R-Square being 0.97, however adjusted R-Square value is 0.96. Overall, the findings indicate that the study's model is reliable and well fitted.

17.4.4 Sensitivity Estimates

Results presented in Table 17.5 reveal that there is no serial correlation in the model, confirmed by Breusch–Godfrey serial correlation L.M. test. Besides, to check for autoregressive conditional heteroscedasticity, Breusch–Pagan–Godfrey and Glejser were run. The results revealed that there is no sign of heteroscedasticity as the values of *F*-statistics being greater than 0.05, which indicates a 5% significance level. Thus, these findings represent that the model is the best fit and perfect.

17.4.5 Stability Estimate

This test is applied to check whether the model is stable or does it possess any structural breaks. Here structural break refers to a sudden jump or fall in the time series that occurs due to regime shift or external shock. There are various tests apart from the Cusum test which can be applied to know about that, which does include Chou test, Durban Watson test, etc. There is a rule of thumb in Cusum test for concluding whether the model is stable or not. If the blue line in the plot of Cusum test is found to be inside the two red lines therein, one can conclude that the model is

Table 17.5 Sensitivity Estimates

	*Obs*R-Square*	*F-statistic*	*Probability*
Breusch–Godfrey serial *correlation LM test*	*0.655*	*0.21*	*0.72*
Heteroskedasticity test Breusch–Pagan–Godfrey	*6.00*	*0.66*	*0.64*
Heteroskedasticity test Glejser	*3.651*	*1.140*	*0.34*

Source: Authors' calculations.

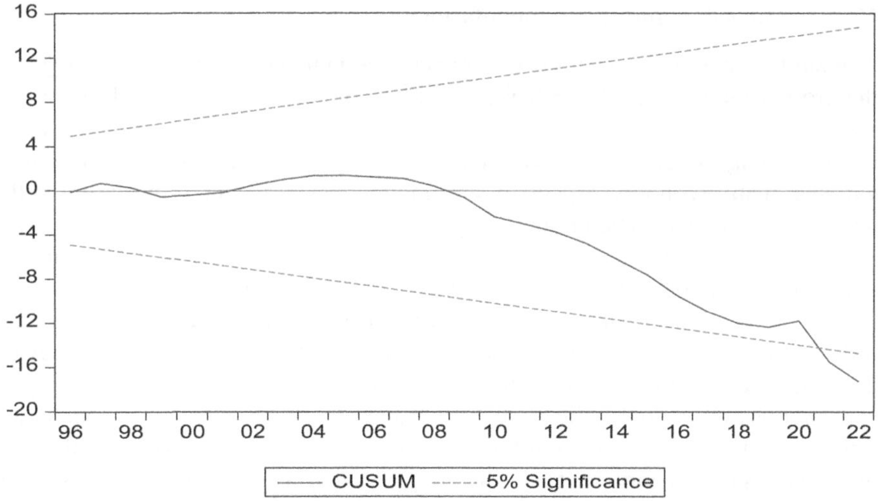

Figure 17.1 Cusum

stable at 5% level of significance and hence does not possess any structural shift. These two red lines indicate the level of significance of 5% (Figures 17.1 and 17.2).

Stability estimates reveal that the model used in the study is stable and free from any structural break. The results of these tests add further confidence to the robustness and reliability of the findings obtained from the econometric analysis. By employing these advanced stability tests, the study ensures that the underlying model's relationship between variables remains consistent and reliable throughout.

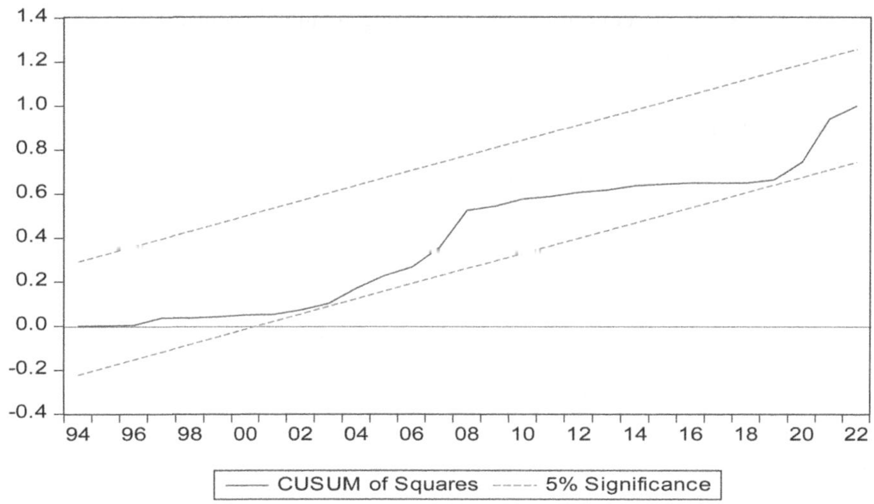

Figure 17.2 Cusum squares

17.5 Conclusion and Recommendations

This study attempted to examine the impact of certain macroeconomic variables on the gross saving rate in the Indian economy in the post-reform period. It emphasizes the role of financial inclusion, income levels and inflation, and rate of interest in shaping the country's saving habits. Saving rate being an important policy variable in any economy, especially developing ones, it is vital to nurture it in the best possible manner. The findings of the study can aid and strengthen the existing literature on the particular matter. Based on the findings of the study it would be suggested that in order to encourage savings rates and ensure stability policymakers should focus on initiatives that improve access to financial services and control inflation. It is essential to expand banking services in rural areas to promote saving and financial security. Additionally, implementing financial education programs can empower individuals with knowledge that motivates them to save. Maintaining inflation control policies is vital for safeguarding the value of savings. Balancing interest rates is also important as it encourages saving while promoting investment. Lastly, policymakers should prioritize strategies that foster economic growth and increase, per capita income as these factors play a role in encouraging savings.

17.6 Policy Implications

The study's findings emphasize the critical importance of enhancing financial inclusion, controlling inflation, and sustaining economic growth for fostering higher savings rates in India. To achieve this, policymakers should prioritize expanding access to banking services, promoting digital financial solutions, implementing financial literacy programs, and maintaining stable real interest rates. Additionally, focusing on inclusive, long-term savings options, regular monitoring and evaluation, and learning from global best practices can further bolster the stability and growth of the Indian economy while promoting financial security and future economic development.

Conflict of Interest

We ratify that both the authors of the manuscript have no conflicts of interest to declare.

Acknowledgement

We are thankful to both the editors for giving us this opportunity to contribute to this book. Also we are thankful to reviewers for their comments which made this work more concrete and insightful.

Funding

No funding has been received for this research work.

Contribution

This research work is a result of joint efforts from both the authors.

Data Availability

The data will be available on request.

References

Abou El-Seoud, M. S. (2014). The effect of interest rate, inflation rate, and GDP on national savings rate. *Global Journal of Economics and Management Perspective*, *3*(3), 1–7.

Adelakun, O. J. (2015). An investigation of the determinants of savings and investment in Nigeria. *International Economics and Business*, *1*(2), 1–16.

Adewuyi, A. O., Bankole, A. S., & Arawomo, D. F. (2010). What determines saving in the economic community of West African State (ECOWAS). *Journal of Monetary and Economic Integration*, *10*(2), 71–99.

Agrawal, P., Sahoo, P., & Dash, R. K. (2009). Savings behaviour in South Asia. *Journal of Policy Modeling*, *31*(2), 208–224.

Agrawal, P., Sahoo, P., & Dash, R. K. (2010). Savings behavior in India: Co-integration and causality evidence. *The Singapore Economic Review*, *55*(02), 273–295..

Ahmad Malik, F., & Yadav, D. K. (2022a). Financial inclusion schemes and changing socio economic status of poorest of the poor. In *Financial inclusion schemes in India* (pp. 109–130). Singapore: Springer Nature Singapore.

Ahmad Malik, F., & Yadav, D. K. (2022b). Impact of recent financial inclusion schemes on status of financial inclusion in India: Secondary data analysis. In *Financial inclusion schemes in India* (pp. 37–51). Singapore: Springer Nature Singapore.

Ahmad, S. W., & Wongsurawat, W. (2023). Mobile financial services and household welfare in a developing economy: Boon and bane. *Journal of Science and Technology Policy Management*, *14*(6), 1–20.

Aleemi, A. R., Ahmed, S., & Tariq, M. (2015). The determinants of savings: Empirical evidence from Pakistan. *International Journal of Management Sciences and Business Research*, *4*(1), 63–71.

Ando, A., & Modigliani, F. (1963). The "life cycle" hypothesis of saving: Aggregate implications and tests. *The American Economic Review*, *53*(1), 55–84.

Ang, J. (2009). Household saving behaviour in an extended life cycle model: A comparative study of China and India. *Journal of Development Studies*, *45*(8), 1344–1359.

Ang, J. B., & Sen, K. (2011). Private saving in India and Malaysia compared: The roles of financial liberalization and expected pension benefits. *Empirical Economics*, *41*, 247–267.

Ansong, A., Marfo-Yiadom, E., & Ekow-Asmah, E. (2011). The effects of financial innovation on financial savings: Evidence from an economy in transition. *Journal of African Business*, *12*(1), 93–113.

Ariç, K. H. (2015). Determinants of savings in the APEC countries. *Theoretical & Applied Economics*, *22*(2), 113–122.

Athukorala, P. C., & Sen, K. (2004). The determinants of private saving in India. *World Development*, *32*(3), 491–503.

Azimova, T., & Mollaahmetoglu, E. (2017). Innovation in financial markets and its impact on savings. *Journal of Business Economics and Finance*, *6*(2), 147–154.

Baharumshah, A. Z., & Thanoon, M. A. (2003). Determinants of gross national saving in Malaysia: A macroeconomic analysis 1960–2000. *Savings and Development*, *27*(4), 421–440.

Bashir, M. F., Shahzad, U., Latif, S., & Bashir, M. (2015). The nexus between economic indicators and economic growth in Brazil. *Nexus*, *13*(1), 1–8.
Bayar, Y. (2014). Financial development and domestic savings in emerging Asian countries. *Theoretical & Applied Economics*, *21*(7), 55–66.
Bhatia, G. K., & Tyagi, M. (2018). An impact of socio-economic factors on saving behaviour of individuals. *Asian Journal of Management*, *9*(1), 64–68.
Burgess, R., & Pande, R. (2005). Do rural banks matter? Evidence from the Indian social banking experiment. *American Economic Review*, *95*(3), 780–795.
Chaturvedi, V., Dholakia, R. H., & Kumar, B. (2009). Inter-relationship between economic growth, savings and inflation in Asia. *Journal of International Economic Studies*, *23*, 1–22.
Chigusiwa, L., Bindu, S., Mudavanhu, V., Muchabaiwa, L., & Mazambani, D. (2011). Export-led growth hypothesis in Zimbabwe: Does export composition matter?. *International Journal of Economic Research*, *2*(4), 111–129.
Dash, S. K., & Kumar, L. (2018). Does inflation affect savings non-linearly? Evidence from India. *Margin: The Journal of Applied Economic Research*, *12*(4), 431–457.
Demirgüç-Kunt, A., & Klapper, L. F. (2012). Financial inclusion in Africa: An overview. *World Bank policy research working paper* (6088).
Desroches, B., & Francis, M. (2010). World real interest rates: A global savings and investment perspective. *Applied Economics*, *42*(22), 2801–2816.
Duasa, J. (2007). Determinants of Malaysian trade balance: An ARDL bound testing approach. *Global Economic Review*, *36*(1), 89–102.
Duran, E., Uzgur Duran, B., Akay, D., & Boran, F. E. (2017). Grey relational analysis between Turkey's macroeconomic indicators and domestic savings. *Grey Systems: Theory and Application*, *7*(1), 45–59.
Engle, R. F., & Granger, C. W. (1987). Co-integration and error correction: Representation, estimation, and testing. *Econometrica: Journal of the Econometric Society*, *55*(2), 251–276.
Epaphra, M. (2014). Empirical investigation of the determinants of Tanzania's national savings. *Journal of Economics and Development Studies*, *2*(4), 223–241.
Filipiak, U., Grohmann, A., & Heyerhorst, F. (2017). Female empowerment, cultural effects and savings: Empirical evidence from India, *Universitat Gottingen* Discussion Paper No. 234
Gleizer, D. L. (1991). Saving and real interest rates in Brazil. *Brazilian Review of Econometrics*, *11*(1), 63–92.
Granger, C. W. (1981). Some properties of time series data and their use in econometric model specification. *Journal of Econometrics*, *16*(1), 121–130.
Gupta, K. L. (1987). Aggregate savings, financial intermediation, and interest rate. *The Review of Economics and Statistics*, *69*(2), 303–311.
Harrod, R. F. (1939). An essay in dynamic theory. *The Economic Journal*, *49*(193), 14–33.
Heer, B., & Süssmuth, B. (2009). The savings-inflation puzzle. *Applied Economics Letters*, *16*(6), 615–617.
Hondroyiannis, G. (2006). Private saving determinants in European countries: A panel cointegration approach. *The Social Science Journal*, *43*(4), 553–569.
Horioka, C. Y., & Terada-Hagiwara, A. (2012). The determinants and long-term projections of saving rates in developing Asia. *Japan and the World Economy*, *24*(2), 128–137.
Jain, N., & Goli, S. (2022). Demographic change and private savings in India. *Journal of Social and Economic Development*, *24*(1), 1–29.
Jangili, R. (2011). Causal relationship between saving, investment and economic growth for India – what does the relation imply? *Reserve Bank of India Occasional Papers*, *32*(1), 25–39.
Johansen, S., & Juselius, K. (1990). Maximum likelihood estimation and inference on cointegration—with applications to the demand for money. *Oxford Bulletin of Economics and Statistics*, *52*(2), 169–210.

Keynes, J. M. (1936). *The general theory of employment, interest and money*. New York: Harcourt, Brace.

Khan, M. I., Khan, M. K., Rehan, M., & Abasimi, I. (2018). Determinants of gross domestic saving: An evidence from Asian countries. *Economic Research*, *2*(10), 1–14.

Khan, A., & Sarker, S. (2016). Determinants of gross domestic savings in Bangladesh: evidence from time series analysis. In *Proceedings of Dhaka International Business and Social Science Research Conference, Westin Hotel and Uttara University, Dhaka, Bangladesh* (Vol. 333, p. 352).

Khan, M. I., Teng, J. Z., Khan, M. K., Jadoon, A. U., & Rehan, M. U. H. A. M. M. A. D. (2017). Factors affecting the rate of gross domestic saving in different countries. *European Academic Research*, *5*(8), 42–62.

Khatkhate, D. R. (1988). Assessing the impact of interest rates in less developed countries. *World Development*, *16*(5), 577–588.

Lenka, S. K. (2022). Relationship between financial inclusion and financial development in India: Is there any link? *Journal of Public Affairs*, *22*, e2722.

Lewis, W. A. (2013). The Theory of Economic Growth. Richard D. Irwin, Routledge: Homewood, IL.

Malik, F. A., & Yadav, D. K. (2022). *Financial inclusion schemes in India*. Springer.

Malik, F. A., Yadav, D. K., Adam, H., & Omrane, A. (2020). The urban poor and their financial behavior: A case study of slum dwellers in Lucknow (India). In *Sustainable entrepreneurship, renewable energy-based projects, and digitalization* (pp. 305–315). CRC Press.

Malik, F. A., Yadav, D. K., Lone, N. A., & Adam, H. (2021). An investigation into the dynamics of financial inclusion in south Asian countries. *Pakistan Economic and Social Review*, *59*(2), 231.

Mowafy, M. A. A. S., & Ela, H. H. A. A. (2020). Using The ARDL and ECM Models to Measure the Impact of Financial and Monetary Policies on the Domestic Saving in Egypt. *Far East Journal of Theoretical Statistics*, *58*(1), 37–58.

Nagawa, V., Wasswa, F., & Bbaale, E. (2020). Determinants of gross domestic savings in Uganda: An autoregressive distributed lag (ARDL) approach to cointegration. *Journal of Economic Structures*, *9*(1), 1–19.

Narayan, P. K. (2005). The saving and investment nexus for China: Evidence from cointegration tests. *Applied Economics*, *37*(17), 1979–1990.

Narayan, P., & Siyabi, S. A. (2005). An empirical investigation of the determinants of Oman's national savings. *Economics Bulletin*, *3*(51), 1–7.

Nkoro, E., & Uko, A. K. (2016). Autoregressive distributed lag (ARDL) cointegration technique: Application and interpretation. *Journal of Statistical and Econometric Methods*, *5*(4), 63–91.

Nwachukwu, T. (2012). Determinants of private saving in Nigeria. *Journal of Monetary and Economic Integration*, *11*(2), 83–106.

Okun, A.M. (1962). Potential GNP: Its measurement and significance. In *Proceedings of the business and economics statistics*, Washington, DC: American Statistical Association, 98–104.

Ogaki, M., Ostry, J. D., & Reinhart, C. M. (1996). Saving behavior in low-and middle-income developing countries: A comparison. *Staff Papers*, *43*(1), 38–71.

Ogwumike, F. O., & Ofoegbu, D. I. (2012). Financial liberalisation and domestic savings in Nigeria. *The Social Sciences*, *7*(4), 635–646.

Ouma, S. A., Odongo, T. M., & Were, M. (2017). Mobile financial services and financial inclusion: Is it a boon for savings mobilization? *Review of Development Finance*, *7*(1), 29–35.

Patra, S. K., Murthy, D. S., Kuruva, M. B., & Mohanty, A. (2017). Revisiting the causal nexus between savings and economic growth in India: An empirical analysis. *Economia*, *18*(3), 380–391.

Pesaran, M. H., & Shin, Y. (1995). *An autoregressive distributed lag modelling approach to cointegration analysis* (Vol. 9514). Cambridge, UK: Department of Applied Economics, University of Cambridge.

Pesaran, M. H., Shin, Y., & Smith, R. P. (1999). Pooled mean group estimation of dynamic heterogeneous panels. *Journal of the American statistical Association*, *94*(446), 621–634.

Pesaran, M. H., Shin, Y., & Smith, R. J. (2001). Bounds testing approaches to the analysis of level relationships. *Journal of Applied Econometrics*, *16*(3), 289–326.

Pesaran, M. H., & Shin, Y. (1996). Cointegration and speed of convergence to equilibrium. *Journal of Econometrics*, *71*(1–2), 117–143.

Premik, F., & Stanisławska, E. (2017). The impact of inflation expectations on Polish consumers' spending and saving. *Eastern European Economics*, *55*(1), 3–28.

Ribaj, A., & Mexhuani, F. (2021). The impact of savings on economic growth in a developing country (the case of Kosovo). *Journal of Innovation and Entrepreneurship*, *10*, 1–13.

Salahuddin, M., & Islam, M. R. (2008). Factors affecting investment in developing countries: A panel data study. *The Journal of Developing Areas*, *42*(1), 21–37.

Samantaraya, A., & Patra, S. K. (2014). Determinants of household savings in India: An empirical analysis using ARDL approach. *Economics Research International*, *2014*, 1–8.

Samuelson, P. A., & Modigliani, F. (1966). The Pasinetti paradox in neoclassical and more general models. *The Review of Economic Studies*, *33*(4), 269–301.

Seraphin, P. Y., & Cesar, K. Y. (2023). Analysis of the determinants of domestic savings in the WAEMU. *International Journal of Business and Management*, *16*(9), 1–71.

Shrestha, R., & Nursamsu, S. (2021). Financial inclusion and savings in Indonesia. In *Financial inclusion in Asia and beyond: Measurement, development gaps, and economic consequences* (Vol. 344, pp. 227–250). Routledge.

Solow, R. M. (1956). A contribution to the theory of economic growth. *The Quarterly Journal of Economics*, *70*(1), 65–94.

Solow, R. M. (1970). Growth theory: An exposition. Cambridge University Press, London.

Teeli, A. A., Wani, S. H., & Reshi, A. H. (2023). Determinants of total factor productivity in India: An econometric analysis. *Statistika: Statistics & Economy Journal*, *103*(4).

Touny, M. A. (2008). Determinants of domestic saving performance in Egypt: An empirical study. *Journal of Commercial Studies and Researches*, *1*, 1–23.

von Ungern-Sternberg, T. (1981). Inflation and savings: International evidence on inflation-induced income losses. *The Economic Journal*, *91*(364), 961–976.

Yadav, I. S., Goyari, P., & Mishra, R. K. (2018). Saving, investment and growth in India: Evidence from cointegration and causality tests. *Economic Alternatives*, *1*, 55–68.

18 Financial Inclusion in Emerging Market

A Synthesis of Theory and Practicality

Tarika Singh Sikarwar, Firdous Ahmad Malik, and Nidhi Jain

18.1 Introduction

Financial inclusion is currently a buzzword and has recently garnered international attention. According to King, (Ouma, S. A., et al 2017), "financial inclusion" is a process that assures all members of an economy have easy access to, availability of, and utilisation of the formal financial system. Access to finance by the poor and vulnerable groups is necessary for poverty reduction, employment, economic progress, and social cohesion and will empower the inhabitants of developing and undeveloped countries. India is an economy in development. According to The Hindu's Census Report, more than 70 per cent of the Indian population resides in rural areas, making this problem even more significant. This word also refers to the provision of inexpensive financial services to economically disadvantaged parts of society, such as credit availability and banking services. It provides financial assistance to low-income community members at low prices. Multiple institutions, including microfinance institutions, regional rural banks, and payment banks, have attempted to provide financial services at the nearest locations. Financial inclusion in rural India has progressed since January 2020. Government programmes such as Pradhan Mantri Jan Dhan Yojana (PMJDY), Pradhan Mantri Mudra Yojana (PMMY), Atal Pension Yojana (APY), and Rashtriya Swasthya Bima Yojana (RSBY), among others, have been established to aid economically disadvantaged individuals. Children, the elderly, low-income parts of society, and women, particularly in rural areas, are the deprived individuals who are financially excluded. The base of the pyramid of unbanked people is in the mainstream, and the government of India has taken a few steps to provide financial services at an accessible price. This paper is an attempt to synthesise the work on financial inclusion in emerging economies, beginning with understanding the various theories of financial inclusion, factors affecting financial inclusion in emerging markets, regulations, reforms, the most recent financial inclusion models developed, and the conclusion and implications of the work.

18.2 Theories of Financial Inclusion

Inclusion fosters the premise that everyone is entitled to access and the opportunity for success. Individuals advocating for inclusion argue that it will increase social contact at all levels of human interaction and help people respect diversity, fostering an accepting

DOI: 10.4324/9781032655185-24

society (Clark et al., 1999; Mallory & New, 1994). Through inclusion, individuals will encounter individuals and groups who believe and behave differently from them, and they will need to learn how to get along with and collaborate with these individuals and groups. Financial inclusion is a complex problem influenced by various political, geographical, economic, sociological, and psychological factors. Several ideas and approaches are employed to describe and analyse the issue. These ideas explain not only financial inclusion but also financial exclusion. Financial exclusion, like other types of exclusion, has a theoretical basis (Buckland, 2012). The complex subject of financial exclusion has been investigated from various theoretical perspectives, including neoclassical economic, institutional, and political economy theories. These exclusion theories can be broadly classified as either economic (such as new-Keynesian theory and neoclassical economic theory) or interdisciplinary (i.e., behavioural economics, institutional theories, political-economy theories, poverty and community-based analyses, geographic spatial analyses, and household economy). Institutional behaviour and human reason are the two significant presumptions. Buckland (2012) put these ideas into rationalist institutional "space." The alternative rational choice theory, commonly known as choice theory or reasonable action theory, is a framework for understanding and typically replicating both individual and group behaviour.

After financial inclusion, social constructivism theory helps explain inclusion. According to the social constructivist approach, language is used to build reality in social interactions and is primarily influenced by biological characteristics, the past, society, and culture (Berger & Luckmann, 1977). It demonstrates that nature and nurture have a role in forming people's perceptions of reality by emphasising how cultural and biological variables interact to shape people's views of reality (Teater, 2015). According to the social constructivist perspective, a person's likelihood of equal access to and opportunities in all aspects of society depends primarily on biological variables (individual characteristics and eccentricities) and societal forces that restrict or promote inclusion. The social constructivist theory has implications for financial inclusion, indicating that physical and other social traits that favour or oppose financial inclusion may influence an individual's propensity to have access to funding in the formal financial sector. Natural features, such as health problems, physical ability or handicap, behavioural traits, and habits, can either hinder or promote financial inclusion. Social factors such as culture, customs, language, education, entrepreneurial potential, a language barrier, and religious belief can also make financial inclusion more challenging to attain.

Present-day financial inclusion research is founded on the proposed economic interconnectedness ratio (Goldsmith, 1975). Goldsmith (1975) utilised this ratio to illustrate how a more significant client base could contribute to financial system penetration (Nwidobie, 2019). The four fundamental financial inclusion theories – welfare, monetary, regulatory, and development –are based on measuring variables used to determine and gauge the level of financial inclusion in each country (Nwidobie, 2019). According to these views, there are supply- and demand-side indicators of financial inclusion. According to financial inclusion theories, inequality and economic growth are directly connected with financial inclusion (Ozili, 2020). Inclusion is a civil rights concept that advocates for equitable access and equal opportunity for all individuals. Proponents of inclusion, or those who favour inclusion, claim that inclusion will promote social connection at all levels of human contact and that these interactions allow individuals to comprehend diversity, hence fostering an open-minded society (Clark et al., 1999; Mallory & New, 1994). Persons will be exposed to individuals and groups that do not share their beliefs and behaviours and will need to learn how to work with and interact with them.

Financial inclusion is a complex topic comprising various psychological, sociological, geographical, economic, and political elements. Numerous theories and methodologies are utilised to describe and analyse this topic. Specifically, neoclassical economic, institutional, and political economy theories have been used to investigate the complicated phenomenon of financial exclusion. Financial exclusion has a similar theoretical foundation (Buckland, 2012), and the exclusion theories fall into two broad categories: economic (i.e., neoclassical and new-Keynesian) and interdisciplinary (i.e., behavioural economics, institutional approaches, political-economy ideas, poverty and community-based analyses, geographic and spatial analyses, and household economy). The two most important assumptions are human rationality and the function of institutions. Buckland (2012) contextualised these theories within the institutional nationalist framework. The alternative rational choice theory, often known as choice theory or reasonable action theory, is a framework for analysing and frequently modelling individual, societal, and economic behaviour.

Social constructivist theory aids in comprehending inclusion, followed by financial inclusion. The social constructivist theory asserts that reality is formed through biological processes and the use of language in social interactions, primarily influenced by biological features, history, society, and culture (Berger & Luckmann, 1966; Teater, 2015). It emphasises that cultural and natural variables contribute to the formation of a person's reality or that reality construction is influenced by both nature and nurture (Teater, 2015). The social constructivist theory has implications for inclusion, namely that an individual's propensity to have equal rights (or access) and equal opportunities in all aspects of society largely depends on biological factors (individual traits and idiosyncrasies) and social factors that impede or facilitate inclusion (Ozili, 2021). The social constructivist theory also has implications for financial inclusion, namely that a person's inclination to have access to finance in the formal financial sector may be influenced by biological traits and other social factors that restrict or facilitate financial inclusion. Natural characteristics, such as health issues, physical ability or disability, behavioural attributes, and behaviours, might determine or permit financial inclusion. Social variables such as culture, customs, language, education, entrepreneurial skill, a language barrier, and religious conviction can also impede financial inclusion. The proposed financial interconnectedness ratio (Goldsmith, 1975) is the basis for contemporary financial inclusion research. Goldsmith (1975) used this ratio to demonstrate that financial system penetration is possible by expanding the client base (Nwidobie, 2019). Each of the four identified financial inclusion theories, namely the welfare, monetary, regulatory, and development theories (Nwidobie, 2019), is based on metrics for determining and assessing the level of financial inclusion in each country. The financial inclusion metrics are derived from both the supply and demand sides of the market.

The ideas of financial inclusion demonstrate a clear relationship between inequality and economic prosperity (Ozili, 2020).

18.3 Factors Affecting Financial Inclusion in Emerging Markets

A review of existing literature is conducted to understand the background of financial exclusion. According to the literature, there are two types of financial exclusion (Figure 18.1): voluntary and involuntary (Jaramillo et al., 2013). The concept of supply and demand for financial services has developed the fundamental equations of access and non-access (Talledo, 2015). Determinants of financial inclusion are defined by the supply of financial services, price, and consumer income. This mechanism is quite similar to the concept of demand for a product by a consumer. As we all know, demand for a commodity or product is based on its price and income at a particular time (Dymski, 2005). The trade-off is only possible if demand and supply meet at a point that benefits producers and consumers, called market demand in economics. The market demand is a defined line that qualifies people for access or non-access to financial services. The other reasons are financial illiteracy, cultural barriers, a lack of need, and perceptions of individual creditworthiness, which may all contribute to financial access and usage restrictions on the demand side.

In terms of financial inclusion, financial institutions help to allocate resources efficiently, theoretically lowering the cost of capital and reducing the rise of informal loan sources (Ardic et al., 2011; Sarma & Pais, 2011; Sotomayor et al., 2018). Access to competent financial services can also help daily financial management (Allen et al., 2016). Lack of access to official financial institutions makes it difficult for the poor to save money, accumulate assets, and invest in income-generating initiatives. For more equitable economic systems, the focus has shifted from financial sector expansion to factors of access depth and breadth (Aparicio et al., 2016; Hannig & Jansen, 2010). Adults without bank accounts, approximately 1.4 billion of them, cite a lack of finances, distance to the nearest financial institution, and missing documentation as the primary reasons. Governments, telecommunications firms, and financial services firms must invest in rules and governance to ensure that all people can access simple products and services (Demirguc-Kunt et al., 2022). In developing economies, 64 per cent of unbanked people claimed they could not open an account at a financial institution without assistance. In Brazil, unbanked

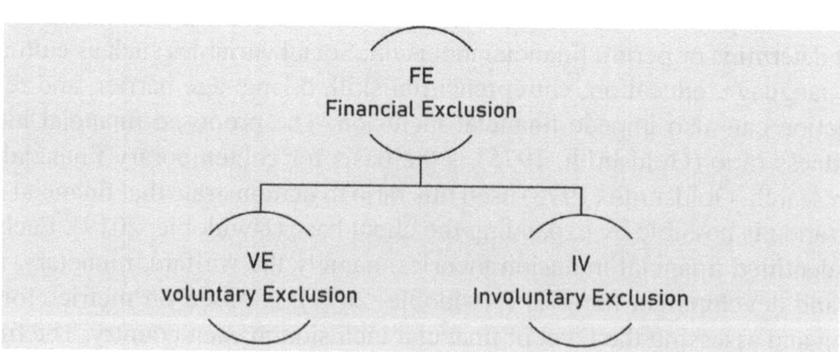

Figure 18.1 Financial exclusion

women are 31 percentage points more likely than unbanked men to indicate that they would require assistance opening a bank account. Governments must set and implement consumer protection legislation. Financial service providers must ensure that staff and agents offer comprehensive and correct information (Demirguc-Kunt et al., 2022). All users, particularly those with limited reading and numeracy skills, must have access to and afford digital financial services. Governments must ensure that adequate rules and consumer protection safeguards are in place to ensure that all users can benefit from digital financial services (Demirguc-Kunt et al., 2022).

18.4 Regulations

Ozili (2018) investigated the growth of digital finance in emerging economies and concluded that it does not benefit those who do not have smartphones or other digital devices; the introduction of the technology is critical, as coerced adoption may result in an unwilling population to use it. There is no substitute for an in-depth examination of an applicant's abilities, expertise, and capacity to manage their organisation. Banerjee et al. (2019) argue similarly. Additionally, it is critical to stress that, aside from these two studies, the launch of mobile applications and the extension of statewide 4G networks will not impact eliminating financial exclusion. According to research, poverty has a detrimental effect on financial inclusion (unfulfilled basic requirements). That reaffirms that unmet demands affect asset ownership and, consequently, one's ability to engage in the financial markets Ozili, (2021). The more money you have, the more likely you will be able to enter the financial industry.

18.5 Reforms

Financial inclusion is working to combat financial exclusion so that poverty is eliminated globally. Global organisations such as the World Bank initiate policies and programmes aimed at alleviating poverty. The IMF, the Asian Development Bank, and many other organisations are jointly working with countries, NGOs, and private and public organisations for the welfare of the people. Similarly, each country is following its own strategies to tackle the problem of financial exclusion by announcing programmes and schemes. Scientists, researchers, policymakers, academicians, and bureaucrats are drafting policies to benefit poor people. Most of the policies, particularly financial inclusion policies, are supply-driven. They are following institutional settings and targeting exclusion. They are targeting the problem, like providing good food to a sick person, but instead of the ill person needing the proper treatment, they are boasting with temporary solutions, like poor people needing income to buy financial services; the institutions are significant across the world and are providing him money for the time being. The disease of sickness remains, the problem remains, and poverty exists. The cell phone has a significantly greater impact on access to finance than the banking system. Cheap and ubiquitous Internet connectivity is necessary for ongoing development. Financial education programmes are one of the strategies to consider. The gender gap in financial access has shrunk, yet it still exists (Table 18.1) (Demirguc-Kunt et al., 2022).

Table 18.1 Summary of previous studies

	Factors affecting financial inclusion in emerging markets			
	Author	*Theme*	*Methodology*	*Conclusion*
1	Yangdol and Sarma (2019)	Demand-side factors for financial inclusion: A cross-country empirical analysis	Financial inclusion, logistic regression model	Negative associations exist between women, less education, unemployment, and poverty with the financial inclusion of individuals
2	Alam et al. (2017)	Measuring financial condition of urban local government: A study of municipalities in Bangladesh	Composite index	Regional differences in financial inclusion
3	Bozkurt et al. (2018)	Spatial determinants of financial inclusion over time	Index of financial inclusion, Global Moran's Index.	Social, banking, and political factors are crucial in determining the direction of progress in financial inclusion
4	Ozturk and Ullah (2022)	Does digital financial inclusion matter for economic growth and environmental sustainability in OBRI economies? An empirical analysis	Pooled ordinary least squares (OLS), two-stage least squares (2SLS), and generalised method of moments (GMM) approaches	Digital financial inclusion increases economic growth but diminishes environmental quality due to a rise in CO2 emissions
5	Lee et al. (2022)	Financial aid and financial inclusion: Does risk uncertainty matter?	Ordinary least square (OLS) and fixed effect (FE) regression model	Financial assistance is a crucial predictor of a company's and nation's financial inclusion
6	Demir et al. (2022)	Fintech, financial inclusion, and income inequality: a quantile regression approach	Quantile regression model	Financial inclusion is an essential FinTech conduit for reducing income inequality
7	Khera et al. (2022)	Measuring digital financial inclusion in emerging market and developing economies: a new index	Digital financial inclusion index	Adoption of digital financial services has been a crucial factor in the advancement of financial inclusion

(Continued)

Table 18.1 (Continued)

	Author	*Theme*	*Methodology*	*Conclusion*
Financial inclusion reforms and regulations				
8	Besong et al. (2022)	An empirical analysis of the impact of banking regulations on sustainable financial inclusion in the CEMAC region	Financial inclusion ndex Panel regression model	Banking regulation positively impacts financial incl
9	Ofoeda (2022)	Anti-money laundering regulations and financial inclusion: empirical evidence across the globe	Panel regression model	Below the threshold of AML regulations, financial inclusion is aided by AML laws, however over the threshold, AML requirements are detrimental to Financial Inclusion.
10	Yakubi et al. (2022)	The Impact of Digital Technology and Business Regulations on Financial Inclusion and Socio-Economic Development in Low-Income Countries	Structural equation modelling (SEM)	Financial inclusion as a means to an end
11	Malik et al. (2022)	Financial stability of Asian nations: governance quality and financial inclusion	GMM estimations; principal component analysis (PCA)	The relationship between governance quality and financial stability is mediated by financial inclusion
12	Senyo et al. (2022)	FinTech ecosystem practices shaping financial inclusion: the case of mobile money in Ghana	Theoretical sampling approach	Financial inclusion is being scaled and developed in terms of players, connections, and practices in developing nations
13	Tian and Li (2022)	Impact of financial inclusion and globalisation on environmental quality: evidence from G20 economies. Environmental Science and Pollution Research, 1-12	PCA; autoregressive distributed lag (CS-ARDL) VECM Granger causality method	Governments must integrate financial inclusion objectives with renewable energy consumption patterns and environmental policies

(Continued)

Table 18.1 (Continued)

	Author	*Theme*	*Methodology*	*Conclusion*
14	Khan et al. (2021)	Does financial inclusion induce poverty, income inequality, and financial stability: empirical evidence from the 54 African countries? *Journal of Economic Studies*	Multiple regressions across an unbalanced panel	Financial inclusion is a valuable indicator; it reduces poverty and income inequality while enhancing financial stability

Explain the persistence of poverty as one of the fundamental reasons for financial exclusion (Caplan et al., 2021; Lyons & Kass-Hanna, 2021; Mosley & Lenton, 2011). The reasons for financial exclusion are voluntary and involuntary (Mahalika et al., 2021; Mossie, 2022; Motta & Gonzalez Farias, 2022). We are more interested in understanding involuntary exclusion (Andani, 2021). The backdrop of involuntary exclusion is due to a policy mismatch between supply and demand (Jin, 2022; Jungo et al., 2022; Singh & Stakic, 2021). The suggested model recommends treatment to overcome policy-oriented bottlenecks (Figures 18.2–18.6). We also need inclusive development programmes or schemes that meet the needs of excluded people (Aziz & Naima, 2021; Pradhan et al., 2021). Existing literature and studies show that development programmes alleviate poverty, and financial inclusion promotes financial inclusion (Huang et al., 2021; Ozili, 2021, October). As poverty is reduced, so is financial exclusion, which aids financial inclusion.

Problems of risk and uncertainty like earthquakes, tsunamis, floods, economic crises, inflation, health problems like the spread of viruses, COVID 19, and other

Financial Inclusion Model (Malik F.A.& Singh. Tarika, 2022)

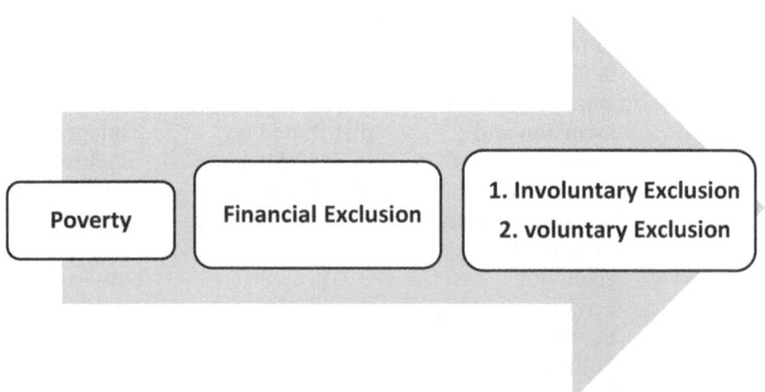

Figure 18.2 Reasons for financial exclusion

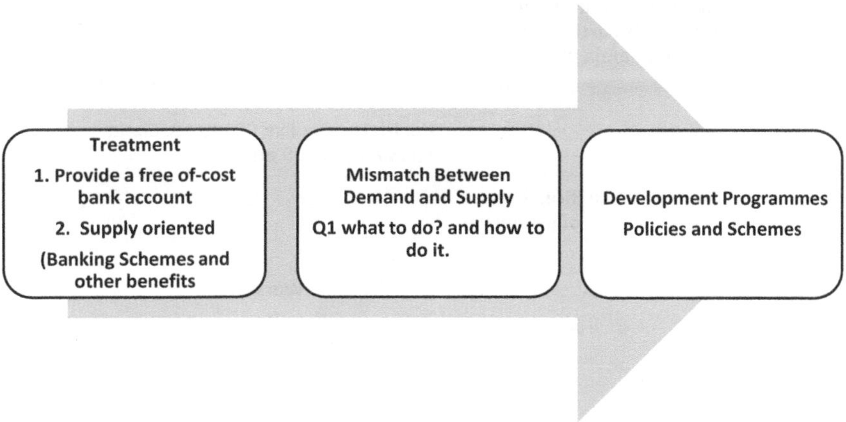

Figure 18.3 Policy mismatch and reforms

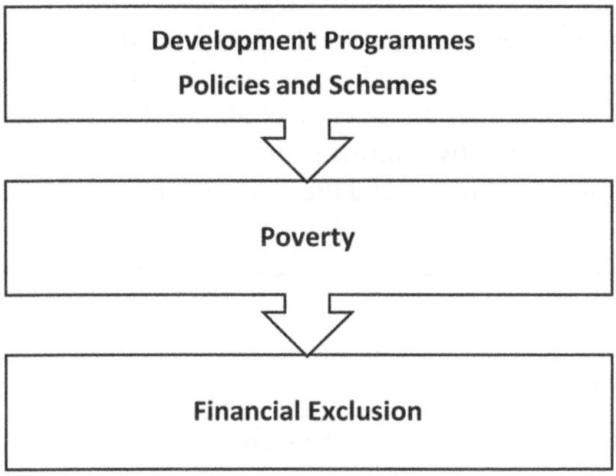

Figure 18.4 Policy output lowers financial exclusion

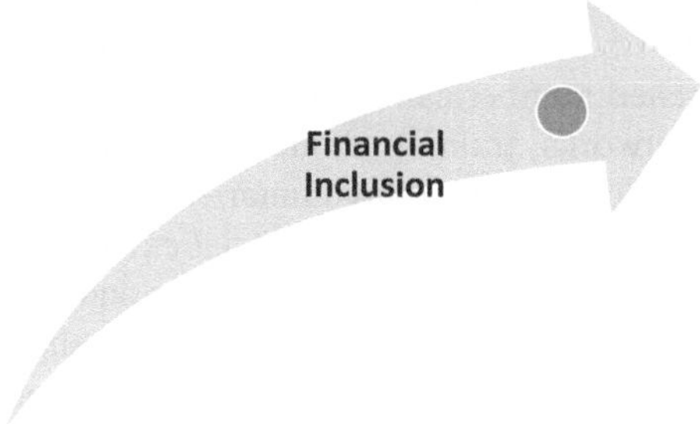

Figure 18.5 Achieving financial inclusion

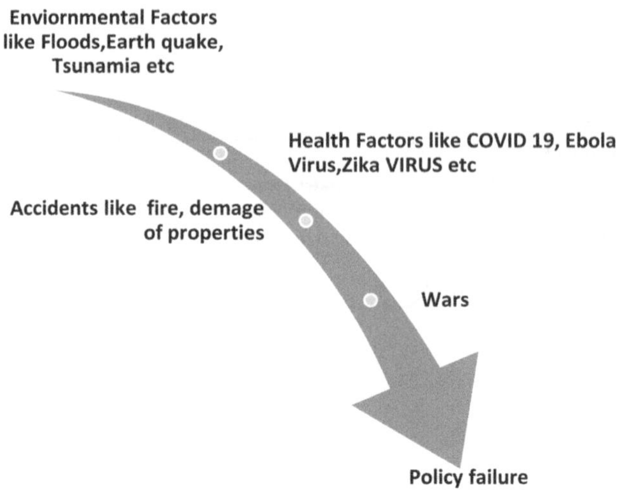

Figure 18.6 Unrecognised risk and uncertain factors lead to policy failure

related accidents or issues need to be addressed immediately to lower the pressure of being disaster-prone and to save human resources from the threats of increasing poverty (Chen & Sivakumar, 2021; Garz et al., 2021; Lee et al., 2022). Risk and uncertainty hinder the effective implementation of policies or programs. Identifying the gaps in existing literature and their impact on policy execution is essential, which is why we recommend that policies account for these risk and uncertainty forces. (Arbulú et al., 2021; Cantú et al., 2021; Chenet et al., 2021; Dogan et al., 2021).

18.6 Conclusion

The paper intends to study Financial Inclusion in Emerging Markets: A Synthesis of Theory and Practicality. Financial inclusion can be understood precisely by understanding financial exclusion, which is of two types. Voluntary exclusion and involuntary exclusion. Unlike voluntary exclusion, involuntary exclusion can be treated through various initiatives, like free bank accounts offered by the government or other banking schemes and benefits like PJMDY and Start-up India. According to the study, there is a mismatch between the demand and supply of digitally literate people. This mismatched number can be improved by providing free cell phones, telecommunication networks, training about usage, improving security, and winning the trust of the citizens who are involuntarily excluded from digital financial literacy. One of the strongest reasons for financial exclusion is poverty, which can be reduced by increasing policies related to start-ups and employment so that people can have money and accordingly have the urge to use digital financial platforms by generating income sources to increase the disposable personal income of the citizens, which could help citizens of emerging countries like India to be able to enter the financial industry (Demirguc-Kunt et al., 2022).

World organisations such as the World Bank. The IMF, the Asian Development Bank, and many other organisations are jointly working with countries, NGOs, and private and public organisations for the welfare of the people. Such relationships among organisations must be promoted to increase affordability among citizens. Scientists, researchers, policymakers, academicians, and bureaucrats are drafting policies to benefit poor people. The cell phone has a significantly greater impact on access to finance than the banking system. Cheap and ubiquitous Internet connectivity is necessary for ongoing development. Hence, telecommunication services must be improved so that non-volunteers can access digital financial services.

18.7 Implications

Theoretically, the present research effectively contributes to the existing body of knowledge by building the literature for the Social Construction Theory, which says both nature and nurture have a role in forming people's perceptions of reality by emphasising how cultural and biological variables interact to shape people's views of reality (Teater, 2015). Financial products like loans, savings accounts, insurance, and payment systems combined with financial inclusion led to the economic growth and development of any country. If implemented right, this study will be helpful to all the poor people who can improve their living standards by having a secure future after learning the importance and usage of digital financial literacy, which will promote the urge to invest, making it beneficial for both individuals and the economy as well. This study will also be helpful to bureaucrats, scientists, researchers, policymakers, and academicians by studying financial inclusion in emerging markets: a synthesis of theory and practicality.

References

Alam, A. M., Alam, M., & Hoque, A. (2017). Measuring financial condition of urban local government: A study of municipalities in Bangladesh. *The Journal of Developing Areas, 51*(2),71–85.

Allen, F., Demirguc-Kunt, A., Klapper, L., & Martinez, M. (2016). The foundations of financial inclusion: Understanding ownership and use of formal accounts. *Journal of Financial Intermediation, 27*, 1–30.

Andani, H. M. (2021). *Financial Exclusion due to Religious Reasons: Examining Sociodemographic Factors* (Doctoral dissertation, Hamad Bin Khalifa University (Qatar)).

Aparicio, C., Huayta, K., & Bohórquez, D. (2016). Access to financial services through retail agents and household expenditures: Evidence from Peru. *Journal of Financial Issues SBS, 12*(1), 1–26.

Arbulú, I., Razumova, M., Rey-Maquieira, J., & Sastre, F. (2021). Measuring risks and vulnerability of tourism to the COVID-19 crisis in the context of extreme uncertainty: The case of the Balearic Islands. *Tourism Management Perspectives, 39*, 100857.

Ardic, O. P., Heimann, M., & Mylenko, N. (2011). Access to financial services and the financial inclusion agenda around the world: a cross-country analysis with a new data set. Policy Research working paper, WPS 5537. Washington: World Bank.

Aziz, A., & Naima, U. (2021). Rethinking digital financial inclusion: Evidence from Bangladesh. *Technology in Society*, *64*, 101509.
Banerjee, A., Breza, E., Duflo, E., & Kinnan, C. (2019). Can Microfinance Unlock a Poverty Trap for Some Entrepreneurs? NBER Working Paper No. w26346.
Barr, M. S., & Sherraden, M. W. (2005). Institutions and inclusion in saving policy.
Berger, P., & Luckmann, T. (1966). The reality of everyday life. *The social construction of reality: A treatise in the sociology of knowledge*, 33–42.
Berger, P. L., & Luckmann, T. (1977). *The Social Construction of Reality. New York: Anchor.*
Besong, S. E., Okanda, T. L., & Ndip, S. A. (2022). An empirical analysis of the impact of banking regulations on sustainable financial inclusion in the CEMAC region. *Economic Systems*, *46*(1), 100935.
Bozkurt, İ, Karakuş, R., & Yildiz, M. (2018). Spatial determinants of financial inclusion over time. *Journal of International Development*, *30*(8), 1474–1504.
Buckland, J. (2012). *Hard choices: Financial exclusion, fringe banks, and poverty in urban Canada*. Toronto: University of Toronto Press.
Cantú, A., Aguiñaga, E., & Scheel, C. (2021). Learning from failure and success: The challenges for circular economy implementation in SMEs in an emerging economy. *Sustainability*, *13*(3), 1529.
Caplan, M. A., Birkenmaier, J., & Bae, J. (2021). Financial exclusion in OECD countries: A scoping review. *International Journal of Social Welfare*, *30*(1), 58–71.
Chen, Y., Kumara, E. K., & Sivakumar, V. (2021). Invesitigation of finance industry on risk awareness model and digital economic growth. *Annals of Operations Research*, 1–22.
Chen, Y., & Sivakumar, V. (2021). Investigation of finance industry on risk awareness model and digital economic growth. *Annals of Operations Research*, *326*, 1–22. Volume 326, page 15.
Chenet, H., Ryan-Collins, J., & van Lerven, F. (2021). Finance, climate-change and radical uncertainty: Towards a precautionary approach to financial policy. *Ecological Economics*, *183*, 106957.
Clark, C., Dyson, A., Millward, A., & Robson, S. (1999). Theories of inclusion, theories of schools: Deconstructing and reconstructing the ‘inclusive school’. *British Educational Research Journal*, *25*(2), 157–177.
Demir, A., Pesqué-Cela, V., Altunbas, Y., & Murinde, V. (2022). Fintech, financial inclusion and income inequality: A quantile regression approach. *The European Journal of Finance*, *28*(1), 86–107.
Demirguc-Kunt, A., Klapper, L., Singer, D., & Ansar, S. (2022). The Global Findex Database 2021: *Financial inclusion, digital payments, and resilience in the age of COVID-19*. World Bank Publications.
Dogan, E., Madaleno, M., & Taskin, D. (2021). Which households are more energy vulnerable? Energy poverty and financial inclusion in Turkey. *Energy Economics*, *99*, 105306.
Dymski, G. A. (2005). Financial globalization, social exclusion and financial crisis. *International Review of Applied Economics*, *19*(4), 439–457.
Garz, S., Giné, X., Karlan, D., Mazer, R., Sanford, C., & Zinman, J. (2021). Consumer protection for financial inclusion in low-and middle-income countries: Bridging regulator and academic perspectives. *Annual Review of Financial Economics*, *13*, 219–246.
Goldsmith, R. W. (1975). *Financial structure and development*. New Haven: Yale University Press.
Hannig, A., & Jansen, S. (2010). *Financial inclusion and financial stability: Current policy issues*. ADBI Working Paper 259. Tokyo: Asian Development Bank Institute. https://www.adb.org/sites/default/files/publication/156114/adbi-wp259.pdf.
Huang, R., Kale, S., Paramati, S. R., & Taghizadeh-Hesary, F. (2021). The nexus between financial inclusion and economic development: Comparison of old and new EU member countries. *Economic Analysis and Policy*, *69*, 1–15.
Jaramillo, M., Aparicio, C., & Cevallos, B. (2013). Quéfactoresexplican las diferenciasenelacceso al sistemafinanciero?: evidencia a nivel de hogaresenel Perú. Documento de Trabajo/03/2018, Lima: SBS.

Jin, S. (2022). *Financial Inclusion towards economic Inclusion: empirical evidence from China's rural households: A thesis submitted in partial fulfilment of the requirements for the Degree of Master at Lincoln University* (Doctoral dissertation, Lincoln University).

Jungo, J., Madaleno, M., & Botelho, A. (2022). The relationship between financial inclusion and monetary policy: A comparative study of countries in Sub-Saharan Africa and Latin America and the Caribbean. *Journal of African Business*, *23*(3), 794–815.

Khan, I., Khan, I., Sayal, A. U., & Khan, M. Z. (2021). Does financial inclusion induce poverty, income inequality, and financial stability: Empirical evidence from the 54 African countries? *Journal of Economic Studies*, *49*(2), 303–314.

Khera, P., Ng, S., Ogawa, S., & Sahay, R. (2022). Measuring digital financial Inclusion in emerging market and developing economies: A new index. *Asian Economic Policy Review*, *17*(2), 213–230.

Lee, C. C., Wang, C. W., & Ho, S. J. (2022). Financial aid and financial inclusion: Does risk uncertainty matter? *Pacific-Basin Finance Journal*, *71*, 101700.

Lyons, A. C., & Kass-Hanna, J. (2021). Financial inclusion, financial literacy and economically vulnerable populations in the Middle East and North Africa. *Emerging Markets Finance and Trade*, *57*(9), 2699–2738.

Mahalika, R., Matsebula, V., & Yu, D. (2021). Investigating the relationship between financial inclusion and poverty in South Africa. *Development Southern Africa*, 40, 109–132.

Malik, A. H., bin Md Isa, A. H., bin Jais, M., Rehman, A. U., & Khan, M. A. (2022). Financial stability of Asian nations: Governance quality and financial inclusion. *Borsa Istanbul Review*, *22*(2), 377–387.

Mallory, B. L., & New, R. S. (1994). Social constructivist theory and principles of inclusion: Challenges for early childhood special education. *The Journal of Special Education*, *28*(3), 322–337.

Mosley, P., & Lenton, P. (2011). *Financial exclusion and the poverty trap: Overcoming deprivation in the inner city* (1st ed.). Routledge. https://doi.org/10.4324/9780203802373

Mossie, W. A. (2022). Understanding financial inclusion in Ethiopia. *Cogent Economics & Finance*, *10*(1), 2071385.

Motta, V., & Gonzalez Farias, L. E. (2022). Determinants of financial inclusion in Latin America and the Caribbean. *Development in Practice*, 1–15., *32*(8), 1063–1077.

Nwidobie, B. M. (2019). Financial inclusion index in Nigeria: An exploratory analysis. *International Journal of Publication and Social Studies*, *4*(1), 26–36. https://doi.org/10.18488/journal.135.2019.41.26.36

Ofoeda, I. (2022). Anti-money laundering regulations and financial inclusion: empirical evidence across the globe. *Journal of Financial Regulation and Compliance*, *30*(5), 646–664.

Ostrom, E. (2009). *Understanding institutional diversity*. Princeton: Princeton University Press.

Ouma, S. A., Odongo, T. M., & Were, M. (2017). Mobile financial services and financial inclusion: Is it a boon for savings mobilization?. *Review of Development Finance*, *7*(1), 29–35.

Ozili, P. (2018). Impact of digital finance on financial inclusion and stability. *Borsa Istanbul Review*, *18*(4), 329–340.

Ozili, P. K. (2020). Theories of financial inclusion. In *Uncertainty and challenges in contemporary economic behavior* (pp. 89–115). Emerald Publishing Limited.

Ozili, P. K. (2021, October). Financial inclusion research around the world: A review. In *Forum for social economics* (Vol. 50, No. 4, pp. 457–479). Abingdon: Routledge.

Ozturk, I., & Ullah, S. (2022). Does digital financial inclusion matter for economic growth and environmental sustainability in OBRI economies? An empirical analysis. *Resources, Conservation and Recycling*, *185*, 106489.

Pradhan, R. P., Arvin, M. B., Nair, M. S., Hall, J. H., & Bennett, S. E. (2021). Sustainable economic development in India: The dynamics between financial inclusion, ICT development, and economic growth. *Technological Forecasting and Social Change*, *169*, 120758.

Sarma, M., & Pais, J. (2011). Financial inclusion and development. *Journal of International and Development*, *23*(5), 613–628.
Ouma, S. A., Odongo, T. M., & Were, M. (2017). Mobile financial services and financial inclusion: Is it a boon for savings mobilization?. *Review of development finance*, *7*(1), 29–35.
Senyo, P. K., Karanasios, S., Gozman, D., & Baba, M. (2022). FinTech ecosystem practices shaping financial inclusion: The case of mobile money in Ghana. *European Journal of Information Systems*, *31*(1), 112–127.
Singh, D., & Stakic, N. (2021). Financial inclusion and economic growth nexus: Evidence from SAARC countries. *South Asia Research*, *41*(2), 238–258.
Sotomayor, N., Talledo, J., & Wong, S. (2018). Determinants of financial Inclusion in Peru: Recent Evidence from the Demand Side. DT/06, Lima: SBS.
Talledo, J. (2015). Access to and use of financial services: Evidence from Peru. *Journal of Financial Issues SBS*, *11*(1), 1–49.
Tian, Y., & Li, L. (2022). Impact of financial inclusion and globalization on environmental quality: Evidence from G20 economies. *Environmental Science and Pollution Research*, 1–12. DOI 10.1007/s11356-022-19618-9
Yakubi, Y. A. Y., Basuki, B., Purwono, R., & Usman, I. (2022). The impact of digital technology and business regulations on financial inclusion and socio-economic development in low-income countries. *SAGE Open*, *12*(3), 21582440221116112.
Yangdol, R., & Sarma, M. (2019). Demand-side factors for financial inclusion: A cross-country empirical analysis. *International Studies*, *56*(2–3), 163–185.

19 Financial Inclusion and Tax Revenue

Evidence from Asian Countries

Tanya Nautiyal

19.1 Introduction

Financial inclusion aims to ensure widespread availability, easy accessibility and affordable usage of formal financial system to every individual in an economy. A comprehensive financial system will help in development and upliftment of the economy by generating new employment opportunities and reducing poverty. Financial inclusion is the main element of social inclusion, particularly useful in opening the blocked advancement opportunities for the poor sections of the society. A well-structured and well-defined financial system is necessary for economic growth and it can attract investment which is required to direct a country's development. This development will further lead to more use of financial services or more inclusive financial system in the country. Policymakers can facilitate financial services by modifying the existing laws. An undeveloped financial system can be costly for individuals planning to use financial services (Kempson & Whyley, 1999), and the disadvantage of underdevelopment includes financial exclusion of people especially the poorer group in society and reductions in economic growth.

Inclusive growth is one of the most important policy goals. Economists and government administrators all over the world have given emphasis to economic and social inclusion, like access to education, health, affordable transport, social security, clean water and sanitation. Financial inclusion is the recent term and item to be added to the social inclusion agenda and promotes the need for access to a range of financial services to all sections of society. Financial inclusion is now a global agenda (ADB, 2014). In Asia several countries have included financial Inclusion as an important tool of their strategies to achieve inclusive growth and higher GDP. The Asia-Pacific Economic Cooperation (APEC) Finance Minister has dedicated a specific and serious platform looking at the issue of financial inclusion. Financial reforms have played a critical role in the success of financial inclusion. Every country in Asia has adopted different approaches for its success, for example Thailand's approach for financial inclusion is primarily driven by the government sector (ADB, 2014). In India, the need to empower the poor section came into light in 1950s and many banking centric approaches were seriously taken, e.g. Regional Rural Banks, nationalization of banks, etc. In addition, recently, India

DOI: 10.4324/9781032655185-25

launched a flagship programme for enhancing financial inclusion called PMJDY, Pradhan Mantri Jan Dhan Yojana. Despite the achievements there still exist widespread disparities in the use of formal financial services among the countries. One reason for these disparities is the difference in the financial sector operations and developments across countries, difference in GDP, etc. (ADB, 2014).

Government's chief source of income is tax and nontax revenue from economic activities. In recent years, majority of the countries around the world have seen privatization, which has decreased the percentage of the public sector in the economy. As a result, governments of the countries now rely primarily on tax collection as their prime source of revenue. Because of privatization, tax revenue has become increasingly vital source of income for the government in order to be able to provide public services in the country. Policymakers and administration of both developing and developed countries are apprehensive about tax revenue variability and volatility, as it may cause variations in public spending and public investment, all of which can impact economic growth negatively. Economic growth, in turn, is a critical factor in determining the tax base of the country and as a result tax collection. In order to finance the development plans and projects in both developed and developing countries, government needs to increase its tax revenue. Tax law enforcement and collection of taxes are strenuous to enforce in both developed and developing economies. At the same time, estimating tax revenue and identifying prominent factors of tax revenue have become an adjuvant issue in the formation of economic policies. Policymakers can directly increase revenues by focusing on determinants of tax revenue. There are many research papers in the literature that have focused on various determinants of tax revenue (Addison & Levin, 2012; Karagoz, 2013; Stoilova, 2017).

One such determinant is financial development which can affect direct tax income in a variety of ways. First, economic growth increases the number of economic activities which are taxable and which expands direct tax income. Second, increased economic businesses generate income and increases demand for various products and services, resulting in fresh investment. As a result, the income tax base expands, which accompanies the increase in direct tax revenue. From this perspective, financial sector developments and improvement in the financial infrastructure have the potential to enlarge tax collection by expanding economic activities and diminishing the shadow economy. As a result of this, most governments have begun to take a variety of measures to reduce the existence of the shadow economy and increase total tax revenue.

The remaining part of the paper is organized as follows. Section 19.1 gives a brief overview about the Asian countries. It talks about the geographical history of Asia and regional division of Asian countries. Section 19.2 explains the association between tax revenue and financial inclusion, tax revenue and GDP and tax revenue and inflation. Review of literature is discussed in Section 19.3 followed with research gap. The next section, i.e. Section 19.4, explains the methodology adopted in the paper followed by empirical analysis in Section 19.5. Last section of the paper, i.e. Section 19.6, gives the conclusion and policy recommendations.

19.1.1 Asian Countries

Asia is the world largest and diverse continent on planet Earth in terms of area and population. Asia covers an area of about 49.7 million km[2] (19,189,277 square miles), which corresponds to about 30 per cent of the Earth's total land area. Asia is divided into six main geographical regions – Northern Asia, Western Asia, South Asia, South East Asia, Eastern Asia and Central Asia. There are total 50 countries in the continent. With respect to area, the largest country in Asia is Russia with more than 17 million km[2], of which 13 million km[2], i.e. 77 per cent are in Asia. China occupies the second position, with an area of 9.6 million km[2] followed by India with an area of 3.28 million km[2]. In Asia, the smallest independent state is the island nation of Maldives with 298 km[2].

Asia's stake in world markets has grown tremendously in the last half-century. Today, some of the top producers of many agricultural, forest, fishing, mining, and industrial products are countries located in Asia. This increased production has led to pros and cons both in terms of extreme wealth and negative environmental impacts to the continent.

19.1.2 Asia

19.1.2.1 Tax Revenue and GDP Per Capita

Figure 19.1 shows the association of tax revenue and GDP per capita of 35 Asian countries. A country's GDP and tax revenue relationship is complex and changes from time to time, depending upon the economic strength of the country. A higher

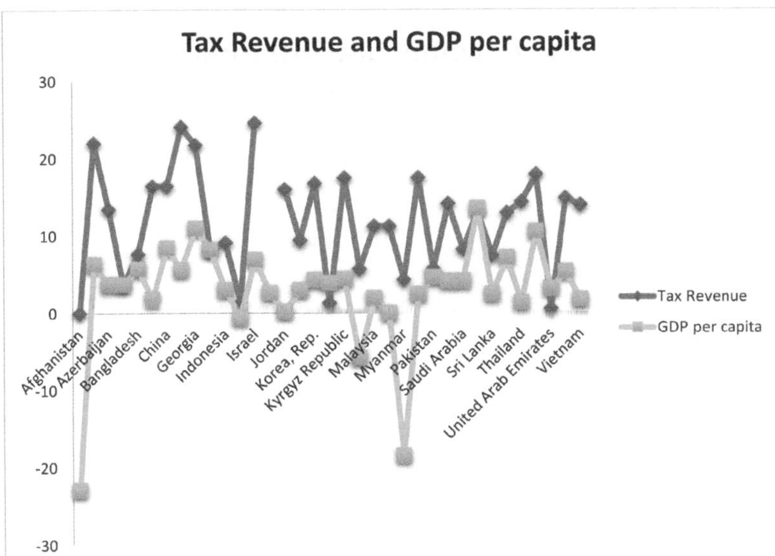

Figure 19.1 Tax revenue and GDP per capita

GDP indicates higher tax revenue for the country which in turn shows strong financial position of the country. A country's tax revenue is positively related to its potential GDP, thereby maintain strong tax buoyancy. Both GDP and tax revenue play a significant role in understanding the economic condition of the nation. Change in tax policies and tax rates can affect economic activities. This affects economic output of the country and GDP (Andrasic et al., 2017; Odum et al., 2018). Contrary to it, many studies also show that changes in economic activities and GDP cause changes in tax revenues (Zeng et al., 2013). The figure below shows the tax revenue and GDP per capita for the year 2021. The top countries in tax revenue are Israel, Cyprus, Georgia and Turkey whereas the lowest tax revenue has been in UAE, Iraq, Kuwait and Bahrain. The top and lowest countries in terms of tax revenue are primarily located in the western parts of Asia. On the GDP per capita side, Singapore, Georgia, Turkey, China and India are in top five lists whereas Afghanistan, Myanmar, Lebanon, Iraq and Jordan are on the lowest scale.

19.1.2.2 Tax Revenue and Inflation

Figure 19.2, Tax Revenue and Financial inclusion, shows the relationship between inflation and tax revenue of Asian countries, where Lebanon, Turkey, Kyrgyz Republic, Uzbekistan and Georgia have the highest inflation rates. These countries are situated in the western and central parts of Asia. The countries with lowest inflation rates are Bahrain, Japan, UAE, China and Jordan. These countries are mostly located in western and eastern parts of Asia. Lebanon saw the highest inflation rate of 154.8 in 2021, mainly because of the collapse of the economic system. Lebanon

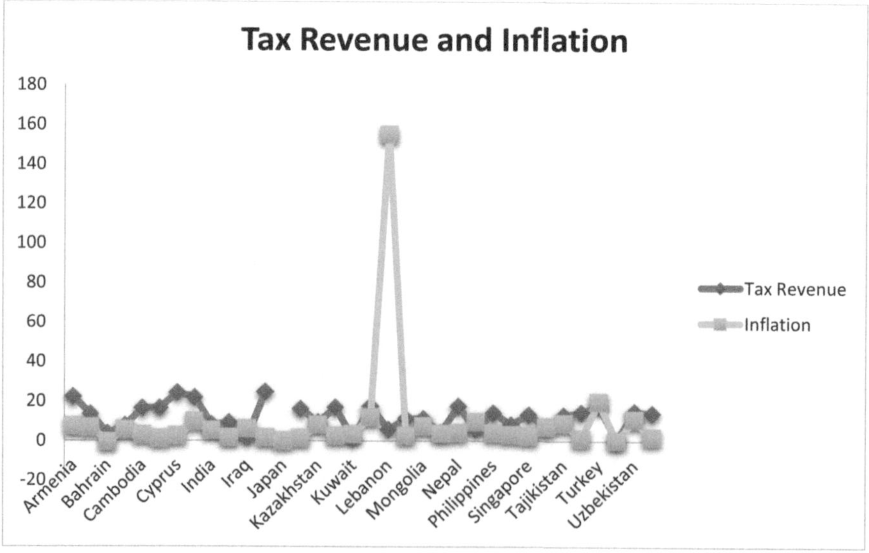

Figure 19.2 Tax revenue and inflation rates

is profoundly vulnerable to the broader impact that the Ukraine conflict has had on commodity prices, as well as losing access to proximately located markets upon which it was previously dependent (Mercy Corps, 2023).

19.1.2.3 Tax Revenue and Financial Inclusion

The economy theory indicates a positive relation between access to institutional finance and economic growth (Aghion & Bolton, 1997; Aghion et al., 2009). There are many studies in the literature which has examined the relationship between financial inclusion and economic growth. Increased financial inclusion increases inclusive economic growth (Beck et al., 2004). Access to formal financial services improves local economic activities which further increases tax revenues of the country. There are many findings which indicate that market capitalization and large number of bank branches have a significant, positive and considerable impact on tax collection and tax revenue in the long run (Ahamed, 2016). Other studies postulate that financial inclusion is an adjuvant determinant of tax revenue receipts (Oz-Yalaman, 2019). Figure 19.3, Tax revenue and percentage of people reported having a bank account (financial inclusion), shows the amount of tax revenue and percentage of respondents reported having a bank account. Bank account ownership is taken as a proxy of financial inclusion which comes under the usability aspect of financial inclusion. The countries having highest number of people with bank accounts are Korea, Japan, Singapore, Thailand and Israel which are in the Eastern and western parts of Asia. Further, countries having the lowest number of bank accounts are Afghanistan, Iraq, Lebanon, Pakistan and Tajikistan, majority of which are located in Western Asia, South Asia and Central Asia. According to

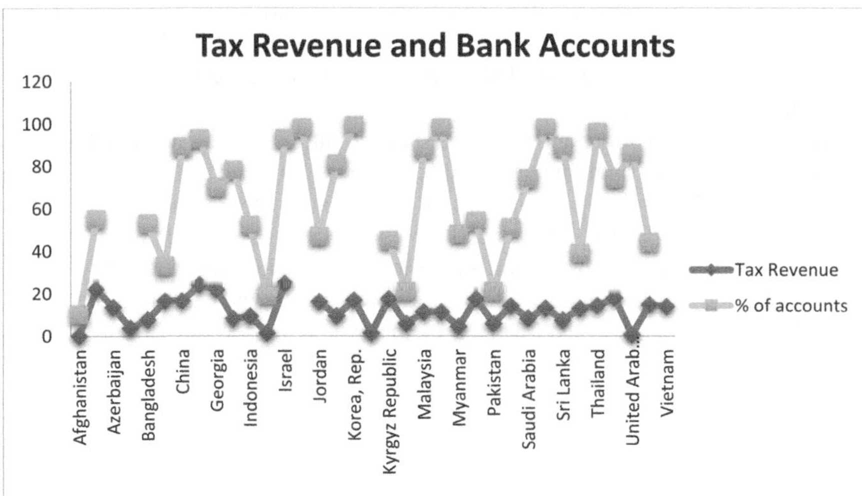

Figure 19.3 Tax revenue and percentage of people reported having a bank account (financial inclusion)

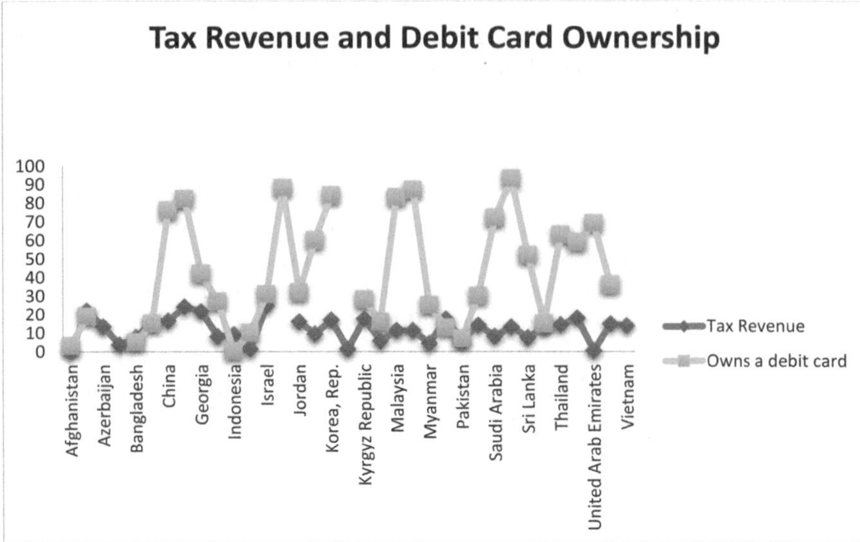

Figure 19.4 Tax revenue and percentage of people reported owing a debit card (financial inclusion)

Global Findex report, the global account ownership growth has changed in recent years. Different economies saw different rates of bank account growth and same is the case with Asia.

Another proxy variable for financial inclusion is ownership of debit cards. The countries with highest debit account ownership are Singapore, Japan, Mongolia, Korea and Malaysia which belongs to the western and south-east parts of Asia. Further, countries in Asia where debit account ownership is the lowest are Indonesia, Afghanistan, Bangladesh, Pakistan and Iraq which are majorly from South Asia and Western Asia.

Korea, Japan, Singapore and Cyprus are the countries which are on high index of financial inclusion for both ownership of bank account as well as ownership of debit cards, whereas Afghanistan, Pakistan, Iraq and Lebanon are on the lowest index of financial inclusion. The lowest financial inclusion is mostly found in South Asia and Central Asia. Iraq, Afghanistan and Lebanon are the countries which have lowest tax revenue and lowest financial inclusion which clearly indicates that there exists a positive association between financial inclusion and tax revenue (Figure 19.4).

19.2 Review of Literature

There have been many studies in the past which supports the hypothesis that financial inclusion can be a factor which can bring huge amount of income and economic growth in the nation. Financial inclusion is one of the major initiative and policy tools which can reduce poverty, increase wellness and welfare and maintain macroeconomic stability (Beck et al., 2004; Han & Melecky, 2013; Kim, 2016;

Kempson & Whyley, 1999). Literature has also postulated a causal relationship from financial development to economic growth, which means planned building of financial institutions and markets, boosts the financial services supply and thus leads to real economic growth. Various empirical as well as theoretical writings on this subject have shown that financial development is adjuvant and causes economic growth.

There is a huge literature exploring the various determinants of tax revenue. Inflation, capital flows, trade openness, per capita income, GDP, sectoral growth, agriculture sector, industrial sector and unemployment are generally taken as the prime determinants of tax revenue (Bird et al., 2008; Castro & Camarillo, 2014; Macek, 2014 2010; Odum et.al, 2018; Karagoz, 2013; Hannig & Jansen, 2010). Additionally, several studies have researched on the association between financial inclusion and tax revenue. Examining different indicators with different samples, researchers have found that financial development has a significant positive impact on the tax collection and tax revenue of the country. Akram, (2016) found that financial inclusion has a favourable impact in direct tax revenue collection in Turkey. The result of the research shows that banking and non-banking financial development leads to increase in direct tax-revenue in the long-run, whereas in the short-run only banking financial development causes increase in direct tax-revenue.

Apart from this, various authors have studied about impact of taxes on economic growth of the nation. According to Hannig and Jansen (2010) there is a strong positive relationship between a country's GDP and a country's ability to pay taxes. Economic growth has an impact on increasing tax revenue. Further, McMahon & Boediono (1992) in his work explained economic growth as a process of increasing output in the long run. Economic growth will happen if there is a tendency from the internal processes of the country, meaning that it happens from the forces within the economy itself. The effect of taxation on economic growth is a major concern for the policymakers and tax administrators of the country. Over the years academicians and researchers have also developed their interest in the following area. From a realistic point of view, tax policy is used for the economic and social development of the country. It can help in resource allocation through higher savings generated internally, controlling the production stable prices, and consumption level indirectly through sales taxes, and increasing growth of the economy. Over the years, economists and researchers have been investigating various factors causing different economies to grow at different rates and conquer different levels of capital accumulation. However, several economists favour taxation as one of the influential and significant factors that discovers the productive capacity of the country (Stoilova, 2017).

According to the review of literature, there are few studies in the literature investigating the relationship between tax revenue and financial inclusion using Global Findex Database (Maherali, 2017; Oz-Yalaman, 2019). To the best of our knowledge and literature reviewed there are very few studies investigating the factors affecting tax revenue in Asian countries using Global Findex Database. To fill the gap in literature, the present research uses the Global Findex Database to examine the factors affecting the tax revenue in Asian Countries. In the present research data on 35 Asian countries has been collected and analysed. The data for all the Asian countries was not available so the paper has taken the available data of 35 Asian countries.

19.3 Research Methodology

The present research is primarily based on secondary data. The secondary information has been collected from the following sources Global Findex Database Reports, IMF and World Bank database. Since the research consist of 35 cross-sectional units and four years of time dimension, i.e. 2011, 2014, 2017 and 2021, it is more appropriate to run panel estimation methods. Panel data estimation technique is expected to deal better with the issue of limited degrees of freedom and the problem of measurement bias.

The Global Findex Report has published datasets covering 140 countries, interviewing 150,000 people in 2011, 2014 and 2017. The report has used over 100 indicators for financial inclusion. This regularly published dataset helps out to test the linkages between financial inclusion indicators and tax revenue using panel data methodology. Panel data methodology is important and accurate because the model is based on comprehensive observations derived from both "cross-sectional" data and "time-series" data, which increases degree of freedom and ensures estimation of a more robust model with lesser problems (Baltagi, 1995).

In this research, tax revenue is used as a dependent variable. Tax revenue is taken as a proportion of GDP. The data on tax revenue (% of GDP) was collected from the World Databank Indicators. As discussed earlier that financial inclusion is a broader concept and has many indicators, the study has used two indicators for financial inclusion. The dataset of the dimensions included in the calculation of financial inclusion are number of bank accounts of people above the age of 15 and ownership of debit cards. These two variables are taken as a proxy variable for financial inclusion. Tax revenue can be determined and affected by factors other than financial inclusion. So, GDP per capita and inflation rate calculated using consumer prices annually in percentage are included in the model. Data for these variables was obtained from the World Databank Indicators. Table 19.1 presents the definitions of variables used in the model and sources of the variables.

Table 19.1 Variables, their definitions and sources of the variables

S. No.	*Name of the variable*	*Definition*	*Data sources*
1.	TR	Tax Revenue as a percentage of GDP	World bank database
2.	GDPPC	GDP per capita	World bank database
3.	IN	Inflation, consumer prices in percentage (annual)	World bank database
4.	$FI_{account}$ (accounts)	Percentage of people having bank account (% of people age >15)	Global Findex Database Reports (2011, 2014, 2017, 2021)
5.	FI_{debit} (card)	Debit card ownership (% of people age >15)	Global Findex Database Reports (2011, 2014, 2017, 2021)

The following panel data model is used to test the linkages between tax revenue, financial inclusion, economic growth and inflation; the following model has been made and analysed:

$$TR_{it} = \alpha + \beta_1(\text{FI}_{\text{account}}) + \beta_2(\text{FI}_{\text{debit}}) + \beta_3(GDPPC) + \beta_4(IN) + \varepsilon_{it}$$

where for $i = 1, 2, \ldots, N$; $t = 1, 2, \ldots, T$ and ε_{it} is a disturbance term.

In the above model tax revenue is taken as a dependent variable and number of bank accounts (% of people age >15), ownership of debit cards (% of people age >15), GDP per capita and inflation as independent variables. Because the dependent variable in the regressions is a ratio such as tax revenues/GDP, we use logistic transformation of dependent variables to fit a model (Macek, 2014; Maherali, 2017; Stoilova, 2017; Ugwunta & Ugwuanyi, 2015).

It is foremost to choose appropriate panel model for estimation from a fixed effect model or a random effect model. For selection of model, Hausman specification test has been applied. The Hausman test statistic follows Chi-square distribution with k degrees of freedom. If p-value of Chi-square statistics is <0.05, then we reject the null hypothesis and conclude fixed effect model is the appropriate choice for panel estimations. However, if p-value >0.05 we will accept the H_0 concluding that random effect model is the right choice.

19.4 Empirical Analysis

The table below (Table 19.2) shows the result of panel data regression with fixed effect. The result of the analysis shows GDP, inflation, number of bank accounts and ownership of debit cards as significant factors. GDP, number of bank accounts and ownership of debit cards are found to be positive and significant factors which means as GDP of a country increases its tax revenue also shows a positive increase. Further number of bank accounts and ownership of debit cards are the proxy variables for financial inclusion which are positive and significant. This means that level of financial inclusion and tax revenue are positively related. The results indicate that 1 per cent increase in number of bank accounts increases tax revenue by

Table 19.2 Panel data regression results (fixed effect model)

Variable	*Coefficient*	*Standard error*	*t*	*P > [t]*
GDP	.1980206	.0732735	2.70	0.008
Inflation	–.0619671	.0179743	–.345	0.001
Logit-transformed financial inclusion	39.65297	13.65772	2.90	0.005
Logit-transformed card	37.67281	12.30626	3.06	0.003
Constant	14.50245	5.514467	2.63	0.010
R-sq (within)		0.2380	F (4, 93)	7.26
R-sq (between)		0.0972	Prob > F	0.000
R-sq (overall)		0.0958	Number of Obs	132
Corr (u_i, Xb)		0.0791	Number of groups	35

Table 19.3 Panel data regression results (random effect model)

Variable	*Coefficient*	*Standard error*	*z*	*P > [z]*
GDP	.2324444	.0722652	3.22	0.001
Inflation	–.0582514	.0181015	–3.22	0.001
Logit-transformed financial inclusion	40.82424	13.62843	3.00	0.003
Logit-transformed card	40.24628	12.25575	3.28	0.003
Constant	12.82458	5.627398	2.28	0.023
R-sq (within)		0.2358	Wald chi2 (4)	31.61
R-sq (between)		0.1172	Prob > chi2	0.000
R-sq (overall)		0.1089	Number of Obs	132
Corr (u_i, Xb)		0 (assumed)	Number of groups	35

36.6 per cent. Further 1 per cent increase in debit card ownership will increase tax revenue by 37.6 per cent.

Inflation is found to be negatively related with tax revenue. The result indicates that 1 per cent increase in inflation will decrease tax revenue by 0.06 per cent. Further the overall significance of the model is seen by F-test in the model which is found to be significant and which indicates that the regression model fits the data better than the model with no independent variables.

Next are the results of random effect model (Table 19.3). The analysis reveals all four variables, i.e. GDP, inflation, number of bank accounts and debit card ownership as significant factors. GDP and financial inclusion are found to be positively related with tax revenue. The result indicates 1 per cent increase in the number of accounts of people; tax revenue will increase by 40.8 per cent. Further 1 per cent increase in debit card ownership will increase tax revenue by 40.2 per cent. Therefore, the empirical result indicates that financial inclusion leads to increase in tax revenue of the government.

Inflation is found to be negatively related with tax revenue. The result indicates that 1 per cent increase in inflation will decrease tax revenue by 0.05 per cent. Further the overall significance of the model is seen by Wald chi2 test in the model which is found to be significant and which indicates that the regression model fits the data better than the model with no explanatory variables.

19.4.1 Model Validation Test

The causality result has been examined through panel data regression. Table 19.4, Hausmen specification, presents the result of Hausmen specification test. This test

Table 19.4 Hausman specification

Dependent variable – tax revenue		
Null hypothesis	*Chi2(1) = (b – B)'[(V_b – V_B)^(–1)](b – B)*	*Probability*
Ho: difference in coefficients not systematic	2.42	0.6594

is done for the selection of model between random effect and fixed effect. The probability value below is more than the critical value, which indicates that random effect model is valid on the basis of Hausman specification test.

19.5 Conclusion and Policy Recommendations

Taxation is a critical part of a modern economy, as the government of each economy targets to maximize tax revenue collection for smooth functioning of the country and finance its spending needs. Taxes are also related with a country's economic growth, financial inclusion of the country and other macro-economic variables. Because of the significance of taxation, the goal of this study is to investigate the prime determinants of tax revenue and analyse them. Researchers and policymakers study the prime determinants of tax revenue. One of the determinants of tax revenue is financial inclusion. Exploring parameters of financial inclusion is a major concern for policymakers.

The present research provides some powerful empirical evidence for a significant and positive relationship between tax revenue and financial inclusion indicators. The results are robust with respect to the effects of different proxy of financial inclusion and tax revenue. As more people come under the ambit of financial inclusion their income grows over time, which will in turn increase their tax contributions to the government. It is important for government and policymakers to understand how the increased financial inclusion of their economy will affect their tax revenues. GDP is also found to be positive and significant factor in increasing tax revenue of the country. However, inflation is found to be negative and significant. This means that macro-economic variables also determine tax revenue of the country.

Furthermore, policymakers and government must prioritize measures for increasing financial inclusion with its powerful tax revenue-enhancing effects. In conclusion, this research can help policymakers and decision-makers to find the ideal degree of financial inclusion, specifically in countries where financial inclusion is low. As a result, administers and government can set policies to bag the appropriate degree of financial inclusion to get the optimum tax collection and tax revenue.

References

Addison, T., & Levin, J. (2012). The determinants of tax revenue in sub-Saharan Africa. Unpublished.

Aghion, P., Bacchetta, P., Ranciere, R., & Rogoff, K. (2009). Exchange rate volatility and productivity growth: The role of financial development. *Journal of Monetary Economics*, *56*(4), 494-513.

Aghion, P., & Bolton, P. (1997). A theory of trickle-down growth and development. The review of economic studies, *64*(2), 151–172.

Ahamed, M. M. (2016). Does inclusive financial development matter for firms' tax evasion? Evidence from developing countries. *Economics Letters*, *149*, 15–19.

Akçay, S., Sagbas, I., & Demirtas, G. (2016). Financial development and tax revenue nexus in Turkey. *Journal of Economic and Development Studies*, *4*(1), 103e108.

Akram, N. (2016). Do financial sector activities affect tax revenue in Pakistan? *The Lahore Journal of Economics*, *21*(2), Winter 2016.
Andrasic, J., Kalas, B., & Mirovic, V. (2017). Estimating the impact of taxes on the economic growth in the United States. *Economic Themes*, *55*(4), 481–499.
Beck, A. T., Baruch, E., Balter, J. M., Steer, R. A., & Warman, D. M. (2004). A new instrument for measuring insight: the Beck Cognitive Insight Scale. *Schizophrenia Research*, *68*(2–3), 319–329.
Beck, T., Demirguc-Kunt, A., & Levine, R. (2004). Finance, Inequality, and Poverty: Cross-Country Evidence. Working Paper 10979. The World Bank.
Becker, M. C., & Knudsen, T. (2002). Schumpeter 1911: Farsighted visions on economic development. *American Journal of Economics and Sociology*, *61*(2), 387–403.
Bird, R. M., Martinez-Vazquez, J., & Torgler, B. (2008). Tax effort in developing countries and high income countries: The impact of corruption, voice and accountability. *Economic Analysis and Policy*, *38*(1), 55e71.
Castro, G. A., & Camarillo, D. B. R. (2014). Determinants of tax revenue in OECD countries over the period 2001e2011. *Contaduría y Administración*, *59*(3), 35e59.
Han, R., & Melecky, M. (2013). Financial inclusion for financial stability: Access to bank deposits and the growth of deposits in the global financial crisis. World bank policy research working paper, (6577).
Hannig, A., & Jansen, S. (2010). Financial inclusion and financial stability: Current policy issues.
Karagoz, K. (2013). Determinants of tax revenue: Does sectorial composition matter? *Journal of Finance, Accounting & Management*, *4*(2), 50-63.
Kim, J. H. (2016). A study on the effect of financial inclusion on the relationship between income inequality and economic growth. *Emerging Markets Finance and Trade*, *52*(2), 498e512.
King, R. G., & Levine, R. (1993). Finance and growth: Schumpeter might be right. *Quarterly Journal of Economics*, *108*, 13–737.
Macek, R. (2014). The impact of taxation on economic growth: Case study of OECD countries. *Review of Economic Perspectives*, *14*(4), 309.
McMahon, W. W., & Boediono, W. W. (1992). Universal basic education: An overall strategy of investment priorities for economic growth. *Economics of Education Review*, *11*(2), 137–151.
Maherali, A. (2017). Financial Inclusion, Digital Payments and Their Impact on Income and Tax Revenue Around the World. Master's thesis. Harvard Extension School.
Mercy Corps. (2023). Effect of the Ukraine conflict on Lebanon's economic and humanitarian crises – one year on. *Thematic Report,* Lebanon Crisis Analytics Team.
Odum, A. N., Odum, C. G., & Egbunike, F. C. (2018). Effect of direct income tax on GDP: Evidence from Nigeria fiscal policy framework. *Indonesian Journal of Applied Business and Economic Research*, *1*(1), 59–66.
Oz-Yalaman, G. (2019). Financial inclusion and tax revenue. *Central Bank Review*, *19*(3), 107–113.
Stoilova, D. (2017). Tax structure and economic growth: Evidence from the European Union. *Contaduría y Administración*, *62*(3), 1041–1057.
Ugwunta, O. D., & Ugwuanyi, U. B. (2015). Effect of distortionary and non-distortionary taxes on economic growth: Evidence from Sub-Saharan African countries. *Journal of Accounting and Taxation*, *7*(6), 106–112.
World Bank. (2017). Global Findex Database. Retrieved from https://globalfindex.worldbank.org/
Zeng, K., Li, S., & Li, Q. (2013). The impact of economic growth and tax reform on tax revenue and structure: Evidence from China experience. *Modern Economy*, *4*(12), 839–851.

Index

Note: *Italicized* and **bold** pages refer to figures and tables respectively, and page numbers followed by "n" refer to notes.

For Product Safety Concerns and Information please contact our
EU representative GPSR@taylorandfrancis.com Taylor & Francis
Verlag GmbH, Kaufingerstraße 24, 80331 München, Germany